THE FRESHWATER FISHES OF MANITOBA

THE LARGEST FISH EVER CAUGHT IN MANITOBA

A 184.6 kg lake sturgeon caught in the Roseau River, east of Dominion City, by Sandy Waddell (back row, fifth from left in picture), on October 3, 1903. The fish was a female "full of roe." It was found in a pool in the Roseau River by Sandy's son, Jim (back row, fourth from left in picture), who called his dad for help. Sandy killed it with an axe and they roped it and dragged it from the river with Sandy's team of horses. They loaded it onto a seven-foot Democrat wagon and hauled it to Dominion City, where it was measured and weighed at the grain elevator, and this picture was taken.

Back row (L. to R.): Bill Morkill, Earl Quantz, Dave Waddell, Jim Waddell, Sandy Waddell, Henry Lawson
Front row (L. to R.): Roy Ginn, Heck Miller, Henry Simpson, Bill Barber, Bill Campbell
Photo by George Barraclough
This print is made from a scan done by the Manitoba Museum of a print held by the Franklin Museum, Dominion City.

THE FRESHWATER FISHES OF MANITOBA

KENNETH W. STEWART AND DOUGLAS A. WATKINSON

UNIVERSITY OF MANITOBA PRESS

© Kenneth W. Stewart and Douglas A. Watkinson, 2004

University of Manitoba Press
Winnipeg, Manitoba R3T 2N2 Canada
www.umanitoba.ca/uofmpress

Printed in Canada by Friesens.

All rights reserved. No part of this publication may be reproduced or transmitted in any form or by any means, or stored in a database and retrieval system, without the prior written permission of University of Manitoba Press, or, in the case of photocopying or other reprographic copying, a licence from ACCESS COPYRIGHT (Canadian Copyright Licensing Agency), 6 Adelaide Street East, Suite 900, Toronto, Ontario M5C 1H6.

Design: Doowah Design

National Library of Canada Cataloguing in Publication Data
Stewart Kenneth, 1936-
Freshwater fishes of Manitoba / Kenneth Stewart, Douglas Watkinson.
Includes bibliographical references.
ISBN 0-88755-176-9 (bound).—ISBN 0-88755-678-7 (pbk.)
1. Freshwater fishes—Manitoba. 2. Freshwater fishes—Manitoba—Identification. I. Watkinson, Douglas, 1974- II. Title.
QL626.5.M3S74 2004   597.176'097127   C2004-901611-3

The University of Manitoba Press gratefully acknowledges the financial support for its publication program provided by the Government of Canada through the Book Publishing Industry Development Program (BPIDP); the Canada Council for the Arts; the Manitoba Arts Council; and the Manitoba Department of Culture, Heritage and Tourism.

IN MEMORY OF DR. E.J. CROSSMAN

The late Dr. E.J. Crossman, Curator Emeritus of Fishes of the Royal Ontario Museum (ROM), and Professor Emeritus in the Department of Zoology, University of Toronto, contributed to this book in countless ways. He provided a handwritten catalogue of Manitoba fishes in the ROM collection long before there was a computerized database of their collection records. He loaned us specimens of Manitoba fishes and identified reference specimens of Hudson Bay Drainage fish species found upstream from Manitoba. These were invaluable for examination and use in developing the keys to our fishes. He gave encouragement at all stages of the project, even though it took 20 years to complete and there was a long interval during which little or no progress was made. Finally, he read the first draft of the book, made many suggestions, and caught a lot of errors. He was a constant and willing source of information, inspiration, and encouragement. This book is much stronger and more useful because of all he did for us. We regret we can't give Ed a copy of *Freshwater Fishes of Manitoba*. We hope the final result justifies his efforts on our behalf, and that he would have found it useful and informative. Thanks, Ed!

K.W. Stewart
D. A. Watkinson
March 8, 2004

PERMISSIONS

The authors and publisher gratefully acknowledge the following for permission to reprint photographs. Copyright holders and page numbers where their photographs appear are listed below. Photographs may not be reproduced without permission.

Jason Barnucz: 220. Ronald Bretecher: 17 (top). Randy Brown: 165. Neil Fisher: 42 (top). William Franzin: 12. Harold Funk: 15 (top). Gavin Hanke: 198, 214, 215. Claire Herbert: 11 (bottom), 153. Kimberly Howland: 179. James Johnson: 175 (top and bottom). Allan Kristofferson: 177 (middle). Casimir Lindsey: 171 (bottom), 217, 235. John Lyons, © Wisconsin Department of Natural Resources: 64, 81, 121, 122, 129, 134, 188, 193, 225, 230, 232. Donald MacDonell: 16 (bottom). S.M.D. Matkowski: 177 (bottom). Lee Murray: 164. Norwegian Seafood Export Council: 152. Richard Remnant: 15 (bottom), 16 (top), 17 (bottom). Konrad Schmidt: 146, 223. John Shearer: 13 (bottom), 14 (top and bottom). Kenneth Stewart: 8 (bottom), 10, 11 (top), 13 (top), 29 (bottom), 40 (top), 49, 51, 63, 83 (bottom), 95 (bottom), 104, 132 (top and bottom), 135, 137 (bottom), 168, 169, 171 (top). Peter Vanriel: 166. Douglas Watkinson: 7 (top and bottom), 8 (top), 9 (top and bottom), 28 (top and bottom), 29 (top), 38 (top and bottom), 40 (bottom), 42 (bottom), 45, 53, 54, 65, 66, 68, 69, 71, 73 (top and bottom), 74, 76, 77, 79, 82, 83 (top), 85 (top and bottom), 86, 88, 89, 91, 92 (top and bottom), 94, 95 (top), 97, 99, 100, 102, 105, 106 (top and bottom), 108 (top and bottom), 109, 116, 118, 119, 123, 124 (top and bottom), 126 (top and bottom), 127 (top and bottom), 137 (top), 140, 142, 145, 149, 160, 162, 173 (top and bottom), 177 (top), 182, 185, 191, 194, 199, 200, 202, 203, 204, 205, 208, 213, 218, 221, 226, 231, 233, 236, 238, 239, 240, 242 (top and bottom), 246.

ACKNOWLEDGEMENT OF SPONSORS

Funding for publication of this book has been provided by a partnership between the Government of Manitoba, a Crown Corporation, private businesses, environmental consulting firms, and non-profit conservation organizations. The names and logos of these sponsoring organizations appear in alphabetical order below.

Fish Futures, Inc.,
200-1555 St. James Street,
Winnipeg, Manitoba, R3H 1B5

LP Canada, Ltd.
Swan River, Manitoba,
R0L 1Z0

Manitoba Government, Fisheries Branch,
Department of Water Stewardship,
200 Saulteaux Crescent, Winnipeg,
Manitoba, R3J 3W3

Manitoba Hydro,
820 Taylor Avenue,
Winnipeg, Manitoba,
R3M 3T1

Manitoba Wildlife Federation,
70 Stevenson Road
Winnipeg, Manitoba,
R3H 0W7

7 Oaks Game and Fish Association,
Brian Strauman, 42 Gardner Cove,
Winnipeg, Manitoba, R2C 4X8

75 Game and Fish Association,
Ted Finlay,
285 Kirkbridge Drive Winnipeg,
Manitoba, R3T 4W5

North/South Consultants, Inc.,
83 Scurfield Boulevard,
Winnipeg, Manitoba, R3Y 1G4

TetrES Consultants, Inc.
603-386 Broadway,
Winnipeg, Manitoba, R3C 3R6

TABLE OF CONTENTS

ACKNOWLEDGEMENTS | xii

CHECKLIST OF THE FRESHWATER FISH SPECIES FOUND IN MANITOBA | xiv

INTRODUCTION | 3

    THE BIOGEOGRAPHY OF THE FRESHWATER FISH FAUNA OF MANITOBA | 3

    THE GEOGRAPHY OF MANITOBA'S WATERSHEDS AND FISH SPECIES DIVERSITY | 6

    PATTERN OF FISH SPECIES DIVERSITY | 18

    POSTGLACIAL COLONIZATION OF FISH | 18

    ORGANIZATION OF THE SPECIES ACCOUNTS | 22

    COMMON AND SCIENTIFIC NAMES OF FISHES | 25

    Common Names | 25

    Scientific Names | 25

    Pronunciation Guide for Scientific Names | 25

    DOCUMENTATION AND PRESERVATION OF FISH SPECIMENS FOR IDENTIFICATION | 26

    Documentation of Fish Collections | 26

    Preservation of Fish Specimens | 27

GENERAL FEATURES AND MEASUREMENTS OF FISH | 28

    Lateral Views, Whole Body | 28

    Features and Measurements on the Head | 29

    How to Use the Keys in This Book | 30

    Where to Get Help with Fish Identification | 30

KEY TO THE FAMILIES OF FRESHWATER FISHES OF MANITOBA AND ADJACENT AREAS OF THE HUDSON BAY DRAINAGE | 31

SPECIES ACCOUNTS | 35

Lampreys, Order Petromyzontiformes | 36

    Lampreys, Family Petromyzontidae | 36

    Key to the Ammocoetes Larvae of Lampreys Found in Manitoba | 37

    Key to the Adult Lampreys Found in Manitoba | 37

    Ichthyomyzon castaneus, chestnut lamprey; lamproie brune | 38

    Ichthyomyzon fossor, northern brook lamprey; lamproie du nord | 40

    Ichthyomyzon unicuspis, silver lamprey; lamproie argentée | 42

Sturgeons and Paddlefishes, Order Acipenseriformes | 44

    Sturgeons, Family Acipenseridae | 44

    Acipenser fulvescens, lake sturgeon; esturgeon jaune | 45

Gars and Their Extinct Relatives, Order Semionotiformes | 48

    Gars, Family Lepisosteidae | 48

    Lepisosteus osseus, longnose gar; lépisosté osseux | 49

Bowfin and Its Extinct Relatives, Order Amiiformes | 50

    Bowfin, Family Amiidae | 50

    Amia calva, bowfin; poisson-castor | 51

Bony-Tongued Fishes, Order Osteoglossiformes | **52**
   Goldeye and Mooneye, Family Hiodontidae | **52**
      Key to the Goldeye and Mooneye | **53**
      Hiodon alosoides, goldeye; laquaiche aux yeux d'or | **53**
      Hiodon tergisus, mooneye; laquaiche argentée | **54**
Minnows, Suckers, and Loaches, Order Cypriniformes | **56**
   Minnows and Carp, Family Cyprinidae | **56**
      Key to the Minnows Found in Manitoba and Adjacent Areas of the Hudson Bay Drainage | **57**
      Campostoma anomalum, central stoneroller; roule-caillou | **63**
      Campostoma oligolepis, largescale stoneroller; roule-caillou à grandes écailles | **64**
      Carassius auratus, goldfish; poisson doré | **65**
      Couesius plumbeus, lake chub; méné de lac | **66**
      Cyprinella spiloptera, spotfin shiner; méné bleu | **68**
      Cyprinus carpio, common carp; carpe | **69**
      Hybognathus hankinsoni, brassy minnow; méné laiton | **71**
      Luxilus cornutus, common shiner; méné à nageoires rouges | **73**
      Macrhybopsis storeriana, silver chub; méné à grandes écailles | **74**
      Margariscus margarita, pearl dace; mulet perlé | **76**
      Nocomis biguttatus, hornyhead chub; tête à taches rouges | **77**
      Notemigonus crysoleucas, golden shiner; méné jaune | **79**
      Note on the Identification of Manitoba Minnows of the Genus *Notropis* | **80**
      Notropis anogenus, pugnose shiner; méné camus | **81**
      Notropis atherinoides, emerald shiner; méné émeraude | **82**
      Notropis blennius, river shiner; méné de rivière | **83**
      Notropis dorsalis, bigmouth shiner; méné à grande bouche | **85**
      Notropis heterodon, blackchin shiner; menton noir | **86**
      Notropis heterolepis, blacknose shiner; museau noir | **88**
      Notropis hudsonius, spottail shiner; queue à tache noire | **89**
      Notropis percobromus, carmine shiner; méné carminé | **91**
      Notropis stramineus, sand shiner; méné paille | **92**
      Notropis texanus, weed shiner; méné diamant | **94**
      Notropis volucellus, mimic shiner; méné pâle | **95**
      Phoxinus eos, northern redbelly dace; ventre rouge du nord | **97**
      Phoxinus neogaeus, finescale dace; ventre citron | **99**
      Pimephales notatus, bluntnose minnow; ventre-pourri | **100**
      Pimephales promelas, fathead minnow; tête-de-boule | **102**
      Pimephales vigilax, bullhead minnow; tête barbotte | **104**
      Platygobio gracilis, flathead chub; méné à tête plate | **105**
      Zoogeographic Note on Species of *Rhinichthys* | **106**
      Rhinichthys cataractae, longnose dace; naseux de rapides | **106**
      Rhinichthys obtusus, western blacknose dace; naseux noir de l'ouest | **108**
      Semotilus atromaculatus, creek chub; mulet à cornes | **109**

    Suckers, Family Catostomidae | **112**
        Key to the Suckers Found in Manitoba and Adjacent Areas of the Hudson Bar Drainage | **113**
        Carpiodes cyprinus, quillback; couette | **116**
        Catostomus catostomus, longnose sucker; meunier rouge | **118**
        Catostomus commersoni, white sucker; meunier noir | **119**
        Hypentelium nigricans, northern hog sucker; meunier à tête carrée | **121**
        Ictiobus bubalus, smallmouth buffalo; buffalo à petite bouche | **122**
        Ictiobus cyprinellus, bigmouth buffalo; buffalo à grande bouche | **123**
        Moxostoma anisurum, silver redhorse; chevalier blanc | **124**
        Moxostoma erythrurum, golden redhorse; chevalier doré | **126**
        Moxostoma macrolepidotum, shorthead redhorse; chevalier rouge | **127**
        Moxostoma valenciennesi, greater redhorse; chevalier jaune | **129**
Catfishes, Order Siluriformes | 130
    North American Freshwater Catfishes, Family Ictaluridae | 130
        Key to the Catfishes Found in Manitoba and Adjacent Areas of the Hudson Bay Drainage | **131**
        Ameiurus melas, black bullhead; barbotte noire | **132**
        Ameiurus natalis, yellow bullhead; barbotte jaune | **134**
        Ameiurus nebulosus, brown bullhead; barbotte brune | **135**
        Ictalurus punctatus, channel catfish; barbue de rivière | **137**
        Noturus flavus, stonecat; barbotte des rapides | **140**
        Noturus gyrinus, tadpole madtom; chat-fou brun | **142**
Pike-Like Fishes, Order Esociformes | 144
    Pike and Muskellunge, Family Esocidae | 144
        Key to the Pike and Muskellunge | **145**
        Esox lucius, northern pike; grand brochet | **145**
        Esox masquinongy, muskellunge; maskinongé | **146**
    Mudminnows, Family Umbridae | 148
        Umbra limi, central mudminnow; umbre de vase | **149**
Smelt-Like Fishes, Order Osmeriformes | 151
    Smelts, Family Osmeridae | 151
        Key to the Smelts Found in Manitoba | **152**
        Mallotus villosus, capelin; capelan | **152**
        Osmerus mordax, rainbow smelt; éperlan arc-en-ciel | **153**
Trout-Like Fishes, Order Salmoniformes | 155
    Whitefish, Grayling, Char, Trout, and Salmon, Family Salmonidae | 155
        Key to the Whitefish, Grayling, Char, Trout, and Salmon Found in Manitoba | **157**
        Note on the Species Differentiation of Ciscoes in Manitoba | **159**
        Coregonus artedi, cisco; cisco de lac | **160**
        Coregonus clupeaformis, lake whitefish; grand corégone | **162**
        Coregonus zenithicus, shortjaw cisco; cisco à mâchoires égales | **164**
        Prosopium cylindraceum, round whitefish; ménomini rond | **165**

Thymallus arcticus, Arctic grayling; ombre arctique | 166
Oncorhynchus clarkii lewisi, westslope cutthroat trout; truite fardée | 168
Oncorhynchus mykiss, rainbow trout; truite arc-en-ciel | 169
Oncorhynchus nerka, kokanee; kokani | 171
Salmo trutta, brown trout; truite brune | 173
"tiger trout" truite tigre (brown trout X brook trout hybrid) | 173
Salvelinus alpinus, arctic char; omble chevalier | 175
Salvelinus fontinalis, brook trout; omble de fontaine | 177
"splake" truite moulac (brook trout X lake trout hybrid) | 177
Salvelinus namaycush, lake trout; touladi | 179

Troutperches, Pirate Perch, and Cavefishes, Order Percopsiformes | 181
  Troutperches, Family Percopsidae | 181
    Percopsis omiscomaycus, troutperch; omisco | 182

Cod-Like Fishes, Order Gadiformes | 184
  Codfishes, Family Gadidae | 184
    Lota lota, burbot; lotte | 185

Topminnows, Order Cyprinodontiformes | 187
  Killifishes, Family Fundulidae | 187
    Fundulus diaphanus, banded killifish; fondule barrée | 188

Sticklebacks, Pipefishes, Seahorses, and Related Families, Order Gasterosteiformes | 190
  Sticklebacks: Family Gasterosteidae | 190
    Key to the Sticklebacks Found in Manitoba | 191
    Culaea inconstans, brook stickleback; épinoche à cinq épines | 191
    Gasterosteus aculeatus species complex, threespine stickleback; épinoche à trois épines | 193
    Pungitius pungitius, ninespine stickleback; épinoche à neuf épines | 194

Scorpionfishes and Related Families, Order Scorpaeniformes | 196
  Sculpins, Family Cottidae | 196
    Key to the Freshwater Sculpins and Marine Sculpins of the Genus *Myoxocephalus* Found in Manitoba | 197
    Cottus bairdi, mottled sculpin; chabot tacheté | 198
    Cottus cognatus, slimy sculpin; chabot visqueux | 199
    Cottus ricei, spoonhead sculpin; chabot à tête plate | 200
    Myoxocephalus quadricornis, fourhorn sculpin; chaboisseau à quatre cornes | 202
    Myoxocephalus scorpioides, Arctic sculpin; chaboisseau arctique | 203
    Myoxocephalus scorpius, shorthorn sculpin; chaboisseau à épines courtes | 204
    Myoxocephalus thompsoni, deepwater sculpin; chabot de profondeur | 205

Perch-Like Fishes, Order Perciformes | 207
  Temperate Basses, Family Moronidae | 207
    Morone chrysops, white bass; bar blanc | 208
  Bass, Crappies, and Sunfishes, Family Centrarchidae | 210
    Key to the Bass, Crappies, and Sunfishes Found in Manitoba and Adjacent Areas of the Hudson Bay Drainage | 211
    Ambloplites rupestris, rock bass; crapet de roche | 213

Lepomis cyanellus, green sunfish; crapet vert | **214**

Lepomis gibbosus, pumpkinseed; crapet-soleil | **215**

Lepomis humilis, orangespotted sunfish; crapet menu | **217**

Lepomis macrochirus, bluegill; crapet arlequin | **218**

Lepomis megalotis, longear sunfish; crapet à longues oreilles | **220**

Micropterus dolomieu, smallmouth bass; achigan à petite bouche | **221**

Micropterus salmoides, largemouth bass; achigan à grande bouche | **223**

Pomoxis annularis, white crappie; marigane blanche | **225**

Pomoxis nigromaculatus, black crappie; marigane noire | **226**

Darters, Perch, Sauger, and Walleye, Family Percidae | 228

Key to the Darters, Perch, Sauger, and Walleye Found in Manitoba and Adjacent Areas of the Hudson Bay Drainage | **229**

Etheostoma caeruleum, rainbow darter; dard arc-en-ciel | **230**

Etheostoma exile, Iowa darter; dard à ventre jaune | **231**

Etheostoma microperca, least darter; petit dard | **232**

Etheostoma nigrum, johnny darter; raseux-de-terre | **233**

Perca flavescens, yellow perch; perchaude | **235**

Percina caprodes, logperch; fouille-roche | **236**

Percina maculata, blackside darter; dard noir | **238**

Percina shumardi, river darter; dard de rivière | **239**

Sander canadensis, sauger; doré noir | **240**

Sander vitreus, walleye; doré jaune | **242**

Drums, Family Sciaenidae | 245

Aplodinotus grunniens, freshwater drum; malachigan | **246**

APPENDIX: DISTRIBUTION OF MANITOBA FRESHWATER FISHES BY WATERSHED | 249

GLOSSARY | 259

REFERENCES | 269

ACKNOWLEDGEMENTS

We are indebted to many people and organizations who have contributed their support, both moral and material, to our work on this book.

The senior author's wife, Bessie Stewart, provided constant support and understanding, and help in the field, in the lab, and at the computer. She has also put up with his moods and idiosyncrasies for the last 48 years, for which he is eternally grateful.

The junior author wishes to thank his wife, Kimberly Watkinson, for her love and support. He also thanks his supervisor, Bill Franzin, for his encouragement and for allowing the time required to complete this book to be taken from other duties.

Funding for preparation of the first draft of this book was provided by two contracts from Fisheries and Oceans Canada. Richard Janusz, of Fisheries and Oceans Canada, took care of all the development and administrative aspects of the contracts for production of the first draft of this book. Without his initiative, this project may never have begun. We would also like to thank Andries Blouw, of Fisheries and Oceans Canada, for his help and encouragement with all aspects of proposal development and fundraising for this book for final publication. Fisheries and Oceans Canada also provided specimens, internal reports, and field records, added records to the distribution database, and entered the database into Arc View[tm], a GIS application, which made creating the distribution maps possible. Bill Franzin and Pat Nelson in particular have shared their data on fish distributions in southern Manitoba.

The personnel of the Fisheries Branch of the Manitoba Department of Water Stewardship provided distribution records, internal reports, and specimens, and loaned equipment, helped with fieldwork, and exchanged and criticized ideas with us. Art Derksen, Shelly Matkowski, Joel Hunt, Keith Kristofferson, Jim Beyette, and Lionel Robert were sources of a wealth of information.

The Royal Ontario Museum, and especially the late Ed Crossman, and Erling Holm, provided the collection records of Manitoba fishes in the Royal Ontario Museum and loaned many specimens to us. Dr. Crossman also was an invaluable source of ideas and suggestions. He reviewed the first draft and provided criticism and questions that have greatly improved this book.

The National Museum of Canada, especially Charles Gruchy, Brian Coad, and the late Don McAllister, also provided their collection records and the loan of specimens. The Manitoba Museum, and especially William Preston and Brian McKillop, Janis Klapecki, and Gavin Hanke, also provided their collection records and specimens for examination. We hope that the material sent to them helps to pay some of our debt to those institutions.

Ed Crossman and Joe Nelson provided information on recent changes to nomenclature of the fish species in our area. Fernand Saurette provided and checked the accuracy of French common names.

Donna Grassia of L.P. Canada, Ltd. sent us specimens from the Porcupine Mountains area. She has also been a constant source of encouragement to get this book finished and published.

Rick Moodie of the University of Winnipeg provided his Manitoba collecting records and also provided specimens for examination. North-South Consultants provided an electrofishing boat and operator for fish collections in the Red River. They have also provided field data and specimens for examination. TetrES Consultants also provided data and specimens.

Bruce McCulloch, David Tyson, and Gavin Hanke put in many hours in the field, collecting fish, and more in the laboratory, identifying them and entering records in the distribution database. During that work, they also managed to do their own research and write excellent theses on the stonecat, channel catfish, and the ecology of Lake Winnipeg shore fish communities, respectively. The largest single body of knowledge about our freshwater fishes is contained in the theses of graduate students, mainly from the Department of Zoology and the Natural Resources Institute of the University of Manitoba. We have drawn heavily on their work in this book. Stephanie Backhouse, Jeff Eastman, Richard Penner, and Tommy Sheldon aided with the collection of many of the fish that appear as illustrations in this book. A host of graduate and undergraduate students contributed their efforts to collecting fish, especially during the Biology of Fishes class fieldtrips. We hope the experience and knowledge they gained repaid their efforts.

Non-professional people and organizations have also helped us. In particular, we would like to thank David Carrick and Stuart McKay for reviewing the first draft of this book from the viewpoint of non-professionals. In addition, Stuart McKay provided valuable information about the lower Red River and its fish. The senior author's son, John Stewart, and David Pannu helped with fieldwork.

Peer review and editing of the revised draft of the book was done by Gavin Hanke and Art Derksen. Nick Barnes of Manitoba Hydro also provided comments on the revised draft.

Finally, during the process of producing this book, several individuals stand out as having always been available for fieldwork, discussions, criticism of ideas, and, more recently, prodding, coaxing, pushing, and even pleading to get this book done! The constant moral support, encouragement, feedback, and nattering from Art Derksen, Bill Franzin, Francis Cook, Ray Ratynski, Pat Nelson, and Beverly Horn are much appreciated. It must have seemed to you like you were pulling teeth at times!

We apologize to any people or organizations we have failed to mention. To all those who helped, our sincerest thanks. We hope this book justifies the effort you put in on our behalf.

K.W. Stewart
D.A. Watkinson
March 8, 2004

CHECKLIST OF THE FRESHWATER FISHES OF MANITOBA

NOTES ON THE ORGANIZATION OF THE CHECKLIST

1. Species are listed in the same order in which they appear in the Table of Contents and in the Species Accounts.

2. The number on the left side of the left-hand column of the table is the number of species, including the one in that row, listed up to that point in the table.

3. Orders and families are numbered serially as they appear in the table. The order and family are listed in the two rows at the head of the rows listing the genera and species in that family. Where there is more than one family in an order, the order name and number are not repeated after the first family.

Species	Common Names		Native, Native and Transplanted, Reintroduced to Former Range, or Introduced
	English	French	
Order 1, Lampreys, Petromyzontiformes			
Family 1, Lampreys, Petromyzontidae			
1 *Ichthyomyzon castaneus*	chestnut lamprey	lamproie brune	Native
2 *Ichthyomyzon fossor*	northern brook lamprey	lamproie du nord	Native
3 *Ichthyomyzon unicuspis*	silver lamprey	lamproie argentée	Native
Order 2, Sturgeons and Paddlefishes, Acipenseriformes			
Family 2, Sturgeons, Acipenseridae			
4 *Acipenser fulvescens*	lake sturgeon	esturgeon jaune	Native Reintroduced
Order 3, Bony-Tongued Fishes, Osteoglossiformes			
Family 3, Goldeye and Mooneye, Hiodontidae			
5 *Hiodon alosoides*	goldeye	laquaiche aux yeux d'or	Native
6 *Hiodon tergisus*	mooneye	laquaiche argentée	Native
Order 4, Minnows, Suckers, and Loaches, Cypriniformes			
Family 4, Minnows and Carp, Cyprinidae			
7 *Carassius auratus*	goldfish	poisson doré	Introduced
8 *Couesius plumbeus*	lake chub	méné de lac	Native
9 *Cyprinella spiloptera*	spotfin shiner	méné bleu	Native
10 *Cyprinus carpio*	common carp	carpe	Introduced
11 *Hybognathus hankinsoni*	brassy minnow	méné laiton	Native
12 *Luxilus cornutus*	common shiner	méné à nageoires rouges	Native
13 *Macrhybopsis storeriana*	silver chub	méné à grandes écailles	Native
14 *Margariscus margarita*	pearl dace	mulet perlé	Native
15 *Nocomis biguttatus*	hornyhead chub	tête á taches rouges	Native
16 *Notemigonus crysoleucas*	golden shiner	méné jaune	Native
17 *Notropis atherinoides*	emerald shiner	méné émeraude	Native
18 *Notropis blennius*	river shiner	méné de rivière	Native
19 *Notropis dorsalis*	bigmouth shiner	méné à grande bouche	Native
20 *Notropis heterodon*	blackchin shiner	menton noir	Native
21 *Notropis heterolepis*	blacknose shiner	museau noir	Native
22 *Notropis hudsonius*	spottail shiner	queue à tache noir	Native

Family 4, Minnows and Carp, Cyprinidae (Cont'd)

23	*Notropis percobromus*	carmine shiner	méné carminé	Native
24	*Notropis stramineus*	sand shiner	méné paille	Native
25	*Notropis texanus*	weed shiner	méné diamant	Native
26	*Notropis volucellus*	mimic shiner	méné pâle	Native
27	*Phoxinus eos*	northern redbelly dace	ventre rouge du nord	Native
28	*Phoxinus neogaeus*	finescale dace	ventre citron	Native
29	*Pimephales notatus*	bluntnose minnow	ventre-pourri	Native
30	*Pimephales promelas*	fathead minnow	tête-de-boule	Native
31	*Platygobio gracilis*	flathead chub	méné à tête plate	Native
32	*Rhinichthys cataractae*	longnose dace	naseux de rapides	Native
33	*Rhinichthys obtusus*	western blacknose dace	naseux noir de l'ouest	Native
34	*Semotilus atromaculatus*	creek chub	mulet à cornes	Native

Order 4, Family 5, Suckers, Catostomidae

35	*Carpiodes cyprinus*	quillback	couette	Native
36	*Catostomus catostomus*	longnose sucker	meunier rouge	Native
37	*Catostomus commersoni*	white sucker	muenier noir	Native
38	*Ictiobus cyprinellus*	bigmouth buffalo	buffalo à grande bouche	Native
39	*Moxostoma anisurum*	silver redhorse	chevalier blanc	Native
40	*Moxostoma erythrurum*	golden redhorse	chevalier doré	Native
41	*Moxostoma macrolepidotum*	shorthead redhorse	chevalier rouge	Native

Order 5, Catfishes, Siluriformes
Family 6, North American Freshwater Catfishes, Ictaluridae

42	*Ameiurus melas*	black bullhead	barbotte noir	Native
43	*Ameiurus nebulosus*	brown bullhead	barbotte brune	Native
44	*Ictalurus punctatus*	channel catfish	barbue de rivière	Native
45	*Noturus flavus*	stonecat	barbotte des rapides	Native
46	*Noturus gyrinus*	tadpole madtom	chat-fou brun	Native

Order 6, Pike-Like Fishes, Esociformes
Family 7, Pike and Muskellunge, Esocidae

47	*Esox lucius*	northern pike	grand brochet	Native
48	*Esox masquinongy*	muskellunge	maskinongé	Native Transplanted

Order 6, Family 8, Mudminnows, Umbridae

49	*Umbra limi*	central mudminnow	umbre de vase	Native

Order 7, Smelt-Like Fishes, Osmeriformes
Family 9, Smelt, Osmeridae

50	*Mallotus villosus*	capelin	capelan	Marine (Estuarine)
51	*Osmerus mordax*	rainbow smelt	éperlan arc-en-ciel	Introduced

Order 8, Trout-Like Fishes, Salmoniformes
Family 10, Whitefishes, Graylings, Trout, and Salmon, Salmonidae

52	*Coregonus artedi*	cisco	cisco de lac	Native
53	*Coregonus clupeaformis*	lake whitefish	grand corégone	Native Transplanted
54	*Coregonus zenithicus*	shortjaw cisco	cisco à mâchoires égales	Native
55	*Prosopium cylindraceum*	round whitefish	ménomini rond	Native

Family 10, Whitefishes, Graylings, Trout, and Salmon, Salmonidae (Cont'd)				
56	*Thymallus arcticus*	Arctic grayling	ombre arctique	Native Transplanted
57	*Oncorhynchus clarkii lewisi*	westslope cutthroat trout	truite fardée	Introduced
58	*Oncorhynchus mykiss*	rainbow trout	truite arc-en-ciel	Introduced
59	*Oncorhynchus nerka*	kokanee	kokani	Introduced
60	*Salmo trutta*	brown trout	truite brun	Introduced
61	*Salmo trutta* X *Salvelinus fontinalis* Hybrid	"tiger trout" brown trout X brook trout hybrid	truite tigre	Human-made hybrid
62	*Salvelinus alpinus*	Arctic char	omble chevalier	Native Transplanted
63	*Salvelinus fontinalis*	brook trout	omble de fontaine	Native Transplanted
64	*Salvelinus fontinalis* X *Salvelinus namaycush* Hybrid	"splake" brook trout X lake trout hybrid	truite moulac	Human-made hybrid
65	*Salvelinus namaycush*	lake trout	touladi	Native Transplanted
Order 9, Troutperch, Percopsiformes				
Family 11 Troutperch, Percopsidae				
66	*Percopsis omiscomaycus*	troutperch	omisco	Native
Order 10, Cod-Like Fishes, Gadiformes				
Family 12, Codfishes, Gadidae				
67	*Lota lota*	burbot	lotte	Native
Order 11, Topminnows, Cyprinodontiformes				
Family 13, Topminnows and Killifishes, Fundulidae				
68	*Fundulus diaphanus*	banded killifish	fondule barrée	Native
Order 12, Sticklebacks, Pipefishes, and Seahorses, Gasterosteiformes				
Family 14, Sticklebacks, Gasterosteidae				
69	*Culaea inconstans*	brook stickleback	épinoche à cinq épines	Native
70	*Gasterosteus aculeatus*	threespine stickleback	épinoche à trois épines	Native
71	*Pungitius pungitius*	ninespine stickleback	épinoche à neuf épines	Native
Order 13, Scorpionfishes and Related Families, Scorpaeniformes				
Family 15, Cottidae, Sculpins				
72	*Cottus bairdi*	mottled sculpin	chabot tacheté	Native
73	*Cottus cognatus*	slimy sculpin	chabot visqueux	Native
74	*Cottus ricei*	spoonhead sculpin	chabot à tête plate	Native
75	*Myoxocephalus quadricornis*	fourhorned sculpin	chaboisseau à quatre cornes	Marine (Estuarine)
76	*Myoxocephalus scorpioides*	Arctic sculpin	chaboisseau arctique	Marine (Estuarine)
77	*Myoxocephalus scorpius*	shorthorn sculpin	chaboisseau à épines courtes	Marine (Estuarine)
78	*Myoxocephalus thompsoni*	deepwater sculpin	chabot de profondeur	Native
Order 14, Perch-Like Fishes, Perciformes				
Family 16, Temperate Basses, Moronidae				
79	*Morone chrysops*	white bass	bar blanc	Introduced
Order 14, Family 17, Bass, Crappies, and Sunfishes, Centrarchidae				
80	*Ambloplites rupestris*	rock bass	crapet de roche	Native
81	*Lepomis gibbosus*	pumpkinseed	crapet-soleil	Native Transplanted

	Order 14, Family 17, Bass, Crappies, and Sunfishes, Centrarchidae (Cont'd)			
82	*Lepomis macrochirus*	bluegill	crapet arlequin	Native
83	*Micropterus dolomieu*	smallmouth bass	achigan à petite bouche	Introduced
84	*Micropterus salmoides*	largemouth bass	achigan à grande bouche	Introduced
85	*Pomoxis annularis*	white crappie	marigane blanc	Native
86	*Pomoxis nigromaculatus*	black crappie	marigane noir	Native Transplanted
	Order 14, Family 18, Darters, Perch, Sauger, Walleye, Percidae			
87	*Etheostoma exile*	Iowa darter	dard à ventre jaune	Native
88	*Etheostoma nigrum*	johnny darter	raseux-de-terre	Native
89	*Perca flavescens*	yellow perch	perchaude	Native
90	*Percina caprodes*	logperch	fouille-roche	Native
91	*Percina maculata*	blackside darter	dard noir	Native
92	*Percina shumardi*	river darter	dard de rivière	Native
93	*Sander canadensis*	sauger	doré noir	Native
94	*Sander vitreus*	walleye	doré jaune	Native
	Order 14, Family 19, Drums, Sciaenidae			
95	*Aplodinotus grunniens*	freshwater drum	malachigan	Native

SUMMARY OF FISHES FOUND IN MANITOBA	
TOTAL ORDERS:	14
TOTAL FAMILIES:	19
TOTAL GENERA:	53
TOTAL SPECIES:	95
NATIVE FRESHWATER SPECIES:	79
NATIVE SPECIES REINTRODUCED TO FORMER RANGE AFTER EXTIRPATION:	1
NATIVE SPECIES TRANSPLANTED OUTSIDE NATIVE RANGE IN MANITOBA:	8
INTRODUCED SPECIES:	10
HUMAN-MADE HYBRIDS:	2
MARINE SPECIES FOUND IN ESTUARIES ON HUDSON BAY COAST:	4

THE FRESHWATER FISHES OF MANITOBA

INTRODUCTION

This book is meant to provide its users, including students, professional fish biologists, and interested members of the general public, with an accurate, reliable, and up-to-date means of identifying our freshwater fishes and obtaining at least basic information on their biology. Where it is available, we have provided more specific, Manitoba-based information on species than would be contained in a popular-level field guide. We have also cited the sources of our information and given a full citation for each of our literature sources, which is not usually done in popular-level field guides. At the same time, we have tried to avoid technical terms as much as possible, and to provide definitions for the specialized terms we did use. We hope that interested anglers, commercial fishers, and the public in general will find the information in this book interesting and easily accessible. In fact, we will gauge the success of this book, in part, by whether it generates increased interest and enquiries about fish from the public. We also hope it will stimulate interested young people to pursue a career in fish biology.

Manitoba has the third most diverse freshwater fish fauna in Canada, after Ontario and Québec, with 95 species (including ten introduced species and two human-made hybrids). This book covers the native and introduced freshwater fishes found in Manitoba, with the following additions. We have included the capelin, *Mallotus villosus*, fourhorn sculpin, *Myoxocephalus quadricornis*, Arctic sculpin, *Myoxocephalus scorpioides*, and shorthorn sculpin, *Myoxocephalus scorpius*, all marine species in Hudson Bay that have been collected in estuaries. This is admittedly an arbitrary decision. Species such as the Arctic flounder, *Liopsetta glacialis*, Greenland cod, *Gadus ogac*, lumpfish, *Cyclopterus lumpus*, sand lance, *Ammodytes hexapterus*, and a variety of eelpouts (Zoarcidae), pricklebacks (Stichaeidae), and snailfish (Liparidae), for which there are no records in our database, must also get into estuaries. We considered it useful to include those marine species we have records for, but the necessary data on which to base a complete book on the marine shore fishes of Manitoba remain to be collected.

We have also included 15 freshwater species that have not been found in Manitoba, but occur in the Hudson Bay Drainage, in one or more of northwestern Ontario, northwestern Minnesota, eastern North Dakota, and extreme northeastern South Dakota. Since 1966, six species from those areas have been found here. Three of these, the stonecat, the spotfin shiner, and the rainbow smelt, are apparently the result of dispersal over the last 30 years. The other three, the blackchin shiner, the golden redhorse, and the weed shiner, probably have been in Manitoba longer, but, until recently, were misidentified. At least some species from adjacent areas will likely be found here in the near future. The yellow bullhead, notably, has been found in the Bois de Sioux River and several Minnesota tributaries of the Red River, including the Roseau River (Renard, Hanson, and Enblom, 1983, 1985; Koel, 1997), and it may already be north of the US-Canada border. If global warming continues, the rate of northward and westward dispersal of fish species may accelerate in the future.

THE BIOGEOGRAPHY OF THE FRESHWATER FISH FAUNA OF MANITOBA

The wide variety and distribution of our freshwater fishes are the result of three factors. First, fish survived glaciation in different refugia, which made different routes available to them to reach Manitoba during and after the retreat of the ice sheet. Second, different species of fishes have different ecological requirements, which limited the routes they may have been able to use to reach Manitoba and also limit the waters they can colonize today. Third, the distribution of different types of fish habitat in Manitoba determined where species could survive once they arrived. This is largely delimited by the geology of the province.

Manitoba's freshwater fish fauna has a close relationship to the fish faunas of the Mississippi River and Laurentian Great Lakes. Four species are found in both the Mississippi headwaters and upper Missouri, and 27 species occur in the Lake Superior watershed, Mississippi headwaters, and the upper Missouri watershed. In contrast to this, 13 species of our native freshwater fish are found in Mississippi River headwaters in Minnesota, but not in the Lake Superior watershed or the upper Missouri watershed, and 20 species occur in the Mississippi headwaters and the Lake Superior watershed, but not in the upper Missouri. Only two species of native freshwater fish in Manitoba, the goldeye and the flathead chub, are found today in the upper Missouri River, but not in the Mississippi River headwaters in Minnesota. Two minnow species, the bigmouth shiner and sand shiner, have recognized subspecies in the Mississippi/Great Lakes watersheds that are different from their subspecies in the Missouri River watershed. In both cases, the Manitoba form agrees with the Mississippi/Great Lakes subspecies, not the Missouri River

INTRODUCTION

subspecies (see Table I). The close relationship between the aquatic fauna of the upper Mississippi River and that of southern Manitoba was also observed by Clarke (1981), who noted the relationship between the freshwater mollusk fauna of southern Manitoba and that of the upper Mississippi River.

TABLE I. [1,2]Watersheds Adjacent to the Hudson Bay Drainage in which Manitoba Native Freshwater Fish Species Are Found

WATERSHED		
Lake Superior	**Upper Mississippi and Lake Superior**	**Upper Mississippi**
lake chub; *Couesius plumbeus*	northern brook lamprey; *Ichthyomyzon fossor*	chestnut lamprey; *Ichthyomyzon castaneus*
longnose sucker; *Catostomus catostomus*	silver lamprey; *Ichthyomyzon unicuspis*	mooneye; *Hiodon tergisus*
shortjaw cisco; *Coregonus zenithicus*	lake sturgeon; *Acipenser fulvescens*	spotfin shiner; *Cyprinella spiloptera*
[2]round whitefish; *Prosopium cylindraceum*	hornyhead chub; *Nocomis biguttatus*	silver chub; *Macrhybopsis storeriana*
[2]Arctic grayling; *Thymallus arcticus*	blackchin shiner; *Notropis heterodon*	river shiner; *Notropis blennius*
lake trout; *Salvelinus namaycush*	spottail shiner; *Notropis hudsonius*	carmine shiner; *Notropis percobromus*
ninespine stickleback; *Pungitius pungitius*	mimic shiner; *Notropis volucellus*	weed shiner; *Notropis texanus*
spoonhead sculpin; *Cottus ricei*	bluntnose minnow; *Pimephales notatus*	quillback; *Carpiodes cyprinus*
deepwater sculpin; *Myoxocephalus thompsoni*	western blacknose dace; *Rhinichthys obtusus*	golden redhorse; *Moxostoma erythrurum*
	silver redhorse; *Moxostoma anisurum*	pumpkinseed; *Lepomis gibbosus*
	tadpole madtom; *Noturus gyrinus*	white crappie; *Pomoxis annularis*
	muskellunge; *Esox masquinongy*	blackside darter; *Percina maculata*
	central mudminnow; *Umbra limi*	river darter; *Percina shumardi*
	cisco; *Coregonus artedi*	
	lake whitefish; *Coregonus clupeaformis*	
	brook trout; *Salvelinus fontinalis*	
	mottled sculpin; *Cottus bairdi*	
	slimy sculpin; *Cottus cognatus*	
	rock bass; *Ambloplites rupestris*	
	bluegill; *Lepomis macrochirus*	
	black crappie; *Pomoxis nigromaculatus*	
	logperch; *Percina caprodes*	
Total 9	Total 22	Total 13

1. The Arctic char and threespine stickleback do not occur naturally in any drainage adjacent to the Hudson Bay Drainage except the Arctic Ocean coastal drainages. Therefore, they do not appear in this table or in the species number totals. Their inclusion in the totals brings the total number of native freshwater species in Manitoba to 79.
2. The round whitefish and Arctic grayling both have extensive distributions across northern Canada, south to the Peace and Churchill river watersheds. They both also have (or had) outlier distributions to the south, the round whitefish in the Lake Superior watershed, and the Arctic grayling in the Great Lakes and upper Missouri River watersheds. The Manitoba distribution of both is continuous with the northern Canadian distribution and widely disjunct from the southern outlier distributions.
3. The bigmouth shiner, *Notropis dorsalis*, and sand shiner, *N. stramineus*, both have different subspecies in the Mississippi and Missouri river watersheds. In both species, the Manitoba form agrees with the Mississippi, not the Missouri, subspecies.

WATERSHED		
Upper Mississippi and Upper Missouri	**Upper Missouri**	**Lake Superior, Upper Mississippi, and Upper Missouri**
[3]bigmouth shiner; *Notropis dorsalis*	goldeye; *Hiodon alosoides*	brassy minnow; *Hybognathus hankinsoni*
bigmouth buffalo; *Ictiobus cyprinellus*	flathead chub; *Platygobio gracilis*	common shiner; *Luxilus cornutus*
banded killifish; *Fundulus diaphanus*		pearl dace; *Margariscus margarita*
freshwater drum; *Aplodinotus grunniens*		golden shiner; *Notemigonus crysoleucas*
		emerald shiner; *Notropis atherinoides*
		blacknose shiner; *Notropis heterolepis*
		[3]sand shiner; *Notropis stramineus*
		northern redbelly dace; *Phoxinus eos*
		finescale dace; *Phoxinus neogaeus*
		fathead minnow; *Pimephales promelas*
		longnose dace; *Rhinichthys cataractae*
		creek chub; *Semotilus atromaculatus*
		white sucker; *Catostomus commersoni*
		shorthead redhorse; *Moxostoma macrolepidotum*
		black bullhead; *Ameiurus melas*
		brown bullhead; *Ameiurus nebulosus*
		channel catfish; *Ictalurus punctatus*
		stonecat; *Noturus flavus*
		northern pike; *Esox lucius*
		troutperch; *Percopsis omiscomaycus*
		burbot; *Lota lota*
		brook stickleback; *Culaea inconstans*
		Iowa darter; *Etheostoma exile*
		johnny darter; *Etheostoma nigrum*
		yellow perch; *Perca flavescens*
		sauger; *Sander canadensis*
		walleye; *Sander vitreus*
Total 4	Total 2	Total 27
		Grand Total[1] 77[1]

INTRODUCTION

THE GEOGRAPHY OF MANITOBA'S WATERSHEDS AND FISH SPECIES DIVERSITY

We have distinguished four physiographic regions of Manitoba—the prairies, the Manitoba Great Lakes, the Canadian Shield, and the Hudson Bay coastal plain. Each region has watersheds with distinctive characteristics and assemblages of fish species. The geographic pattern of our watersheds determines which areas are accessible to fish, and watershed characteristics determine which species can survive there. Below is a map of the watersheds we considered in studying the distribution of our freshwater fishes. A list of the species and the status of each in the watersheds in Manitoba and adjacent areas is given in the Appendix.

From south to north, the watersheds of the Red River, the Assiniboine River, the western tributaries of Lake Winnipeg, lakes Manitoba, Dauphin, and Winnipegosis, and the Saskatchewan River lie wholly within the prairie and/or aspen parkland portion of Manitoba. The Winnipeg River watershed and all the eastern tributaries of Lake Winnipeg flow over the Canadian Shield. The watersheds of the Hayes, Nelson, Churchill, and Seal rivers lie on the Canadian Shield for most of their length, but descend onto the Hudson Bay coastal plain.

THE MAJOR WATERSHEDS OF MANITOBA

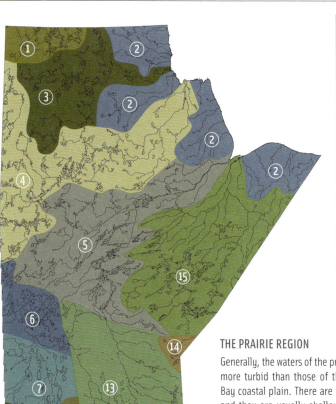

1	Thlewiaza River
2	Coastal
3	Seal River
4	Churchill River
5	Nelson River
6	Cedar Lake
7	Lake Winnipegosis
8	Lake Dauphin
9	Assiniboine River
10	Red River
11	Lake Manitoba
12	Winnipeg River
13	Lake Winnipeg
14	Severn River
15	Hayes River

THE PRAIRIE REGION

Generally, the waters of the prairie region are warmer and often more turbid than those of the Canadian Shield and Hudson Bay coastal plain. There are fewer lakes in the prairie region and they are usually shallow, with gently contoured basins and fine sediment substrates. Prairie streams typically have low gradients, low to moderate water velocities, and meandering courses. The most notable exceptions to these generalizations are the lakes and streams on the high-standing areas of the Manitoba Escarpment—the Turtle, Riding, Duck, and Porcupine mountains. In these areas, there are spring-fed, clear, cool lakes and streams. Streams draining the escarpment typically have some higher gradient sections and higher velocity. They have also incised valleys through the relatively soft Mesozoic sediments that underlie these elevated areas. The elevated areas of the Manitoba Escarpment are also the main areas west of the Canadian Shield in which bog habitats can be found. Another exception is the northwestern portion of the prairie region in Manitoba, which encompasses the watersheds of the north basins of Lake Winnipeg (west side) and Lake Manitoba, and much of the watershed of Lake Winnipegosis. This area is underlain by Paleozoic limestone and lacks the overlay of clay sediments deposited by Glacial Lake Agassiz that covers it to the south and east. Consequently, the streams and lakes of this area are clear and relatively cool.

The Red River south of Winnipeg has a meandering course through the low-lying, flat Red River Plain. Although it consists of mostly uniform, low-velocity runs, the surface uniformity and turbid water conceal a wide variety of habitat beneath the surface. The substrate can vary from mud and silt to sand, gravel, and rubble, with submerged large woody debris and some glacially transported boulders. This habitat diversity, the accessibility to fish of hundreds of kilometres of river habitat, and the reliability of flows in the large rivers make them our most diverse flowing-water fish communities.

The Assiniboine River at the Brandon Rapid, just east of Brandon. Both the Assiniboine and Red rivers have riffle or rapid sections where the river flows over glacial till or a bedrock outcrop that constricts or partially dams the channel. These provide additional habitat diversity and spawning habitat for some fish species, most notably the lake sturgeon.

INTRODUCTION

Aerial view of Big Island Lake (centre) and the Assiniboine River (flowing around it) in Spruce Woods Provincial Park. The oxbow lakes along the Assiniboine River are clear, cool, and have heavy growths of aquatic plants. The most abundant fish species in the oxbow lakes are the golden shiner, *Notemigonus crysoleucas*, and three species of black-striped *Notropis* shiners. One of the latter three, the weed shiner, *Notropis texanus*, is not found in any other Canadian province.

The Pembina River southwest of Morden occupies a large valley cut by glacial meltwater. In smaller streams, habitat variety is more easily seen than in large rivers. From foreground (downstream) to background (upstream), there is a run, a riffle where shale boulders constrict the channel, and a pool and braided channel at the bend farthest upstream. Moderate to high turbidity in these streams prevents development of extensive growth of aquatic plants. Small prairie streams support a distinctive assemblage of fish species, which, in western Manitoba, includes the bigmouth shiner, *Notropis dorsalis*, a species found nowhere else in Canada.

INTRODUCTION

The Brokenhead River, like many streams near the eastern edge of the prairie in Manitoba, is clear but stained brown. The clear water allows the growth of aquatic plants like those seen in the left foreground. Weedbeds such as this are important spawning and juvenile habitat for many species of fish.

Hazel Creek flows through low-lying peat lands interspersed with low ridges composed of glacial till and/or Lake Agassiz beach ridge deposits. In places, it lacks a well-defined channel. This view shows a channel flowing through an open bog, flanked by a higher standing glacial till ridge. This is an example of the bog habitat, which contains a distinctive fish species assemblage. See the pearl dace, *Margariscus margarita*, species account for a discussion.

THE MANITOBA GREAT LAKES

Lakes Winnipeg, Manitoba, Winnipegosis, and Dauphin comprise a cluster of large lakes in the central portion of southern Manitoba. The east side of Lake Winnipeg overlies the western boundary of the Canadian Shield, and the west side is in the prairie region. Lakes Dauphin, Winnipegosis, and Manitoba are wholly within the prairie region, and drain into Lake Winnipeg. With the exception of much of the east side of Lake Winnipeg, these lakes are similar to other prairie lakes in being shallow, with gently contoured basins and fine sediment substrates. The south basins of lakes Winnipeg and Manitoba, and all of Lake Dauphin, are turbid during the open-water season.

INTRODUCTION

The north basins of lakes Winnipeg and Manitoba, and all of Lake Winnipegosis, are relatively clear. This is because much of the turbidity load contributed by their southern tributaries settles out in the south basins of lakes Winnipeg and Manitoba, and the watersheds of their north basins and Lake Winnipegosis do not have the overlay of Lake Agassiz sediments found to the south, which contributes suspended matter. Additionally, impoundments on the Saskatchewan River allow much of the suspended material it carries to settle before it reaches Lake Winnipeg.

Of the Manitoba Great Lakes, Lake Winnipeg deserves special mention. First, in surface area, it is the tenth largest lake in the world, and second, its watershed includes four Canadian provinces and three states in the United States, extending from the Continental Divide on the Alberta-British Columbia border in the west, east to the divide between the Lake Superior and Hudson Bay drainages in northwestern Ontario, and south to the divide between the Mississippi/Missouri Drainage and the Hudson Bay Drainage, in Minnesota, South Dakota, and North Dakota. No other watershed in Canada is this large. Because Lake Winnipeg is at the downstream end of this far-flung area, it is at the hub of the post-Glacial Lake Agassiz freshwater-access routes available to fish entering Manitoba. It also makes Lake Winnipeg vulnerable to colonization by exotic species of aquatic organisms that have been introduced into upstream areas of its watershed.

The west side of Lake Winnipeg is underlain by flat-lying Paleozoic limestone beds. Where these are resistant to weathering and erosion, they can form low cliffs along the shoreline, with limestone boulder talus extending onto the lake bottom from their base. These local rocky littoral habitats provide cover and spawning habitat for many smaller fish species living in nearshore habitats.

INTRODUCTION

The eastern shore of Lake Winnipeg lies on the Canadian Shield. This bay on the east side of the lake has a granite bedrock shoreline with more relief than the west shore. The great size of the lake, its variety of shoreline habitats, and the fact that it receives tributaries from the Canadian Shield to the east, and the prairies and the Rocky Mountains in the west, has enabled it to be reached and colonized by the largest number of freshwater fish species in any single lake in Canada, west of the Great Lakes.

CCGS *Namao*, currently used for research, on the north basin of Lake Winnipeg. Like an increasing number of lakes, Lake Winnipeg is subject to a high level of nutrient pollution from municipal, industrial, and agricultural wastewater delivered by its tributaries. Note the dark stains, just above the waterline, forward and to the rear on the hull. These consist of algae from a plankton bloom caused by the excessive nutrient loading in the lake.

THE CANADIAN SHIELD

Waters of the Canadian Shield region generally occupy low areas, which are the result of glacial sculpting of the bedrock or are structural low areas. There has not been enough time since deglaciation for streams to incise valleys in the hard granitic rock of the Canadian Shield. Watercourses in Shield country consist of flowing sections alternating with expanded lake sections and bogs. The flowing sections of streams are typically either short, relatively steep-gradient, sections or meandering bog sections. Lake substrates vary from clay sediments to plant debris (sapropel) to boulders and bedrock. Lake basins can vary from shallow and gently contoured, where sapropel or fine sediments have been deposited, to irregular with precipitous drop-offs, and reefs, where the lake bottom consists of exposed bedrock. Shield lakes in Manitoba vary in depth from 111 m, for West Hawk Lake, in Whiteshell Provincial Park, to 1-3 m where the basin has been filled in with sediment or peat. The water in Canadian Shield lakes is clear and often stained brown, and is usually cooler than prairie waters. Lakes with small watersheds with little or no peat are clear and unstained. The clear water also supports more frequent and larger beds of aquatic plants in Shield lakes and streams than in the more turbid prairie waters.

The Whitemouth River, like many Canadian Shield streams, has relatively clear, brown-stained water from the peat lands over which its headwaters flow. The Whitemouth River has a unique fish community containing the northern brook lamprey, *Ichthyomyzon fossor*, which is known only from the Whitemouth, and the hornyhead chub, *Nocomis biguttatus*, and carmine shiner, *Notropis percobromus*, whose distributions in Manitoba are centred on the Whitemouth River.

INTRODUCTION

Whitemouth Falls, seen here during spring runoff, is one of several short rapid/fall sections of the Whitemouth River. The presence of several widely distributed, typically large river or lacustrine fish species, including the silver and shorthead redhorses, *Moxostoma anisurum* and *M. macrolepidotum*, the walleye, *Sander vitreus*, and the rock bass, *Ambloplites rupestris*, in the Whitemouth River suggests that the rapid/fall sections are, at least seasonally, passable to fish.

Much of the length of Canadian Shield streams meanders through peat-filled low areas, interspersed with higher standing hummocks and ridges of bedrock. Current velocities are low, the water is brown-stained, and the characteristic assemblage of eight fish species associated with bogs comprises most of the fish fauna.

INTRODUCTION

Canadian Shield lakes usually have a complex shape, subdivided into bays and arms and dotted with islands because of the irregular, glacially carved basins they occupy.

The shorelines of Shield lakes are often exposed bedrock, and, if the watershed does not contain much peat, the water is clear and not stained.

THE HUDSON BAY COASTAL PLAIN

The Hudson Bay coastal plain is underlain by Paleozoic sedimentary rock covered by glacial till, with an overlay of clay. The streams usually flow over glacial till, but have cut down to the underlying limestone in places. At high flows, they erode the clay, which may be redeposited in protected waters along their margins. Coastal plain streams usually have low gradients, and often have meandering, or even braided, courses. Unlike Shield streams, which have convoluted valleys that follow structural or glacially sculpted low areas, coastal plain streams have cut relatively straight, if shallow, valleys into the clay and glacial till overlaying the coastal plain. As on the prairies, lakes are less common, and tend to be shallow and have gently contoured bottoms, with fine sediment substrates. Except for areas where clay banks are being eroded, the water is clear, sometimes stained brown, and there may be large beds of aquatic plants in quiet waters where there is fine sediment on the bottom.

The bank of the Nelson River shows the glacial till the river flows over, and a steep face of exposed clay above it. Eroding clay banks are the source of turbidity in the water.

The lower Churchill River runs over glacial till, which creates a rocky bottom ranging from cobble to large boulders that protrude above the water at low flows.

INTRODUCTION

This reach of Moondance Creek flows over flat-lying Paleozoic limestone beds, which create a series of low falls with riffles or rapids between them.

Lower Limestone Rapids on the Nelson River is another example of a low falls where the river flows over an exposed limestone bedrock ledge. Fast, shallow water, such as this, is typical spawning habitat for lake sturgeon.

INTRODUCTION

Beaver dams, such as this one on Moondance Creek, make temporary impoundments on headwater streams everywhere in Manitoba. They increase the variety of aquatic habitats available, create or expand peripheral marshland around the impoundment, and can increase water clarity downstream because fine sediments will settle out in the impoundment. They are temporary, however, and may cause flash flooding when they inevitably fail.

This pool along the shore of the lower Churchill River has a fine sediment substrate and a large bed of aquatic plants.

PATTERN OF FISH SPECIES DIVERSITY

The pattern of fish species diversity in Manitoba reflects the paths by which most fish species entered the area. The watersheds with the greatest diversity of native fishes are the Red River watershed, with 57 native species, the Winnipeg River watershed, with 61 native species, and the Lake Winnipeg watershed, which both the Red and Winnipeg rivers flow into and which has 60 native species of fishes. The headwaters of the Red and Winnipeg rivers reach the boundaries between the Hudson Bay Drainage, and the Mississippi/Missouri and Lake Superior drainages, respectively. These two drainages were the main entry routes into Manitoba since deglaciation. They occupy areas that discharged water from Lake Agassiz at least some of the time during glacial recession. Lake Winnipeg and its tributaries have habitats that cover the range available in both the Canadian Shield and the prairie region. This provides fishes from both sources with suitable habitat. Beyond Lake Winnipeg, species diversity declines. The Saskatchewan River (36 native species in Manitoba) and Nelson River (30 native species), respectively a tributary to, and the outlet of, Lake Winnipeg, have the next greatest species diversity (see Appendix).

POSTGLACIAL COLONIZATION OF FISH

Manitoba was completely covered by the ice of the Laurentide Ice Sheet until about 11,000 years ago, when the melting ice had receded north and Manitoba was uncovered from the southwest to the northeast. Every species of plant and animal in the province has come here since the ice sheet began to melt. This event is so recent that the melting of the ice sheet and the meltwater lakes and rivers that drained the water away remain the most obvious and important factors determining the distribution of our fishes today.

Glacial Lake Agassiz was a meltwater lake that covered much of Manitoba as the ice melted. During its existence, between about 11,000 and 7800 years ago, its discharge and inflow channels provided routes by which fish could reach Manitoba and then spread over and beyond our area through the lake or its marginal waters. Lake Agassiz discharged first into the Mississippi River via the Minnesota Spillway or River Warren. Today, the valley created by discharge from Lake Agassiz is occupied by the Minnesota River. Later, Lake Agassiz flowed into the progenitors of Lake Superior and Lake Michigan, and then into the Mississippi River. Later still, it discharged eastwards via Glacial Lake Barlow-Ojibway (now in the James Bay watershed) into the St. Lawrence River. Finally, about 7800 years ago, the last ice covering northeastern Manitoba melted and Lake Agassiz drained into Hudson Bay through channels occupied today by the Hayes, Nelson, Churchill, and Seal rivers. During its existence, Lake Agassiz received meltwater from the margin of the ice sheet from what would become the James Bay watershed in the east, northwest to the headwaters of the Lake Athabasca watershed and west to the Rocky Mountains (Table II).

Our freshwater fish fauna arrived during three time intervals, the first two from natural dispersal, and the third by human introduction: (1) the melting of the Laurentide Ice Sheet; (2) natural colonization after the drainage of Glacial Lake Agassiz, and continuing to the present; and (3) human introductions since the arrival of Europeans in the Hudson Bay Drainage.

The earliest fish to arrive were cold-water species, which colonized Manitoba as the Laurentide Ice Sheet melted. Those fish that survived glaciation south of the Laurentide Ice Sheet presumably followed the receding ice margin northward, entered Lake Agassiz via one or more of its outlet channels, and dispersed through the lake and its marginal waters and beyond through its tributaries and inlet channels. These species typically are widely distributed across Canada from the Rocky Mountains and the Mackenzie River watershed eastwards to the James Bay and Great Lakes/St. Lawrence watersheds, and often extend north into the Arctic. A few of them are also found west of the Continental Divide. Some of the early colonizers, such as the lake trout, brook trout (considering only its native range), and Arctic grayling, now are absent from the prairie region, although they likely passed through the prairies during deglaciation. In addition, at least some of the fish that survived glaciation along the east coast of North America probably followed the Arctic Ocean and Hudson Bay coastline as it emerged from the melting ice. Species such as the Arctic char, threespine stickleback, and other coastal and estuarine fishes of Hudson Bay probably arrived via this coastal route. Dispersal as the ice sheet melted, however, accounts for only 36 of the 91 species of fishes that spawn in fresh water in Manitoba (Table II).

Forty-three of our native freshwater fish species seem to have reached Manitoba after the ice sheet had melted and Lake Agassiz had drained into Hudson Bay (the second time interval). None of these species is found north of the Churchill River watershed, and none is found in the Athabasca/Mackenzie system. Their distributions in Canada show four patterns.

INTRODUCTION

First, there are 20 species (Table II) that are either absent from, or have restricted distributions in, Lake Superior and/or its northern tributaries and in the Lake of the Woods watershed in northwestern Ontario. These species are found in Mississippi River headwaters in Minnesota, the upper Red River and/or its tributaries in northwestern Minnesota, and in at least parts of the watersheds of the Red River, the Manitoba Great Lakes, the Nelson River, and often also in the Saskatchewan River. The simplest interpretation of this pattern is that these species entered the Red River mainstem via Big Stone Lake and Lake Traverse, or entered Red River tributaries from Mississippi River tributaries in Minnesota. Subsequently, they dispersed downstream in the Red River and spread outward from the Red/Nelson river system via tributaries.

The second distribution pattern explains the distribution of only two species, the northern brook lamprey and the shortjaw cisco (which may have arisen *in situ*), which are both found in Lake Superior and some of its northern tributaries, and are absent from the Mississippi Drainage in Minnesota. These species probably were able to get into the Lake of the Woods watershed from Lake Superior and spread downstream into Manitoba (Table II). If this is true, additional locations for these species should eventually be found in the Rainy/English/Wabigoon watershed in northwestern Ontario and Minnesota.

The third distribution pattern includes 16 species found in Mississippi River headwaters, the Lake Superior watershed, the Rainy/English/Wabigoon system in northwestern Ontario, and the Red River headwaters in Minnesota. These could have entered Manitoba from either or both of the Great Lakes and the Upper Mississippi watersheds via the Winnipeg River and/or Red River watersheds (Table II).

The fourth distribution pattern for fish arriving after Glacial Lake Agassiz had drained is shared by five species. Their distributions differ from the fishes included in the third pattern by being absent from the Red River and its tributaries in Manitoba, although they may be present in Red River tributaries, but not the mainstem of the Red River, in Minnesota (Table II). In Manitoba, these species are found in the Winnipeg River watershed and Lake Winnipeg and/or its eastern tributaries. Three of them, the blackchin shiner, weed shiner, and mimic shiner, are found in the Icelandic River, on the west side of the Lake Winnipeg Narrows. The blackchin shiner and weed shiner are also found in the Dauphin Lake watershed and in spring-fed oxbow lakes of the Assiniboine River in Spruce Woods Provincial Park. This suggests the possibility of a northern dispersal track through lakes Manitoba and Winnipegosis into Lake Dauphin and southward via Lake Dauphin and Assiniboine headwaters in Riding Mountain National Park. Again, this implies that these species will be found in other locations in the central portion of the Interlake region, as well as in lakes Manitoba and Winnipegosis. These areas are poorly surveyed, especially for small fish, and the species in question were misidentified as blackchin shiners until recently (Stewart, 1988).

The most recent additions to our fish fauna are the result of human-made introductions. Ten species of fish and two human-made hybrids have been introduced into Manitoba or invaded Manitoba from points of introduction in North Dakota or northwestern Ontario (Table II). Four of these exotics are the rainbow trout, cutthroat trout, kokanee salmon, and brown trout. The two hybrids are the "splake," a brook trout X lake trout hybrid, and the "tiger trout," a brook trout X brown trout hybrid. All these have been and/or are being planted in many lakes, small streams, and impoundments in Manitoba at least as far north as Flin Flon. None of these exotic species reproduces in the wild in Manitoba, nor has any spread beyond the areas where they have been planted. Since their presence is dependent on continued planting, they may not all be present in the province at any given time.

In addition, two exotic species, which are also the result of planned introductions, do reproduce in the wild in some places in Manitoba. The smallmouth bass and largemouth bass were introduced in many locations in southern Manitoba, and as far north and west as Lake Athapapuskow.

The bluegill may be native in the Red River watershed in Manitoba, but introduced in the Winnipeg River watershed. However, even in the Red River watershed, its distribution and abundance have probably been increased by unintentional introductions of bluegills as contaminants in plantings of largemouth and smallmouth bass and black crappies. See the Distribution in Manitoba section of the bluegill species account for a more complete discussion.

Koel (1997) also lists the white crappie as native to the Red River watershed in Minnesota. There is no record of either crappie species in Henry's (1897) journal or in Coues's (Henry's editor) attached notes. Like the bluegill, there are no recorded introductions of white crappie in Manitoba. There are no records of the white crappie in Manitoba until 1982 but, since only six specimens have been collected, earlier captures may have been misidentified as the black crappie. We have classified the white crappie as probably native, since it was not found in a location into which other centrarchids were introduced. See the Distribution in Manitoba section of the white crappie account for further discussion.

TABLE II. Probable Time and Entry Routes of Manitoba Freshwater Fishes

SPECIES THAT ENTERED DURING GLACIAL RECESSION	SPECIES THAT ENTERED DURING POST-GLACIAL TIMES NATIVE SPECIES	
	From Upper Mississippi via Red River	From Great Lakes via Winnipeg River
silver lamprey; *Ichthyomyzon unicuspis*	chestnut lamprey; *Ichthyomyzon castaneus*	northern brook lamprey; *Ichthyomyzon fossor*
lake sturgeon; *Acipenser fulvescens*	spotfin shiner; *Cyprinella spiloptera*	[1]shortjaw cisco; *Coregonus zenithicus*
goldeye; *Hiodon alosoides*	silver chub; *Macrhybopsis storeriana*	
lake chub; *Couesius plumbeus*	river shiner; *Notropis blennius*	
brassy minnow; *Hybognathus hankinsoni*	bigmouth shiner; *Notropis dorsalis*	
pearl dace; *Margariscus margarita*	carmine shiner; *Notropis percobromus*	
emerald shiner; *Notropis atherinoides*	sand shiner; *Notropis stramineus*	
blacknose shiner; *Notropis heterolepis*	quillback; *Carpiodes cyprinus*	
spottail shiner; *Notropis hudsonius*	bigmouth buffalo; *Ictiobus cyprinellus*	
northern redbelly dace; *Phoxinus eos*	black bullhead; *Ameiurus melas*	
finescale dace; *Phoxinus neogaeus*	brown bullhead; *Ameiurus nebulosus*	
fathead minnow; *Pimephales promelas*	channel catfish; *Ictalurus punctatus*	
flathead chub; *Platygobio gracilis*	stonecat; *Noturus flavus*	
longnose dace; *Rhinichthys cataractae*	central mudminnow; *Umbra limi*	
longnose sucker; *Catostomus catostomus*	banded killifish; *Fundulus diaphanus*	
white sucker; *Catostomus commersoni*	bluegill; *Lepomis macrochirus*	
northern pike; *Esox lucius*	white crappie; *Pomoxis annularis*	
cisco; *Coregonus artedi*	blackside darter; *Percina maculata*	
lake whitefish; *Coregonus clupeaformis*	river darter; *Percina shumardi*	
round whitefish; *Prosopium cylindraceum*	freshwater drum; *Aplodinotus grunniens*	
Arctic grayling; *Thymallus arcticus*		
Arctic char; *Salvelinus alpinus*		
brook trout; *Salvelinus fontinalis*		
lake trout; *Salvelinus namaycush*		
troutperch; *Percopsis omiscomaycus*		
burbot; *Lota lota*		
brook stickleback; *Culaea inconstans*		
threespine stickleback; *Gasterosteus aculeatus*		
ninespine stickleback; *Pungitius pungitius*		
slimy sculpin; *Cottus cognatus*		
spoonhead sculpin; *Cottus ricei*		
deepwater sculpin; *Myoxocephalus thompsoni*		
Iowa darter; *Etheostoma exile*		
johnny darter; *Etheostoma nigrum*		
yellow perch; *Perca flavescens*		
walleye; *Sander vitreus*		
Total 36	Total 20	Total 2

1. Shortjaw cisco (*Coregonus zenithicus*)-like forms may have arisen *in situ* from the cisco, *C. artedi*, in lakes where it is found. (See the note on cisco differentiation in Manitoba.)
2. These species do not reproduce in the wild in Manitoba and may not be present at a given time unless they have been stocked recently.

SPECIES THAT ENTERED DURING POST-GLACIAL TIMES		INTRODUCED SPECIES AND HUMAN-MADE HYBRIDS
NATIVE SPECIES		
From Both Mississippi and Great Lakes via Winnipeg and Red Rivers	From Both Mississippi and Great Lakes via Winnipeg River	
mooneye; *Hiodon tergisus*	blackchin shiner; *Notropis heterodon*	goldfish; *Carassius auratus*
common shiner; *Luxilus cornutus*	weed shiner; *Notropis texanus*	common carp; *Cyprinus carpio*
hornyhead chub; *Nocomis biguttatus*	mimic shiner; *Notropis volucellus*	rainbow smelt; *Osmerus mordax*
golden shiner; *Notemigonus crysoleucas*	muskellunge; *Esox masquinongy*	[2]cutthroat trout; *Oncorhynchus clarki*
bluntnose minnow; *Pimephales notatus*	pumpkinseed; *Lepomis gibbosus*	[2]rainbow trout; *Oncorhynchus mykiss*
western blacknose dace; *Rhinichthys obtusus*		[2]kokanee salmon; *Oncorhynchus nerka*
creek chub; *Semotilus atromaculatus*		[2]brown trout; *Salmo trutta*
silver redhorse; *Moxostoma anisurum*		[2]"splake" (brook X lake trout hybrid)
golden redhorse; *Moxostoma erythrurum*		[2]"tiger trout" (brook X brown trout hybrid)
shorthead redhorse; *Moxostoma macrolepidotum*		white bass; *Morone chrysops*
tadpole madtom; *Noturus gyrinus*		smallmouth bass; *Micropterus dolomieu*
mottled sculpin; *Cottus bairdi*		largemouth bass; *Micropterus salmoides*
rock bass; *Ambloplites rupestris*		
black crappie; *Pomoxis nigromaculatus*		
logperch; *Percina caprodes*		
sauger; *Sander canadensis*		
Total 16	Total 5 Total native species 79	Total introduced species 12
	GRAND TOTAL (LESS 4 MARINE SPECIES) 91	

INTRODUCTION

Two of the remaining four exotic species, the rainbow smelt and white bass, were introduced into the Hudson Bay Drainage outside Manitoba and spread into Manitoba. Rainbow smelt were introduced unintentionally and/or illegally at several points in the Rainy, English, and Wabigoon river watersheds in northwestern Minnesota and northwestern Ontario (Franzin et al., 1994; Stewart et al., 2001), and probably invaded Manitoba by downstream dispersal in the Winnipeg River. It is also possible, however, that rainbow smelt were introduced into the Red River watershed, perhaps as early as the 1960s, and had spread downstream into Manitoba before the Rainy/English/Wabigoon river introductions reached even Lake of the Woods. This is based on an anecdotal report by Vanreil (pers. comm., 2002) of having angled two rainbow smelt from the tailrace of the St. Andrews Dam on the Red River in the spring of 1976. The white bass was introduced intentionally into Lake Ashtabula, a reservoir on the Sheyenne River (Red River watershed) in North Dakota (Koel, 1997). It dispersed downstream in the Sheyenne and Red rivers.

The third species, the common carp, was introduced into both the Red and Assiniboine river watersheds in Manitoba in 1886. It was also introduced into the Red River watershed in North Dakota at about the same time. The common carp was first caught in the wild in Manitoba in the Red River, below the St. Andrews Dam at Lockport, in 1938. Since then, it has spread throughout the accessible reaches of the larger streams in southern Manitoba and throughout the Manitoba Great Lakes. All three of these species breed in the wild and have spread rapidly in southern Manitoba. The fourth, the goldfish, got into the wild in Manitoba by illegal releases of aquarium fish. It is probably breeding in the wild in Rock Lake, on the Pembina River, and is definitely breeding in the wild in at least one impoundment in south Winnipeg that drains into the Red River.

Additionally, nine native species have been introduced outside their native ranges in Manitoba. The Arctic char, brook trout, lake trout, and Arctic grayling have been introduced in a number of locations across southern Manitoba, with the brook trout being the most extensively planted. The pumpkinseed and black crappie have also been planted outside their native ranges in southern Manitoba. These introductions are the result of a combination of planned releases, in the case of the black crappie, and unplanned release of both as contaminants in plantings of largemouth or smallmouth bass.

Crossman and McAllister (1986) presented a comprehensive account of the zoogeography of freshwater fishes of the Hudson Bay Drainage. Stewart and Lindsey (1983) gave a general discussion of the dispersal of fishes into the Hudson Bay Drainage during deglaciation, and Franzin et al. (2003) present a discussion of the postglacial dispersal of freshwater fishes in Manitoba relative to Lake Winnipeg.

ORGANIZATION OF THE SPECIES ACCOUNTS

All animals are classified into a series of groupings. In this book, the most general grouping we use is the **order**. Each order contains one or more **families**, and each of those contains one or more **genera**. Each genus contains one or more **species**, the lowest grouping used in this book. The orders and families in this book are presented in an evolutionary sequence, with those of the most ancient origin appearing first. The genera in each family are arranged alphabetically, and the species in each genus are also arranged alphabetically.

There is an introduction to each family of fishes that includes:

• common name and Latin name of the order of fishes (e.g., catfishes, Order Siluriformes). The names used are those given in Nelson (1994).

• common name and Latin name for the family of fishes (e.g., North American Freshwater Catfishes, Family Ictaluridae). The names used are those given in Nelson (1994).

• a brief discussion of the order and family, including its relationships to other major groups of fishes, its diversity, history, and any unique adaptations. There is a summary of the characteristics that distinguish members of the family from members of other families in our area. Also, any special notes on classification or species identification are given.

• for families in which there is more than one species in our area, a key to the species of fishes of that family in our area.

INTRODUCTION

For each species, the account is organized as follows:

1. The scientific name (e.g., *Ameiurus melas*) is given, and the English and French common names (e.g., black bullhead; barbotte noir) are given. Robbins et al. (1991) is the source for all but a few of the scientific names and English common names. French common names are those currently used in Québec, and have been checked by Fernand Saurette, Instructor in Biology, St. Boniface College. In a very few cases, we have had to coin French common names for species that do not occur in Québec, and have not been given a French name up to now. In every case, the newly coined named is a French translation of the English common name.

Note: Robbins et al. (1991) is currently under revision by the American Fisheries Society Committee on Names of Fishes. Some of the names in Robbins et al. have been changed, and the names given here are those that will be in the new list, when it is published. In each case where a new name is used, the source is cited as "(Nelson, pers. comm., 2003)." J.S. Nelson is the current Chair of the Committee on Names of Fishes.

2. A colour photograph of a specimen is given. The background has been removed and the image of the fish scaled to a standard size. The type of specimen (e.g., live, fresh, or preserved) is given, and a scale bar is provided to give an idea of the size of the specimen. Where necessary, images have been digitally processed to repair damaged fins and scales, eliminate glare, and correct colours.

3. A map of Manitoba with the distribution of the species is provided. For native species, the shaded area indicates the part of Manitoba where the species is continuously distributed. Red spots within the shaded area indicate known locations where the species has been collected. Red spots outside the shaded area indicate isolated records or, for rare species, there may be no shaded area. For introduced species, known locations are indicated by black spots, and there is no area of continuous distribution indicated.

4. Identification. A summary is provided of the features that distinguish this species from all other similar species of fish found in Manitoba.

5. Distribution in Manitoba. A written summary of the distribution of the species in Manitoba is provided as a supplement to the map.

6. Biological Notes. Biological information is presented, where possible, for the species in Manitoba. Unfortunately, Manitoba or other Canadian populations of many of our species are poorly studied. In these cases, we have presented information from studies in other areas.

Spawning: The spawning information consists of time of spawning, spawning habits, and habitat, or such information as may be available for each species.

Growth and adult size: This information consists of the size range of adults of the species and age attained. For most game fish species, the Manitoba angling record size, the name of the water body where the fish was caught, and the year in which it was caught are also included. For the mooneye, rock bass, and sauger, the published records are based on misidentifications of goldeye, smallmouth bass, and walleye, respectively. No Manitoba angling records are given for these species.

Feeding: This includes the types of food taken and whether the species feeds on the bottom, midwater, surface, or a combination of habitats.

Habitat: This is a statement of the habitat of non-spawning adults of the species.

Ecological role: This is a brief statement of the trophic position of each species (e.g., "benthic, middle-level consumer"). It may include information on predators. There is also a statement of the importance of each species in the food web of aquatic communities.

7. Importance to People. A note on the species' importance to people gives the commercial, subsistence, angling, and aesthetic values of the species and also states the importance of its ecological role in human terms. In the species accounts for some of the species introduced into the Hudson Bay Drainage, and one recent, apparently natural, immigrant species, the term "invasive" is used in describing their ecological role and/or importance to people. It is meant to indicate a species that is able to spread beyond the point(s) of introduction or entry into Manitoba and successfully establish itself in the aquatic communities that it encounters. For example, the common carp and rainbow smelt are examples of invasive introduced species. The stonecat is an example of an invasive, apparently natural, immigrant.

INTRODUCTION

8. COSEWIC, MBESA, and MBCDC Status: The status of species is periodically evaluated at both national and provincial levels. The status of a species is that which applied as recently as possible before this book went to the printer. Changes are to be expected over time. The reader can access both COSEWIC and Manitoba Conservation Data Centre at the following Internet Web sites: COSEWIC http://www.cosewic.gc.ca and Manitoba Conservation Data Centre http://www.gov.mb.ca/conservation/cdc. In addition to the current species-at-risk status, these sites provide reports of species studies and other species-at-risk information.

COSEWIC Status as of January 1, 2004: The Committee on the Status of Endangered Wildlife in Canada (COSEWIC) ranks the status of plant and animal species. These ranks are for Canada as a whole. A given species may be Not at Risk over the entire country, but be of Special Concern in a particular province. The COSEWIC status ranking is given for each species.

Extinct: The species no longer exists.

Extirpated: The species no longer exists in the wild in Canada, but occurs elsewhere.

Endangered: A species faces imminent extirpation or extinction.

Threatened: A species is likely to become endangered if limiting factors are not reversed.

Special Concern: A species is of special concern because of characteristics that make it particularly sensitive to human activities or natural events but is not an endangered or threatened species.

Data Deficient: A species for which there is inadequate information to make a direct, or indirect, assessment of its risk of extinction.

Not at Risk: A species that has been evaluated and found not to be at risk.

Not Listed: A species that has not been evaluated.

MBESA Status as of January 1, 2004: The Manitoba Endangered Species Act (MBESA) gives protection to species classed as Endangered, Threatened, or of Special Concern.

MBCDC Status as of January 1, 2004: The Manitoba Conservation Data Centre (MBCDC) is an office within Manitoba Conservation. It ranks species found in Manitoba based mainly on the numbers of records of the species occurrence. Two ranks are given. The first is based on the species abundance over its entire range (G) and the second is based on its abundance in Manitoba (S). The ranking system is as follows:

Rank	Definition
1	Very rare throughout its range (G1) or in the province (S1) (5 or fewer occurrences, or very few remaining individuals). May be especially vulnerable to extirpation.
2	Rare throughout its range (G2) or in the province (S2) (6-20 occurrences). May be vulnerable to extirpation.
3	Uncommon throughout its range (G3) or in the province (S3) (21-100 occurrences).
4	Widespread, abundant, and apparently secure throughout its range (G4) or in the province (S4) (> 100 occurrences). There is still, however, reason for long-term concern.
5	Demonstrably widespread, abundant, and secure throughout its range (G5) or in the province (S5), and essentially ineradicable under present conditions.
U	Possibly in peril, but status uncertain; more information needed.
H	Historically known; may be rediscovered.
X	Believed to be extinct; historical records only, continue search. In addition, the following modifiers are used in the rankings for fish: G#G#, S#S# This gives a range for the rank (G4G5, S2S3, for example).

E	Designates an exotic species in the province. The brown trout, for example, is G5, SE.
P	The species may potentially occur in the province. The northern hog sucker, for example, is ranked G5, SP.
T	A rank given to a subspecies. The inland Columbia Basin redband trout, for example, is a subspecies of the rainbow trout. It is ranked G5T4?, SE.
?	Inexact or uncertain for numeric ranks; denotes inexactness.

COMMON AND SCIENTIFIC NAMES OF FISHES

COMMON NAMES

The common names of fishes change in different languages and from place to place, even in areas where the same language is spoken. In Manitoba, for example, the freshwater drum is called "silver bass" or sheepshead by anglophone anglers, "sunfish" by anglophone commercial fishers, and "malachigan" by francophone Manitobans. Notably, the French common names for several species of fish in our area are the same as, or derived from, an Aboriginal name for the species. In Manitoba, the Cree, Ojibwe, and Saulteaux languages have contributed French common names to fishes. "Malachigan" (freshwater drum), "laquaiche" (goldeye and mooneye), "omisco" for the troutperch, and "achigan" for the smallmouth and largemouth basses are examples.

SCIENTIFIC NAMES

Scientific names are intended to be standard reference names, which are the same in all languages and throughout the world. In addition to being a standard reference, scientific names are also intended to show the evolutionary relationships among species. Because these relationships are the subject of continuing study, new findings can cause changes in the scientific name of a fish. Unlike common names, which change only slowly as languages evolve, scientific names may change frequently in groups being studied.

The scientific name is a two-part name applied to each species of fish. The first word in a scientific name is the name of the genus of fishes and the second word is the name of the species. A genus is a group of related species, so species that share the same generic name are all closely related to one another. The walleye and sauger, for example, are two species of the genus *Sander* (*Sander vitreus* for the walleye and *Sander canadensis* for the sauger). Their close relationship is obvious, even to a casual observer, in their similar appearance. The specific name denotes one particular species, such as *vitreus* for the walleye and *canadensis* for the sauger. The specific name must always be used with the genus name.

Scientific names are always given the form of Latin words, even though they may not ever have been part of the Latin language. To use the walleye and sauger example, the genus name *Sander* is the Latinized form of the German word "zander," which is one of the common names for the pike-perch, a European relative of the walleye and sauger, and another member of the genus *Sander* (*Sander luciopercus*). Because the scientific name is in Latin, it is always italicized. Scientific names may be derived from a common name, like *Sander*. They may describe a distinctive feature of the fish, like the specific name of the walleye, *vitreus*, which describes the large, glassy-looking eye of a walleye. They may be named for an area where a fish is found, like *canadensis* (of Canada) for the sauger. Or, they may be named after a person, like *Couesius*, the genus name for the lake chub, a minnow, which is named after Elliott Coues, an American explorer and botanist during the 19th century.

PRONUNCIATION GUIDE FOR SCIENTIFIC NAMES

Pronouncing scientific names can be cumbersome, even for people trained in their use. Since the words are in Latin form, they are often long and have many syllables. They also may present combinations of letters that are unfamiliar to anglophones, especially. There are no set rules for pronouncing scientific names. We suggest the following guidelines to help:

a. Use the sounds for letters that are familiar in your language. Don't try to say it like a Roman would have unless you are a student of Latin. (Our apologies to Latin scholars who may read this book.)

b. Break each word into syllables that reflect the roots of which it is composed and pronounce it and accent the syllables so that the roots are distinct. For example, the genus name of the white and longnose suckers is *Catostomus*. Break the word into four syllables, Cat-o-stom-us, and accent the third syllable, Cat-o-*stom*-us. The species of the white sucker is *commersoni*, named after the French naturalist Commerson. Pronounce it as you would the naturalist's name (*comm*-er-son-i). In general, where a person's name is the basis for the scientific name, the first syllable is accented, as it would be in saying the name. Shorter names of two syllables usually have the accent on the first syllable. For example, the genus name of the northern pike and muskellunge, *Esox*, should be pronounced *E*-sox, and the genus of the yellow perch (*Perca*) should be pronounced *Per*-ka. Really long names may have accents on more than one syllable. For example, the freshwater drum genus, *Aplodinotus*, should be broken down and pronounced *Ap*-lo-din-*ot*-us, and the deepwater sculpin genus, *Myoxocephalus*, pronounced My-*ox*-o-*kef*-al-us (or My-*ox*-o-*sef*-al-us); Latin pronunciation would use a hard c or k sound, but a soft c or s sound is more frequently used today.

DOCUMENTATION AND PRESERVATION OF FISH SPECIMENS FOR IDENTIFICATION

Fish specimens kept in collections are valuable for resource managers, environmental managers, and scientists. Preserved specimens are the foundation for our information on species distributions. Because they can be re-examined, they are the only verifiable records of species in an area. Preserved specimens allow comparisons to be made over time to detect possible changes in morphology, growth, size, age, time of sexual maturity, and other characteristics used to assess the health of populations and changes in species composition and diversity. New specimens may be compared with previous collections to ensure the accuracy of species identification.

Even adults of some of our larger fish species may be confused with other similar species on casual examination, so fieldworkers should retain at least a few specimens of each type of fish collected from a site for laboratory examination as a check on field identifications. For example, juvenile northern pike are often marked with wavy, diagonal bars, which has led inexperienced workers to confuse them with the muskellunge. The golden redhorse was probably confused with the silver and shorthead redhorses in Manitoba before Franzin, Parker, and Harbicht (1986) identified it in collections from the Red River. Walleye and sauger sometimes interbreed and the hybrids may be hard to distinguish from the sauger under field conditions.

When smaller species or early life-history stages of any of our fish are being studied, examination under magnification and comparison with identified reference specimens are often necessary to identify species correctly. Juveniles and small species should be collected and returned to the laboratory for identification.

DOCUMENTATION OF FISH COLLECTIONS

Any fish that are collected must be documented and preserved in order to be useful in the laboratory. A basic set of data with each collection increases the value of the specimens to future workers, and should be recorded both in the fieldnotes and on a waterproof label kept in the container with the specimens. The following data should be noted.

- An identifying serial number for the collection, which matches the serial number in the fieldnotes.
- Date of the collection and time of day.
- Name(s) of the collector(s).
- The location of the field site, either in latitude and longitude, or UTM coordinates. If differential GPS was used to determine location, also give the datum for the ground station.
- Name of the water body and the specific location, if it has a name. Use the place names published in the *Gazetteer* for the area. If there is a local name that isn't in the *Gazetteer*, record it and identify it as a local name.
- Method of collection (e.g., angling, seine, minnow trap, etc.) and some measure of effort (length of seine haul, duration of a trap or gillnet set, for example).
- Habitat notes (water temperature, depth, colour and clarity, current or wave action, cover, substrate type, etc.).

Labels placed in containers with specimens should be resistant to tearing, be waterproof, and retain writing. We have used Fisher Polypaper™, a paper-like plastic fiber product, writing on it with an H or HB pencil. Tyvek™ is another paper-like plastic fiber product that works if written on with a moderately soft pencil. It is extremely important to use a strong, waterproof product for specimen labels. Ordinary paper can disintegrate after only a few days in a specimen container under field conditions.

PRESERVATION OF FISH SPECIMENS

For anglers or other members of the general public who wish to save a fish specimen for identification, the safest and best way to preserve a fish specimen is to freeze it whole. If a freezer isn't available close by, refrigerate the specimen. Place the fish in a large enough bag so that it can lay out straight, add a label with as much of the above information as is available, and seal the bag as tightly as possible before it is put in the freezer to prevent drying.

For people who are making collections for field projects, specimens should be preserved so as to meet the specific needs of their work. Additional specimens or fish from which samples are removed should be frozen for further study in the laboratory or fixed in the field to prevent decomposition.

The best fixative for preserving fish is formalin. **Formaldehyde is carcinogenic, allergenic, and a powerful irritant. Formalin vapours are inflammable and produce toxic fumes when they burn. Formalin solutions should never be used by the general public. Professionals who use them should do so only in a well-ventilated place outdoors or under an exhaust fan or fume hood in the laboratory. Eye protection should always be used and hands should be protected by non-allergenic vinyl examination gloves when using formalin solutions. Transport Canada requires a permit for transport of commercial formaldehyde**.

For most fish, use a 10% (vol./vol.) formalin solution. For specimens smaller than about 50 mm, or for larval or early juvenile fish, a 5% formalin (vol./vol.) solution can be used. These are prepared by adding 1 part of commercial formalin (37% formaldehyde gas) to 9 parts water for the 10% solution, or 1 part commercial formalin to 19 parts water for the 5% solution. Specimens larger than about 100 mm total length should have the body cavity opened by a small slit through the abdominal wall on **the lower right side**. This allows the formalin to preserve the viscera before they begin to decompose. This is especially important for plant- and detritus-eating fish such as all suckers and the common carp.

Canadian Council on Animal Care standards require that fish must be euthanized before being placed in formalin solution. 2-Phenoxyethanol, added to the water the fish are held in at a concentration of about 0.1%, will anaesthetize and kill fish, without causing apparent distress, in about five minutes. It is not classified as a hazardous material.

If fish are to be kept in formalin longer than about a month, a small amount of calcium carbonate (chalk dust or limestone chips) should be added to the formalin solution to prevent it from becoming acidic and decalcifying fish bones. Fish specimens may be kept indefinitely in formalin solution buffered with calcium carbonate.

INTRODUCTION

GENERAL FEATURES AND MEASUREMENTS OF FISH

LATERAL VIEWS, WHOLE BODY

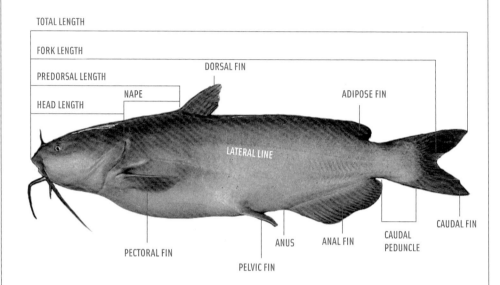

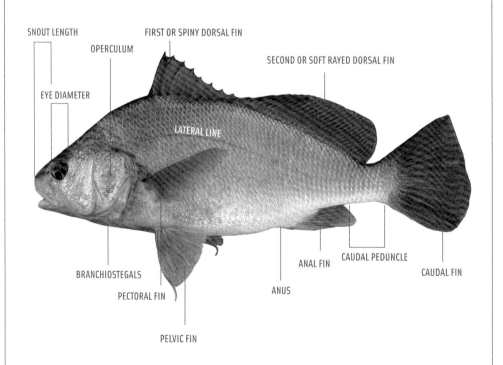

FEATURES AND MEASUREMENTS ON THE HEAD

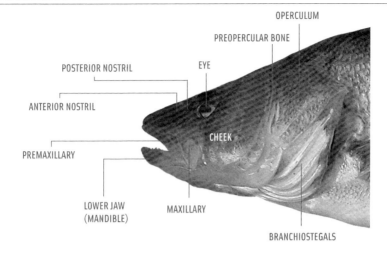

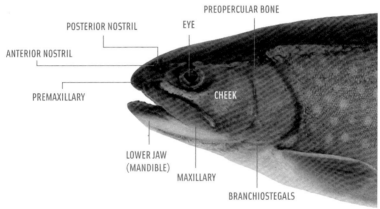

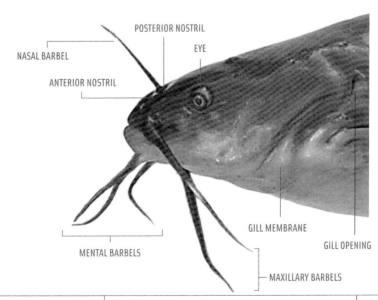

HOW TO USE THE KEYS IN THIS BOOK

The keys in this book present a series of choices that help you to identify our freshwater fishes. Immediately following this section is a key to the families of fishes found in fresh water in Manitoba. In cases where there is only one species in a family, the species is given with the family in this key. For families with more than one species in Manitoba, there is a separate key to the species of each family following the introductory section for that family in the species accounts.

To use a key, it is best to have a specimen of the fish you are trying to identify at hand. If only a picture is available, it may work, but a picture likely won't show all the features you need to make full use of the key. Each step in a key consists of two alternate choices. Read each choice, examine your specimen, and decide which of the two fits your specimen. Below each choice will be either the name of the species or a note telling you to go to a particular numbered choice farther along in the key. **Read each choice carefully. If you are not familiar with some of the terms in the choice, look them up in the Glossary. Most choices present more than one feature. Be sure to examine all the features before making a choice.** Make sure you **go to the correct next choice or the correct page number** for the species description or the next key. **Write down any counts or measurements you make. You may need them for a later choice.**

When you reach an identification, go to the species account, **examine the species illustration**, and **read the Identification section** of the account. Also **check the distribution map** and the Distribution in Manitoba section of the text. If you have a good match between your specimen, the species illustration, and the Identification section, and the distribution agrees with where you found the specimen, you can be confident of your identification. If your specimen doesn't match what you identified it to be, you will need to go back over your choices and find the mistake. Did you **understand all the terms correctly**? Did you **check all the features presented in each choice**? Did you **go to the correct next choice every time**? These are some of the most common mistakes people make when using a key.

Finally, **no key is infallible**! Fish vary, and you may have found a specimen that is outside the known variation for its species. Also, some species are just hard to identify because they are very similar to one or more other species. This is true of some of the minnow species, the ciscoes, and two of the sculpins in this book. Keep working at the hard ones and you will improve quickly with experience. Also, keep in mind that many areas in Manitoba are poorly sampled, and you could have a correct identification, but found the species outside its known range in Manitoba. **New locations for species can be important**. If you think you have one, contact any of the organizations listed below. You will need to have the specimen, or a good photograph of it, and notes on where it was found, when, and by whom. **If you find a specimen that doesn't fit anything in the book, you may have something new**. Again, in that case, contact one of the organizations listed below for help. If your specimen is new to the province, they will identify it and make its presence known, so that research, conservation, and management planning can take it into account.

WHERE TO GET HELP WITH FISH IDENTIFICATION

You can report occurrences of fish (always include the specimen or a photograph) or get specimens collected in our area identified at any of the following institutions.

Department of Zoology	Fisheries Branch	Fisheries and Oceans Canada	The Manitoba Museum
Duff Roblin Building	Manitoba Department of	Freshwater Institute	Natural History Division
University of Manitoba	Water Stewardship	501 University Crescent	190 Rupert Avenue
Winnipeg, Manitoba	200 Saulteaux Crescent	Winnipeg, Manitoba	Winnipeg, Manitoba
R3T 2N2	Winnipeg, Manitoba	R3T 2N6	R3B 0N2
(204) 474-9245	R3J 3W3	(204) 983-5000	(204) 956-2830
	(204) 945-8105		

KEY TO THE FAMILIES OF FRESHWATER FISHES OF MANITOBA AND ADJACENT AREAS OF THE HUDSON BAY DRAINAGE

1A Jaws and paired fins lacking. In adults, mouth circular, funnel-shaped when open, armed with spiral rows of horny teeth. Mouth closes to a longitudinal slit. In ammocoetes larvae, mouth toothless, surrounded by an oral hood. Seven pairs of external gill openings.

Lampreys, family Petromyzontidae page 36

ADULT LAMPREY LATERAL VIEW

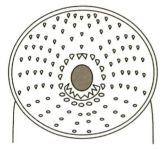

VENTRAL VIEW ADULT LAMPREY MOUTHPARTS (MOUTH OPEN)

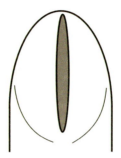

VENTRAL VIEW ADULT LAMPREY MOUTHPARTS (MOUTH CLOSED)

VENTRAL VIEW AMMOCOETES LARVAL MOUTHPARTS

1B Jaws and paired fins present. Jaws with true teeth or toothless, not horny teeth. Mouth closes to a transverse slit. One pair of external gill openings.

go to choice 2

2A (1B) Caudal fin heterocercal, with body extending into upper lobe, which is longer than lower lobe. Mouth ventral, overhung by long snout, with 4 barbels anterior to mouth.

Sturgeons, family Acipenseridae page 44

1 species, lake sturgeon, *Acipenser fulvescens* page 45

2B Caudal fin homocercal, body not extending into upper lobe, and fin symmetrical, or nearly so. Mouth superior, terminal, or inferior, not ventral, and overhung by snout. Barbels may be present, but never anterior to mouth.

go to choice 3

3A (2B) Jaws elongated into beak, with strong teeth. Body covered by rhombic, ganoid scales.

Gars, family Lepisosteidae page 48

1 species, longnose gar, *Lepisosteus osseus* page 49

RED RIVER, USA ONLY, NO RECENT RECORDS

3B Jaws not elongated into beak. Scales cycloid, ctenoid, or absent.

go to choice 4

KEY TO THE FAMILIES

4A (3B) Pectoral fins low on sides, pelvic fins far back on abdomen. Posterior tips of depressed pectoral fins not reaching base of pelvic fins.
go to choice 5

4B Pectoral fins higher on sides, pelvic fins farther forward. Posterior tips of depressed pectorals reach at least to base of pelvic fins.
go to choice 15

5A (4A) Adipose fin present.
go to choice 6

5B Adipose fin absent.
go to choice 8

6A (5A) Scales absent, mouth surrounded by 8 barbels.
Catfish, family Ictaluridae page 130

6B Scales present (but may be small and imbedded), barbels absent.
go to choice 7

7A (6B) Pelvic axillary process present.
Trout and Whitefish, family Salmonidae page 155

7B Pelvic axillary process absent.
Smelts, family Osmeridae page 151

8A (5B) Teeth present (may be small).
go to choice 9

8B Teeth absent.
go to choice 13

9A (8A) Teeth on maxillae and tongue. Anal fin with 26 or more rays, its base longer than the head. Body deep and strongly compressed.
Mooneyes and Goldeyes, family Hiodontidae page 52

9B Teeth on maxillae but not tongue, or absent from both maxillae and tongue.
go to choice 10

10A (9B) Teeth on maxillae. Dorsal fin long and low, starting anterior to pelvic fins, and extending nearly to base of caudal fin. A broad, flat, bony plate covers underside of head between the sides of the lower jaw.
Bowfin, family Amiidae page 50
1 species, bowfin, *Amia calva* page 51
RED RIVER HEADWATERS IN MN, INTRODUCED INTO LAKE OF THE WOODS IN 1984

10B No teeth on maxillae or tongue. Dorsal fin shorter, and starting over or behind pelvic fins. No bony plate on underside of head between lower jaws.
go to choice 11

11A (10B) Head long, the snout depressed and pointed. Strong, fang-like teeth on lower jaw, premaxillae, and roof of mouth.
Pike and Muskellunge, family Esocidae, page 144

11B Head shorter, the snout not depressed. Teeth small, and may be difficult to see without magnification.
go to choice 12

KEY TO THE FAMILIES

12A (11B) Mouth reaching to below eye. Premaxillae immovably joined to snout.
Mudminnows, family Umbridae page 148
1 species, central mudminnow, *Umbra limi* page 149

12B Mouth not reaching to below eye. Premaxillae movably joined to snout.
Topminnows, family Fundulidae page 187
1 species, banded killifish, *Fundulus diaphanus* page 188

13A (8B) Lips with fleshy expansions. Mouth inferior.
Suckers, family Catostomidae page 112
(see also choice **14A**)

13B Lips without fleshy expansions. Mouth usually terminal, but may be subterminal or inferior.
go to choice 14

14A (13B) Anal fin set far back, the distance between anal origin and middle of caudal base equal to 1/2 or less the distance from anal origin to posterior margin of operculum.
Suckers, family Catostomidae page 112

14B Anal fin set farther forward, the distance from anal origin to middle of caudal base equal to more than 1/2 the distance from anal origin to posterior margin of operculum.
Minnows, family Cyprinidae page 56

15A (4B) Fins without spines, or spines, if present, flexible and weak, not strong, rigid, and sharp.
go to choice 16

15B Strong, rigid, sharp spines present in some or all of anterior dorsal, anal, and pelvic fins.
go to choice 18

16A (15A) Body eel-like, fins lacking spines, and scales tiny, imbedded, and not obvious without close inspection. A single barbel at tip of chin.
Codfishes, family Gadidae page 184
1 species, burbot, *Lota lota* page 185

16B Body deeper, not eel-like. One or more weak spines present, at least in dorsal fin. Scales may be ctenoid and larger, modified into prickles, or absent.
go to choice 17

17A (16B) Adipose fin present, scales ctenoid, normally developed. One dorsal fin with 1 or 2 weak spines at leading edge. One weak spine at leading edge of anal fin.
Troutperch, family Percopsidae page 181
1 species, troutperch, *Percopsis omiscomaycus* page 182

17B Adipose fin absent. Scales absent or modified into prickles. Two dorsal fins, the anterior one composed of weak spines. A weak spine present at the leading edge of each pelvic fin.
Sculpins, family Cottidae page 196

18A (15B) Anterior dorsal fin composed of free spines, not joined by a fin membrane. Pelvic fins reduced to a single spine each, with no rays. Scales absent, or modified into a series of enlarged lateral plates.
Sticklebacks, family Gasterosteidae page 190

18B Spines in anterior dorsal fin connected by a fin membrane. Pelvic fins with a spine at leading edge connected to 5 branched rays by a fin membrane. Scales always ctenoid and normally developed.
go to choice 19

KEY TO THE FAMILIES

19A (18B) Anal fin with 2 or fewer spines.
go to choice 20
19B Anal fin with 3 or more spines.
go to choice 21

20A (19A) Posterior dorsal fin with 1 spine and 25 or more rays, its base longer than the head. Second anal spine thickened and much longer than first. Lateral line extending to the rear margin of the caudal fin.
Drums, family Sciaenidae page 245
1 species, freshwater drum, *Aplodinotus grunniens* page 246
20B Posterior dorsal fin base shorter than head, with 1 spine and 22 or fewer rays. Second anal spine slender, and not much longer than first, or absent. Lateral line extending onto the base of the caudal fin only in the walleye and sauger.
Perch, family Percidae page 228

21A (19B) Posterior dorsal and anal fins falcate. Anterior and posterior dorsal fins separate. Posterior margin of opercular bone with a spine. A series of 6–8 narrow, longitudinal dark stripes on sides.
Temperate Basses, family Moronidae page 207
1 species, white bass, *Morone chrysops* page 208
INTRODUCED
21B Posterior dorsal and anal fins with convex, rounded margins. Anterior and posterior dorsal fins connected by at least a narrow fin membrane, and usually broadly connected. Posterior margin of opercular bone without a spine. Markings various, including sometimes a single mid-lateral dark band, but never 6–8 narrow longitudinal stripes.
Sunfishes, family Centrarchidae page 210

SPECIES ACCOUNTS

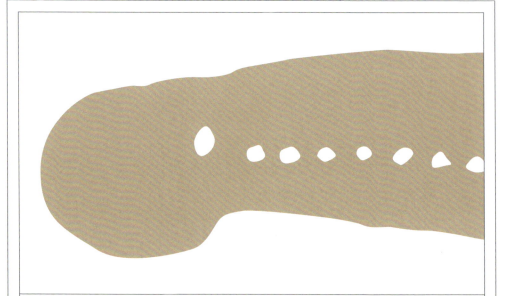

LAMPREYS, ORDER PETROMYZONTIFORMES
LAMPREYS, FAMILY PETROMYZONTIDAE

ORDER PETROMYZONTIFORMES

The Order Petromyzontiformes is the only surviving group of jawless fishes. Members of this order are living descendants of the extinct, jawless fishes (agnathans), which are some of the most ancient fishes known. The order contains six living genera and about 41 living species. Three genera and 37 species are found in the temperate zone of the northern hemisphere and two genera and four species are found in the temperate zone of the southern hemisphere. The basic life-history pattern of members of the order is anadromy. Spawning occurs in fresh water, with eggs hatching into ammocoetes larvae. After a period of a variable number of years, the larvae transform into adults, migrate to the ocean, and grow to maturity by feeding on the blood of fish, to which they attach with their sucking mouthparts. Mature adults migrate back to fresh water to spawn, and die after spawning. Freshwater lampreys may arise from populations of anadromous species that fail to migrate to the sea for a variety of reasons. This has happened a number of times over the history of the group. It has resulted in freshwater forms that are the same species as their marine ancestor, such as the sea lamprey in the Great Lakes, and, over much longer periods, has led to the evolution of wholly freshwater genera with no anadromous species. The three Manitoba species, all members of the genus *Ichthyomyzon*, are examples of this. Finally, some freshwater lampreys have evolved non-parasitic forms, which never feed as adults, and spawn and die during the spring following their transformation from the larval to the adult stage.

FAMILY PETROMYZONTIDAE

Lampreys have slender, eel-like bodies and **lack paired fins and jaws**. There are **seven gill openings on each side** behind the head. Adult lampreys have a circular, sucking mouth or **oral disc** armed with **spiral rows of horny teeth**. All our lamprey species live their entire lives in fresh water. Two of our three lamprey species are parasites on other fish as adults. They feed by attaching to a host fish with their oral disc, rasping a hole through its skin with horny teeth on their tongue, and sucking blood from the host. The third species is a dwarfed form, which does not feed as an adult. Lampreys have a larval stage, the **ammocoetes larva**, which lasts between five and seven years in Canadian waters. Ammocoetes larvae differ from adults by **lacking well-developed eyes** and having an **oral hood that lacks teeth** and surrounds the mouth cavity. Ammocoetes larvae burrow in the stream bottom, usually preferring a mud-sand substrate, and feed by filtering microscopic algae, protozoans, and detritus from water pumped through their gills. The food particles are trapped on mucous that covers the basket-like gill structure. The largest ammocoetes

LAMPREYS, FAMILY PETROMYZONTIDAE

larvae in the University of Manitoba collection are 105–122 mm long. The smallest adult-stage lampreys of all species in the collection are 95–117 mm long. This suggests that transformation from the larval to the adult stage occurs at about the same size in all three species. We have adapted Lanteigne's (1988) key to the ammocoetes larvae of the *Ichthyomyzon* species to identify only our three lamprey species.

KEY TO THE AMMOCOETES LARVAE OF LAMPREYS FOUND IN MANITOBA (After Lanteigne 1988)

1A Lateral line pores on the head and body above the gill openings have dark pigment, giving the appearance of scattered dark spots.

chestnut lamprey, *Ichthyomyzon castaneus* page 38

1B Lateral line pores on head and body over gill openings not pigmented; whitish in colour.

go to choice 2

2A (1B) Areas of the head below the eye and anterior to the gill openings have dusky pigment. There is a whitish band 1 mm wide above the gill openings.

northern brook lamprey, *Ichthyomyzon fossor* page 40

2B Areas of the head below the eye and anterior to the gill openings are only weakly pigmented. Whitish band above gill openings is about 3 mm wide.

silver lamprey, *Ichthyomyzon unicuspis* page 42

KEY TO THE ADULT LAMPREYS FOUND IN MANITOBA

1A At least 1 inner lateral tooth on one side of mouth opening, at centre of buccal funnel, with 2 cusps. Usually 2 or more teeth on each side with 2 cusps (see Diagram 1).

chestnut lamprey, *Ichthyomyzon castaneus* page 38

1B All lateral teeth unicuspid.

go to choice 2

2A (1B) Oral disc wider than the branchial region of the body, armed with strong, sharp teeth. Infraoral lamina with 5–11 sharp cusps.

silver lamprey, *Ichthyomyzon unicuspis* page 42

2B Oral disc narrower than branchial region. Teeth few and weakly developed. Infraoral lamina with 6–11 blunt, knoblike cusps (see Diagram 2).

northern brook lamprey, *Ichthyomyzon fossor* page 40

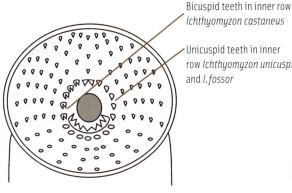

DIAGRAM 1
VENTRAL VIEW ORAL DISC AND TEETH

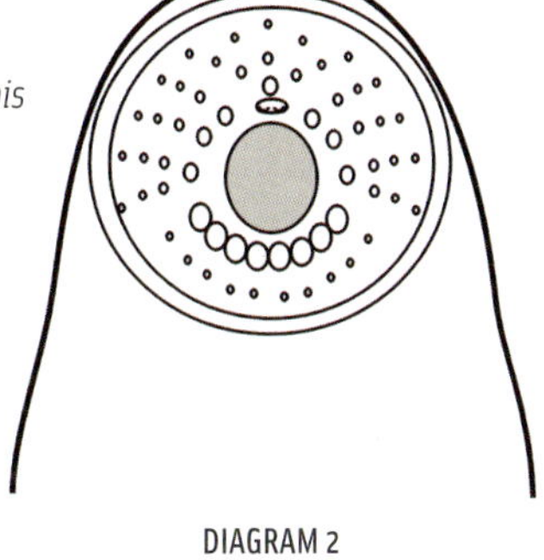

Bicuspid teeth in inner row *Ichthyomyzon castaneus*

Unicuspid teeth in inner row *Ichthyomyzon unicuspis* and *I. fossor*

DIAGRAM 2
VENTRAL VIEW NORTHERN BROOK LAMPREY
Ichthyomyzon fossor

LAMPREYS, FAMILY PETROMYZONTIDAE

CHESTNUT LAMPREY; LAMPROIE BRUNE | *Ichthyomyzon castaneus*

5 CM — FRESH SPECIMEN

1 CM — PRESERVED SPECIMEN

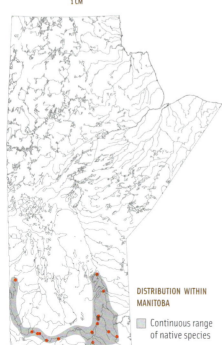

DISTRIBUTION WITHIN MANITOBA
- Continuous range of native species
- Known occurrences

IDENTIFICATION

The chestnut lamprey is distinguished from the northern brook lamprey by having the **oral disc as wide as or wider than the body**. Distinguished from the silver lamprey by having **one or more bicuspid teeth in the inner lateral tooth row**.

DISTRIBUTION IN MANITOBA

Chestnut lampreys are found in most streams and lakes in southern Manitoba, northward to Dog Head Point, Lake Winnipeg. This is the most commonly collected of our three lamprey species, but, as with all lampreys, they are not effectively sampled by any collecting gear, and they may be more common and widespread than our data suggest.

BIOLOGICAL NOTES

SPAWNING: The chestnut lamprey ascends streams to spawn in mid- to late June. Adults cease feeding and the digestive tract degenerates when they mature. Case (1970b) described the spawning behaviour of chestnut lampreys in the Rat River at St. Malo. Spawning took place during the last two weeks of June. A school of spawning lampreys constructed a communal nest by moving gravel with their oral discs. Spawning progressed upstream, with the downstream section of the nest being filled in with gravel removed from the newer upstream section. Chestnut lampreys, like all lampreys, die after spawning. Mature adult chestnut lampreys have been collected in the Roseau River at the Dominion City Dam in mid- to late June, and dead, spawned-out chestnut and silver lampreys have been found in the Rat River at St. Malo in early July.

GROWTH AND ADULT SIZE: The chestnut lamprey, like all other lampreys, has the life history divided into two phases. The ammocoetes larva lives for five to seven years (Scott and Crossman, 1979), probably seven years in Manitoba, and grows to a length of 105–122 mm. Transformation to the adult form is probably completed in the fall. The length actually shortens during transformation to the adult stage, with the smallest adults we have measured being 100–125 mm long. The adult stage lasts for one year and mature adults collected from a spawning run in the Roseau River measured 265–282 mm long.

LAMPREYS, FAMILY PETROMYZONTIDAE

FEEDING: As ammocoetes larvae, lampreys filter-feed on organic detritus, microscopic algae, and protozoa. Adult chestnut lampreys have been observed attached to a variety of fish, including the white sucker, shorthead redhorse, silver redhorse, common carp, bullheads, channel catfish, walleye, and sauger. Typically, the lamprey is attached, or a wound or circular scar consistent with a lamprey attack, is located on the back or on the side, just above or behind a pectoral fin.

HABITAT: Ammocoetes larvae burrow in firm sand-mud substrates in fast-flowing water, presumably near the site where they hatched (Scott and Crossman, 1979). Adult chestnut lampreys move downstream into larger rivers and apparently migrate upstream into tributaries to spawn. Whether spawning takes place in the natal stream is unknown. Nothing is known about preferred substrates, water depths, or velocities for non-spawning adults. Presumably, the presence of suitable host species is the most important factor in determining habitat suitability.

ECOLOGICAL ROLE: The ecological role of lampreys is unique. The ammocoetes larvae are, at least partially, first-level consumers, which is unusual for North American fishes in general. Adults are parasitic on other fishes, a feeding role not used by any other family of fish in Manitoba. Both ammocoetes larvae and adults would be subject to predation by other fish, but their importance as forage species is unknown in Manitoba.

IMPORTANCE TO PEOPLE

The chestnut lamprey has no economic importance. Its parasitism on fish has no apparent effect on populations of its host species. Chestnut lampreys only grow to about half the size of adult non-migratory sea lampreys, and are much less abundant, so relatively few fish are parasitized, and those that are, are more likely to survive than lake trout parasitized by sea lampreys. The species that are parasitized also appear to be more tolerant of lamprey attacks than lake trout.

COSEWIC Status as of January 1, 2004: Special Concern
MBESA Status as of January 1, 2004: Not Listed
MBCDC Status as of January 1, 2004: G4, S3S4

NORTHERN BROOK LAMPREY; LAMPROIE DU NORD — *Ichthyomyzon fossor*

LAMPREYS, FAMILY PETROMYZONTIDAE

2 CM — PRESERVED SPECIMEN

1 CM — PRESERVED SPECIMEN

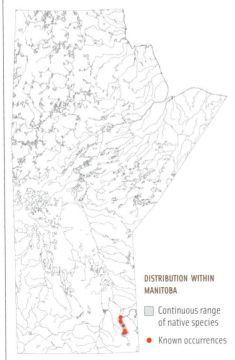

DISTRIBUTION WITHIN MANITOBA

- Continuous range of native species
- Known occurrences

IDENTIFICATION

The northern brook lamprey is distinguished from both the chestnut and silver lampreys by having an **oral disc that is narrower than the body**, armed with **few, poorly developed, unicuspid teeth**. The largest adult northern brook lamprey we have measured is 117 mm long. Typically, adults grow to a **length of 80–100 mm**.

DISTRIBUTION IN MANITOBA

In Manitoba, the northern brook lamprey has been found in the Whitemouth River watershed, including the Whitemouth, Birch, and Bog rivers, Hazel Creek, and in the Winnipeg River at the mouth of the Whitemouth River. Within the Whitemouth River watershed, they are apparently absent from the bog habitat in upper reaches. Although the data on their distribution in the Whitemouth River are soundly based, the northern brook lamprey may be more widespread than available data indicate.

BIOLOGICAL NOTES

SPAWNING: Dead, spawned-out northern brook lampreys have been found in mid-June in riffle areas immediately adjacent to silty shallows with ammocoetes larvae, at several locations in the Whitemouth River north of the Trans-Canada Highway. The spawning substrate is clean gravel and rubble in riffles up to 30 cm deep. There is no apparent migration. Spawning behaviour in the brook lamprey is similar to that of other *Ichthyomyzon* species.

GROWTH AND ADULT SIZE: Ammocoetes larvae of the northern brook lamprey grow to about the same size as the other two lamprey species in Manitoba. Age at transformation is reported to be between three and six years old (Becker, 1983) and five to seven years (Scott and Crossman, 1979). The largest ammocoetes larvae from the Whitemouth River are 105–122 mm long. Adults do not feed, and lose length during transformation. They range 95–117 mm long in the Whitemouth River, about the same size as the smallest transformed lampreys of the other two Manitoba species. A 110 mm ammocoetes larva identified as *I. fossor* was caught from the Winnipeg River at the mouth of the Whitemouth River on July 18, 2003. It showed reduction of the buccal cirri, and thickening of the margin of the oral hood. It also had well-formed lenses in its eyes, indicating that transformation to the adult form was in progress by that time. Transformation is complete in at least some individuals by late September. Adults apparently overwinter in the substrate and emerge and spawn the following spring.

FEEDING: Ammocoetes larvae are filter feeders like those of the chestnut and silver lampreys. Northern brook lampreys do not feed after transformation.

HABITAT: In the Whitemouth River, larval northern brook lampreys burrow in silt-sand substrate in shallow, slow-moving water, up to 40 cm deep. We have observed undisturbed northern brook lampreys swimming for short distances and then burrowing in new locations or possibly entering existing burrows.

ECOLOGICAL ROLE: Northern brook lampreys are first-level consumers in their food web. They are abundant enough in the Whitemouth River and its tributaries that they may have some importance as forage for larger benthivores and piscivores. This has not been demonstrated, however.

IMPORTANCE TO PEOPLE

The northern brook lamprey has no economic importance. Its small size, relatively large numbers, and its position near the base of the food web in the Whitemouth River, raise the possibility that it may have ecological importance where it occurs. Its unique life history and adaptations are a significant addition to the interest and diversity of Manitoba's fish fauna.

COSEWIC Status as of January 1, 2004: Special Concern
MBESA Status as of January 1, 2004: Not Listed
MBCDC Status as of January 1, 2004: G4, S2

LAMPREYS, FAMILY PETROMYZONTIDAE

SILVER LAMPREY; LAMPROIE ARGENTÉE | *Ichthyomyzon unicuspis*

FRESH SPECIMEN
5 CM

PRESERVED SPECIMEN
1 CM

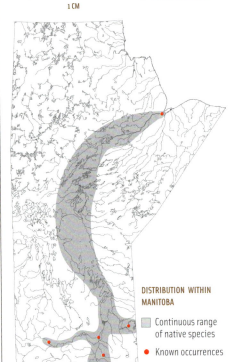

DISTRIBUTION WITHIN MANITOBA

- Continuous range of native species
- Known occurrences

IDENTIFICATION

The silver lamprey is distinguished from the northern brook lamprey by having the **oral disc as wide as or wider than the body**. Distinguished from the chestnut lamprey by having **only unicuspid teeth in the inner lateral tooth row**.

DISTRIBUTION IN MANITOBA

The silver lamprey is known in Manitoba only from the Red, Rat, Assiniboine, Winnipeg, and Nelson rivers, northward to Seal Creek, near the mouth of the Nelson River. As with the chestnut lamprey, this is probably not an accurate estimate of either their distribution or abundance in Manitoba. Misidentification of lamprey species may also give a false idea of silver lamprey distribution in Manitoba. While collecting data on lampreys, we reidentified most of the "silver lampreys" in the University of Manitoba collection as chestnut lampreys, on the basis of having one or more bicuspid, inner lateral, oral teeth. This reduced the number of records for the silver lamprey in Manitoba by about half.

BIOLOGICAL NOTES

Virtually nothing is known of the biology of this species in Manitoba.

SPAWNING: Silver lampreys ascend larger rivers to spawn in May and June in Québec (Scott and Crossman, 1979). A nest is excavated in gravel substrate by transporting stones in the mouth. As with other lampreys, silver lampreys die after spawning.

GROWTH AND ADULT SIZE: The silver lamprey, like all other lampreys, has the life history divided into two phases. The ammocoetes larva lives for five to seven years (Scott and Crossman, 1979), probably seven years in Manitoba. Transformation to the adult form is probably completed in the fall. The silver lamprey may feed as an adult for more than one summer in Manitoba. Two females with mature ovaries, collected in the fall of different years, from the Winnipeg River, measured 255 mm (with part of the tail missing) and 295 mm, respectively, while three other fall-caught individuals (all caught in different years) lacked mature gonads and were 235, 240, and 247 mm long.

FEEDING: As ammocoetes larvae, lampreys filter-feed on organic detritus, microscopic algae, and protozoa. Silver lampreys have been observed attached to walleye, shorthead redhorse, white sucker, and lake sturgeon. Scott and Crossman (1979) suggest that the silver lamprey may continue some parasitism on fish during the winter prior to spawning.

HABITAT: The specimens in the University of Manitoba collection came from large rivers or impounded, lake-like sections of the Winnipeg River.

ECOLOGICAL ROLE: The ecological role of lampreys is unique. The ammocoetes larvae are, at least partially, first-level consumers, which is unusual for North American fishes in general. Adults are parasitic on other fishes. Both ammocoetes larvae and adults would be subject to predation by other fish, but their importance as forage species is unknown in Manitoba. If the silver lamprey is as rare as the available records suggest, it is only of minor ecological importance in Manitoba.

IMPORTANCE TO PEOPLE

Like the chestnut lamprey, the fish parasitism of the silver lamprey apparently has no significant effect on its host species. Like all lampreys, its unique form, life history, and adaptations add interest and diversity to our fish fauna.

COSEWIC Status as of January 1, 2004: Not Listed
MBESA Status as of January 1, 2004: Not Listed
MBCDC Status as of January 1, 2004: G5, S3

STURGEONS AND PADDLEFISHES, ORDER ACIPENSERIFORMES

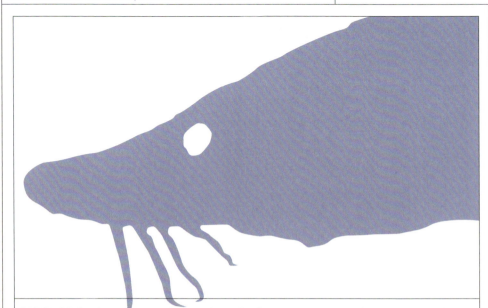

STURGEONS AND PADDLEFISHES, ORDER ACIPENSERIFORMES

STURGEON, FAMILY ACIPENSERIDAE

Sturgeon and paddlefishes are descendants of an ancient lineage of bony fishes. They have lost much of the bone in their skeletons. Their ancestors were covered by an armour of edge-to-edge-joined, rhombic, ganoid scales that are retained in sturgeon only on the sides of the tail, where the body extends into the upper lobe of the tail. Sturgeons have become specialized for bottom feeding, using their barbels to detect food, and their ventral, toothless, protrusible mouths to suck in food.

FAMILY ACIPENSERIDAE

The sturgeons comprise about 24 species of anadromous and freshwater fish living in warm temperate to cool temperate waters in North America and Eurasia. Most species of sturgeon live to a great age and grow to large size. The largest sturgeon in Canada is the white sturgeon, an anadromous sturgeon of the Pacific coast of North America, which can weigh up to 630 kg.

All sturgeon can be recognized by the **shark-like, heterocercal tail**, with the **body turning into the upper lobe of the tail**. This is also the most visible evidence of their ancient origin. Sturgeon have a **long, depressed, and bluntly pointed snout**, with the **toothless, protrusible mouth underneath it**. The streamlined, torpedo-shaped body has a **row of enlarged bony plates or scutes down the back** and **two rows on each side**. Sturgeon are mainly bottom feeders that suck in prey with their protrusible mouths. Young sturgeon feed on invertebrates, but larger individuals become fish predators. While a number of sturgeon species are migratory and move between the sea and fresh water, the lake sturgeon never leaves fresh water.

LAKE STURGEON; ESTURGEON JAUNE | *Acipenser fulvescens*

FRESH SPECIMEN
10 CM

IDENTIFICATION
The lake sturgeon is the only freshwater fish in Manitoba with a **shark-like tail, rows of large plates down the back and sides**, the **mouth on the underside of a long snout**, and a **row of four barbels** across the snout **in front of the mouth**.

DISTRIBUTION
Historically, lake sturgeon were found in all the larger rivers and lakes in Manitoba north to the Seal River. In southern Manitoba, they have become rare to absent in the Manitoba Great Lakes and the Winnipeg, Red, and Assiniboine river watersheds. Since about 1997, the Manitoba Fisheries Branch and the University of Manitoba have planted juvenile lake sturgeon in the Assiniboine River and the state of Minnesota has planted them in the Red River. As a result of these plantings, sturgeon are now being caught by anglers occasionally in both the Red and Assiniboine rivers. Also, reports of larger sturgeon being caught or observed in Lake Winnipeg and the Red River below the St. Andrews Dam at Lockport, Manitoba, have become more frequent recently.

BIOLOGICAL NOTES
SPAWNING: Lake sturgeon spawn in late May to mid-June in Manitoba when water temperature approaches 11°C (Bayette, pers. comm., 2002). They migrate to fast water, such as rapids or the bases of impassable falls, to spawn. The eggs are scattered over hard substrate, such as boulders or bedrock, and adhere to the bottom.

Since dams are usually built at the downstream end of steep-gradient sections of streams, they may cut off access of sturgeon to their spawning grounds. Hydroelectric dams also typically have large fluctuations in water discharge, as power generation is adjusted to meet changes in electricity demand. Sturgeon that have been cut off from their spawning grounds by construction of the dam often begin to spawn in the tailrace of the dam. When this happens, their eggs are often left exposed and killed when the water level below the dam drops abruptly as discharge is reduced during periods of low electric power consumption.

In the past in southern Manitoba, there must have been very long migrations, often ending in tributaries, in low-gradient rivers such as the Red River. A 1903 record for the Roseau River (Waddell, 1970) and the 1799 to 1814 journals of Alexander Henry (Henry and Thompson, 1897) both provide evidence of the upstream abundance and distribution of sturgeon in the Red River drainage.

GROWTH AND ADULT SIZE: Lake sturgeon grow slowly, requiring as many as 25 years to reach sexual maturity in the Nelson River (Scott and Crossman, 1979). After maturity, females do not spawn every year. They are also long-lived, and ages of 50 years for males and 80 years for females are known (Scott and Crossman). Becker (1983) reports an estimated age of 100 years for a female sturgeon collected from Lake Superior in 1921, and Waddell (1970) reported an estimated age of 150 years for a female taken from the Roseau River, Manitoba, in 1903.

Block (2001) studied the growth of lake sturgeon in two impounded reaches of the Winnipeg River and in Round Lake, a small natural lake on the Pigeon River (Lake Winnipeg watershed). The age-length curves were similar for the three areas, with sturgeon living to a maximum of 80 years and growing to 1200–1400 mm total length.

STURGEONS, FAMILY ACIPENSERIDAE

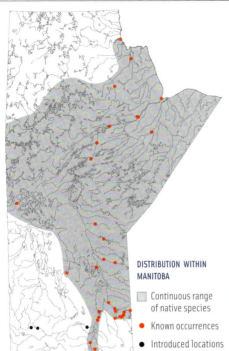

DISTRIBUTION WITHIN MANITOBA

- Continuous range of native species
- Known occurrences
- Introduced locations

The lake sturgeon is the largest species of freshwater fish in Manitoba. The largest documented record for a lake sturgeon in Manitoba, and apparently for lake sturgeon anywhere, is in a photograph taken by George Barraclough, which is included in Waddell's (1970) history of the Dominion City area (see Frontispiece). It shows a sturgeon that was caught by Sandy Waddell from the Roseau River east of Dominion City, Manitoba, on October 27, 1903. Information written on the photograph states that "it was a female, full of caviar, and was 15 feet long and weighed 406 lbs. The age of this fish was recorded as 150 years...." There is no information as to how the age was determined. In metric units the reported size is 4.572 m and 184.57 kg. Waddell gives a first-hand account of its capture.

Note: A comparison of the lengths of the image of the sturgeon and the images of three people in this photograph suggests that the sturgeon was actually about 3 m long. A weight of 184 kg, however, is within the weight range to be expected if a scatter plot of length against weight for large sturgeon reported by Scott and Crossman (1979), Becker (1983), and Block (2001) is extrapolated to a length of 3 m. A length: weight regression for 1964 female lake sturgeon from the Wolf River, Wisconsin (Bruch, pers. comm., 2004), also yields a predicted length of 3.12 m for a 184.57 kg fish. If the length were 4.57 m, as reported, the predicted weight would be 470.79 kg, more than twice the reported weight. The angling record for the lake sturgeon in Manitoba is a 199 cm fish caught from the Red River in 1996.

FEEDING: Lake sturgeon feed mainly on small food items such as aquatic insects, crayfish, and other benthic invertebrates. A wide variety of food items have been reported, however, ranging from plant material such as algae or spilled grain, to small fish, to carrion. Their food, which they detect using chemoreceptors on their barbels, is nearly always benthic in origin, and they suck food in, using their protrusible mouths.

HABITAT: Lake sturgeon inhabit larger lakes and rivers. Although they are considered to be mainly benthic, Block (2001) found that they spent significant amounts of time above the bottom. When they were on the bottom, they were most often on fine to medium sand substrates. He also found that sturgeon were most densely distributed in areas with current. In the Winnipeg River impoundments, sturgeon were absent from standing water but present in areas where current approximated pre-impoundment conditions.

Lake sturgeon apparently school and undergo extensive movements at all phases of their life history, but are no longer abundant enough in southern Manitoba to provide a basis for detailed study of their movements.

Becker (1983) notes that sturgeon move over wide ranges and also notes the effect of dams in cutting them off from spawning habitat and isolating groups of sturgeon in short reaches of streams, which results in their eventual extirpation.

In the Red and Assiniboine rivers, the construction of the St. Andrews Dam on the Red River at Lockport in 1910 flooded the St. Andrews Rapid, likely an important spawning area for sturgeon. The dam is also impassable to fish when the movable barrier is not in place, and the fishway is not passable to large adult sturgeon because its cells are too small and the clearance between the baffles and side walls is too narrow. The St. Andrews Dam was probably the final blow, after about a quarter-century of overexploitation, that led to the near-extirpation of the lake sturgeon from the Red and Assiniboine rivers.

ECOLOGICAL ROLE: Lake sturgeon are middle-level consumers that rely on aquatic invertebrates for most of their food. Considering their abundance in the Red River in the early 19th century, as reported by Henry and Thompson (1897), they must have been one of the most important species at that level in aquatic communities in our lakes and larger streams. This suggests that these waters have undergone major reorganization of their aquatic communities over the past century.

IMPORTANCE TO PEOPLE

Historically, sturgeon were an important food fish for Aboriginal people. Harkness (1936) traces the increasing intensity of the commercial sturgeon fishery in the Manitoba Great Lakes and the rivers in southern Manitoba during the late 19th and early 20th centuries. With a heavy commercial harvest from many lakes and rivers, sturgeon had become rare over most of their range in southern Manitoba by the late 1920s. The construction of dams on the Red, Winnipeg, Saskatchewan, Nelson, Burntwood, and Churchill rivers during the 20th century has severely reduced the suitability of these waters as sturgeon habitat for the reasons noted above.

Sturgeon habitat requirements are incompatible with economic development of our rivers, which involves extensive construction of dams. The identification, designation, and protection of streams that still support healthy sturgeon spawning stocks, combined with initial prohibition, followed by stringent limitation, of harvest of sturgeon would seem to be the most likely way to ensure recovery and long-term survival of the species in at least some watersheds in Manitoba. The most likely candidates for consideration as designated protected areas for sturgeon would include the eastern tributary rivers to Lake Winnipeg and the Hayes/God's River watershed. Some reaches of the Saskatchewan and Winnipeg rivers with remnant sturgeon stocks could also be candidates for designation as sturgeon habitat if they are protected from overexploitation and any further degradation of their habitat.

It may also be possible to rehabilitate the Red and Assiniboine rivers for sturgeon if modifications could be made to the St. Andrews Dam and the Assiniboine River Floodway Control Structure at Portage la Prairie to allow free passage of sturgeon at all water stages, other barriers to fish movement were removed from at least the lower reaches of the tributaries of these rivers, and no additional barriers constructed. The passability to sturgeon of the Red River Floodway Control Structure at St. Norbert would also have to be determined, and, if necessary, mitigation measures taken to ensure free passage. There would also have to be prohibition of harvest of sturgeon at least until stocks increased to a level at which a limited harvest might be considered. If sturgeon could be restored in the Red and Assiniboine rivers, they would contribute, along with those from the eastern tributaries of Lake Winnipeg, to significant rehabilitation of sturgeon in Lake Winnipeg.

Recently, lake sturgeon have acquired minor importance as a game fish. Unless steps are taken to promote recovery of at least some stocks, as noted above, their potential economic importance will remain small.

The lake sturgeon is the most distinctive of our fish species. Its bizarre, shark-like appearance, archaic structure, large size, and historical importance to both Aboriginal people and more recent immigrants make it highly desirable that this species be conserved and perhaps restored to its former abundance, at least in some of its native range in Manitoba.

COSEWIC Classification as of January 1, 2004: Not at Risk
MBESA Status as of January 1, 2004: Not Listed
MBCDC Status as of January 1, 2004: G3, S2S3

GARS AND THEIR EXTINCT RELATIVES, ORDER SEMIONOTIFORMES

GARS, FAMILY LEPISOSTEIDAE

ORDER SEMIONOTIFORMES

The gars are the only survivors of this ancient lineage of bony fishes whose roots extend back to the late Paleozoic Era. This order was diverse and widespread during the late Paleozoic and early Mesozoic eras. Fish of this order retain the rhombic ganoid scales of the earliest bony fishes and the upper jaw is immovably attached to the skull, rather than being movable, as it is in more advanced fishes. The body does not extend along the full length of the upper lobe of the tail, as it does in the sturgeon, however.

FAMILY LEPISOSTEIDAE

During the late Cretaceous period, between about 90 million and 65 million years ago, gars lived in Europe, West Africa, and India, as well as what is now the western Great Plains and Rocky Mountain region of North America. Today, two genera and seven species of gars survive in eastern North America, Cuba, and Central America. Only one species, the longnose gar, *Lepisosteus osseus*, has been found in the wild in the Hudson Bay Drainage.

Gars can be distinguished from all other fish in the Hudson Bay Drainage by the **elongated, beak-like jaws**, which are armed with many **needle-like teeth**, and the **interlocking, rhombic, ganoid scales**, which have a **dense, shiny, enamel-like surface**.

GARS, FAMILY LEPISOSTEIDAE

LONGNOSE GAR; LÉPISOSTÉ OSSEUX | *Lepisosteus osseus*

NOTE: Not found in Manitoba; Lake Traverse, Minnesota/South Dakota

5 CM — FRESH SPECIMEN

IDENTIFICATION

The longnose gar has **elongated, beak-like jaws** armed with **needle-like teeth**. The body is covered with **interlocking, rhombic, ganoid scales**, which have a **dense, shiny, enamel-like surface**.

DISTRIBUTION IN MANITOBA

The longnose gar has not been found in Manitoba. There is a single record of the longnose gar from Lake Traverse, at the head of the Bois de Sioux River, on the Minnesota/South Dakota border, collected in 1928. Considering the long period since with no additional reports, it is probable that the longnose gar is no longer present in the Hudson Bay Drainage. There is a continuing possibility of reintroduction from the periodic connection established between the Little Minnesota River (Mississippi River Drainage) and Lake Traverse due to flooding on the Little Minnesota River (Stewart and Lindsey, 1970). Also, juvenile longnose, shortnose, and spotted gar appear occasionally in the aquarium trade in Manitoba, raising the additional possibility that any or all of these three species could be introduced into Manitoba by release of aquarium fish (Stewart et al., 2001).

BIOLOGICAL NOTES

SPAWNING: Longnose gar spawn in late spring to early summer over flooded vegetation or aquatic plants. Several males accompany a single female, and the eggs sink into the weeds after fertilization.

GROWTH AND ADULT SIZE: Underyearling longnose gar grow more rapidly than any other North American freshwater fish. Longnose gar in Wisconsin grow at about 2.3 mm/day. They also live to great age and grow to large size. In Lake Mendota, Wisconsin, female longnose gar live to 32 years and grow up to 1230 mm long. Males live to 27 years and grow to 990 mm (Becker, 1983).

FEEDING: The longnose gar is a fish predator at all except the smallest sizes. It is an ambush predator, which usually lives in the cover of weedbeds. Prey fish that pass too close are caught with a quick dart forward or a sideways sweep of the head, with the jaws agape. The jaws snap shut when the prey contacts them.

HABITAT: Longnose gar prefer quiet marginal waters of lakes and large rivers. Although they tolerate turbidity, they are most often found in clear water, in weedbeds. Like all other gar species, the longnose gar can breathe air, which enables it to survive in oxygen-depleted water.

ECOLOGICAL ROLE: The longnose gar is a top-level predator. It is vulnerable to predation only in its young stages before its size and armour of ganoid scales make it invulnerable to other predators.

IMPORTANCE TO PEOPLE

The longnose gar is of no importance to people in the Hudson Bay Drainage. **The eggs of all gars are poisonous to all mammals, *including humans***. The flesh of gars, if carefully cleaned and not contaminated by eggs, is considered very good to eat and is usually prepared by smoking in the southeastern United States. Given the difficulty of getting through the armour of ganoid scales to remove eggs and viscera without contaminating the meat, eating gar is not recommended.

Longnose gar have been used successfully to control populations of green sunfish in stocked farm ponds (Becker, 1983).

COSEWIC Status as of January 1, 2004: Not Listed
MBESA Status as of January 1, 2004: Not Listed
MBCDC Status as of January 1, 2004: G5, SR

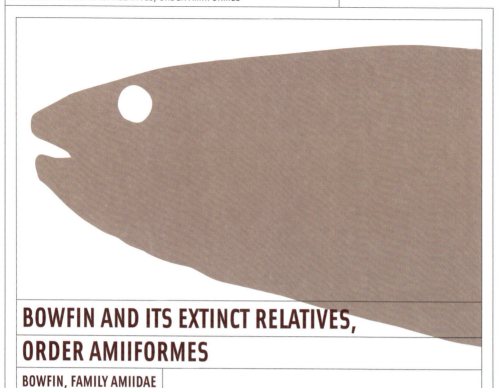

BOWFIN AND ITS EXTINCT RELATIVES, ORDER AMIIFORMES

BOWFIN, FAMILY AMIIDAE

ORDER AMIIFORMES

The bowfin is the only surviving member of this group of fishes, which was diverse and widely distributed in both fresh water and marine habitats during the Mesozoic Era. Amiiforms have overlapping cycloid scales, like most living bony fishes, instead of the rhombic, enamel-covered ganoid scales seen in the sturgeons and gars. Fossil bones of a swordfish-like marine relative of the bowfin, named *Protosphyrena*, which date from the late Cretaceous Period, can be found in the Cretaceous shales of the Manitoba Escarpment.

FAMILY AMIIDAE

The bowfin is the only survivor of its order and family. Its distribution is restricted to eastern North America. The bowfin differs from all other fish in our area in having a **bony plate in the floor of the mouth** and a single, **long, low dorsal fin, with only soft rays**, that begins over or just behind the tips of the pectoral fins and extends almost to the base of the tail. The jaws are armed with **strong, fang-like teeth** and there are **pads of smaller teeth** on the roof of the mouth and along the inner surfaces of the lower jaws.

BOWFIN; POISSON-CASTOR | *Amia calva*

NOTE: Not found in Manitoba; Red River watershed, Minnesota, Lake of the Woods, Ontario

FRESH SPECIMEN
5 CM

IDENTIFICATION

The **bony plate in the floor of the mouth** and the **long, low dorsal fin with only soft rays** distinguish the bowfin from any other fish in our area. Northern pike have strong teeth, but the maxilla is toothless, and walleye and sauger have strong teeth on both upper and lower jaws, but they also have two dorsal fins, the first being spiny. Burbot have two soft dorsal fins, with the second being long, and do not have strong, fang-like teeth in the jaws.

DISTRIBUTION IN MANITOBA

The bowfin does not occur in Manitoba. It is found in tributaries to the Red River in Minnesota and was introduced into Lake of the Woods in 1984. It is included here because it may eventually be found in Manitoba, either as a result of downstream dispersal or with human help. It is seen in aquarium shops in Winnipeg occasionally, and there is a risk of its being illegally released into the wild by ill-informed aquarists.

BIOLOGICAL NOTES

SPAWNING: Bowfin spawn in mid- to late spring, in vegetation. Males clear a nest and mate with one or more females. The male guards the nest and also herds the young into a tight school. Males guard the young vigorously, and have attacked human observers or their nets and other implements placed in the water near the school. Guarding of young ceases by late summer, and the schools disperse.

GROWTH AND ADULT SIZE: Female bowfins grow larger than males, reaching 650 and 700 mm in Ontario and Wisconsin, respectively (Scott and Crossman, 1979; Becker, 1983). Males grow to 500–650 mm.

FEEDING: The bowfin preys on fish and larger aquatic invertebrates. In their weedy habitat, bowfin hunt from ambush or can stalk prey. They are extremely manoeuvrable in heavy cover, swimming both forward and backward with almost no disturbance of the water, by passing undulations along the dorsal fin.

HABITAT: The bowfin seems to prefer shallow, clear, weedy water of lakes or protected marginal waters in rivers. It is tolerant of turbid water, however, and does well in backwaters of large rivers like the Mississippi. Bowfin are also able to breathe air, using their swim bladder to extract oxygen. They can be seen coming to the surface to gulp air even in well-oxygenated water. This enables them to survive in habitats that are cut off by falling water levels and become hypoxic. It also allows them to forage for extended periods in densely vegetated habitats, which are subject to oxygen depletion due to restricted water circulation and decomposition of organic debris.

ECOLOGICAL ROLE: The bowfin is a top-level predator, similar to the northern pike. Although bowfins can be found with northern pike, they tend to occupy shallower, warmer, and more heavily vegetated water than pike. Their air-breathing ability allows them to utilize habitats along shorelines that are not accessible to pike.

IMPORTANCE TO PEOPLE

The bowfin is of secondary importance as an angling species where it is found. It will strike a lure as readily as a bass or pike, grows as large as bass, and battles furiously when hooked. Unfortunately, its flesh is soft, bland-tasting, and of poor texture. Like the goldeye and mooneye, which share this trait, it is reported to be good when smoked.

COSEWIC Status as of January 1, 2004: Not Listed
MBESA Status as of January 1, 2004: Not Listed
MBCDC Status as of January 1, 2004: G5, SP

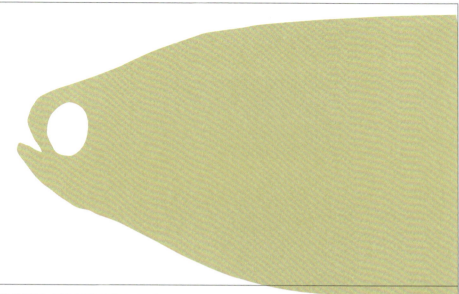

BONY-TONGUED FISHES, ORDER OSTEOGLOSSIFORMES
GOLDEYE AND MOONEYE, FAMILY HIODONTIDAE

ORDER OSTEOGLOSSIFORMES

Most fish in this order have teeth on the tongue that bite against teeth on the roof of the mouth. The closest relatives of the mooneye and goldeye are tropical fish such as the giant (4.5 m long, 200 kg) arapaima (*Arapiama*) of the Amazon River; the arawannas of South America (*Osteoglossum*), Southeast Asia (*Scleropages*), and western Africa (*Heterotis*); the featherbacks (*Notopterus*) of Southeast Asia; and the elephant-nosed fishes and their relatives (families Mormyridae and Gymnarchidae) of Africa. This order is related to an extinct, giant marine fish, the 5 m long *Xiphactinus audax* that lived in the inland sea that covered Manitoba during the Cretaceous period. *Xiphactinus* bones can be found today in the Cretaceous shales of the Manitoba Escarpment, along with those of plesiosaurs, mosasaurs, and giant marine turtles. Fossil bones of this fish are displayed in the Manitoba Museum in Winnipeg, the Morden and District Museum in Morden, and the foyer of the Wallace Building (Geological Sciences Department) on the University of Manitoba campus.

FAMILY HIODONTIDAE

The mooneye and goldeye are silvery, midwater- to surface-feeding, open-water fish. They prey mostly on aquatic insect larvae and emerging adult insects near the water surface and on small fish. They have **large eyes**, the **mouth is moderately large and oblique**, and the tongue and roof of the mouth are armed with **strong, fang-like teeth**. Their **bodies are streamlined and compressed**, and the **tail deeply forked**. The **scales are large**. These two species are the only living members of the family.

GOLDEYE AND MOONEYE, FAMILY HIODONTIDAE

KEY TO THE GOLDEYE AND MOONEYE

1A Origin of the dorsal fin anterior to the origin of the anal fin. The belly behind the pelvic fins is rounded across the midline and covered by scales.

mooneye, *Hiodon tergisus* page 54

1B Origin of the dorsal fin posterior to the origin of the anal fin. The belly behind the pelvic fins is keeled, and scales are not continuous across the midline.

goldeye, *Hiodon alosoides* page 53

GOLDEYE; LAQUAICHE AUX YEUX D'OR | *Hiodon alosoides*

FRESH SPECIMEN
5 CM

IDENTIFICATION

The goldeye may be distinguished from the mooneye by having the **origin of the dorsal fin behind a line drawn vertically up from the origin of the anal fin**. The goldeye also has a **fleshy keel, which is not covered by scales**, on the midline of the abdomen behind the pelvic fins. There is no such keel, and the midline of the belly is covered by scales, in the mooneye. The body of the goldeye is **not as deep** as the mooneye, the **dorsal profile is straight** rather than arched, and the **eye is smaller** than in the mooneye. In life, the **back is olive or brown**, rather than blue, and the **iris of the eye is yellow**, rather than silvery.

DISTRIBUTION IN MANITOBA

The goldeye is found in all medium and larger rivers and lakes from southern Manitoba northward into the Churchill River. In the southeast, it has not been taken in the Winnipeg River upstream of the MacArthur Falls Dam.

BIOLOGICAL NOTES

SPAWNING: The goldeye spawns in midwater in larger turbid rivers. The eggs are buoyant, so substrate is not an important factor in spawning habitat. Goldeye have never been observed during spawning because of the turbidity of the water they inhabit. In the Red River, spawning must occur during spring runoff, because all the females we have examined (from mid-May and later) have spent or recovering ovaries.

GROWTH AND ADULT SIZE: In southern Manitoba, goldeye can grow to about 400 mm long and weigh up to about 700 g. The Manitoba angling record is a 48 cm goldeye from the Saskatchewan River, caught in 1996.

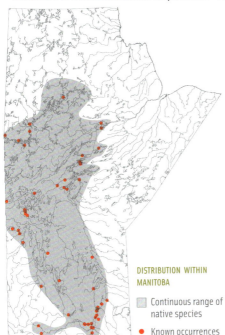

DISTRIBUTION WITHIN MANITOBA

▨ Continuous range of native species

● Known occurrences

GOLDEYE AND MOONEYE, FAMILY HIODONTIDAE

FEEDING: Goldeye are midwater- to surface-feeding fish, which feed mainly on aquatic insect larvae, and emerging and flying insects, including terrestrial insects that fall into the water. They will also take small fish, the emerald shiner (*Notropis atherinoides*) being the most common prey species in stomachs of goldeye taken in the lower Red River.

HABITAT: In Manitoba, the goldeye prefers turbid water in larger rivers and lakes. Because of its midwater- to surface-feeding and reproductive habits, water depth and substrate type are apparently not important habitat factors. In the water velocity range found in the Red and lower Assiniboine rivers, there is no apparent preference for faster or slower current. In areas where mooneye and goldeye are found together, goldeye are the more common species in flowing, turbid water.

ECOLOGICAL ROLE: The goldeye is a second- to third-level consumer in the food web of their community, feeding mostly on aquatic insects but also taking smaller fish. It is one of the larger species that is important as a forage fish for large predatory fish. It is an important food of the channel catfish in the Red and Assiniboine rivers. It may contribute significantly in the growth of channel catfish to the large size they attain in southern Manitoba. Goldeye are also found in the stomach contents of walleye and northern pike.

IMPORTANCE TO PEOPLE

The goldeye is an important commercial fish when smoked and sold as "Winnipeg Goldeye." Most of the goldeye in this trade are imported as frozen fish for processing in Manitoba, although some are harvested from Lake Winnipeg. In southern Manitoba, goldeye contribute significantly to the sport fishery catch. Most anglers fish for them with a float and a natural bait such as a worm or small minnow. They also provide excellent fly fishing opportunities when they are feeding on insects. Most often, anglers smoke their catch for their own consumption, but a significant portion of the angler catch in the lower Red River is used as bait for channel catfish. Their greatest economic value, however, probably lies in their role as prey of the two most important recreational fish species in southern Manitoba, the channel catfish and walleye.

COSEWIC Status as of January 1, 2004: Not Listed
MBESA Status as of January 1, 2004: Not Listed
MBCDC Status as of January 1, 2004: G5, S5

MOONEYE; LAQUAICHE ARGENTÉE | *Hiodon tergisus*

5 CM — FRESH SPECIMEN

IDENTIFICATION

The mooneye may be distinguished from the goldeye by the **origin of its dorsal fin being forward** of a line drawn vertically up from **the origin of the anal fin**. The mooneye also **lacks the fleshy keel on the midline of the abdomen posterior to the pelvic fins**. The **body is deeper** than in the goldeye, the **dorsal profile is arched**, rather than straight, and the **eye is larger** than in the goldeye. In life, the **back is blue**, rather than olive or brown, and the **iris of the eye is silvery**, rather than yellow.

GOLDEYE AND MOONEYE, FAMILY HIODONTIDAE

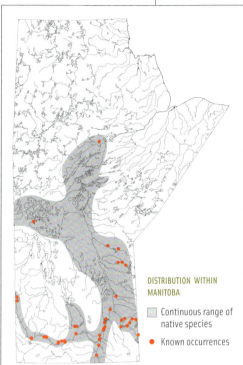

DISTRIBUTION WITHIN MANITOBA
☐ Continuous range of native species
● Known occurrences

DISTRIBUTION IN MANITOBA

Mooneye are found in medium to large lakes and rivers in southern Manitoba, northeastward into the Nelson River, and northwestward into the Saskatchewan River into eastern Saskatchewan. In the Winnipeg River watershed, they are found upstream into Lake of the Woods and above in the Rainy River.

BIOLOGICAL NOTES

SPAWNING: Like the goldeye, the mooneye spawns in midwater and the eggs are buoyant. In the Red River, they probably spawn somewhat later than goldeye, because females with mature eggs have been taken in mid- to late May below the St. Andrews Dam at Lockport. Spawning has never been observed in the mooneye, notwithstanding that they can be found in relatively clear water in some places.

GROWTH AND ADULT SIZE: Mooneye grow to about 400 mm long in Manitoba, but they have deeper bodies and attain somewhat greater weights than the goldeye. Two specimens in the University of Manitoba collection from the Winnipeg River below Lamprey Falls weighed 750 gm when caught. The Manitoba angling record for the mooneye is a 44 cm fish caught in 1996 from Amphibian Lake.

FEEDING: The mooneye feeds on the same food items as the goldeye, and also is a midwater to surface feeder.

HABITAT: In general, the mooneye is more common than the goldeye in less turbid and slower moving water. The local distribution of the two is complex, however, and requires detailed study in Manitoba. For example, contrary to expectation from the preceding, mooneye are more common than goldeye in the upper Assiniboine River in the vicinity of Brandon. Mooneye also are common in the Red River above Winnipeg, although they do not outnumber goldeye.

ECOLOGICAL ROLE: Like the goldeye, the mooneye is a middle-level consumer in its community. Because mooneye are not as abundant as goldeye in the Red River, they are probably less important as a forage fish for the channel catfish. In the Winnipeg River above the Seven Sisters Dam, however, their importance as a large prey species for walleye and northern pike probably is significant. This may change, however, since rainbow smelt have been established in the Winnipeg River below Lake of the Woods since the late 1990s. Up to now, nothing is known of the relative abundance of smelt and mooneye, nor is there any information on comparative accessibility or preference for mooneye and smelt by pike and walleye.

IMPORTANCE TO PEOPLE

The mooneye is almost never distinguished from the goldeye by Manitoba fishers. It even appears infrequently in the commercial trade smoked as "Winnipeg Goldeye." Because it is less abundant than the goldeye, it is less important to anglers and as a forage species.

COSEWIC Status as of January 1, 2004: Not Listed
MBESA Status as of January 1, 2004: Not Listed
MBCDC Status as of January 1, 2004: G5, S5

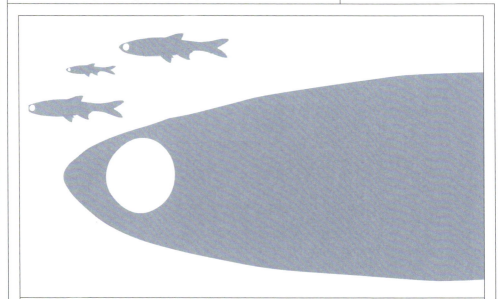

MINNOWS, SUCKERS, AND LOACHES, ORDER CYPRINIFORMES

MINNOWS AND CARP, FAMILY CYPRINIDAE

ORDER CYPRINIFORMES

The Order Cypriniformes is one of four related orders that are characterized by a series of specialized anterior vertebrae and ribs that form a connection between the swim bladder wall and the inner ear. This helps these fish to hear, using the swim bladder wall as an eardrum.

The cypriniform fishes lack teeth in the jaws, but have pharyngeal teeth at the back of the throat. They also lack the adipose fin. The body is covered by normal cycloid scales.

Two families of the Order Cypriniformes, the minnows and carp (Family Cyprinidae), and the suckers (Family Catostomidae), are found in Manitoba.

FAMILY CYPRINIDAE

The Family Cyprinidae is the largest family of vertebrate animals, with an estimated 2010 species worldwide (Nelson, 1994). In biomass and species diversity, minnows are the dominant group of fishes in nearly all of North America's temperate zone watersheds.

The ecological importance of minnows is also great. Minnows are the most common prey of piscivorous fishes in temperate North America. They are the most important single food resource for most of our freshwater game and commercial fish species. The species composition and diversity of minnows in a water body can provide a good indication of the type and quality of habitat. Unlike most other groups of fish in our area, many of our minnow species have relatively narrow habitat requirements, and show partitioning of habitat by water velocity, depth, substrate type, feeding and spawning habits, and habitat. Ten of our native species of minnows have been subject to detailed studies of at least some aspects of their biology in Manitoba. There are also limited data available for three additional native species. In some of these species, significant differences in biology between Manitoba populations and those to the south have been shown. Fourteen of our 26 native species of minnows reach their northern or northwestern limit of distribution in Manitoba, and it is reasonable to expect that there would be significant differences in the biology of species in near-limiting environments. Finally, detection of changes in distribution of these species could provide indications of the ecological effects of climate change.

Minnows display a wider array of feeding and habitat adaptations than suckers, and this is reflected in the large number of genera and species in the family. Manitoba alone has 14 native genera containing 26 native species of minnows

MINNOWS AND CARP, FAMILY CYPRINIDAE

In addition, there are two genera and two species of introduced exotics established in the province. One of these, the common carp, was introduced in Manitoba in 1886, making it the oldest introduced fish species in the province. For all these reasons, our minnows should receive a good deal more attention than they have to date.

Minnows are closely related to the suckers, and, like them, **lack teeth in their jaws**. Instead, as in the suckers, the **fifth or pharyngeal arches**, at the back of the gill chamber, have **one or more rows of strong teeth** that function in food processing. In comparison to suckers, **minnow pharyngeal teeth** are **fewer in number**, more **heavily constructed**, and **widely spaced, often in two or more rows**, and **do not oppose a bony branchial organ in the roof of the pharynx**.

As a group, minnows can be distinguished from all other Manitoba freshwater fishes by a combination of the following characters. The **jaws are toothless**. There are **no fleshy expansions of the lips** and **no adipose fin. The distance from the origin of the anal fin to the middle of the base of the caudal fin is more than half the distance from the origin of the anal fin to the rear margin of the operculum. Carp and goldfish** also have a **spine at the leading edge of the dorsal and anal fins**, and the **carp** has both **maxillary and terminal barbels on the upper jaw**.

All native species of minnows in our area belong to the subfamily Leuciscinae, which is distributed across North America and Eurasia, north of India, and Southeast Asia. Our two introduced species, the carp and goldfish, both belong to the subfamily Cyprininae, which is native to all of Eurasia, including the Indian subcontinent and Africa.

Note: The red shiner, *Cyprinella lutrensis*, has not been found in the wild in the Hudson Bay Drainage, but it does appear occasionally in the tropical aquarium trade in Winnipeg, either misidentified as "Asian rainbow barbs" or in shipments of goldfish. The red shiner is native in the Missouri River in North Dakota and is a favoured bait species in the United States (Stewart et al., 2001). This is an invasive species that has caused the extirpation of populations of native cyprinids in a number of locations where it was introduced in the western United States (Moyle, 1976). The possible introduction of this species into Manitoba should be guarded against and prevented if possible.

KEY TO THE MINNOWS FOUND IN MANITOBA AND ADJACENT AREAS OF THE HUDSON BAY DRAINAGE

1A Dorsal fin long, with more than 11 soft rays and a spine at its leading edge. A spine also present at the leading edge of the anal fin.

go to choice 2

1B Dorsal fin short, with fewer than 11 soft rays and no spine at the leading edge of dorsal and anal fins.

go to choice 3

2A (1A) Upper jaw with 2 barbels on each side. Pharyngeal teeth broad, flat-crowned, and molar-like, in 3 rows.

common carp, *Cyprinus carpio* **page 69**

INTRODUCED

2B No barbels on upper jaw. Pharyngeal teeth slender, with rounded crowns, in 1 row.

goldfish, *Carassius auratus* **page 65**

INTRODUCED

3A (1B) Lower jaw with a cartilaginous cutting edge. Intestine long, and looped in a spiral pattern over the ventral surface of the swim bladder.

go to choice 4

3B Lower jaw without a cartilaginous ridge. Intestine may be long and have extra loops, but not in a spiral pattern over the ventral surface of the swim bladder.

go to choice 5

4A (3A) Usually 39–46 scale rows around the body just in front of the dorsal fin. Usually 49–55 lateral line scales.

central stoneroller, *Campostoma anomalum* **page 63**

OTTER TAIL RIVER (RED RIVER DRAINAGE), USA

4B Usually 31–36 scale rows around the body just in front of the dorsal fin. Usually 43–47 lateral line scales.

largescale stoneroller, *Campostoma oligolepis* **page 64**

FOREST RIVER (RED RIVER DRAINAGE), USA

MINNOWS AND CARP, FAMILY CYPRINIDAE

5A (3B) A slender barbel present at the posterior tip of the upper jaw.
go to choice 6

5B Barbel either absent or forward of posterior tip of upper jaw, and often tiny and difficult to see.
go to choice 12

6A (5A) Groove separating upper lip from snout is interrupted across midline of snout.
genus *Rhinichthys*, go to choice 7

6B Groove separating upper lip from snout is continuous across midline.
go to choice 8

7A (6A) Snout projects beyond tip of lower jaw by a distance equal to or greater than that from tip of lower jaw to angle of mouth.
longnose dace, *Rhinichthys cataractae* page 106

7B Snout projects beyond tip of lower jaw by less than the distance from tip of lower jaw to angle of mouth.
western blacknose dace, *Rhinichthys obtusus* page 108

8A (6B) Well-developed dark lateral band that extends onto the head is present and visible even on faded preserved specimens. *Note:* In lake chub, *Couesius plumbeus*, larger than 60 mm total length, the lateral band becomes weak and is lost in large specimens. They are also keyed out under the alternate choice.
go to choice 9

8B Lateral band absent, or, if present, weakly developed and not extending onto the head.
go to choice 10

9A (8A) Forty-eight or fewer lateral line scales. Lateral band strong, extending onto head and across snout. Posterior end of lateral band ends in a distinct basicaudal spot. Dorsal and caudal fins orange or red in living specimens.
hornyhead chub, *Nocomis biguttatus* page 77

9B Fifty-five or more, usually 59 or more, lateral line scales. Lateral band is less well defined. If it extends onto snout, then the snout portion is offset lower than the portion behind the eye. No black spot at caudal base. Lateral band indistinct to absent on specimens over 60 mm total length. Dorsal and caudal fins dusky, not orange or red in life.
lake chub, *Couesius plumbeus* page 66 (see also choice **11B**)

10A (8B) Posterior margins of pectoral fins straight (in smaller specimens) to distinctly falcate in larger specimens. Head is notably flattened, with a pointed snout, when viewed from the side.
flathead chub, *Platygobio gracilis* page 105

10B Posterior margins of pectoral fins rounded. Head not flattened and snout blunt in lateral view.
go to choice 11

11A (10B) Forty-one or fewer lateral line scales. In specimens over about 70 mm, there is a distinct white stripe along the lower edge of the caudal fin. This stripe is also visible in smaller specimens if magnification is used.
silver chub, *Macrhybopsis storeriana* page 74

11B Fifty-five or more, usually 59 or more, lateral line scales. Lower margin of caudal fin is dusky.
lake chub, *Couesius plumbeus* page 66 (see also choice **9B**)

12A (5B) Fifty-five or more lateral line scales (or scale rows in lateral series, if lateral line not complete).
go to choice 13

12B Fifty-four or fewer lateral line scales (or scale rows in lateral series, if lateral line not complete).
go to choice 16

13A (12A) Lateral line runs full length of body, although it may be interrupted in places. A barbel is usually present, on the upper edge of the maxilla, just ahead of its posterior tip, concealed in, or barely projecting from, the groove between the snout and upper lip, and often tiny and difficult to see.

go to choice 14

13B Lateral line ends over or anterior to pelvic fins. Barbel never present.

genus *Phoxinus*, go to choice 15

14A (13A) Sixty-three or fewer lateral line scales. Mouth extending to below anterior edge of pupil of eye. There is a black basicaudal spot. Barbel easily visible on larger specimens in good condition.

creek chub, *Semotilus atromaculatus* page 109

14B Seventy-one or more lateral line scales. Mouth extending to below or slightly in front of anterior margin of eye. No basicaudal spot, although a prominent dark lateral band is present. Barbel is much harder to see, and may be absent on one or both sides, even on large specimens in good condition.

pearl dace, *Margariscus margarita* page 76

15A (13B) Intestine short, with a single loop running forward along right side of stomach. Mouth reaching to below anterior margin of eye.

finescale dace, *Phoxinus neogaeus* page 99

15B Intestine longer, with two loops crossing from side to side, overlying the stomach. Rear corner of mouth does not reach back as far as anterior margin of eye.

northern redbelly dace, *Phoxinus eos* page 97

16A (12B) First dorsal ray blunt-tipped and separated from second by at least a narrow membrane. (Magnification is required to see this in small specimens.) Predorsal scales distinctly smaller and more crowded than lateral body scales; margin of dorsal fin always rounded.

genus *Pimephales*, go to choice 17

16B First dorsal ray slender, pointed, tapered, and closely bound to second. Predorsal scales as large, or nearly so, as other scales on upper body. Margin of dorsal fin straight or falcate in all Manitoba species EXCEPT *Cyprinella spiloptera*.

go to choice 19

17A (16A) Lateral line not extending full length of body, usually ending in advance of anal fin. Mouth is terminal except in breeding males, in which it is somewhat overhung by the enlarged snout with breeding tubercles.

fathead minnow, *Pimephales promelas* page 102

17B Lateral line extends full length of the body. Mouth subterminal to inferior in both sexes at all stages.

go to choice 18

18A (17B) Mouth distinctly overhung by snout, and snout length is less than eye diameter. Lateral band distinct, extending on head, through eye, and across snout. Lateral band terminating posteriorly in a basicaudal spot. Dorsal fin without a dark blotch in its lower anterior corner. Peritoneum black, and main loop of intestine crossing body cavity anteriorly and extending rearward to left of stomach.

bluntnose minnow, *Pimephales notatus* page 100

18B Mouth nearly terminal, slightly overhung by snout, and snout length equal to or greater than eye diameter. Lateral band less distinct, not extending onto head, and there is no basicaudal spot. Dorsal fin with a dark blotch on its lower anterior corner that may be difficult to see on small or badly faded preserved specimens. Peritoneum silvery, and main loop of intestine not crossing body cavity anteriorly and extending posteriorly to left of stomach.

bullhead minnow, *Pimephales vigilax* page 104

SHEYENNE RIVER (RED RIVER DRAINAGE), USA

MINNOWS AND CARP, FAMILY CYPRINIDAE

19A (16B) Abdomen with a fleshy mid-ventral keel extending from pelvic fins to anus. Lateral line strongly decurved, its lowest point more than 2/3 the distance from top of back to lower edge of belly.

golden shiner, *Notemigonus crysoleucas* page 79

19B No fleshy keel on abdomen. Lateral line may curve downward, but never much lower than halfway between back and belly.

go to choice 20

20A (19B) Intestine very long, with 2 loops coiled into a spiral overlying the stomach.

brassy minnow, *Hybognathus hankinsoni* page 71

20B Intestine short, with only main loop, not coiled into a spiral.

go to choice 21

21A (20B) Anal rays 9 or more. *Note: Luxilus cornutus, Cyprinella spiloptera,* and *Notropis volucellus* may also have 8, or rarely 7, anal rays. They are also keyed out under the alternate choice.

go to choice 22

21B Anal rays 8 or fewer.

go to choice 26

22A (21A) Origin of dorsal fin over or anterior to base of pelvic fins.

go to choice 23

22B Origin of dorsal fin posterior to base of pelvic fins.

go to choice 25

23A (22A) Lateral scales anterior to dorsal fin are more than twice as high as long. Anal rays usually 9, sometimes 8 or 10.

common shiner, *Luxilus cornutus* page 73 (see also choice **34A**)

23B Lateral scales anterior to dorsal fin less than twice as high as long. Anal rays usually 8, rarely 7 or 9.

go to choice 24

24A (23B) Mid-dorsal stripe well developed, continuous around base of dorsal fin. Dorsal fin with dark pigment on membranes between last 3 rays, forming a distinct spot in specimens over about 35 mm total length. Body deep and compressed, with flat sides. Back and belly profiles about equally arched. Posterior margin of anal fin sloping to rear and upward. Pharyngeal teeth usually 1,4-4,0; but may be 1,4-4,1; 0,4-4,1; or, rarely, 0,4-4,0.

spotfin shiner, *Cyprinella spiloptera* page 68 (see also choice **35A**)

24B Mid-dorsal stripe indistinct except for some pigment along base of dorsal fin. No dark pigment on membranes between dorsal fin rays. Body slender, little compressed, and back more arched than belly. Posterior margin of anal fin vertical or sloping forward of vertical. Pharyngeal teeth always 0,4-4,0.

mimic shiner, *Notropis volucellus* page 95 (see also choice **30A**)

25A (22B) Snout long and narrowly pointed, its length nearly equal to eye diameter. Dark lateral band broad and distinct posterior to dorsal fin, and becoming more narrow and indistinct anterior to dorsal fin. Scales on back and upper sides finely outlined with black pigment.

carmine shiner, *Notropis percobromus* page 91

25B Snout shorter and blunter, its length only between 1/2 and 3/4 eye diameter. Lateral band less distinct, and may be completely masked by silver pigment, especially in fresh specimens. Scales on back and upper sides not outlined with black pigment.

emerald shiner, *Notropis atherinoides* page 82

MINNOWS AND CARP, FAMILY CYPRINIDAE

26A (21B) Dark lateral band distinct over entire length of body and on head.

go to choice 27

26B Dark lateral band absent or becoming indistinct anterior to dorsal fin, and never extending onto head.

go to choice 30

27A (26A) Either chin lacks dark pigment, or, if there is any dark pigment on the chin, then the upper lip projects at least slightly beyond the tip of the lower jaw (lower jaw included).

go to choice 28

27B Chin always has black pigment. Upper and lower jaws equal, lower jaw never included.

go to choice 29

28A (27A) Chin lacks black pigment, lower jaw not included. Posterior tip of upper jaw reaching only to below nostril. Pharyngeal teeth always 0,4–4,0. Mid-dorsal stripe indistinct or absent, and lateral stripe continuous across iris of eye.

blacknose shiner, *Notropis heterolepis* **page 88**

28B Some black pigment present on chin, and lateral stripe with a distinct basicaudal spot at its posterior end. Mouth moderately oblique and lower jaw included. Posterior tip of upper jaw reaching to, or nearly to, a point below anterior margin of eye. Pharyngeal teeth in two rows, at least on one side, the count usually 2,4–4,2. Mid-dorsal stripe distinct anterior to dorsal fin, and lateral band not continuous across iris of eye.

weed shiner, *Notropis texanus* **page 94**

29A (27B) Posterior tip of upper jaw reaching only to below nostril. Mouth strongly oblique, inclined at an angle greater than 45° to the horizontal. Peritoneum brown, with an underlay of silvery pigment. Pharyngeal teeth 0,4–4,0.

pugnose shiner, *Notropis anogenus* **page 81**
OTTERTAIL AND SHEYENNE RIVERS (RED RIVER WATERSHED), USA

29B Posterior tip of upper jaw reaching to below anterior margin of eye or nearly so. Mouth moderately oblique. Lateral band without a spot at its posterior end. Peritoneum silvery, with scattered melanophores. Pharyngeal teeth 1,4–4,1.

blackchin shiner, *Notropis heterodon* **page 86**

30A (26B) Mid-dorsal stripe indistinct or absent, except for a short streak of dark pigment on either side of base of dorsal fin in some specimens. Dark pigment present around posterior margin of anus, base of anal fin, and in a narrow, mid-ventral dark band on caudal peduncle. (*Note:* Anal pigmentation may be concealed by swollen vent in mature, spawning fish.) Anal rays always 8 or more.

mimic shiner, *Notropis volucellus* **page 95** (see also choice **24B**)

30B Mid-dorsal stripe well defined, but may not be continuous around base of dorsal fin. No dark pigment around posterior margin of anus (but *Notropis stramineus* may have some dark pigment along base of anal fin and ventral surface of caudal peduncle). Anal rays 6–10.

go to choice 31

31A (30B) Lateral line marked by dark pigment around edges of lateral line pores "mouse tracks."

go to choice 32

31B Little or no dark pigment around edges of lateral line pores, especially posterior to dorsal fin.

go to choice 33

MINNOWS AND CARP, FAMILY CYPRINIDAE

32A (31A) Pharyngeal teeth 1,4–4,1. Posterior tip of upper jaw extends to at least anterior margin of eye. Body profile arched dorsally, nearly flat ventrally. Mid-dorsal stripe relatively broad, tapering toward base of tail, and continuous around base of dorsal fin. Anal rays 8, rarely 7.

bigmouth shiner, *Notropis dorsalis* **page 85**

32B Pharyngeal teeth 0,4–4,0. Posterior tip of upper jaw not reaching to below anterior margin of eye. Both back and belly profiles are arched, the belly less than the back. Mid-dorsal stripe relatively narrow, with a wedge-shaped expansion in front of the leading edge of the dorsal fin, not continuous around the base of the dorsal fin. Anal rays 7, rarely 6.

sand shiner, *Notropis stramineus* **page 92**

33A (31B) Basicaudal spot present.

spottail shiner, *Notropis hudsonius* **page 89**

33B No basicaudal spot.

go to choice 34

34A (33B) Scales on sides anterior to dorsal fin more than twice as high as long. Scales on nape distinctly crowded and smaller than scales on sides. Anal rays 9 or 10, rarely 8.

common shiner, *Luxilus cornutus* **page 73** (see also choice **23A**)

34B Scales on sides less than twice as high as long. Scales on nape about the same size as lateral scales. Anal rays 7–9.

go to choice 35

35A (34B) Dorsal fin with dark pigment on membranes between last 3 rays, forming a distinct spot in specimens over about 35 mm total length. Anal rays 8, sometimes 7 or 9. Pharyngeal teeth usually 1,4–4,0 but may be 1,4–4,1; 0,4–4,1; or, rarely, 0,4–4,0.

spotfin shiner, *Cyprinella spiloptera* **page 68** (see also choice **24A**)

35B Dorsal fin without a dark spot. Dark pigment, if present, not limited to membranes between last 3 rays. Anal rays 7, rarely 8. Pharyngeal teeth usually 2,4–4,2; but may be 2,4–4,1; or 1,4–4,2.

river shiner, *Notropis blennius* **page 83**

CENTRAL STONEROLLER; ROULE-CAILLOU | *Campostoma anomalum*

NOTE: Not found in Manitoba; Red River watershed, Minnesota, and North Dakota

FRESH SPECIMEN
2 CM

IDENTIFICATION

Both stoneroller species differ from all other minnows in Manitoba by having a **sharp, cartilaginous edge on the lower jaw**. The central stoneroller differs from the largescale stoneroller in having **49–55 lateral line scales and 39–46 scale rows around the body**, as opposed to 43–47 lateral line scales and 31–36 scale rows around the body in the largescale stoneroller.

DISTRIBUTION IN MANITOBA

The central stoneroller is not found in Manitoba. It is found in tributaries of the Red River in Minnesota and North Dakota.

BIOLOGICAL NOTES

The following information is summarized from Becker (1983), and applies to Wisconsin.

SPAWNING: Males of both the central and largescale stonerollers show extensive development of breeding tubercles during spawning. The central stoneroller spawns in late May and June in Wisconsin. Fish ascend to the uppermost reaches of streams and spawn in gravel, in which the males excavate a nest. Nesting sites may vary from riffles to quiet water. The eggs are adhesive.

GROWTH AND ADULT SIZE: In Wisconsin, the central stoneroller lives up to three years and grows up to 161 mm long, with males being larger than females (Becker, 1983).

FEEDING: The central stoneroller feeds on algae attached to the substrate, using the cartilaginous edge on its lower jaw to scrape it off the stones.

HABITAT: The central stoneroller prefers fast-flowing headwater streams, but may occur rarely in medium to large rivers. It lives on or near the bottom, over a variety of substrates, with a preference for gravel in riffle-pool sections of streams. It occurs over a wide range of turbidities (Becker, 1983).

ECOLOGICAL ROLE: The central stoneroller is a benthic primary consumer, which is a feeding position not commonly occupied by North American native fishes. Ecologically it is more similar to suckers than to most other cyprinids. Where it is abundant, it is probably an important link in the food web of small-stream communities.

Native North American fishes in this trophic position are probably at greater risk of significant direct impact from the invasion of Eurasian carp species than any other segment of our fish fauna. In stocked trout streams in Wisconsin, the central stoneroller competes with introduced rainbow trout for nesting sites, and will excavate rainbow trout nests while building its own nest.

IMPORTANCE TO PEOPLE

The central stoneroller has no direct economic importance. Its role as a low-level consumer in headwater communities probably enhances the ability of these habitats to produce game fish.

COSEWIC Status as of January 1, 2004: Not at Risk
MBESA Status as of January 1, 2004: Not Listed
MBCDC Status as of January 1, 2004: G5, SP

LARGESCALE STONEROLLER; ROULE-CAILLOU À GRANDES ÉCAILLES | *Campostoma oligolepis*

NOTE: Not found in Manitoba; Red River watershed, North Dakota

2 CM   FRESH SPECIMEN

IDENTIFICATION

Both stoneroller species differ from all other minnows in Manitoba by having **a sharp, cartilaginous edge on the lower jaw**. The largescale stoneroller differs from the central stoneroller in having **43–47 lateral line scales and 31–36 scale rows around the body** as opposed to 49–55 lateral line scales and 39–46 scale rows around the body in the central stoneroller.

DISTRIBUTION IN MANITOBA

The largescale stoneroller does not occur in Manitoba. It has been found in the Forest River, North Dakota (Koel, 1997). Aside from this occurrence, there are no records of this species west of the confluence of the Mississippi and St. Croix rivers in Minnesota/Wisconsin. This record may be the result of an introduction.

BIOLOGICAL NOTES

Becker (1983) provides information on the largescale stoneroller in Wisconsin.

SPAWNING: The largescale stoneroller spawns in June, in deep, fast water, as opposed to the shallower and often quiet water of headwaters used by the central stoneroller. The breeding habits and eggs are similar to those of the central stoneroller.

GROWTH AND ADULT SIZE: Largescale stonerollers in Wisconsin live to an age of three years and grow to a length of 126 mm.

FEEDING: The feeding habits of the largescale stoneroller are similar to the central stoneroller. Both scrape algae from hard surfaces.

HABITAT: The largescale stoneroller prefers medium to large streams and is seldom found in headwaters. It prefers fast water, and, like the central stoneroller, is most common on rocky substrates. It occurs over the same range of substrates as the central stoneroller, although less often over sand.

ECOLOGICAL ROLE: The largescale stoneroller occupies a similar trophic position to the central stoneroller, but lives in faster, deeper water in larger streams. Its use of larger streams may increase its vulnerability to competition for food and space from invading Eurasian carps.

IMPORTANCE TO PEOPLE

Like the central stoneroller, the largescale stoneroller is an important link in the food web of its community and, as such, enhances the production of economically important species. Its distribution in the United States is shrinking, possibly due to the more frequent alteration of larger streams by dams, diversions, etc., than happens in small headwater streams.

COSEWIC Status as of January 1, 2004: Not Listed
MBESA Status as of January 1, 2004: Not Listed
MBCDC Status as of January 1, 2004: G5, SP

MINNOWS AND CARP, FAMILY CYPRINIDAE

GOLDFISH; POISSON DORÉ | *Carassius auratus*

PRESERVED SPECIMEN
1 CM

DISTRIBUTION WITHIN MANITOBA

● Known occurrences

IDENTIFICATION

The goldfish is a **robust, deep-bodied** cyprinid with **large scales**, an **elongate dorsal fin**, and **spines at the leading edges of the dorsal and anal fins**, like the common carp. It differs from the common carp in **lacking a maxillary and terminal barbel on each side of the upper jaw** and in having a **single row** of **four, blunt-crowned pharyngeal teeth** on each side.

Most **feral goldfish** in Manitoba are a **brownish bronze colour**, fading from dark on the back to paler on the sides and underside. Occasionally, a **large specimen** may be **partly or completely reddish gold-coloured** like aquarium goldfish. All of them will **fade to a reddish gold-colour in a few weeks if brought into captivity** and raised as aquarium fish. The goldfish can be distinguished from the quillback, *Carpiodes cyprinus*, and the buffaloes, *Ictiobus* spp., by the **spines at the leading edge of the dorsal and anal fins**, and the **reddish gold to bronze colouration**. Also, the row of **four, stout, blunt-crowned pharyngeal teeth** differ from the comb-like, single row of thin pharyngeal teeth of the quillback and buffaloes.

Note: Rarely, carp with red, black, or white colours, or a combination of these, may be found in the wild in the urban Winnipeg area. These are a domesticated ornamental variety of the carp, the koi, which have either escaped or been illegally released into the wild. Unlike all goldfish, koi always have two barbels on the upper jaw.

DISTRIBUTION IN MANITOBA

The goldfish is an introduced Eurasian species, which probably got into the wild in Manitoba by illegal releases of aquarium fish. Feral goldfish are established and breeding in the Fort Richmond storm water retention ponds in south Winnipeg, which connect with the Red River. Two underyearling goldfish were also found in Rock Lake, on the Pembina River, in 1993. We also have anecdotal reports of goldfish from the Red River at the mouth of the Red River Floodway below Lockport; from Cook's Creek, a Red River tributary north of Selkirk; Crescent Lake, an Assiniboine oxbow lake in Portage la Prairie; Brandon; and a borrow pit along Provincial Highway 10, south of The Pas. It should be noted that at least some of the anecdotal reports apparently refer to reddish gold-coloured fish, which suggests they may have been recent releases/escapees rather than fish breeding in the wild.

MINNOWS AND CARP, FAMILY CYPRINIDAE

BIOLOGICAL NOTES

There are no studies of the biology of the goldfish in Manitoba.

SPAWNING: Becker (1983) reports that, in Wisconsin, goldfish spawn when the water temperature reaches 15.6°C and continue spawning throughout the summer. Eggs are deposited on aquatic vegetation in water over 15 cm deep.

GROWTH AND ADULT SIZE: Adult feral goldfish from the Fort Richmond retention ponds range from 136–160 mm total length. A few dead goldfish washed ashore or thrown onto the shore by anglers were probably close to 250 mm total length when alive. By late summer, the smallest goldfish caught in seine hauls from the Fort Richmond retention ponds and from Rock Lake are about 40 mm total length, suggesting that this is the size attained during the first summer. By contrast, Becker (1983) reports a range of 81–84 mm total length for Age 0 goldfish.

FEEDING: Goldfish are omnivorous feeders, taking mostly aquatic larval insects and adult insects. Mollusks and smaller crustaceans are also reported to be eaten (Scott and Crossman, 1979).

HABITAT: Goldfish prefer quiet, weedy water and are less tolerant of turbidity than carp. In Manitoba, they are found in dense weedbeds with brook sticklebacks and fathead minnows. In the Fort Richmond retention ponds, they apparently move offshore into deeper water beginning in late August. The goldfish is tolerant of hypoxic conditions and can survive winterkill conditions that eliminate most native species of minnows.

ECOLOGICAL ROLE: Goldfish, like many of our native minnows, are low-level consumers. They differ from most native minnows in their preference for dense aquatic vegetation, but are not widespread enough to have a significant role as competitors with native minnows or as food for piscivores. They may become a threat to native minnows that live in similar habitats, should their abundance or distribution increase.

IMPORTANCE TO PEOPLE

Feral goldfish are descended from domesticated aquarium goldfish. In Manitoba, the feral stocks have no economic importance. They have the potential to spread more widely because they are caught and illegally transported by anglers for use as live bait fish.

COSEWIC Status as of January 1, 2004: Not Listed
MBESA Status as of January 1, 2004: Not Listed
MBCDC Status as of January 1, 2004: G5, SE

LAKE CHUB; MÉNÉ DE LAC | *Couesius plumbeus*

2 CM   PRESERVED SPECIMEN

IDENTIFICATION

The lake chub has a **terminal maxillary barbel**. It differs from the longnose and blacknose dace in having a **continuous groove separating the upper lip from the snout**. It differs from all other Manitoba cyprinids with a terminal barbel by having **more than 55 lateral line scales**.

MINNOWS AND CARP, FAMILY CYPRINIDAE

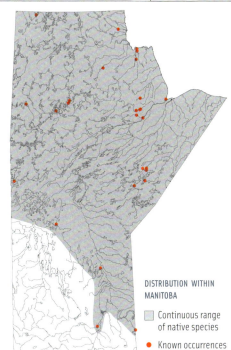

DISTRIBUTION WITHIN MANITOBA
- Continuous range of native species
- Known occurrences

DISTRIBUTION IN MANITOBA

The lake chub is found in the Winnipeg River system, Lake Winnipeg, and all drainages north of the Manitoba Great Lakes. Except for a single record from the Red River at Winnipeg, it is generally absent from the Red and Assiniboine watersheds.

BIOLOGICAL NOTES

There have been no studies of the biology of the lake chub in Manitoba.

SPAWNING: Scott and Crossman (1979) report that the lake chub ascends tributary streams from lakes and has been observed to spawn at temperatures from 14°–19°C. The timing varies from early April in the Great Lakes to May or June in northern Saskatchewan and the Northwest Territories. Sexually mature individuals have been taken as late as August in tundra lakes in Nunavut. Brown, Hammer, and Koshinsky (1970) reported that spawning occurred in 5 cm water depth along the margin of the Montreal River at Lac la Ronge, Saskatchewan. The non-adhesive eggs are deposited among cobble and boulders.

GROWTH AND ADULT SIZE: The lake chub is a large minnow, growing to a maximum adult size of about 220 mm in Québec (Scott and Crossman, 1979). Scott and Crossman report that lake chubs in British Columbia mature at three to four years of age and seldom survive beyond five years old.

FEEDING: Young lake chubs are planktivores and larger lake chubs feed on benthic aquatic insects.

HABITAT: The lake chub prefers cool water in both streams and lakes. It lives over a wide range of depths, from shoals 15 cm deep in streams, to rocky habitats along lakeshores, to depths of 178 m in Lake Superior (Becker, 1983). Its preference for cool water makes the lake chub a good indicator species of water suitable for trout.

ECOLOGICAL ROLE: The lake chub is a benthic, low- to middle-level consumer. It is a significant food source for piscivores, including lake trout and burbot in deep water.

IMPORTANCE TO PEOPLE

The lake chub has no economic significance. Its greatest human importance is as a food resource for game fish in cool lakes and streams, especially in the north.

COSEWIC Status as of January 1, 2004: Not Listed
MBESA Status as of January 1, 2004: Not Listed
MBCDC Status as of January 1, 2004: G5, S5

SPOTFIN SHINER; MÉNÉ BLEU | *Cyprinella spiloptera*

PRESERVED SPECIMEN
1 CM

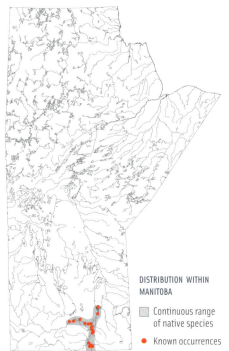

DISTRIBUTION WITHIN MANITOBA

- Continuous range of native species
- Known occurrences

IDENTIFICATION

The spotfin shiner is a **deep-bodied, laterally compressed** shiner that has the **mid-dorsal stripe continuous around the base of the dorsal fin** and has a **dark spot on one to three of the membranes separating the dorsal rays just ahead of the rear margin of the dorsal fin**. It resembles the sand shiner, *Notropis stramineus*, from which it differs by having a **deep, compressed body, the dorsal fin having a convex posterior margin, the mid-dorsal stripe being continuous around the base of the dorsal fin, and in having one inner-row pharyngeal tooth on at least one side**. It is also similar to the common shiner, *Luxilus cornutus*, from which it differs in being **more strongly compressed** and the **anterior scales above the lateral line not being more than twice as high as long**.

DISTRIBUTION IN MANITOBA

The spotfin shiner is a recent, probably natural, addition to Manitoba's fish fauna. It was first found in Manitoba in the Roseau River below Dominion City in 1988. The spotfin shiner is found in Manitoba only in the Red River and lower reaches of its tributaries, and in the Assiniboine River downstream from the Assiniboine River Floodway Control Structure at Portage la Prairie.

BIOLOGICAL NOTES

SPAWNING: Spawning of spotfin shiners has not been observed in Manitoba. Becker (1983) reports that they spawn over most of the late spring and summer, between late May and early September. Single females spawn repeatedly over the summer, at about five-day intervals. Male spotfin shiners select crevices among boulders, the bark of fallen trees, etc., as spawning territories, which they defend. The eggs are adhesive.

GROWTH AND ADULT SIZE: Becker (1983) reports that spotfin shiners live to three years old and grow to 74 mm long. In Manitoba, adult spotfin shiners range from 40–58 mm total length.

FEEDING: Nothing is known of feeding of the spotfin shiner in Manitoba. In Wisconsin, the species feeds mostly on or near the surface, on insects and emerging insect larvae, plankton, and even small fish and drifting fish eggs.

HABITAT: In Manitoba, the spotfin shiner prefers low-velocity, turbid water in large rivers and the lower reaches of tributaries. It is found over substrates ranging from sand to mud and silt, and in water depths less than 50 cm.

ECOLOGICAL ROLE: The spotfin shiner is a benthopelagic, second-level consumer. Because it lives in large rivers and streams, it probably has a significant role in the transfer of nutrients to economically important fishes. It contributes to the diversity and, hence, the stability of riverine aquatic communities.

IMPORTANCE TO PEOPLE

The spotfin shiner has no direct economic importance. Its ecological role defines its main interest for people. It is closely related to the red shiner, *Cyprinella lutrensis*, which appears infrequently in Manitoba in the aquarium fish trade. The red shiner is an aggressive species, which has displaced spotfin shiners and other species in waters in the United States where it has been introduced, and should not be imported into Canada.

COSEWIC Status as of January 1, 2004: Not Listed
MBESA Status as of January 1, 2004: Not Listed
MBCDC Status as of January 1, 2004: G5, S4

COMMON CARP; CARPE | *Cyprinus carpio*
NOTE: Introduced species

10 CM FRESH SPECIMEN

IDENTIFICATION

The common carp is a **large, robust, deep-bodied** cyprinid with **large scales**, an **elongate dorsal fin**, and **spines at the leading edges of the dorsal and anal fins**. It is our only cyprinid with **two barbels on each side of the upper jaw**. The common carp can be distinguished from the deep-bodied suckers—the quillback, *Carpiodes cyprinus*, and buffaloes, *Ictiobus* spp.—by the **spines at the leading edges of the dorsal and anal fins**, the **barbels**, and the **brassy yellow body colour**. Also, the **three rows of strong, molar-like pharyngeal teeth** differ from the comb-like, single row of thin pharyngeal teeth of all suckers.

Note: Two variant forms of the common carp have been found in the wild in Manitoba. Both are the result of selective breeding of domesticated carp for ornamental purposes. (1) The **"mirror carp"** differs from the common or wild carp in having **fewer, larger, and often misshapen scales on the body**. There are **often areas where there are no scales**. (2) The **koi has colours similar to domesticated goldfish. Red, black, and white** are the most commonly seen colour variants, and **some individuals may be parti-coloured** and show **any two or all three of these colours** in an **irregular, patchy pattern**. These highly coloured fish probably originate as escapees or illegal releases of aquarium fish. They are rare, isolated occurrences that have shown up only in the urban Winnipeg area so far.

DISTRIBUTION IN MANITOBA

The common carp was first introduced in Manitoba in 1886, in the Assiniboine River watershed southeast of Brandon. It was also introduced in a dugout east of Winnipeg. Neither of these introductions appears to have succeeded. Common carp were first caught in the wild in Manitoba in the tailrace of the St. Andrews Dam at Lockport in 1938. By 1954, they were abundant enough in the south basin of Lake Winnipeg to have become a nuisance to commercial fishers (Hinks, 1957). Today, the common carp occurs in all watersheds in southern Manitoba northward in

MINNOWS AND CARP, FAMILY CYPRINIDAE

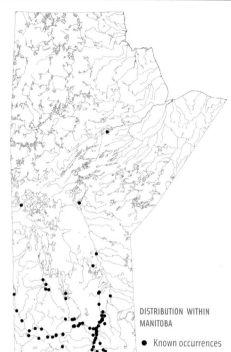

DISTRIBUTION WITHIN MANITOBA
• Known occurrences

the Nelson River, to York Factory (Derksen, pers. comm., 2003). Derksen also reports having identified scales taken from a fish caught in the lower Hayes River as carp scales, and having observed schools of common carp in Lake Winnipegosis. The common carp is absent from the Winnipeg River above the Pine Falls Dam and from higher elevation lakes and streams of the Turtle, Riding, Duck, and Porcupine mountains.

BIOLOGICAL NOTES

SPAWNING: In the Red River and the marshes on the southern margins of lakes Winnipeg and Manitoba, common carp spawn in May and early June. There is a well-marked upstream movement of common carp prior to spawning. In the Red River, this leads to large concentrations of mature carp below the St. Andrews Dam at Lockport, and dams on Red River tributaries such as the LaSalle River at La Barriere Park. A concentration of common carp also develops each spring in Lake Manitoba at the lip of the Assiniboine River Floodway. Spawning is done in vegetation along shorelines or in flooded areas. Small groups of carp, consisting of a single female and a few males, move through vegetation, often in water so shallow that their backs are exposed. Spawning is accompanied by splashing and movement of emergent vegetation, and doesn't easily escape notice. The adhesive eggs are scattered and attach to submerged vegetation. Common carp are extremely fecund, and females of 400–500 mm total length will produce 50,000–100,000 eggs. An 851 mm fish produced 2,208,000 eggs (Swee and McCrimmon, 1966).

GROWTH AND ADULT SIZE: Common carp grow rapidly. We have measured underyearlings in ponds in Winnipeg that were 100 mm total length by late August. The Manitoba angling record common carp is a 108 cm fish caught from the Red River in 1997. Scott and Crossman (1979) report that male carp mature at Age III or IV and females at Age IV or V. The largest common carp they reported in Canada was from near Port Dover on Lake Erie and weighed 17 kg. An age of about 20 years appears to be the maximum attained in Canada.

FEEDING: Common carp are usually benthic-feeding omnivores, consuming detritus, vegetation, a wide variety of invertebrates, and even small fish and some carrion. We have also observed them surface-feeding on floating seeds, such as cottonwood or elm tree seeds.

HABITAT: Common carp are found in slow-moving or still waters ranging from streams and ponds to large rivers and lakes. They can be found over all substrates, but prefer shallow water with soft substrates for feeding.

ECOLOGICAL ROLE: The common carp is a low- to middle-level benthopelagic consumer. It probably has the broadest food preferences of all Manitoba cyprinids. Because of its rapid growth, the dorsal and anal spines, and the large scales, it is only available as prey for piscivorous fish for a short time during its first summer.

IMPORTANCE TO PEOPLE

The common carp is a truly domesticated fish species. North American carp originate from pond-cultured carp brought from Great Britain during the 19th century. In North America, the common carp has escaped into the wild and become an invasive exotic that kills aquatic vegetation and increases turbidity by rooting in the substrate as it feeds. Common carp and water-level regulation by humans are the two most destructive agencies acting on the coastal marshes of lakes Winnipeg and Manitoba.

During the 1950s, unsuccessful attempts were made to remove common carp from the Netley-Libau marshes at the south end of Lake Winnipeg (Derksen, pers. comm., 2003). In the 1960s, attempts were made to exclude them from the Delta Marsh at the south end of Lake Manitoba by fencing. These too were unsuccessful (Derksen, pers. comm., 2003).

Common carp are caught often by anglers and commercial fishers. In most areas, they are discarded as unwanted bycatch, although the Delta Marsh supports a large spring commercial fishery for them (Derksen, pers. comm., 2003). Most of the catch is exported by the Freshwater Fish Marketing Commission. This trade does not begin to absorb all the common carp that are caught, however. There is a significant tourism value to the recreational fishery for common carp in the lower Red River, which attracts carp anglers from Europe. Recently, the Freshwater Fish Marketing Corporation has been processing carp roe for caviar. Although carp are valued as food in Eurasia, their flesh does not adapt well to the "fillet and fry" approach to fish cooking used so commonly in North America. The flesh of carp is very oily and there are many intermuscular bones. Salting and smoking carp yield a tasty product, as does pickling. Carp also are good when used in curries or chowders, or when baked.

COSEWIC Status as of January 1, 2004: Not Listed
MBESA Status as of January 1, 2004: Not Listed
MBCDC Status as of January 1, 2004: G5, SE4

BRASSY MINNOW; MÉNÉ LAITON | *Hybognathus hankinsoni*

PRESERVED SPECIMEN
1 CM

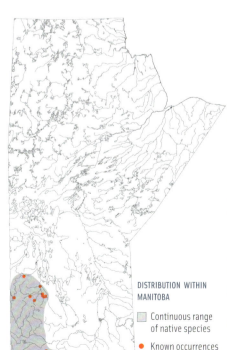

DISTRIBUTION WITHIN MANITOBA

- Continuous range of native species
- Known occurrences

IDENTIFICATION

The brassy minnow is most similar to the shiners of the genus *Notropis*. It differs from all Manitoba species of *Notropis* in having a **long, complexly coiled gut, in which two loops are coiled into a spiral overlying the stomach**. The **peritoneum is black**, which can usually be seen through the abdominal wall in preserved specimens. Also, unlike our *Notropis* species, the **snout overhangs the mouth**. As the common name suggests, **live or fresh specimens have a brassy, yellowish sheen** instead of the silvery colour of *Notropis* species.

Note: There is one record of the Mississippi silvery minnow, *Hybognathus nuchalis*, from the Souris River in Manitoba (Scott and Crossman, 1979). The specimen was re-examined, along with a specimen from the Fisheries Branch (with no collection data), which had also been identified as *H. nuchalis*. Both specimens were found to be the brassy minnow, *H. hankinsoni*.

DISTRIBUTION IN MANITOBA

The brassy minnow has a scattered distribution in Manitoba. It is found mostly in tributaries of the Red and Assiniboine rivers above the Manitoba Escarpment (Harbicht, Franzin, and Stewart, 1988). The pattern of its distribution parallels the southwestern shoreline of Glacial Lake Agassiz.

This species apparently was able to colonize glacial meltwaters and spread along the margin of the receding Laurentide Ice Sheet. It is one of only a few eastern fish species that occurs west of the Continental Divide, in headwaters of the Fraser River in eastern British Columbia.

BIOLOGICAL NOTES

SPAWNING: Spawning of brassy minnows has not been observed in Manitoba. In Wisconsin, spawning occurs in May and June, over vegetation along stream margins or flooded marshes. The eggs are broadcast over the vegetation (Becker, 1983).

GROWTH AND ADULT SIZE: Adult brassy minnows from the Pembina River range from 77–87 mm total length. In Wisconsin, scale ages of up to three years and lengths of 85 mm are reported by Becker (1983).

FEEDING: The brassy minnow is an opportunistic feeder, but feeds mainly on algae and organic detritus. It will also feed rarely on zooplankton and small aquatic insect larvae. Unlike the stonerollers, the brassy minnow lacks a cutting edge on the lower jaw, but the pharyngeal teeth have cutting edges, which presumably help it process filamentous algae.

HABITAT: In Manitoba, brassy minnows are found in small- to medium-sized streams, usually in pools or slower runs. They live over substrates of gravel, sand, or mud, and the water may vary from turbid to clear. They can be very abundant in local areas of streams, but separated from other areas of abundance by long stretches where there are few or no brassy minnows.

ECOLOGICAL ROLE: Brassy minnows are benthic first-level consumers. They are mainly algivores and detritivores. As such, they are important in transferring nutrients to higher trophic levels in their communities. Their abundance, small size, and distribution in tributaries of our large rivers suggest that they contribute significantly to the production of economically important species.

IMPORTANCE TO PEOPLE

The brassy minnow has no direct economic importance. Its main value is in its ecological role and in contributing to the diversity and stability of the communities that produce our economically important species.

COSEWIC Status as of January 1, 2004: Not Listed
MBESA Status as of January 1, 2004: Not Listed
MBCDC Status as of January 1, 2004: G5, S4

COMMON SHINER; MÉNÉ À NAGEOIRES ROUGES | *Luxilus cornutus*

PRESERVED SPECIMEN, IMMATURE
1 CM

PRESERVED SPECIMEN, MATURE
3 CM

IDENTIFICATION

The common shiner has a **robust body** with the **greatest depth at the front of the dorsal fin**. The **anal fin is long, with nine or more rays**, and the **scales on the sides anterior to the dorsal fin are more than twice as high as long**.

DISTRIBUTION IN MANITOBA

The common shiner occurs in most of the tributaries of the Red and Assiniboine rivers, tributaries of the south basin of Lake Winnipeg, and of lakes Dauphin and Winnipegosis. The common shiner also occurs in littoral habitats in these lakes and smaller lakes tributary to them. It is found rarely in the Red and Assiniboine mainstems. It is absent from the Lake Manitoba watershed.

BIOLOGICAL NOTES

SPAWNING: There are no accounts of common shiner spawning reported for Manitoba. In Wisconsin, spawning is protracted, lasting from late May to late July. Breder and Rosen (1966) give a temperature range of 15.6°–18.3°C for spawning. The common shiner often uses nests excavated by other species, in gravel in flowing or still water. The use of nests of other species is reported to be commensal, with the common shiner not interfering with the host species nesting, and helping with guarding the nest

DISTRIBUTION WITHIN MANITOBA
- Continuous range of native species
- Known occurrences

against intruders. Alternatively, the male common shiner excavates a nest in gravel in running water. They apparently spawn in streams exclusively (Becker, 1983).

GROWTH AND ADULT SIZE: Adult common shiners from the Pembina River, in the University of Manitoba collection, range from 135–141 mm total length. Their ages were not determined, but the species is reported to live to four years old in Michigan (Becker, 1983).

FEEDING: The common shiner is an opportunistic, omnivorous feeder, consuming filamentous algae, a variety of aquatic invertebrates, and also adult insects from the surface of the water. Large adults also can take small fish. Becker (1983) reports that plant material comprises about 50% of the stomach contents of common shiners from Wisconsin.

HABITAT: The common shiner prefers pools and slower stretches of medium- and small-sized streams. It occurs over a variety of substrates, ranging from silt and sand to gravel. It appears to prefer open water with beds of aquatic vegetation. Valiant (1975) found the common shiner to be most strongly associated with pools located below riffles (0–15 cm/s water velocity, depth 35–100 cm, and gravel substrate) in five Manitoba Escarpment streams.

ECOLOGICAL ROLE: The common shiner is a benthopelagic, broadly adapted, low-level consumer and is often the most abundant minnow species in its habitat. It is probably one of the more important links in the food web of small- to medium-sized streams in southern Manitoba.

IMPORTANCE TO PEOPLE

The common shiner has no direct economic importance. Its greatest importance to people lies in its role as prey for game and commercial fish species that use its habitat.

COSEWIC Status as of January 1, 2004: Not Listed
MBESA Status as of January 1, 2004: Not Listed
MBCDC Status as of January 1, 2004: G5, S5

SILVER CHUB; MÉNÉ À GRANDES ÉCAILLES | *Macrhybopsis storeriana*

1 CM   PRESERVED SPECIMEN

IDENTIFICATION

The silver chub resembles the shiners (genus *Notropis*) in having **large scales** and **bright silver sides**. It differs from all shiners in having a **terminal maxillary barbel**, a **markedly inferior mouth**, and a **pale streak along the lower edge of the caudal fin**.

DISTRIBUTION IN MANITOBA

In Manitoba, the silver chub is found in the Red and Assiniboine rivers. It has been found in the Assiniboine as far upstream as the Treesbank Ferry southeast of Brandon. It has also been found at Patricia and Hillside beaches, on the east shore of the south basin of Lake Winnipeg, and near Riverton, on the west shore of the south basin of Lake Winnipeg.

MINNOWS AND CARP, FAMILY CYPRINIDAE

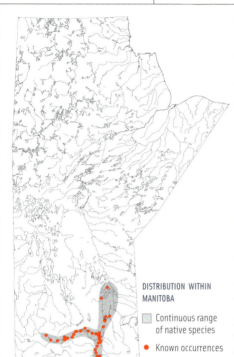

DISTRIBUTION WITHIN MANITOBA

☐ Continuous range of native species
● Known occurrences

BIOLOGICAL NOTES

The biology of the silver chub has not been studied in Manitoba. Becker (1983) gives information on it for the upper Mississippi River in Wisconsin and that is summarized here.

SPAWNING: In Wisconsin, the silver chub spawns in June and July. In Lake Erie, spawning occurred during the same period, at water temperatures over 21°C (Scott and Crossman, 1979). In the Red River south of Winnipeg, we have collected large numbers of early young-of-the-year silver chubs in late July, although we have never seen an adult in spawning condition. We have also not observed dead, spawned-out adults as Scott and Crossman report for Lake Erie. Spawning habitat, behaviour, and whether eggs are demersal, adhesive, or pelagic are unknown.

GROWTH AND ADULT SIZE: In Manitoba, adult silver chub range from 150 mm to a maximum of 210 mm total length. Maximum age (based on scale annuli) is reported to be three years (Becker, 1983).

FEEDING: The silver chub is reported to be a benthic feeder, taking aquatic insect larvae, mainly caddis flies, mayflies, and amphipods (Becker, 1983). In the Red River above Winnipeg, we have observed adult silver chubs rising to the surface in the evening in late July and August, apparently feeding on emerging mayflies.

HABITAT: In Manitoba, the silver chub is abundant only in the mainstems of the Red and lower Assiniboine rivers and the lowermost reaches of their tributaries. It is found more often in slower moving water, over soft substrates, than in riffles. It is one of the three most abundant fish species in the Red River above the St. Andrews Dam. The other two are the river shiner and the emerald shiner.

ECOLOGICAL ROLE: The silver chub is a middle-level consumer that feeds from the bottom to the surface in Manitoba. Because of its abundance in the Red River, the silver chub is probably an important link in the food web. It is found in the stomach contents of walleye, sauger, channel catfish, and northern pike caught in the Red River, but there are no data on its rate of occurrence relative to other prey species.

IMPORTANCE TO PEOPLE

The silver chub has little direct economic importance. It appears uncommonly in the frozen bait minnow trade, and it is occasionally caught by anglers fishing for goldeye. Its main value to people is its contribution to the food web that sustains the game fish species in the Red and Assiniboine rivers. It should be noted that the silver chub is declining in the upper Mississippi River and Lake Erie. The Red River population is one of the few, if not the only, apparently healthy and abundant population of this species that remains.

COSEWIC Status as of January 1, 2004: Special Concern
MBESA Status as of January 1, 2004: Not Listed
MBCDC Status as of January 1, 2004: G5, S3

MINNOWS AND CARP, FAMILY CYPRINIDAE

PEARL DACE; MULET PERLÉ | *Margariscus margarita*

PRESERVED SPECIMEN
1 CM

IDENTIFICATION

The pearl dace differs from the longnose and blacknose daces (*Rhinichthys*) in the following characters. **The upper lip is separated from the snout by a groove continuous across the midline of the snout**, and the **terminal maxillary barbel is absent**, but there is a **small barbel ahead of the tip of the maxillary, in the groove between the upper lip and the snout**. This may be difficult or impossible to find on smaller specimens. It differs from the redbelly and finescale daces (*Phoxinus*) in having the **anterior maxillary barbel**, and the **lateral line is complete to the base of the tail**. It differs from the creek chub (*Semotilus*) in having the **mouth extending back only to below the anterior margin of the eye**, rather than to below the front of the pupil of the eye.

DISTRIBUTION IN MANITOBA

The pearl dace has a disjunct distribution in Manitoba, similar to the distributions of the northern redbelly dace and the finescale dace. In western Manitoba, it is found from the headwaters of the Nelson River southeastwards along the Manitoba Escarpment to the headwaters of the Pembina River. In the east, it is in the Winnipeg River watershed and in tributaries to the south basin of Lake Winnipeg. The widely disjunct records from the Hayes, Hudson Bay coastal, and Churchill watersheds suggest that more thorough sampling would probably reveal that the pearl dace is widely distributed north of the Winnipeg River to the lower Churchill River.

DISTRIBUTION WITHIN MANITOBA

☐ Continuous range of native species
● Known occurrences

BIOLOGICAL NOTES

SPAWNING: In Manitoba, the pearl dace is an early spawner for a minnow. Males with a brilliant red lateral band and running milt can be found by late April or early May, at water temperatures as low as 16°C. Tallman (1980) inferred that spawning occurred before the beginning of May from the continuous increase he observed in the ratio of gonad weight to body weight in both sexes from early May to early November in the Brokenhead River (Lake Winnipeg watershed). Langlois (1929) gives a detailed description of spawning behaviour. Spawning occurs over substrates ranging from gravel to silt, in quiet or flowing water usually 45–60 cm deep. Males defend a territory, but do not construct a nest. The male curls his body around the female, pressing her vent and tail closely to the substrate as the eggs are expelled.

GROWTH AND ADULT SIZE: Large adult pearl dace from the Brokenhead River range from 123–133 mm total length. The maximum age is reported to be three years in Ontario (Scott and Crossman, 1979).

FEEDING: Tallman (1980) found that aquatic insect larvae are the most common food of pearl dace in the Brokenhead River, but terrestrial insects are also taken. We have observed them rising to the surface to take emerging insects or insects that have landed on the water. McPhail and Lindsey (1970) also report filamentous algae and *Chara* from their stomachs. In stocked trout streams in eastern Manitoba, pearl dace are commonly caught by fly fishers angling for trout with dry flies.

HABITAT: The pearl dace prefers cool, clear, slow-flowing waters. It is usually found in stained, tea-coloured water. Valiant (1975) found the pearl dace to be most strongly associated with pools located below riffles (0–15 cm/s water velocity, depth 35–100 cm, and gravel substrate) in five Manitoba Escarpment streams. Tallman (1980) found adult pearl dace most commonly in deep pools in the Brokenhead River, while underyearlings and yearlings occupied shallower water. They were also confined to the upper reaches of the river, which passes through coniferous forest, including some black spruce muskeg. It is one of the eight species of fishes associated with bog habitats in headwater streams and ponds in Manitoba. The others are the northern redbelly dace, the finescale dace, the fathead minnow, the white sucker (typically as dwarfed individuals that can be sexually mature at lengths of 150 mm), the central mudminnow, the brook stickleback, and the Iowa darter.

ECOLOGICAL ROLE: The pearl dace is a middle-level consumer in headwater bog habitats. It can be very abundant, and is probably an important prey species for juvenile stages of larger piscivorous fishes that spawn in headwater habitats. The impact of live bait harvesting from headwater habitats, and of stocking trout in some headwater streams, on the diversity and abundance of the assemblage of fish species associated with headwater bog habitats requires study in Manitoba.

IMPORTANCE TO PEOPLE

The pearl dace is one of four species of minnows that constitute the bulk of the live bait minnow trade in Manitoba. The others are the northern redbelly dace, the finescale dace, and the fathead minnow. In addition, the pearl dace probably contributes significantly to the diet of juvenile game fish like northern pike, which spawn in headwater habitats.

COSEWIC Status as of January 1, 2004: Not Listed
MBESA Status as of January 1, 2004: Not Listed
MBCDC Status as of January 1, 2004: G5, S5

HORNYHEAD CHUB; TÊTE À TACHES ROUGES | *Nocomis biguttatus*

2 CM   PRESERVED SPECIMEN

IDENTIFICATION

The hornyhead chub is distinguished by having **orange-coloured dorsal and caudal fins in life**, a **terminal maxillary barbel**, a **strong, dark lateral band ending in a distinct basicaudal spot**, and **fewer than 48 scales in the lateral line**.

DISTRIBUTION IN MANITOBA

The hornyhead chub occurs in Manitoba only in the Whitemouth River watershed and the Brokenhead River downstream from Provincial Highway 15. The hornyhead chub apparently reached the Brokenhead River via the headwater capture of Hazel Creek, formerly a Whitemouth River tributary, by the Brokenhead River in historic times.

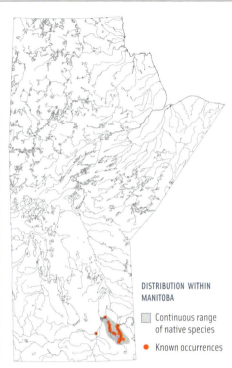

DISTRIBUTION WITHIN MANITOBA

☐ Continuous range of native species
● Known occurrences

There is a single record of the hornyhead chub from the Red River at Winnipeg (Clarke, Boychuck, and Hodgins, 1980), but we have not been able to locate the specimen on which it is based.

BIOLOGICAL NOTES

SPAWNING: Spawning of the hornyhead chub has not been observed in Manitoba. Scott and Crossman (1979) report that spawning begins in May in Ontario. Becker (1983) reports that it lasts into July in Wisconsin. This suggests that the spawning period is probably protracted in Manitoba. Male hornyhead chub clean a nest area in gravel, in flowing water 30–100 cm deep. Cleaned pebbles are carried onto the nest area by the male. Males spawn with a succession of females, expanding the nest as required. The eggs are adhesive (Becker, 1983).

GROWTH AND ADULT SIZE: Adult hornyhead chub from the Brokenhead River range from 105–160 mm total length. They are reported to reach an age of four years in Wisconsin (Becker, 1983).

FEEDING: Juvenile hornyhead chub are reported to feed on benthic aquatic invertebrates. Adults are reported to consume 44% filamentous algae, along with aquatic invertebrates (Becker, 1983).

HABITAT: In the Whitemouth and Brokenhead rivers, adult hornyhead chubs are found on the bottom, over gravel to boulder substrates in water up to about 2 m deep. They are usually found in low to moderate water velocities in runs or pools. Juveniles are found along the shorelines, most commonly in beds of aquatic vegetation, in water depths of 30 cm to 1 m, over silty sand or gravel substrates. By late summer and early fall, young-of-the-year hornyhead chubs can be the most abundant fish species in this habitat.

ECOLOGICAL ROLE: The hornyhead chub is a low- to middle-level consumer. It is unusual in that it shifts its trophic position downward with age. Its abundance in the Whitemouth and Brokenhead rivers suggests that it is important in transfer of nutrients in its community.

IMPORTANCE TO PEOPLE

The hornyhead chub has no direct economic importance. Like most minnows, it contributes to the diversity and, hence, stability of its community. Its distinctive colour pattern makes it an attractive fish in aquaria, and it has been used in native fish aquaria by some Manitobans.

COSEWIC Status as of January 1, 2004: Not at Risk
MBESA Status as of January 1, 2004: Not Listed
MBCDC Status as of January 1, 2004: G5, S2

GOLDEN SHINER; MÉNÉ JAUNE | *Notemigonus crysoleucas*

1 CM — PRESERVED SPECIMEN

DISTRIBUTION WITHIN MANITOBA
- Continuous range of native species
- Known occurrences

IDENTIFICATION

The golden, emerald, and carmine shiners differ from all other minnows in Manitoba by having the **origin of the dorsal fin located behind a line drawn upward from the insertion of the pelvic fins**. The golden shiner can be distinguished from all other minnows in Manitoba by: (1) the **fleshy keel on the midline of the abdomen between the pelvic fins and the anus**; (2) **the strongly decurved lateral line, which curves down to more than two-thirds the distance from the top of the back to the lower edge of the belly**; and (3) the **upward-tilted, superior mouth**.

DISTRIBUTION IN MANITOBA

The golden shiner has a scattered distribution in southern Manitoba northward to the Lake Winnipegosis watershed. In habitats where it is present, it is often one of the most abundant species.

BIOLOGICAL NOTES

SPAWNING: Golden shiner spawning has not been studied in Manitoba. Becker (1983) reports that spawning begins when the water temperature reaches 20°C and continues for the entire summer in Wisconsin and Michigan. In Manitoba, it is usually mid- to late June by the time water temperatures reach 20°C, especially in spring-fed habitats like the Assiniboine River oxbows, where the golden shiner is abundant. The eggs are broadcast over submerged aquatic vegetation. In Minnesota, golden shiners will deposit eggs in the nests of largemouth bass, *Micropterus salmoides*. They are not attacked by the male bass guarding the nest. They apparently take advantage of the nest guarding and fanning by the male largemouth bass to protect and ventilate their eggs (Kramer and Smith, 1960). It is not known whether the golden shiner in Manitoba has a similar association with any other species. Golden shiners have not been found in any of the locations in Manitoba where largemouth bass are found, and there are no similar reports for smallmouth bass, *Micropterus dolomieu*, or rock bass, *Ambloplites rupestris*, which are more widely distributed here and have similar nesting behaviour to the largemouth bass.

GROWTH AND ADULT SIZE: Golden shiners in Manitoba range from 98–107 mm total length as adults. Becker (1983) reports a maximum age of five years, but these fish were almost twice the length of the largest specimens we have seen in Manitoba.

FEEDING: Golden shiners are midwater to surface feeders. They are known to consume a wide variety of planktonic invertebrates, with cladocerans, entomostracans, and insect larvae being most common. They may also consume a significant amount of plant material (Scott and Crossman, 1979).

HABITAT: The golden shiner prefers quiet, usually clear, water with aquatic vegetation cover, in ponds, oxbow lakes, or streams. It is usually found over soft substrates in water less than 2 m deep. It can be one of the most abundant species in suitable habitat. The golden shiner is known to be tolerant of low oxygen and can survive in waters subject to winterkill.

ECOLOGICAL ROLE: The golden shiner is a low- to middle-level consumer. It is an important prey species for large piscivores over much of its range. Its scattered distribution in Manitoba probably reduces its importance as a prey species relative to more abundant and generally distributed species such as emerald and spottail shiners.

IMPORTANCE TO PEOPLE

In Manitoba, the golden shiner has no direct economic importance. Its abundance in areas where it occurs suggests that it contributes significantly to the integrity and stability of those communities. In the United States, the golden shiner is both collected from the wild and cultured for use as a live bait fish. Its tolerance of low oxygen allows it to survive well in a bait bucket, and its large size and bright, reflective sides make it a very effective bait minnow.

COSEWIC Status as of January 1, 2004: Not Listed
MBESA Status as of January 1, 2004: Not Listed
MBCDC Status as of January 1, 2004: G5, S5

NOTE ON THE IDENTIFICATION OF MANITOBA MINNOWS OF THE GENUS *NOTROPIS*

The genus *Notropis* is one of the two most diverse genera of freshwater fishes in North America. There are 10 species of *Notropis* in Manitoba, more species than any other single genus, or, indeed, than most families of fish in our area. Also included here is *N. anogenus*, which has not been found in Manitoba, but occurs in the Red River watershed in Minnesota. Because these species are closely related, they are also similar to one another and often are difficult to identify. For the purpose of identification of the species in Manitoba, it is useful to think of four groupings of *Notropis* species.

1. Minnows with a **sharply defined, black lateral stripe that extends onto the head and around the tip of the snout.** In our area, this group contains the **pugnose shiner**, *Notropis anogenus* (not found in Manitoba), the **blackchin shiner**, *N. heterodon*, the **blacknose shiner**, *N. heterolepis*, and the **weed shiner**, *N. texanus*.

2. Midwater- and surface-living minnows that are **laterally compressed, slender, streamlined shiners** with the **origin of the dorsal fin behind the insertion of the pelvic fins.** In our area, these are the **emerald shiner**, *N. atherinoides*, and the **carmine shiner**, *N. percobromus*.

3. The **spottail shiner**, *N. hudsonius*, which has a **basicaudal spot** but **lacks the distinguishing features seen in groups (1) and (2) above.**

4. Minnows that **lack all the distinguishing features given for groups (1), (2), and (3) above**. These contain the species that are the most difficult of all our shiners to identify. This group consists of the **river shiner**, *N. blennius*, the **bigmouth shiner**, *N. dorsalis*, the **sand shiner**, *N. stramineus*, and the **mimic shiner**, *N. volucellus*.

The above groups are **not** an indication of evolutionary relationship among the species included. They are based only on external features as an aid to identification **in our area only**. They are applicable in our area because we have only a small number of the species of *Notropis*. In an area with more species of *Notropis*, such as the upper Mississippi River, these groupings will quickly become ambiguous and, hence, useless.

PUGNOSE SHINER; MÉNÉ CAMUS | *Notropis anogenus*

NOTE: Not found in Manitoba; Red River watershed, Minnesota

FRESH SPECIMEN
1 CM

IDENTIFICATION

The pugnose, blackchin, blacknose, and weed shiners are the only shiners in our area that have a **strong, lateral dark stripe that extends onto the head and around the snout**. In live or fresh specimens, the lateral stripe may be masked by silvery pigment, as is shown in the illustration. The pugnose shiner differs from the blacknose shiner in **having black pigment on the tip of the lower jaw** and in having the **lateral stripe end in a basicaudal spot**. It differs from the blackchin and weed shiners in **lacking the inner row of pharyngeal teeth**, and the **mouth is strongly oblique, reaching only to below the nostril, rather than to below the front of the eye**.

DISTRIBUTION IN MANITOBA

The pugnose shiner is not found in Manitoba. It is found in the headwaters of tributaries of the Red River in northwestern Minnesota. Its distribution in the Hudson Bay Drainage is similar to that of the blacknose and weed shiners. This suggests that it may eventually be found in the Rainy/Winnipeg River system in northwestern Ontario and possibly in Manitoba.

BIOLOGICAL NOTES

The pugnose shiner has not been studied in Canada. The following information is summarized from Becker (1983).

SPAWNING: In Wisconsin, spawning females have been found from mid-May to July. Spawning habits and habitat are unknown. See further comments in the blacknose shiner species account.

GROWTH AND ADULT SIZE: Becker (1983) reports a maximum length of 60 mm and an age of three years for this species.

FEEDING: In Wisconsin, pugnose shiners feed on about equal proportions of cladocera and filamentous algae.

HABITAT: The pugnose shiner is restricted to clear, cool, weedy, protected waters of lakes and low-gradient streams. Gilbert (1978) notes that it is rare wherever it is found and often missing in apparently suitable habitat within its range.

ECOLOGICAL ROLE: The pugnose shiner, like most minnows, is a low- to middle-level consumer. Its rarity probably limits its significance in nutrient transfer in its communities.

IMPORTANCE TO PEOPLE

The pugnose shiner is too rare to have any direct economic impact. Its tenuous status over its known range has significance for people. All the black-striped shiners in our area have similar habitat requirements and are declining over much of their ranges. The apparently healthy populations of blackchin, blacknose, and weed shiners (*Notropis heterodon*, *N. heterolepis*, and *N. texanus*, respectively) in Manitoba constitute a refuge for these species. The persistence and health of populations of these species are a good indicator of the health of the ecosystems of which they are a part.

COSEWIC Status as of January 1, 2004: Endangered
MBESA Status as of January 1, 2004: Not Listed
MBCDC Status as of January 1, 2004: G3, SP

EMERALD SHINER; MÉNÉ ÉMERAUDE | *Notropis atherinoides*

PRESERVED SPECIMEN
1 CM

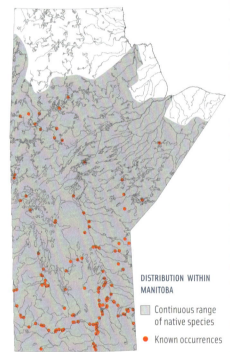

DISTRIBUTION WITHIN MANITOBA

- Continuous range of native species
- Known occurrences

IDENTIFICATION

The emerald, golden, and carmine shiners differ from all other minnows in Manitoba by having the **origin of the dorsal fin located behind a line drawn upward from the insertion of the pelvic fins**. The emerald shiner is distinguished from the golden shiner by **lacking the fleshy keel on the abdomen** and **lacking the strongly decurved lateral line**. It differs from the carmine shiner in having **the snout length equal to only between one-half and three-fourths of the eye diameter** instead of being equal to the eye diameter.

DISTRIBUTION IN MANITOBA

The emerald shiner occurs generally from the Churchill River southwards in Manitoba.

BIOLOGICAL NOTES

SPAWNING: Rowes (1994) found larval emerald shiners in Lake Dauphin from July 7 to August 8, at water temperatures over 21°C. From this, he inferred that spawning extended from the last week in June to early August, a period in which water temperatures varied from 21°C –24°C. Emerald shiners spawn offshore, at night, in midwater, 30–60 cm below the surface. The eggs are not adhesive, but sink to the bottom (Scott and Crossman, 1979). Water depth and substrate are apparently not significant in determining suitability of spawning habitat.

GROWTH AND ADULT SIZE: The largest emerald shiner known from Manitoba is a 103 mm fork length specimen collected from Lake Winnipeg. This makes them one of the two largest species of *Notropis* in our area, the other being the spottail shiner, *N. hudsonius*. Both Becker (1983) and Scott and Crossman (1979) report three years as the maximum age for this species.

FEEDING: Adult emerald shiners are schooling, pelagic predators on larval and adult insects and planktonic crustaceans. Juveniles are also pelagic, feeding on rotifers, ciliated protozoa, and algae (Scott and Crossman, 1979). Hanke (1996) found that, in Lake Winnipeg, planktonic crustaceans formed the dominant component of the diet of emerald shiners less than 43 mm total length. Emerald shiners over that size consumed insects, with dipteran pupae being dominant. He did not find plant material in any of the three size groups of emerald shiners in his samples.

HABITAT: The emerald shiner is a midwater- to surface-living pelagic minnow. It is found in our large, slow-moving streams and in lakes. It is tolerant of turbid water. The emerald shiner is usually collected with the silver chub, river shiner, spottail shiner, juvenile white bass, and juvenile cisco.

MINNOWS AND CARP, FAMILY CYPRINIDAE

ECOLOGICAL ROLE: The emerald shiner is a schooling, pelagic, middle-level consumer. In the Manitoba Great Lakes and larger rivers within its range, the emerald shiner is one of the most abundant fish species. By midsummer, large schools of emerald shiners can be seen near the shoreline of Lake Winnipeg and in the Red River. Until the appearance of rainbow smelt in Lake Winnipeg in 1990 (Campbell et al., 1991) the emerald shiner was probably the most important prey species in the lake.

IMPORTANCE TO PEOPLE

The emerald shiner is one of the two most important species in the frozen bait minnow trade in Manitoba. Most of the harvest of emerald shiners for this trade takes place in the lower Red River and the south basin of Lake Winnipeg. The other common frozen bait species is the spottail shiner, *Notropis hudsonius*.

The emerald shiner is also probably the most important single prey species for commercial and game fish in lakes and larger rivers within its range. In Lake Winnipeg, the establishment of the introduced white bass, *Morone chrysops*, since 1962 has added a voracious and abundant piscivore to the community. Unlike the native larger piscivores in the lake, the white bass is a schooling, midwater- to surface-living predator that spends all its time in the same part of the water column as the emerald shiner. Hanke (1996) did not find any evidence that white bass had caused any change in abundance or distribution of emerald shiners. More recently, the rainbow smelt, *Osmerus mordax*, also has become established in Lake Winnipeg since 1990. Smelt prey on juvenile emerald shiners, and juvenile smelt compete with all life-history stages of the emerald shiner. Given the importance of emerald shiners to the lake ecosystem, there is reason for concern that the combined impact of these two introductions on the emerald shiner could lead to a major reorganization of trophic relationships, and species abundance and distribution within the lake. The outcome of such a reorganization is by no means certain.

COSEWIC Status as of January 1, 2004: Not Listed
MBESA Status as of January 1, 2004: Not Listed
MBCDC Status as of January 1, 2004: G5, S5

RIVER SHINER; MÉNÉ DE RIVIÈRE | *Notropis blennius*

PRESERVED SPECIMEN
1 CM

PRESERVED SPECIMEN, DORSAL VIEW
1 CM

IDENTIFICATION

The river, bigmouth, sand, and mimic shiners are similar to one another in appearance. Collectively, they differ from all other shiners in our area in the combination of: (1) **lacking a lateral dark stripe that continues onto the head**; (2) **lacking a black spot at the base of either the dorsal or caudal fin**; and (3) **having the base of the dorsal fin located over**

MINNOWS AND CARP, FAMILY CYPRINIDAE

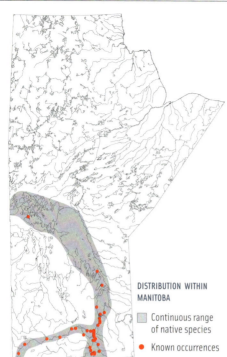

DISTRIBUTION WITHIN MANITOBA

☐ Continuous range of native species
● Known occurrences

the base of the pelvic fins. The river shiner differs from the sand and mimic shiners in having **an inner row of pharyngeal teeth**, and **the mid-dorsal stripe being uniform in width anterior to the dorsal fin and continuous around the base of the dorsal fin**. It differs from the bigmouth shiner in having **two inner-row pharyngeal teeth on at least one side**, instead of only one on both sides, usually **seven anal fin rays** instead of eight, and in **lacking dark markings ("mouse tracks") above and below each lateral line pore**.

DISTRIBUTION IN MANITOBA

The river shiner is found in the Red and lower Assiniboine rivers and in the lower reaches of their tributaries. It is also found in the Saskatchewan River and in the south basin of Lake Winnipeg.

BIOLOGICAL NOTES

SPAWNING: In the Red River above Winnipeg, early young-of-the-year river shiners can be found by early July, sometimes in large numbers. The appearance of juveniles persists into early September. This agrees with reports by Trautman (1957) and others that this species has an extended spawning period. Spawning habitat and habits are undescribed for the river shiner.

GROWTH AND ADULT SIZE: Large adult river shiners from the lower Assiniboine River range from 62–72 mm total length. Early young-of-the-year are 9–11 mm. Becker (1983) gives a maximum age of four years for this species in Wisconsin.

FEEDING: Nothing is known of river shiner feeding in Manitoba. Becker (1983) reports that it feeds mostly on aquatic larval and adult terrestrial and aquatic insects, but also takes planktonic crustacea and some algae.

HABITAT: In Manitoba, the river shiner is found in large, turbid rivers and the lowermost reaches of their tributaries. It is uncommon in littoral habitats in the south basin of Lake Winnipeg. It lives in non-turbulent water at low to moderate water velocities, over substrates ranging from silt to gravel.

ECOLOGICAL ROLE: The river shiner is a middle-level consumer. Because of its abundance, the river shiner is probably an important link in the food web in the Red River above the St. Andrews Dam and the lower Assiniboine River. It should be noted that the frequency of collecting this species in areas in which it was known to occur declined markedly in the late 1980s and early 1990s. This was a warm, dry period during which the spotfin shiner, *Cyprinella spiloptera*, was first collected in Manitoba and spread throughout the Red and lower Assiniboine rivers. During the middle 1990s, the climate became wetter and cooler, and the frequency of collecting river shiners increased and that of spotfin shiners decreased. More recently, both species appear to have decreased in the Red and lower Assiniboine rivers.

IMPORTANCE TO PEOPLE

The primary importance of the river shiner is its role as a prey species for commercial and game fish species in its habitat. Given its abundance in the Red and lower Assiniboine rivers, any large change in its abundance that is not compensated by corresponding increases in other prey species would likely have a significant impact on the production of game fish in those rivers.

COSEWIC Status as of January 1, 2004: Not Listed
MBESA Status as of January 1, 2004: Not Listed
MBCDC Status as of January 1, 2004: G5, S3

BIGMOUTH SHINER; MÉNÉ À GRANDE BOUCHE | *Notropis dorsalis*

1 CM — PRESERVED SPECIMEN

1 CM — PRESERVED SPECIMEN, DORSAL VIEW

IDENTIFICATION

The bigmouth, sand, mimic, and river shiners are similar to one another in appearance. Collectively, they differ from all other shiners in our area in the combination of: (1) **lacking a lateral dark stripe that continues onto the head**; (2) **lacking a black spot at the base of either the dorsal or caudal fin**; and (3) **having the base of the dorsal fin located over the base of the pelvic fins**. The bigmouth shiner differs from the sand and mimic shiners in having **an arched back and flat ventral profile**, having **an inner row of pharyngeal teeth**, and **the mid-dorsal stripe being uniform in width anterior to the dorsal fin and continuous around the base of the dorsal fin**. It differs from the river shiner in having **only one inner-row pharyngeal tooth on both sides** instead of two on at least one side, **usually seven anal fin rays** instead of eight, and in having **dark markings ("mouse tracks") above and below each lateral line pore**.

Note: Bigmouth shiners in Manitoba have scales covering the nape. In this respect, they conform to the subspecies *N. d. dorsalis*, which is found in the upper Mississippi and Great Lakes watersheds. A second nominal subspecies, *N. d. piptolepis*, lacks scales on the nape and is found in the Missouri River and its tributaries northward to near the mouth of the James River (Bailey and Allum, 1962).

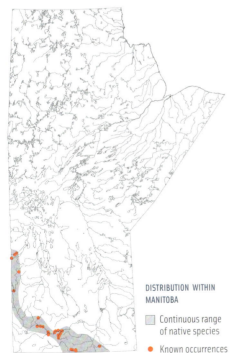

DISTRIBUTION WITHIN MANITOBA

- Continuous range of native species
- Known occurrences

DISTRIBUTION IN MANITOBA

The bigmouth shiner is found mainly in tributaries of the Assiniboine River, where it is often one of the most abundant fish species. It is also found in the Pembina River (abundant) and Roseau River (rarely). These are both Red River tributaries. It has also been found in the Woody and Roaring rivers in the Lake Winnipegosis watershed.

MINNOWS AND CARP, FAMILY CYPRINIDAE

Note: The Woody and Roaring river locations included in the distribution map of *Notropis volucellus* in Scott and Crossman (1979) actually pertain to the bigmouth shiner. Manitoba is the only province where the bigmouth shiner has been found.

BIOLOGICAL NOTES

SPAWNING: Nothing is known about spawning of the bigmouth shiner in Manitoba. Becker (1983) reports that spawning is spread from late May to early August, but gives no information on spawning habitat or behaviour.

GROWTH AND ADULT SIZE: Adult bigmouth shiners from the Pembina River range from 65–74 mm total length. By contrast, Becker reports lengths up to 70 mm in Wisconsin. The oldest age he reports is two years.

FEEDING: Becker (1983) found that bigmouth shiners in Wisconsin fed mostly on aquatic insect larvae, but filamentous algae also appeared in their stomach contents.

HABITAT: Valiant (1975) found the bigmouth shiner to be most strongly associated with pools located below riffles (0–15 cm/s water velocity, depth 35–100 cm, and gravel substrate) in five Manitoba Escarpment streams. In our experience, the bigmouth shiner is more commonly found in riffles and runs. It is usually found in moderately turbid to turbid water, at depths of less than 50 cm. In the Assiniboine River watershed, it is more abundant in the lower reaches of tributaries to the Assiniboine mainstem, but is uncommon to rare in the Assiniboine mainstem. It is benthopelagic and occurs over gravel substrates. It tends to prefer somewhat faster water than the sand shiner, *Notropis stramineus*, being nearer to the upstream ends of riffles and runs than the sand shiner. In addition to the sand shiner, the bigmouth shiner is typically found with the western blacknose dace, *Rhinichthys obtusus*, and less commonly with the longnose dace, *R. cataractae*, which prefers even faster water.

ECOLOGICAL ROLE: The bigmouth shiner is a middle-level consumer. Its abundance in the Pembina River and tributary streams of the Assiniboine River suggests that it is significant in the flow of nutrients in its communities.

IMPORTANCE TO PEOPLE

The bigmouth shiner has no direct economic importance beyond its ecological role in tributary stream habitats. It contributes to the diversity and stability of the communities of which it is a part.

COSEWIC Status as of January 1, 2004: Not at Risk
MBESA Status as of June 2004: Not Listed
MBCDC Status as of January 1, 2004: G5, S3

BLACKCHIN SHINER; MENTON NOIR | *Notropis heterodon*

1 CM   PRESERVED SPECIMEN

IDENTIFICATION

The blackchin, blacknose, weed, and pugnose shiners are the only shiners in our area that have a **strong, lateral dark stripe that extends onto the head and around the tip of the snout**. The blackchin shiner differs from the blacknose shiner in having **black pigment on the tip of the lower jaw**, and in having **an inner row of pharyngeal teeth**. It differs from the weed shiner because the **lateral stripe does not end in a basicaudal spot**, and it has only **one instead of two teeth in the inner pharyngeal tooth row on each side**. It differs from the pugnose shiner in having the **mouth nearly horizontal** and **reaching to, or nearly to, below the front of the eye**.

MINNOWS AND CARP, FAMILY CYPRINIDAE

DISTRIBUTION IN MANITOBA

The blackchin shiner is found in the Winnipeg River, the Lake Dauphin watershed, the Mossy River, which connects lakes Dauphin and Winnipegosis, and in Assiniboine River oxbow lakes in Spruce Woods Provincial Park. Unlike the blacknose shiner, *N. heterolepis*, the distribution of the blackchin shiner in the Hudson Bay Drainage does not suggest that it colonized our area before Lake Agassiz drained out. Instead, the distribution of this species, together with the weed shiner, *N. texanus*, and the mimic shiner, *N. volucellus*, forms a track that supports a post-Glacial Lake Agassiz movement of these species into the Hudson Bay Drainage from upper Mississippi and/or Lake Superior watershed headwaters into Rainy River/Wabigoon River headwaters. Subsequently, downstream dispersal in the Winnipeg River brought these species into Manitoba. Kallemeyn et al. (2003) report collecting blackchin shiners from Rainy Lake, Minnesota, which also supports this dispersal track. The blackchin and weed shiners have also extended west into Lake Dauphin and south into the oxbow lakes of the Assiniboine River in Spruce Woods Provincial Park.

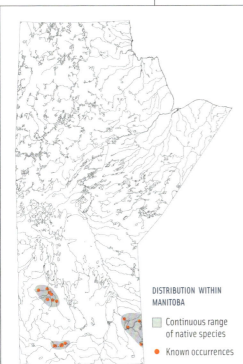

DISTRIBUTION WITHIN MANITOBA
☐ Continuous range of native species
● Known occurrences

BIOLOGICAL NOTES

SPAWNING: Blackchin shiner spawning has not been observed in Manitoba. In Wisconsin, the spawning period extends from June to August. Female blackchin shiners collected in Kichie Manitou Lake, in Spruce Woods Provincial Park, in July and early August, often have apparently mature eggs in their ovaries. There are no reports of spawning habits or habitat. It is noteworthy that there is no detailed knowledge of spawning habits or habitat for any of the four species of black-striped shiners in our area. All of them are closely tied to clear, cool, weedy waters and are declining in the United States. Given the importance of reproductive biology in population maintenance, detailed studies of reproduction of all these species should be given priority.

GROWTH AND ADULT SIZE: Adult blackchin shiners from Kichie Manitou Lake range from 49–53 mm total length. Becker (1983) reports a maximum age of three years.

FEEDING: Becker (1983) reports that the blackchin shiner feeds on crustaceans, oligochaetes, and larval and adult insects that are associated with aquatic vegetation. It apparently does not feed on the bottom and does not take plant material.

HABITAT: The blackchin shiner, like our other black-striped shiners, lives in cool, clear, weedy, protected waters in lakes and marginal waters of rivers in the Canadian Shield in southeastern Manitoba. In Spruce Woods Provincial Park, it is abundant in spring-fed oxbow lakes along the Assiniboine River. In the Assiniboine River oxbow lakes, schools of blackchin shiners can be seen swimming above weedbeds during the summer. They quickly take cover in the weeds when disturbed. Its distribution and abundance are declining in the United States, apparently due to loss of suitable habitat (Becker, 1983). The occurrence of the blackchin, blacknose, and weed shiners in the Assiniboine River oxbow lakes in Spruce Woods Provincial Park suggests that all these black-striped shiners may be tolerant of hypoxic conditions.

ECOLOGICAL ROLE: The blackchin shiner is a middle-level consumer. Its abundance and small size suggest that it may be a significant food source for juvenile northern pike and yellow perch, which share its habitat.

MINNOWS AND CARP, FAMILY CYPRINIDAE

IMPORTANCE TO PEOPLE

The blackchin shiner has no direct economic importance. It is an attractive-looking fish and is sometimes kept in native fish aquaria. It is often easily observed in the wild, and provides enjoyment to people who visit the oxbow lakes in Spruce Woods Provincial Park. Its greatest importance, however, is probably its ecological role in the communities of which it is a part.

COSEWIC Status as of January 1, 2004: Not at Risk
MBESA Status as of January 1, 2004: Not Listed
MBCDC Status as of January 1, 2004: G5, S3

BLACKNOSE SHINER; MUSEAU NOIR | *Notropis heterolepis*

1 CM   PRESERVED SPECIMEN

IDENTIFICATION

The blacknose, weed, pugnose, and blackchin shiners are the only shiners in our area that have a **strong, lateral dark stripe that extends onto the head and around the tip of the snout**. Of these, the blacknose shiner is **more slender** than any of the others and has a **larger eye relative to the length of the head**. The blacknose shiner differs from the blackchin, pugnose, and weed shiners in **lacking black pigment on the tip of the lower jaw**. Also, there is **no basicaudal spot**, and the **mouth is not strongly oblique** as it is in the pugnose shiner. It differs from the blackchin and weed shiners in **lacking the inner row of pharyngeal teeth**, and the **lateral stripe is composed of a series of forward-pointing dark crescents**.

DISTRIBUTION IN MANITOBA

DISTRIBUTION WITHIN MANITOBA
— Continuous range of native species
● Known occurrences

The blacknose shiner is found in the Winnipeg River watershed, lakes Winnipeg, Manitoba, Dauphin, and Winnipegosis, and their tributaries, and northeastward into the Nelson and Hayes river watersheds. It is absent from the Red River. It occurs in the Churchill River in eastern Saskatchewan. The blacknose shiner is more widely distributed than the blackchin shiner, *Notropis heterodon*, and the weed shiner, *N. texanus*. Fossils of the blacknose shiner have been found in the bed of an ice-walled glacial lake in southeastern North Dakota (Cvancara et al., 1971). It is one of only a few fishes for which there is direct evidence of its presence in our area while deglaciation was in progress. Its wide distribution in Manitoba and ocurrence in the Churchill River in Saskatchewan are consistent with its arrival in our area early enough to take advantage of marginal waters around Glacial Lake Agassiz to disperse.

MINNOWS AND CARP, FAMILY CYPRINIDAE

BIOLOGICAL NOTES

SPAWNING: There are no observations of spawning of the blacknose shiner in Manitoba. Scott and Crossman (1979) and Becker (1983) both refer to it spawning over sandy substrate, but no other information on spawning habitat is given. Both also refer to gravid females being found in various localities between June and mid-August. This suggests that the blacknose shiner has a protracted spawning period, like several other species of *Notropis*. See the blackchin shiner species account for additional comments.

GROWTH AND ADULT SIZE: Adult blacknose shiners in the University of Manitoba collection range from 46–56 mm total length. Becker (1983) found no fish older than one year.

FEEDING: The blacknose shiner is reported to feed on planktonic crustaceans, larval and adult insects, small mollusks, and other benthic invertebrates. Some algae also occur in their stomach contents (Becker, 1983).

HABITAT: Unlike most species of *Notropis* in our area, the blacknose shiner is tolerant of hypoxia. It can survive in waters subject to winterkill conditions (Becker, 1983). Like our other black-striped shiners, the blacknose shiner lives in cool, clear, weedy, protected waters in lakes, marginal waters of rivers, and smaller streams in the Canadian Shield. It is also found in the spring-fed oxbow lakes along the Assiniboine River in Spruce Woods Provincial Park. It is declining over the southern part of its range in the United States due to habitat loss (Becker).

ECOLOGICAL ROLE: The small amount of information available suggests that the blackchin shiner is a middle-level consumer. It can be abundant and probably contributes significantly to the food supply of juvenile game fish sharing its habitat. Its ability to survive winterkill conditions probably helps to ensure a supply of prey in habitats used transiently or by early life-history stages of piscivores.

IMPORTANCE TO PEOPLE

The blacknose shiner has no direct economic importance in Manitoba. Because of its tolerance for low dissolved oxygen levels, it is used as a live bait fish in southern Ontario (Scott and Crossman, 1979). It is an attractive-looking fish and is sometimes kept in native fish aquaria. Its greatest importance, however, is probably its ecological role in the communities of which it is a part.

COSEWIC Status as of January 1, 2004: Not Listed
MBESA Status as of January 1, 2004: Not Listed
MBCDC Status as of January 1, 2004: G5, S5

SPOTTAIL SHINER; QUEUE À TACHE NOIRE | *Notropis hudsonius*

1 CM   PRESERVED SPECIMEN

IDENTIFICATION

The spottail shiner differs from all other minnows in our area by the combination of: (1) **having a black basicaudal spot;** (2) **lacking a dark lateral stripe that extends around the head**; and (3) **lacking dark pigment markings ("mouse tracks") above and below the lateral line pores.**

DISTRIBUTION IN MANITOBA

The spottail shiner occurs generally in all watersheds in Manitoba from the Churchill River southwards. It is more common in the lakes and streams of the Canadian Shield than in our prairie waters.

MINNOWS AND CARP, FAMILY CYPRINIDAE

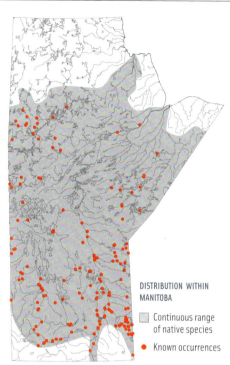

DISTRIBUTION WITHIN MANITOBA

▢ Continuous range of native species
● Known occurrences

BIOLOGICAL NOTES

SPAWNING: Spawning of the spottail shiner has not been studied in Manitoba. Scott and Crossman (1979) report that it spawns in late spring to early summer, ranging from May to July in different areas. They suggest that, in Lake Erie, it may have a protracted spawning period or spawn at different times in different years. Becker (1983) states that spawning can occur in both lakes and streams, over sand or gravel substrates. Spawning is believed to occur in large schools, but there is no description of spawning behaviour.

GROWTH AND ADULT SIZE: Adult spottail shiners in the University of Manitoba collection range from 85–101 mm total length, making this species one of the two largest species of *Notropis* in our area. Becker (1983) reports ages up to five years for this species.

FEEDING: Juvenile spottail shiners feed on planktonic crustaceans and some algae. Larger fish feed on insects and are also reported to feed on spottail shiner eggs to a significant degree (Becker, 1983).

HABITAT: In Manitoba, the spottail shiner is found in lakes, larger streams, and rivers. It tolerates a wide range of turbidity, but is most common in relatively clear water, most often associated with weedbeds. In streams and rivers, it prefers marginal water with little or no current. It is found over a variety of substrates, but most commonly over gravel, sand, or sandy silt in weedbeds.

ECOLOGICAL ROLE: Like most *Notropis* species, the spottail shiner is a middle-level consumer. Its cannibalism of eggs of its own species raises some interesting questions about its ecological role and control of its population density. Because of its abundance, it is one of the most important forage species for game fish in most of our Canadian Shield waters.

IMPORTANCE TO PEOPLE

The spottail shiner is one of the two species commonly sold as frozen bait minnows in Manitoba. The supply is collected farther north than emerald shiners, mostly from northern Lake Winnipeg and the Saskatchewan River.

COSEWIC Status as of January 1, 2004: Not Listed
MBESA Status as of January 1, 2004: Not Listed
MBCDC Status as of January 1, 2004: G5, S5

MINNOWS AND CARP, FAMILY CYPRINIDAE

CARMINE SHINER; MÉNÉ CARMINÉ | *Notropis percobromus*

NOTE: This species was formerly known as *N. rubellus*, rosyface shiner, tête rose

PRESERVED SPECIMEN
1 CM

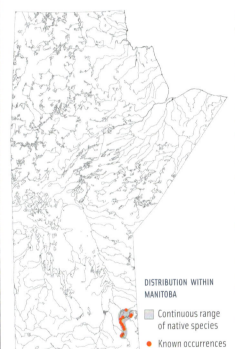
DISTRIBUTION WITHIN MANITOBA
☐ Continuous range of native species
● Known occurrences

IDENTIFICATION

The carmine, emerald, and golden shiners differ from all other minnows in Manitoba by having the **origin of the dorsal fin located behind a line drawn upward from the insertion of the pelvic fins**. The carmine shiner is distinguished from the golden shiner by **lacking the fleshy keel on the abdomen** and **lacking the strongly decurved lateral line**. It differs from the emerald shiner in having the **snout length equal to the eye diameter**, instead of being equal only to between one-half and three-fourths of the eye diameter. In addition, the carmine shiner has **black pigment outlining the scale pockets** dorsally. Freshly caught adult specimens often have **pinkish or rosy pigment on the opercula and cheek**.

DISTRIBUTION IN MANITOBA

In Manitoba, the carmine shiner is found in the Whitemouth River watershed; the Winnipeg River at the mouth of the Whitemouth River; The Old Pinawa Channel at the Pinawa Dam site; Forbes Creek, a tributary of George Lake; Tie Creek, the outlet of George Lake into the Winnipeg River; the Bird River at the mouth of Peterson Creek; and further upstream from Peterson Creek at the first set of rapids on the Bird River.

BIOLOGICAL NOTES

SPAWNING: Spawning of the carmine shiner has not been studied in Manitoba. In Wisconsin, carmine shiners spawn during May and June, in water temperatures above 21°C. They spawn in riffles, on nests built in gravel by hornyhead chubs, *Nocomis biguttatus*, and often also occupied by common shiners, *Luxilus cornutus*. The adhesive eggs are deposited on the substrate in the nest (Becker, 1983).

GROWTH AND ADULT SIZE: Adult carmine shiners from the Whitemouth River are 55–60 mm total length. Becker (1983) gives a maximum age of three years for the species in Wisconsin. Hermaphroditism has been reported for this species (Reed, 1954).

FEEDING: The carmine shiner is omnivorous, taking foods ranging from detritus to algae, insect larvae, and fish eggs (Scott and Crossman, 1979).

HABITAT: Carmine shiners are found in midwater in riffles and runs in the Whitemouth River. They are most often found over substrates ranging from gravel to boulders. Becker (1983) states that the carmine shiner is usually intolerant of turbidity, but that turbidity-tolerant local stocks are found in some streams. Turbidity in the Whitemouth River is usually low, but the Whitemouth River watershed is subject to flash flooding, and turbidity can increase dramatically with heavy rainfall.

ECOLOGICAL ROLE: The carmine shiner is a low- to middle-level consumer. It is uncommon in most areas and, hence, probably has limited significance as a forage fish.

IMPORTANCE TO PEOPLE

The carmine shiner has no direct economic importance. The populations in Manitoba are at the northwestern limit of distribution of this species. They are also separated from the continuous range of the species. Because of the separation from other populations and the location at the limit of distribution of the species, the carmine shiners of the Whitemouth River watershed and areas of the Winnipeg River watershed may be unique. They should be examined for evidence of local adaptation to their habitat and genetic differentiation from other populations of the species.

COSEWIC Status as of January 1, 2004: Threatened
MBESA Status as of February 2004: Not Listed
MBCDC Status as of January 1, 2004: G5, S2

SAND SHINER; MÉNÉ PAILLE | *Notropis stramineus*

PRESERVED SPECIMEN

1 CM

PRESERVED SPECIMEN, DORSAL VIEW

1 CM

IDENTIFICATION

The sand, river, bigmouth, and mimic shiners are similar to one another in appearance. Collectively, they differ from all other shiners in our area in the combination of: (1) **lacking a lateral stripe that continues onto the head;** (2) **lacking a black spot at the bases of either the dorsal or caudal fins;** (3) **having the base of the dorsal fin located over the base of the pelvic fins;** and (4) **the scales on the sides being less than twice as high as long.** The sand shiner differs from the river and bigmouth shiners in (1) **lacking the inner row of pharyngeal teeth;** (2) **the mid-dorsal dark stripe having a wedge-shaped expansion at the front of the dorsal fin;** and (3) **the mid-dorsal dark stripe not being continuous around the base of the dorsal fin.** It differs from the mimic shiner in having: (1) **dark markings ("mouse tracks") above and below each lateral line pore;** (2) **the mid-dorsal stripe well developed anterior and posterior to**

MINNOWS AND CARP, FAMILY CYPRINIDAE

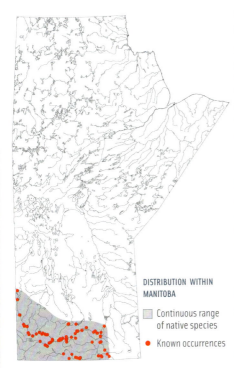

DISTRIBUTION WITHIN MANITOBA

- Continuous range of native species
- Known occurrences

the dorsal fin; and (3) **no black pigment around the anus and front of the anal fin**.

Note: There are two nominal subspecies of the sand shiner. *N. s. stramineus* is found in the Mississippi and Great Lakes watersheds, northwards into the Big Sioux River. It is also found in the Missouri River north into the James River. *N. s. missuriensis* is found in the Missouri River and its tributaries upstream from the mouth of the James River and in most of the Platte River (Bailey and Allum, 1962). Hudson Bay Drainage sand shiners agree with *N. s. stramineus* (Horn, 1993).

DISTRIBUTION IN MANITOBA

In Manitoba, the sand shiner occurs commonly in tributaries of the Red River and uncommonly in the Red River mainstem. It is one of the most abundant fishes in the Assiniboine River mainstem and in the Souris River, but it is replaced by the bigmouth shiner, *Notropis dorsalis*, in tributaries of the Assiniboine River except for the Souris River.

BIOLOGICAL NOTES

SPAWNING: Spawning of the sand shiner has not been observed in Manitoba. Horn (1993) studied changes in gonadosomatic index in both sexes and development of breeding tubercles in males, and their correlation with water temperature. She concluded that sand shiners in Manitoba have a short, well-defined spawning period from mid-June to mid-July. This contrasts with the protracted spawning period she found for sand shiners in southern Ontario. Becker (1983) also reports a protracted spawning period for this species in Wisconsin. Spawning habitat and habits are not described for this species.

GROWTH AND ADULT SIZE: Adult sand shiners from the Assiniboine River range from 55–61 mm total length. Becker (1983) reports a maximum age of three years for this species.

FEEDING: Sand shiners consume a wide variety of foods such as organic detritus, diatoms and other algae, and larval and adult insects. We have observed them rising to the surface for floating insects in the Pembina and Souris rivers and in riffles along the shoreline in the Assiniboine River.

HABITAT: Valiant (1975) found the sand shiner to be most strongly associated with pools located below riffles (0–15 cm/s water velocity, depth 35–100 cm, and gravel substrate) in five Manitoba Escarpment streams. In our experience, the sand shiner lives in somewhat slower water than the bigmouth shiner, preferring the tails of riffles, moderate velocity runs, and similar habitats along the margins of rivers, in water usually less than 30 cm deep. It is most common over gravel or sand substrates and is usually found in moderately turbid water. Its tolerance (or preference) of turbid water in Manitoba is in sharp contrast to its apparent requirement for clear water elsewhere (Becker, 1983; Scott and Crossman, 1979).

ECOLOGICAL ROLE: The sand shiner is a low- to middle-level consumer. Its abundance in the mainstem of the Assiniboine River and generally in the Pembina and Souris rivers suggests that the sand shiner is one of the most important forage species in these rivers.

IMPORTANCE TO PEOPLE

The greatest importance of the sand shiner is its role in the food web of the rivers and streams where it occurs. It is also used in native fish aquaria. It adapts well to aquarium conditions and the purplish iridescence on its sides makes it an attractive-looking fish.

COSEWIC Status as of January 1, 2004: Not Listed
MBESA Status as of January 1, 2004: Not Listed
MBCDC Status as of January 1, 2004: G5, S5

MINNOWS AND CARP, FAMILY CYPRINIDAE

WEED SHINER; MÉNÉ DIAMANT | *Notropis texanus*

1 CM — PRESERVED SPECIMEN

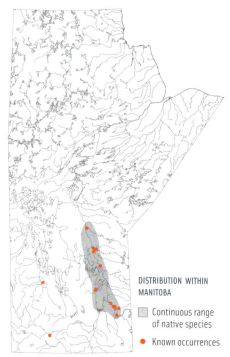

DISTRIBUTION WITHIN MANITOBA

▢ Continuous range of native species
● Known occurrences

IDENTIFICATION

The weed, blacknose, blackchin, and pugnose shiners are the only shiners in our area that have a **strong, lateral dark stripe that extends onto the head and around the tip of the snout**. The weed shiner differs from the blackchin shiner in having **two teeth in the inner pharyngeal tooth row on each side**, and by the **lateral stripe ending in a basicaudal spot**. It differs from the blacknose shiner in having **black pigment on the tip of the lower jaw**, and in having an **inner row of pharyngeal teeth**. It differs from the pugnose shiner in having the **mouth moderately oblique and reaching to below the front of the eye**.

DISTRIBUTION IN MANITOBA

The weed shiner is found in lakes, rivers, and streams in eastern Manitoba northward to at least the Belanger River. Its only known occurrences in tributaries to the west side of Lake Winnipeg are in the Icelandic and Fisher rivers (Hanke, 1996). This suggests that it may have been able to cross Lake Winnipeg using the littoral habitat provided by the shorelines of the Narrows of Lake Winnipeg and the islands to the south of the Narrows. To the west of the Lake Winnipeg watershed, the weed shiner is in Lake Dauphin and in Kichie Manitou Lake, an Assiniboine River oxbow lake in Spruce Woods Provincial Park. Its extensive distribution supports the hypothesis that this species has been in Manitoba for a long time, but has been confused with the blacknose shiner, *Notropis heterolepis*, and the blackchin shiner, *N. heterodon*, until recently. Stewart (1988) presented arguments that the weed shiners in Red River tributaries in northwestern Minnesota are not the source of the weed shiners in Manitoba. The distribution of this species in Manitoba, together with that of the blackchin shiner, *Notropis heterodon*, and the mimic shiner, *N. volucellus*, forms a track that supports a post-Glacial Lake Agassiz movement of these species into the Hudson Bay Drainage from the upper Mississippi and/or Lake Superior watershed headwaters into Rainy River/Wabigoon River headwaters. Subsequently, downstream dispersal in the Winnipeg River brought them into Manitoba. Two of these, the weed shiner and the blackchin shiner, have extended west into the Lake Dauphin watershed and south into the Assiniboine River oxbow lakes in Spruce Woods Provincial Park. Manitoba is the only province in which the weed shiner occurs.

BIOLOGICAL NOTES

SPAWNING: Spawning of the weed shiner has not been studied in Manitoba. In Wisconsin, it spawns in late June and early July (Becker, 1983). See the blackchin shiner species account for further comments.

GROWTH AND ADULT SIZE: Adult weed shiners in the University of Manitoba collection range from 47–56 mm total length. Becker (1983) reports an age of two years for the weed shiner.

FEEDING: In Wisconsin, weed shiners were found to have mostly plant material in their stomachs, with some unidentifiable animal remains (Becker, 1983).

HABITAT: In Manitoba, the weed shiner is found along the shorelines of lakes and larger rivers and in streams. It is in many of the same waters that the mimic shiner inhabits, but, unlike the mimic shiner, it prefers quiet water, in beds of aquatic vegetation. It is found in water depths up to 1 m, over mud, silt, and sand substrates. Like the blackchin shiner, the weed shiner has disappeared from many locations in Wisconsin where it had occurred in the past (Becker, 1983). Apparently, all our black-striped, weed-dwelling shiners are sensitive to alteration of their habitat. The abundance and wide distribution of all these species in Manitoba are probably the best refuge these species have to protect them from eventual extinction due to habitat loss. Like the other black-striped shiners in our area, the weed shiner may be tolerant of hypoxic conditions.

ECOLOGICAL ROLE: The weed shiner is probably a low-level consumer. It can be abundant enough in Manitoba to be significant in the trophic relationships in its community.

IMPORTANCE TO PEOPLE

The weed shiner has no direct economic importance. Because much of its distribution is in areas less accessible to people than the blackchin and blacknose shiners, it has not been used in native fish aquaria. Its greatest importance lies in its ecological role and its contribution to the diversity of our fish fauna.

COSEWIC Status as of January 1, 2004: Not at Risk
MBESA Status as of January 1, 2004: Not Listed
MBCDC Status as of January 1, 2004: G5, S4

MIMIC SHINER; MÉNÉ PÂLE | *Notropis volucellus*

PRESERVED SPECIMEN

1 CM

PRESERVED SPECIMEN, DORSAL VIEW

1 CM

IDENTIFICATION

The mimic, river, bigmouth, and sand shiners are similar to one another in appearance. Collectively, they differ from all other shiners in our area in the combination of: (1) **lacking a lateral dark stripe that continues onto the head**; (2) **lacking a black spot at the base of the dorsal or caudal fin;** (3) having the **base of the dorsal fin located**

MINNOWS AND CARP, FAMILY CYPRINIDAE

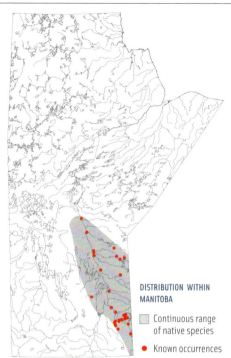

DISTRIBUTION WITHIN MANITOBA

▢ Continuous range of native species
● Known occurrences

over the base of the pelvic fins; and (4) having the **lateral scales anterior to the dorsal fin less than twice as high as long**. The mimic shiner differs from the river and bigmouth shiners in: (1) **lacking the inner row of pharyngeal teeth**; and (2) **lacking a well-developed mid-dorsal dark stripe except for some pigment along either side of the base of the dorsal fin**. It differs from the sand shiner in: (1) **the dark markings ("mouse tracks") above and below each lateral line pore being absent or weakly developed**; (2) **lacking a well-developed mid-dorsal dark stripe, except for some pigment along either side of the base of the dorsal fin**; and (3) having **black pigment around the anus and front of the anal fin**.

DISTRIBUTION IN MANITOBA

The mimic shiner is found in streams and lakes in eastern Manitoba northward at least to the Belanger River. Its westernmost occurrence in Manitoba is in the Icelandic River. This suggests that the mimic shiner may have been able to cross Lake Winnipeg using the littoral habitat provided by the shorelines of the Lake Winnipeg Narrows and the islands to the south of the Narrows. The distribution of this species in Manitoba, together with that of the weed shiner, *Notropis texanus*, and the blackchin shiner, *N. heterodon*, forms a track that supports a post-Glacial Lake Agassiz movement of these species into the Hudson Bay Drainage from upper Mississippi and/or Lake Superior watershed headwaters into Rainy River/Wabigoon River headwaters. Subsequently, downstream dispersal in the Winnipeg River system brought them into Manitoba. *Note:* The Woody and Roaring river locations included in the distribution map of *Notropis volucellus* in Scott and Crossman (1979) actually pertain to *Notropis dorsalis*, the bigmouth shiner.

BIOLOGICAL NOTES

SPAWNING: Horn (1993) found a single, relatively short spawning period for the mimic shiner in Manitoba. The gonadosomatic index of females peaked at a water temperature of 20°C, whereas that of males peaked at 15°C. The spawning period appeared to occupy the last three weeks of July. In Wisconsin, it has a protracted spawning period, extending from May through late July (Becker, 1983). Moyle (1969) found schools of spawning mimic shiners from late July to mid-August in Long Lake, Minnesota. There are no reports of spawning habitat or habits. Horn found evidence for a nighttime onshore movement of mimic shiners in the Winnipeg River. This may be evidence for nocturnal spawning in our area.

GROWTH AND ADULT SIZE: Adult mimic shiners in the University of Manitoba collection range from 46–53 mm total length. Becker (1983) reports that they live to an age of two years.

FEEDING: Moyle (1969) found that mimic shiners in Long Lake, Minnesota, fed in schools, mostly from the surface or midwater. The food taken varied over the course of the day. Planktonic crustacea, especially *Daphnia*, were taken in early morning, and, during the day, feeding shifted to surface insects and also some benthic material, including a significant amount of algae and detritus. During the evening, feeding shifted to pupae of diptera, adult mayflies, and amphipod crustaceans.

HABITAT: The mimic shiner is found along the shorelines of lakes and rivers and in streams in eastern Manitoba. Unlike the weed shiner, with which it shares the same distribution in eastern Manitoba, it lives in open water, often adjacent to rapids in streams. It is collected most often from water less than 1 m deep, over substrates ranging from sand to bedrock. In the Lake Winnipeg tributaries running into the east side of the north basin, the mimic shiner can often be found in water-filled depressions in bedrock outcrops along river shorelines at the bases of rapids or falls. In most cases, the depressions are connected with the river, so the fish are apparently not trapped in the pools by dropping water levels. This pattern suggests that the mimic shiners found in rock pools along the shores of streams in Manitoba may result from a daytime feeding movement.

ECOLOGICAL ROLE: The mimic shiner is a low- to middle-level consumer. Its preference for open-water habitats makes it available as prey to a somewhat different set of species and life-history stages than minnows that live in or near cover.

IMPORTANCE TO PEOPLE

The mimic shiner has no direct economic importance. Its ecological role as a schooling, midwater- to surface-living, open-water forage species for game fish is probably also its most important economic role.

COSEWIC Status as of January 1, 2004: Not Listed
MBESA Status as of January 1, 2004: Not Listed
MBCDC Status as of January 1, 2004: G5, S5

NORTHERN REDBELLY DACE; VENTRE ROUGE DU NORD | *Phoxinus eos*

PRESERVED SPECIMEN
1 CM

IDENTIFICATION

The northern redbelly and finescale daces differ from all other minnows in Manitoba in having an **incomplete lateral line that ends over or in advance of the base of the pelvic fins**, and in having **very small, imbedded scales that are difficult to see without magnification**. The northern redbelly dace differs from the finescale dace in having an **oblique mouth that does not reach or only barely reaches to below the front of the eye**, an **elongated gut with two transverse loops crossing the abdominal cavity overlying the stomach**, and a **black peritoneum. Males in spawning colours are bright red on the belly**.

NATURALLY OCCURRING HYBRID

The northern redbelly dace and finescale dace, *P. neogaeus*, often hybridize. The hybrids are fertile and breed with one another and both parents. In locations where hybridization occurs, the result is a single, variable population in which individuals have a mix of characters of both parents and characters intermediate between the parent species. In these cases, it is impossible to distinguish these species. In northwestern Ontario and the Maritime provinces, all-female, asexually reproducing populations of hybrids between these species are known.

DISTRIBUTION IN MANITOBA

The northern redbelly dace has a disjunct distribution in Manitoba. In the west, it is found in the Lake Dauphin, Lake Manitoba, and Souris River watersheds. In eastern Manitoba, it is found in eastern tributaries to the south basin of Lake Winnipeg, southward into the Winnipeg River watershed and headwaters of eastern tributaries of the Red River.

BIOLOGICAL NOTES

SPAWNING: Like many minnows, the northern redbelly dace has a protracted spawning period. Becker (1983) reports that spawning extends from May to August in Wisconsin. They spawn in masses of filamentous algae, with a female and one to eight males forming a spawning group. The eggs are deposited in the algal masses and are non-adhesive (Hubbs and Cooper, 1936).

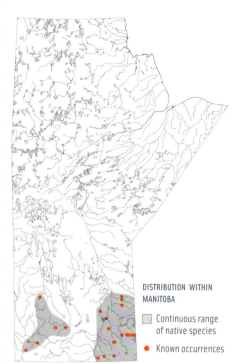

DISTRIBUTION WITHIN MANITOBA

▢ Continuous range of native species
● Known occurrences

GROWTH AND ADULT SIZE: Adult northern redbelly dace in the University of Manitoba collection range from 55–64 mm total length. Becker (1983) found that this species lives to an age of three years.

FEEDING: Manitoba specimens of this species eat mainly filamentous algae, diatoms, unidentified organic (probably plant) detritus, and occasionally insects. This is consistent with their long gut and black peritoneum, characters that usually are correlated with an herbivorous/detritivorous diet.

HABITAT: The northern redbelly dace is found in quiet, clear, cool, often brown-stained waters. It is found over fine substrates including silts and peaty debris (sapropel). It is one of the eight species of fishes found in bog habitats in headwater streams and ponds in Manitoba. See the pearl dace species account for the list of species and additional comments.

ECOLOGICAL ROLE: The northern redbelly dace is a low-level consumer. Because of its abundance, it probably is a significant link in the flow of nutrients in bog/headwater aquatic communities.

IMPORTANCE TO PEOPLE

The northern redbelly dace is one of the four species that are used in the live bait minnow trade in Manitoba and northwestern Ontario. The others are the finescale dace, the pearl dace, and the fathead minnow. Because of its abundance and virtual restriction to bog habitats, it is an important component of the fish community of those habitats. It is also common in native fish aquaria. The hybridization of the northern redbelly dace and finescale dace in Manitoba, and the possibility of existence of all-female, clonally reproducing populations of hybrids here, as occurs in eastern Canada, should be investigated.

COSEWIC Status as of January 1, 2004: Not Listed
MBESA Status as of January 1, 2004: Not Listed
MBCDC Status as of January 1, 2004: G5, S5

FINESCALE DACE; VENTRE CITRON *Phoxinus neogaeus*

1 CM — PRESERVED SPECIMEN

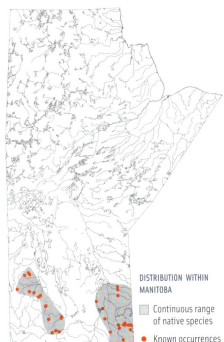

DISTRIBUTION WITHIN MANITOBA
- Continuous range of native species
- Known occurrences

IDENTIFICATION

The finescale and northern redbelly daces differ from all other minnows in Manitoba in having an **incomplete lateral line that ends over or in advance of the base of the pelvic fins**, and in having **very small, imbedded scales that are difficult to see without magnification**. The finescale dace differs from the northern redbelly dace in having a **nearly horizontal mouth that reaches to below or behind the front of the eye**, a shorter gut than the northern redbelly dace, with a single loop that does not cross the abdominal cavity over the stomach, and a **silvery peritoneum with scattered black pigment**. Males in spawning colours are lemon yellow on the belly.

NATURALLY OCCURRING HYBRID

The finescale and northern redbelly dace often hybridize. The hybrids are fertile and breed with one another and both parent species. In locations where hybridization occurs, the result is a single, variable population in which individuals have a mix of characters of both parents and characters intermediate between the parent species. In these cases, it is impossible to distinguish these species. (See note about all-female asexually reproducing hybrids in the *Phoxinus eos* account.)

DISTRIBUTION IN MANITOBA

The finescale dace has a disjunct distribution in Manitoba. In western Manitoba, its range follows the Manitoba Escarpment from the Lake Winnipegosis watershed in the north to the Assiniboine River oxbow lakes in Spruce Woods Provincial Park in the south. In the east, finescale dace are found in tributaries to the east side of the south basin of Lake Winnipeg and southwards in the Winnipeg River watershed and headwaters of eastern tributaries of the Red River.

BIOLOGICAL NOTES

SPAWNING: Unlike the northern redbelly dace, the finescale dace spawns over a shorter period in the spring (Scott and Crossman, 1979; Becker, 1983). Mature males with fully developed spawning colours have been collected in late April from Falcon Creek, Whiteshell Provincial Park. Stasiak (1972) observed finescale dace spawning in depressions covered by submerged logs. One or two males accompanied females, and eggs were deposited on the substrate.

MINNOWS AND CARP, FAMILY CYPRINIDAE

GROWTH AND ADULT SIZE: The finescale dace attains a larger size than the northern redbelly dace. The University of Manitoba collection has adult specimens ranging from 65–90 mm total length. Becker (1983) found that they live to a maximum of four years in Wisconsin.

FEEDING: Unlike the northern redbelly dace, the finescale dace feeds mainly on aquatic invertebrates, including small mollusks and a variety of larval insects. Some filamentous algae can also be found in their gut contents. Their larger mouths, shorter gut, and silvery peritoneum all correlate with more predatory feeding habits than shown by the northern redbelly dace.

HABITAT: Finescale dace are found in bog habitats in small lakes, ponds, and streams. They live in quiet, clear, cool, often brown-stained water. Valiant (1975) found the finescale dace to be most strongly associated with deep, slow channel habitat (0–10 cm/s water velocity, depth 60–110 cm, and silt substrate) in five Manitoba Escarpment streams. Unlike the redbelly dace, they are more common over firmer substrates of gravel or sand. It is one of the eight species of fishes associated with bog habitats in headwater streams and ponds in Manitoba. See the pearl dace species account for a complete list and additional comments.

ECOLOGICAL ROLE: The finescale dace is a middle-level consumer. Like the northern redbelly dace, it is often abundant in headwater/bog habitats. Its abundance suggests that it is probably also an important prey species for the young of game fish using this habitat and for adult game fish, which are transient in this habitat.

IMPORTANCE TO PEOPLE

The finescale dace is one of the four species that are used in the live bait minnow trade in Manitoba and northwestern Ontario. The others are the northern redbelly dace, the pearl dace, and the fathead minnow. It is also an important food source for game fish present in its habitat. It also is kept in native fish aquaria.

COSEWIC Status as of January 1, 2004: Not Listed
MBESA Status as of January 1, 2004: Not Listed
MBCDC Status as of January 1, 2004: G5, S5

BLUNTNOSE MINNOW; VENTRE-POURRI | *Pimephales notatus*

PRESERVED SPECIMEN
1 CM

IDENTIFICATION

All species of *Pimephales* differ from *Notropis* species by the **blunt-tipped first dorsal ray that is separated by a membrane from the second dorsal ray**, and by the **crowded predorsal scales**. The bluntnose minnow differs from the fathead and bullhead minnows in having a **strong lateral dark stripe that extends onto the head and ends posteriorly in a basicaudal spot**, and the **scale pockets being sharply outlined with dark pigment**. Additionally, it differs from the fathead minnow in having a **subterminal mouth**, and a **complete lateral line**.

DISTRIBUTION IN MANITOBA

The bluntnose minnow has been collected at scattered locations in the Winnipeg River, but mainly above the Pointe du Bois Dam. There is also a single record from the Red River below the St. Andrews Dam at Lockport.

BIOLOGICAL NOTES

SPAWNING: In Wisconsin, the bluntnose minnow spawns between May and August (Becker, 1983). None of the fish collected from the Winnipeg River showed nuptial tubercles or any other evidence of sexual maturity. Hubbs and Cooper (1936) stated that bluntnose minnows excavate nests in sand or gravel substrate, under logs, bark, or other covering objects. The eggs are laid on the undersurface of the covering object and are adhesive. The male guards the nest until the young have hatched and left.

GROWTH AND ADULT SIZE: Bluntnose minnows collected from the Winnipeg River above the Pointe du Bois Dam ranged from 52–57 mm total length. This is about the size reported by Scott and Crossman (1979) and Becker (1983) for fish in their second summer of life (Age I+). In the northern USA, bluntnose minnows can grow to just over 100 mm and live up to three years (Becker).

FEEDING: Becker (1983) summarizes several reports of the diet of bluntnose minnows. They are omnivorous, consuming algae, larval and adult insects, and planktonic crustacea. They feed both on the bottom and in midwater. There are seasonal differences in food consumed, with most of the algae (diatoms) being eaten during the winter.

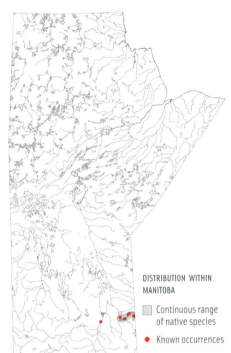

DISTRIBUTION WITHIN MANITOBA

☐ Continuous range of native species

● Known occurrences

HABITAT: Except for the single record from the Red River, the bluntnose minnow in Manitoba is found in protected marginal waters and tributary mouths of the Winnipeg River. It occurs over mud substrates with submerged wood as cover, and on cobble to boulder substrates, in clear or slightly turbid water up to 50 cm deep.

ECOLOGICAL ROLE: The bluntnose minnow is a low- to middle-level consumer. In Manitoba, it is so rare and limited in distribution that it probably does not make a significant contribution to nutrient flow in its communities.

IMPORTANCE TO PEOPLE

In Manitoba, the bluntnose minnow is too uncommon to be of any importance. Elsewhere, it is used in the live bait minnow trade. In southern Ontario and the northern USA, it is one of the most abundant and widely distributed minnows. In those areas, its importance as a forage species for game fish is probably as great as that of the emerald shiner, *Notropis atherinoides*, and the spottail shiner, *N. hudsonius*, in our area.

COSEWIC Status as of January 1, 2004: Not at Risk
MBESA Status as of January 1, 2004: Not Listed
MBCDC Status as of January 1, 2004: G5, S2S3

MINNOWS AND CARP, FAMILY CYPRINIDAE

FATHEAD MINNOW; TÊTE-DE-BOULE | *Pimephales promelas*

FRESH SPECIMEN
1 CM

DISTRIBUTION WITHIN MANITOBA

- Continuous range of native species
- Known occurrences

IDENTIFICATION

All species of *Pimephales* differ from *Notropis* species by the **blunt-tipped first dorsal ray that is separated by a membrane from the second dorsal ray**, and by the **crowded predorsal scales**. The fathead minnow differs from the bullhead and bluntnose minnows in having an **incomplete lateral line**, the **lateral dark stripe being usually less distinct and not extending onto the head**, and the **scale pockets not being outlined with dark pigment**. There is **no basicaudal spot** and the **mouth is inferior only in breeding males with tubercles**. The fathead minnow is misidentified more frequently than any other fish species in our area. Spawning males (see notes on spawning below) are so unusual that they are frequently either misidentified as goldfish or not recognized at all. Juveniles, non-spawning males and females, often (but not always) have a sharply defined, dark lateral stripe, which causes them to be confused with the black-striped *Notropis* shiners. Taking care to look for the **incomplete lateral line**, the **crowded predorsal scales**, and the **blunt-tipped first dorsal ray**, which is **separated by a membrane from the second dorsal ray**, should prevent such identification problems.

DISTRIBUTION IN MANITOBA

The fathead minnow is generally distributed in Manitoba from the upper Nelson and Hayes rivers southward.

BIOLOGICAL NOTES

SPAWNING: In Manitoba, the fathead minnow is a spring spawner. Males showing fully developed nuptial tubercles, enlargement of the snout, a pad of thickened, greyish-coloured skin down the midline of the back, black pigment on the head and general darkening of the body, and a dark band on the dorsal fin can be collected between mid-May and late June in southern Manitoba. Nests are located on soft substrates such as sand or mud. Males construct nests by cleaning the undersides of solid objects such as submerged branches, stones, or articles put into the water by people. If necessary, the male will excavate a cavity under the object. Females enticed into a nest by the male deposit their eggs on the undersurface of the roof, and several females will deposit eggs in a single nest. The eggs are buoyant and adhesive, and adhere to the nest roof. Nests with large masses of eggs attached to the underside of the roof can be collected during most of June and into early July. The male defends his nest against other males.

GROWTH AND ADULT SIZE: Spawning fathead minnows from Whitemouth Lake in the University of Manitoba collection range from 60–74 mm total length. Becker (1983) reports only two age classes for the fathead minnow in Wisconsin. He also reports sexual maturity during the first summer (Age 0). Maximum age and age at maturity are unknown in Manitoba.

FEEDING: Fathead minnows are mainly benthic feeders, consuming a variety of plant materials and detritus as well as aquatic insect larvae. In the often stagnant habitats in which they are found, mosquito larvae can be a significant portion of their stomach contents.

HABITAT: The fathead minnow occurs in a broad range of habitats and water turbidities, from bog ponds and headwater streams to lakes and large, turbid rivers. Within this range, it prefers quiet water, usually with aquatic vegetation as cover. Valiant (1975) found the fathead minnow to be most strongly associated with pools (0–10 cm/s water velocity, depth 35–100 cm, and variable substrate) in five Manitoba Escarpment streams. It tolerates low oxygen levels, and can be one of the most abundant fish species in waters that may winterkill or become stagnant when cut off from their parent streams or lakes. Because of its tolerance of low oxygen, it is often an invader in newly created human-made habitats such as storm water retention ponds, ponded water in drainage ditches, or farm dugouts. It shares this invasiveness with the brook stickleback, *Culaea inconstans*. It is found most often over fine substrates, including sapropel, in waters 1 m or less deep. It is one of the eight species of fishes associated with bog habitats in headwater streams and ponds in Manitoba. See the pearl dace species account for a complete list and additional comments.

ECOLOGICAL ROLE: The fathead minnow is a low- to middle-level consumer. Because of its wide tolerance for oxygen, turbidity, and habitat type, it is present, at least in small numbers, in almost every aquatic habitat within its range. Its ubiquity gives it a place along with the emerald and spottail shiners as one of the most important forage fish species in Manitoba.

IMPORTANCE TO PEOPLE

The fathead minnow is the most common of the four species used in the live bait minnow trade in Manitoba and northwestern Ontario. The others are the northern redbelly dace, the finescale dace, and the pearl dace. In stagnant waters, it is a significant predator on mosquito larvae. Because of its abundance, it can be an important food source for juvenile or adult game fish transiently present in its habitat. Probably because of its broad tolerances, it is usually the most important, and sometimes the only, fish species in human-made habitats like storm water retention ponds. Finally, the abundance of the fathead minnow and its ability to adapt to aquarium conditions have led to its use as a standard species for assaying the toxicity of environmental pollutants.

COSEWIC Status as of January 1, 2004: Not Listed
MBESA Status as of January 1, 2004: Not Listed
MBCDC Status as of January 1, 2004: G5, S5

MINNOWS AND CARP, FAMILY CYPRINIDAE

BULLHEAD MINNOW; TÊTE BARBOTTE | *Pimephales vigilax*

NOTE: Not found in Manitoba, Red River watershed, Minnesota

FRESH SPECIMEN
1 CM

IDENTIFICATION

All species of *Pimephales* differ from *Notropis* species by the **blunt-tipped first dorsal ray that is separated by a membrane from the second dorsal ray**, and by the **crowded predorsal scales**. The bullhead minnow differs from the bluntnose minnow in having the **lateral dark stripe usually less distinct and not extending onto the head**. It differs from the fathead minnow in having a **complete lateral line**, a **basicaudal spot**, and a **spot on the lower front corner of the dorsal fin**. The **mouth is inferior in both sexes at all stages**.

DISTRIBUTION IN MANITOBA

The bullhead minnow does not occur in Manitoba. It is found in Red River tributaries in northwestern Minnesota.

BIOLOGICAL NOTES

SPAWNING: In Wisconsin, the bullhead minnow spawns over most of the summer, after the water temperature reaches 25.6°C. Like the other two *Pimephales* species in our area, the male bullhead minnow builds a nest under solid objects (Becker, 1983).

GROWTH AND ADULT SIZE: Becker (1983) reports two year classes of bullhead minnows, and a maximum size of 79 mm for Wisconsin specimens.

FEEDING: The bullhead minnow is an omnivorous, benthic feeder, as are the other two *Pimephales* species in our area.

HABITAT: The bullhead minnow prefers turbid, slow-moving waters of large rivers, peripheral waters such as oxbows, and the lower reaches of their tributaries. It is most common over soft substrates such as sand, silt, or mud (Becker, 1983).

ECOLOGICAL ROLE: The bullhead minnow has a similar trophic position to the other *Pimephales* species in our area, but is more common in large rivers than either of the others.

IMPORTANCE TO PEOPLE

The bullhead minnow has no direct economic importance. It can be abundant in its preferred habitat, and therefore is probably a significant forage species for game fish.

COSEWIC Status as of January 1, 2004: Not Listed
MBESA Status as of January 1, 2004: Not Listed
MBCDC Status as of January 1, 2004: G5, SP

MINNOWS AND CARP, FAMILY CYPRINIDAE

FLATHEAD CHUB; MÉNÉ À TÊTE PLATE | *Platygobio gracilis*

PRESERVED SPECIMEN
3 CM

IDENTIFICATION

The flathead chub can be distinguished from all other minnows in Manitoba by the combination of: (1) the **falcate pectoral, dorsal, and anal fins**; (2) the **terminal maxillary barbel**; and (3) the **streamlined shape, with a depressed head**. In adults, the large size and graceful, streamlined shape make the flathead chub one of the most distinctive minnow species in Manitoba.

DISTRIBUTION IN MANITOBA

In Manitoba, the flathead chub is found in the mainstem of the Assiniboine River, the Saskatchewan River, Lake Winnipeg, and the Red River below its confluence with the Assiniboine River at Winnipeg.

BIOLOGICAL NOTES

SPAWNING: Spawning has not been described for the flathead chub. Spawning probably occurs in the spring and is not protracted, because mature individuals are not collected during the summer, after water flows are low enough to allow effective collection in their habitat.

DISTRIBUTION WITHIN MANITOBA

☐ Continuous range of native species
● Known occurrences

GROWTH AND ADULT SIZE: The flathead chub is the largest native minnow in Manitoba. Large adults in the University of Manitoba collection range from 270–323 mm total length. Flathead chub collected from the Athabasca River in Alberta by Fisheries and Oceans Canada had a maximum age of five years.

FEEDING: The flathead chub is a predator and consumes a variety of aquatic invertebrates at all life-history stages, as well as small fish, which are consumed by adults. Feeding is mostly benthic, but they occasionally rise to surface insects (Scott and Crossman, 1979).

HABITAT: In Manitoba, adult flathead chub are most often found on the bottom in mid-channel, in fast-flowing sections of larger rivers. They are found on gravel, sand, or, less commonly, rubble. Small schools of flathead chub will congregate in the scour holes found on the downstream side of obstructions such as submerged stumps or glacially deposited boulders in the riverbed. The few flathead chubs from Lake Winnipeg in the University of Manitoba collection were taken in shallow, probably wave-surge-affected water offshore of beaches. Juvenile flathead chub have been collected in the Assiniboine River from shallow riffle sections along the shoreline, over a substrate of shale gravel with silt infill. They share this habitat with the sand shiner, *Notropis stramineus*.

ECOLOGICAL ROLE: The flathead chub is a middle- to upper-level consumer. In the Assiniboine River, it is abundant enough to be an important component of the diet of game fish. Large adult flathead chubs are probably above the range of prey size for all but very large channel catfish, northern pike, and walleye.

MINNOWS AND CARP, FAMILY CYPRINIDAE

IMPORTANCE TO PEOPLE

The flathead chub is caught occasionally by anglers. In the Assiniboine River, it is easily angled by drifting a small hook, baited with a worm, down a riffle. Fly fishers in search of more varied angling opportunities in Manitoba might also try drifting a weighted nymph in the same type of habitat. Its graceful, streamlined body and falcate fins make it a distinctive species of our fast-flowing, shallow prairie rivers.

COSEWIC Status as of January 1, 2004: Not Listed
MBESA Status as of January 1, 2004: Not Listed
MBCDC Status as of January 1, 2004: G5, S4

ZOOGEOGRAPHIC NOTE ON THE SPECIES OF *Rhinichthys*

Our *Rhinichthys* daces and *Catostomus* suckers are the only examples of Pacific Slope fishes native to our area. Most of the evolutionary diversification of *Rhinichthys* took place on the Pacific Slope. Five of the seven species of the genus *Rhinichthys* are found in the Pacific Ocean drainages of North America, but only three, the longnose dace, *R. cataractae*, the eastern blacknose dace, *R. atratulus*, and the western blacknose dace, *R. obtusus*, occur east of the Continental Divide. The longnose dace is found everywhere in Canada except the island of Newfoundland, the Maritime provinces, and Nunavut Territory.

LONGNOSE DACE; NASEUX DE RAPIDES — *Rhinichthys cataractae*

PRESERVED SPECIMEN, IMMATURE — 1 CM

PRESERVED SPECIMEN, SPAWNING MALE — 2 CM

IDENTIFICATION

The *Rhinichthys* daces can be distinguished from all other minnows in Manitoba by the **terminal maxillary barbel**, the **frenum**, and the **inferior mouth**. The longnose dace differs from the western blacknose dace in having the **tip of the snout projecting beyond the tip of the lower jaw by more than the length of the lower jaw**, measured from its tip to the angle of the mouth, and in **lacking, or having fewer, scattered, darkly pigmented scales on the sides and back above the lateral line**.

DISTRIBUTION IN MANITOBA

The longnose dace is generally distributed in Manitoba streams and the Manitoba Great Lakes, from the Churchill River southward. This is the most widely distributed minnow species in Canada. It is absent only from the island of Newfoundland, the Maritime provinces, and the Territory of Nunavut.

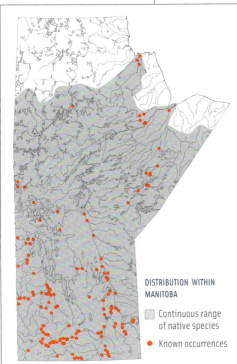

DISTRIBUTION WITHIN MANITOBA

▨ Continuous range of native species

● Known occurrences

BIOLOGICAL NOTES

SPAWNING: Spawning of the longnose dace has been studied in the Mink and Valley rivers (Lake Dauphin watershed) in Manitoba by Bartnick (1970). He found that, although there is significant overlap in their spawning periods, the longnose dace spawns earlier than the western blacknose dace. The percentage of gonad weight in both sexes of longnose dace peaked on May 16 in 1968. This corresponded to a daytime water temperature range of 4°C–16°C. Bartnick also found that spawning longnose dace were most abundant in water velocities from 52.5–60 cm/s and on coarse gravel to rubble substrates with a particle size of 5–20 cm. Although longnose and western blacknose dace may spawn in close proximity to each other, Bartnick found that males of both species were highly territorial, and vigorously defended their spawning stations against intruders. He gave a detailed description of occupation and defense of a spawning territory by male longnose dace. Egg deposition was accompanied by quivering of both the male and female for one to two seconds, during which the eggs were expelled, fertilized, and then sunk into spaces between the stones on the floor of the station. The males expelled females from their territories after the spawning act, although the same female sometimes returned later and spawned again. Males continued to defend nest sites for an interval ranging from several hours to three days after spawning was complete.

GROWTH AND ADULT SIZE: The longnose dace is larger than the western blacknose dace. Adults in the University of Manitoba collection range from 94–103 mm total length. Becker (1983) gives a maximum age of five years for this species in Wisconsin.

FEEDING: McCulloch (1994) compared the habitats and diets of the stonecat, juvenile burbot, and longnose dace at three sites on the Little Saskatchewan River, a tributary of the Assiniboine River. He found that the longnose dace feeds on aquatic insects virtually to the exclusion of other groups. Caddis fly (*Hydropsyche*) and black fly (*Simulium*) larvae comprised the bulk of the food intake. Unlike the stonecat and burbot, the longnose dace fed during daylight hours, but all three species consumed a similar array of prey species.

HABITAT: The longnose dace, perhaps to a greater extent than any other fish in our area, prefers high-energy habitats. Valiant (1975) reported that the longnose dace was most strongly associated with riffle habitat (75–200 cm/s water velocity, 5–25 cm depth, and rocky substrate) in five Manitoba Escarpment streams. The longnose dace is also common along lakeshores subject to wave action. It is tolerant of a wide range of turbidity and water temperature. It is benthic, often living under and in crevices between boulders, where it finds shelter from the current. Two other fish species, the stonecat and juvenile burbot, and one amphibian, the mudpuppy salamander, share the benthic fast-water habitat in southern Manitoba. McCulloch (1994) conducted a detailed, comparative habitat study of the stonecat, juvenile burbot, and longnose dace. All three species share the rocky riffle/rapid habitat, with the longnose dace being more frequent in shallower water with higher current velocity than the other two species.

ECOLOGICAL ROLE: The longnose dace is a benthic-feeding predator on aquatic insects. Its preference for fast-flowing water is shared by only a few other fish species in Manitoba.

IMPORTANCE TO PEOPLE

The longnose dace has no direct economic importance. It occupies a habitat used by only a few other fish species. It contributes to the diversity and, hence, to the stability and productivity, of the aquatic communities in our streams.

COSEWIC Status as of January 1, 2004: Not Listed
MBESA Status as of January 1, 2004: Not Listed
MBCDC Status as of January 1, 2004: G5, S5

MINNOWS AND CARP, FAMILY CYPRINIDAE

WESTERN BLACKNOSE DACE; NASEUX NOIR DE L'OUEST | *Rhinichthys obtusus*

NOTE: This species was formerly known as *R. atratulus*, blacknose dace, naseux noir

PRESERVED SPECIMEN, FEMALE
1 CM

PRESERVED SPECIMEN, MALE
1 CM

DISTRIBUTION WITHIN MANITOBA
- Continuous range of native species
- Known occurrences

IDENTIFICATION

The *Rhinichthys* daces can be distinguished from all other minnows in Manitoba by the **terminal maxillary barbel**, the **frenum**, and the **inferior mouth**. The western blacknose dace differs from the longnose dace in having the **tip of the snout projecting beyond the tip of the lower jaw by less than the length of the lower jaw**, measured from the tip of the lower jaw to the angle of the mouth, and in having **more scattered, darkly pigmented scales** on the sides and back above the lateral line.

DISTRIBUTION IN MANITOBA

The western blacknose dace is found in tributaries of Lake Winnipeg, and the Red and Assiniboine river watersheds northwest into the Lake Winnipegosis watershed.

BIOLOGICAL NOTES

SPAWNING: Spawning of the western blacknose dace has been studied in the Mink and Valley rivers (Lake Dauphin watershed) in Manitoba by Bartnick (1970). He found that, although there is significant overlap in their spawning periods, the western blacknose dace spawns later than the longnose dace. The percentage of gonad weight in both sexes of western blacknose dace peaked on May 27 in 1968. This corresponded to a water temperature range of 9°–18°C for the day. Bartnick also found that spawning western blacknose dace were most abundant in water velocities from 7–45 cm/s and on coarse sand to gravel substrates with a particle size of 5 cm or less, with the majority of nests having particle sizes of 2.5 cm or less. As with the longnose dace, Bartnick found that male western blacknose dace defend a nesting territory. He observed that, during spawning, female western blacknose dace arch their backs and thrust their anal fin into the substrate. The male curls his body around the female and both quiver for about two seconds. The quivering excavates a small depression in the substrate, into which the eggs are deposited. After the spawning act, the male expels the female from the nest. Bartnick found that a male spawns with several females, and that the same female may return to a male's nest and spawn again.

GROWTH AND ADULT SIZE: Adult western blacknose dace in the University of Manitoba collection range from 69–88 mm total length. Becker (1983) reports an age of three years for the blacknose dace.

FEEDING: The western blacknose dace is a benthic-feeding predator on aquatic insect larvae. Plant material may comprise up to 25% of the diet, and fish eggs are also taken (Becker, 1983).

HABITAT: The western blacknose dace prefers current, but is associated with lower water velocities than the longnose dace. Valiant (1975) found that it was most strongly associated with moderately fast channel habitats (15–50 cm/s water velocity, 25–50 cm depth, and gravel substrate) in five Manitoba Escarpment streams. It occurs uncommonly in larger rivers and along the shorelines of lakes. It is found on gravel to rubble substrates, less commonly on sand, in water usually less than 1 m deep. It is often found in the pool at the tail of a rapid that contains longnose dace. The western blacknose dace and bigmouth shiner are found together in streams that have both species.

ECOLOGICAL ROLE: The western blacknose dace is a low- to middle-level benthic consumer. It can be abundant locally, and is probably a significant food source for larger fish in its habitat. There is great diversity of species in our area that fill this role. Each has somewhat different tolerances and adaptations. Together, they contribute stability to their communities, since not all are likely to be affected by a given change in conditions. If this diversity were reduced, the most significant result would probably be a reduction in population size, productivity, and stability of game fish stocks in the community.

IMPORTANCE TO PEOPLE

The western blacknose dace has no direct economic importance. Its greatest importance for people lies in its ecological role as described above. Unlike the longnose dace, it survives well in aquarium conditions, and the pink lateral band of mature males make them attractive for native fish aquaria.

COSEWIC Status as of January 1, 2004: Not Listed
MBESA Status as of January 1, 2004: Not Listed
MBCDC Status as of January 1, 2004: G5, S5

CREEK CHUB; MULET À CORNES | *Semotilus atromaculatus*

PRESERVED SPECIMEN
2 CM

IDENTIFICATION

The creek chub can be distinguished from all other minnows in our area by the **mouth reaching to below the front of the pupil of the eye**, the **spot in the lower anterior corner of the dorsal fin**, and the **small barbel anterior to the tip of the maxilla in the groove between the upper lip and the snout**. Young creek chubs have a distinct, **lateral dark stripe with a basicaudal spot**. The only other Manitoba minnow with a dorsal maxillary barbel is the pearl dace, but in that species, the mouth only extends to below the front of the eye.

MINNOWS AND CARP, FAMILY CYPRINIDAE

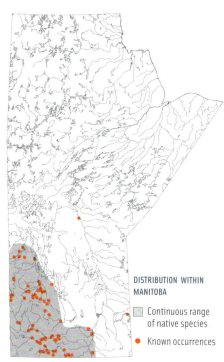

DISTRIBUTION WITHIN MANITOBA
- Continuous range of native species
- Known occurrences

DISTRIBUTION IN MANITOBA

The creek chub is found from the Red River watershed westward in the Assiniboine River watershed and northward into the Lake Winnipegosis watershed. There is also a single record of the creek chub from the Winnipeg River near the Manitoba-Ontario border.

BIOLOGICAL NOTES

SPAWNING: Spawning of the creek chub in the Mink River (Lake Dauphin watershed) in Manitoba was studied by Moshenko (1972). He reported that spawning occurred during the last two weeks of May, starting when daytime water temperature exceeded 14°C. Spawning activity temporarily ceased when water temperature decreased below this value. Spawning activity began at about noon and increased in intensity through the afternoon, peaking between 1600 and 2000 hours. Spawning then declined during sunset. He found that the ratio of gonad weight to body weight peaked on May 19 for females and on May 12 for males. The highest frequency of fish with easily expressed eggs or milt was on May 19 for both sexes, with 80% of females and 75% of males being ripe.

Male creek chubs in the Mink River constructed nests in gravel substrate. A nest consisted of a gravel ridge, parallel to the current, 500–2000 mm long, about 250 mm wide and 50 mm high, with a pit 200–250 mm in diameter and 80–200 mm deep, in which spawning took place. After each spawning, the male would move stones from the downstream end of the pit to the upstream end, to cover the newly deposited eggs. The ridge lengthened as repeated spawnings occurred. Moshenko (1972) observed that 55.6% of the nests were in fast, shallow channels, 30.6% in slow, shallow channels, 8.1% in shallow pools, 2.0% in moderately deep pools, and 4.0% in slow, deep channels.

The male curls his body around the female during spawning. Creek chub eggs varied from 1.5–2.0 mm in diameter, and the fecundity of females increased with size, varying from 1146 eggs in a 100 mm fork length female to 7539 in a 200 mm female.

GROWTH AND ADULT SIZE: The creek chub is the second largest native minnow in Manitoba, after the flathead chub. Large adults from the Boyne River range from 214–236 mm total length. Scales of 150–200 mm total length specimens from Babcock Creek (Red River watershed), west of Roseisle, Manitoba, showed five or six annuli on their scales. Moshenko (1972) found six year classes in Mink River creek chubs. Males were larger than females in each year class. The largest fish in his samples were Age VI males ranging from 192–207 mm fork length.

FEEDING: Moshenko (1972) found that aquatic invertebrates are the most common food items for all age classes of creek chubs. In Age I fish and older, crayfish and fish, mainly juvenile brook sticklebacks and johnny darters, became important food items. These larger food items were taken more frequently later in the summer. Newsome (1975) found that adult creek chubs (>80 mm fork length) in the Mink River (Lake Dauphin watershed) fed mostly on fish during early summer and shifted to mostly crayfish during mid- and late summer. The most common prey fish species was the brook stickleback, followed by the johnny darter, pearl dace, and common shiner.

HABITAT: In Manitoba, the creek chub prefers stream habitats. It can tolerate some turbidity, but is found most often in clear water. Moshenko (1972) stated that non-spawning adult creek chubs are found most often in deeper water (250–500 mm or deeper) of pools and slick runs, or under cut banks. Substrates range from silt in pools to coarse gravel in the runs. Juveniles are often found in shallow riffles or quiet, shallow water, with sand shiners and juvenile common shiners. Valiant (1975) also found creek chubs to be most strongly associated with pool habitat (0–10 cm/s water velocity, depth 35–100 cm, and variable substrate) in five Manitoba Escarpment streams.

ECOLOGICAL ROLE: The creek chub is a middle- to upper-level consumer. Because of its large size and tendency to take small fish, it can be at or near the top of the food web in the small stream communities of which it is a part. It is preyed upon by northern pike, which may be transients in creek chub habitat.

IMPORTANCE TO PEOPLE

Young anglers fishing in our streams frequently catch the creek chub. It can also provide a fine day of fishing for fly fishers willing to extend their experience beyond the usual stocked trout, smallmouth bass, goldeye/mooneye, or northern pike fishing pursued by fly fishers in southern Manitoba.

COSEWIC Status as of January 1, 2004: Not Listed
MBESA Status as of January 1, 2004: Not Listed
MBCDC Status as of January 1, 2004: G5, S5

SUCKERS, FAMILY CATOSTOMIDAE

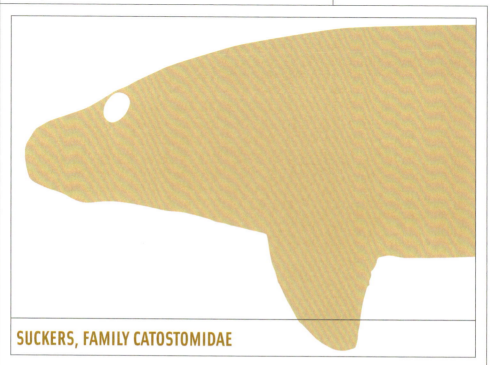

SUCKERS, FAMILY CATOSTOMIDAE

FAMILY CATOSTOMIDAE

Suckers are medium to large fishes closely related to minnows (Family Cyprinidae). All but two species of suckers are found only in North America. The oldest known fossil sucker, *Amyzon aggregatum*, found in Miocene shale in the Horsefly River Canyon in British Columbia, is similar to the living buffalos, genus *Ictiobus* (Smith, 1992).

Suckers have **toothless mouths**. They process food using their pharyngeal teeth, which are located on specialized pharyngeal arches at the rear of the gill chamber. Unlike cyprinids, suckers always have a **single row of pharyngeal teeth** on each side. The teeth vary from slender and closely spaced in small particle feeders like quillback and bigmouth buffalo, to relatively stout and more widely spaced in suckers like the shorthead redhorse and white sucker that feed on larger invertebrates. Uniquely in suckers, there is a **branchial organ**. This is a **bulbous enlargement of the bone of the base of the skull**, which is the base for a hardened area projecting down into the rear of the pharynx. **It provides a hard surface for the pharyngeal teeth to work against** when food is being processed.

Most suckers feed on benthic invertebrates, detritus, and plants. The bigmouth buffalo is an exception, since it may also feed on plankton filtered from the water. In their size and feeding habits, the suckers are similar to the larger cyprinid fishes of Eurasia and Africa, collectively called carp. The evolution of these feeding habits in suckers in North America may explain why no North American minnows have developed large size in association with similar feeding habits. If true, this suggests that the most severe impact of the introduction and spread of a variety of Eurasian carp species in North America will be on the native suckers.

Two subfamilies of suckers are found in Manitoba.

1. **Bigmouth buffalo and quillback, Subfamily Ictiobinae**. The bigmouth buffalo and quillback are **robust, compressed, deep-bodied** fish with **large scales** and a **long dorsal fin**, which is **high in front and lower over most of its length**. They resemble the common carp and goldfish, but differ from them in **lacking a spine at the leading edge of the dorsal and anal fins**. They also differ from the common carp by **not having barbels on the upper jaw**.

2. **Fine-scaled suckers, hog suckers, and redhorses (collectively called "round suckers"), Subfamily Catostominae**. All the rest of our suckers are more **elongate and streamlined**, and they have a **short dorsal fin** with a **straight or slightly rounded edge**.

SUCKERS, FAMILY CATOSTOMIDAE

There are two tribes of "round suckers" in our area.

A. **The white and longnose suckers ("fine-scaled suckers"), Tribe Catostomini.** The species of these suckers found in our area have **small scales, with 53 or more scales in the lateral line**, and **enlarged, fleshy lips with papillae**. This tribe includes all the suckers that occur from the Rocky Mountains west to the Pacific Coast, with four species in Canada found east of the Continental Divide, of which two occur in our area.

B. **The redhorses and hog sucker, Tribe Moxostomatini.** These suckers have **large scales, with 52 or fewer scales in the lateral line** and **enlarged, fleshy lips with folds** (redhorses) **or papillae** (northern hog sucker only). All species in this tribe are found only east of the Rocky Mountains.

Sucker fry in which the fins have developed can be distinguished from minnow fry because the **distance from the origin of the anal fin to the middle of the base of the caudal fin is less than one-half of the distance from the origin of the anal fin to the posterior margin of the operculum. Larval suckers are usually distinguishable from larval minnows by the long, straight rear section of the gut**, which can be seen through the transparent body wall when viewed under magnification.

KEY TO THE SUCKERS FOUND IN MANITOBA AND ADJACENT AREAS OF THE HUDSON BAY DRAINAGE

1A Dorsal fin with 23 or more rays, and the rays of the anterior 1/3 or so notably longer than those of the posterior 2/3 of the fin. The margin of the dorsal fin is steeply concave anteriorly and straight posteriorly. Gill rakers on first arch 30 or more, the longest more than 2% of total length. Lips with little or no fleshy expansion, the greatest anterior-posterior length of the lower lip being 1/3 or less the eye diameter.

go to choice 2

1B Dorsal fin shorter, with 17 or fewer rays, and a smooth gradation in fin ray length from longer anterior to shorter posterior rays. The margin of the dorsal fin is slightly rounded, straight, or falcate. Gill rakers 30 or fewer, the longest 2% or less of the total length. Lips with fleshy expansions, the greatest anterior-posterior length of the lower lip being 1/2 or more the eye diameter.

go to choice 4

2A (1A) Mouth inferior and lower lip with small but distinct fleshy expansions. Longest anterior dorsal rays 4 or more times the length of the shortest dorsal rays.

quillback, *Carpiodes cyprinus* page 116

2B No fleshy expansions of lips. Longest anterior dorsal rays 3 or fewer times the length of the shortest dorsal rays.

go to choice 3

3A (2B) Mouth nearly terminal and oblique. Anterior tip of upper jaw about at same level as the lower margin of the eye.

bigmouth buffalo, *Ictiobus cyprinellus* page 123

3B Mouth inferior, overhung by snout, and nearly horizontal. Anterior tip of upper jaw well below level of lower margin of eye.

smallmouth buffalo, *Ictiobus bubalus* page 122

OTTER TAIL RIVER (RED RIVER DRAINAGE), USA

SUCKERS, FAMILY CATOSTOMIDAE

4A (1B) Fifty-one or fewer scales in lateral line, and scales not notably smaller or crowded on body anterior to dorsal fin. Lips plicate, with longitudinal and often transverse folds, or papillose (hog sucker only) (see Diagram 1).

go to choice 5

4B Fifty-three or more scales in lateral line, and scales anterior to the dorsal fin smaller and more crowded than those on caudal peduncle. Lips always papillose. Margin of dorsal fin straight on our species.

genus *Catostomus*, go to choice 9

DIAGRAM 1

PLICATE LIPS   PAPILLOSE LIPS

5A (4A) Lips papillose. Top of head between eyes is concave. Body marked with a series of 4–6 dark blotches.

northern hog sucker, *Hypentelium nigricans* **page 121**
OTTER TAIL RIVER (RED RIVER DRAINAGE), USA

5B Lips plicate, body colour uniform, without dark blotches.

redhorses, genus *Moxostoma*, go to choice 6

6A (5B) Sixteen scales around caudal peduncle. Lips have longitudinal folds only, no transverse folds. Margin of dorsal fin rounded. Rear margin of lower lip makes a shallow, forward-pointing V.

greater redhorse, *Moxostoma valenciennesi* **page 129**
SHEYENNE RIVER, USA

6B Eleven to 14 scales around caudal peduncle. Lower lip has transverse folds as well as longitudinal folds.

go to choice 7

7A (6B) Dorsal rays usually 15 or more (rarely 14). Lower lip thin, its rear margin forming a deep, forward-pointing V (see Diagram 2). Margin of dorsal fin rounded. Head long, its length contained 3.5 or fewer times in standard length.

silver redhorse, *Moxostoma anisurum* **page 124**

DIAGRAM 2

SILVER REDHORSE LIPS

7B Dorsal rays 14 or fewer. Lower lip thicker, its rear margin nearly straight, or forming a shallow, forward-pointing V. Margin of dorsal fin falcate. Head shorter, its length 1/4 or less (usually 1/5 or less) the standard length.

go to choice 8

8A (7B) Rear margin of lower lip straight, or nearly so (see Diagram 3). Caudal fin red in life.
shorthead redhorse, *Moxostoma macrolepidotum* page 127

DIAGRAM 3

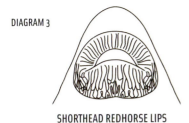

SHORTHEAD REDHORSE LIPS

8B Rear margin of lower lip forming a shallow, forward-pointing V (see Diagram 4). Caudal fin yellow in life.
golden redhorse, *Moxostoma erythrurum* page 126

DIAGRAM 4

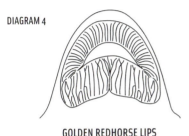

GOLDEN REDHORSE LIPS

9A (4B) More than 90 lateral line scales. Snout projects beyond upper lip by a distance greater than the thickness of the upper lip.
longnose sucker, *Catostomus catostomus* page 118

9B Fewer than 74 lateral line scales. Snout projects beyond upper lip only by a distance equal to or (usually) less than the thickness of the upper lip.
white sucker, *Catostomus commersoni* page 119

SUCKERS, FAMILY CATOSTOMIDAE

QUILLBACK; COUETTE *Carpiodes cyprinus*

FRESH SPECIMEN
5 CM

IDENTIFICATION

The quillback is a **deep-bodied, compressed** sucker with **large scales**, which **resembles the carp, goldfish, and bigmouth buffalo**. It differs from the carp and goldfish by the **dorsal and anal fins not having a spine at their leading edges**, the **mouth being on the underside of the snout**, and **small, fleshy expansions on the lower lip**. It differs from the carp by **lacking barbels** on the upper jaw. It differs from all buffalo in that there are **small, fleshy expansions on the lower lip**, and the **longest anterior dorsal rays are four or more times longer than the shortest**, rather than being three or fewer times longer in the buffaloes.

DISTRIBUTION IN MANITOBA

The quillback is restricted to southern Manitoba, where it is found in the Red and Assiniboine rivers and their larger tributaries, the Winnipeg River below the Pine Falls Dam, and lakes Winnipeg, Manitoba, Winnipegosis, and Dauphin, and the lower reaches of their tributaries.

BIOLOGICAL NOTES

The information reported below is from Parker's (1987) study of quillback biology in Lake Dauphin, Manitoba.

DISTRIBUTION WITHIN MANITOBA
- Continuous range of native species
- Known occurrences

SPAWNING: Quillback in Lake Dauphin ascended the Ochre River to spawn in mid- to late April, when water temperatures reached 5°–6°C. They moved as far as 32 km upstream during years with high discharge and only 2–3 km during years in which discharges were lower. Spent fish migrated downstream between mid-May and early June, with movements in both directions correlated with stream discharge. Spawning occurred over coarse to fine gravel in riffles during high discharge periods and moved to deeper water with sand substrate as water levels declined. The eggs are broadcast over the substrate.

GROWTH AND ADULT SIZE: Female quillback mature at six to eight years old, at a minimum fork length of 345 mm, and males mature at four to six years old, at a minimum fork length of 280 mm. The maximum size and age for females was 548 mm and age 46, and, for males, 463 mm and 52 years. Two large, mature quillback from Lake Dauphin in the University of Manitoba collection measured 443 and 485 mm total length.

FEEDING: Quillback are benthic, small-particle feeders, feeding mainly on chironomid larvae, ostracods, cladocerans, and copepods.

HABITAT: In Manitoba, both juvenile and adult quillback live in turbid water, in lakes and larger streams. Except as noted for spawning, they prefer low water velocities and sand to silt substrates.

ECOLOGICAL ROLE: Quillback are second-level consumers at all life-history stages. Their relatively slow growth rate would make them available as forage species for piscivores for the first and possibly second year of life. Uniquely among North American native freshwater fishes, the suckers collectively are moderate- to large-sized fish that feed at a low level in the food web. In that respect, they have an ecological resemblance to many Eurasian carps such as common carp and grass carp. The carps, however, are rapid growers and some have spines in their dorsal and anal fins. Because of this, the carps are available to most piscivores only for the first few months of their lives. If the introduction and spread of an increasing number of species of Eurasian carps into North America continue, it might be expected that there will be a significant negative impact on the distribution, abundance, and diversity of all suckers in areas where the Eurasian carps become established. Because of the abundance of suckers and their low position in the food web, this will likely have cascading effects on nearly all aquatic communities in North America.

IMPORTANCE TO PEOPLE

Quillback are of no importance as food fish in Manitoba. Their flesh is firm and white, but filled with multi-branched intermuscular bones, making preparation as food tedious at best. Occasionally they are caught by anglers who often mistake them for the common carp. Commercial fishers on lakes Winnipeg and Manitoba recognize them, but they are part of the bycatch in commercial fisheries, with no commercial value. Ecologically, their feeding habits place them as first- or second-level consumers. Because of their feeding habits, this species and the bigmouth buffalo may be affected by the spread of Eurasian carps, especially the silver carp (*Hypophthalmichthys molitrix*) and bighead carp (*Aristichthys nobilis*), should these exotic species reach Manitoba.

COSEWIC Status as of January 1, 2004: Not Listed
MBESA Status as of January 1, 2004: Not Listed
MBCDC Status as of January 1, 2004: G5, S5

SUCKERS, FAMILY CATOSTOMIDAE

LONGNOSE SUCKER; MEUNIER ROUGE — *Catostomus catostomus*

FRESH SPECIMEN

IDENTIFICATION

The longnose sucker is a **terete, small-scaled** sucker with a **short dorsal fin** and **large, fleshy, papillose lips**. It is most similar to the white sucker, from which it differs in having **more than 90 lateral line scales** and in the **long snout, which projects beyond the upper lip by a distance greater than the thickness of the upper lip**.

DISTRIBUTION IN MANITOBA

The longnose sucker is found in most lakes and rivers from Lake Winnipeg northward in Manitoba. It is absent from the prairie/aspen parkland portion of Manitoba, including lakes Manitoba and Dauphin, and the Red and Assiniboine river watersheds. It is present but uncommon in Lake Winnipegosis (Derksen, pers. comm., 2003). The longnose sucker occurs in every province and territory of Canada except Prince Edward Island, Nova Scotia, and Newfoundland.

BIOLOGICAL NOTES

There is no information on this species specific for Manitoba. Scott and Crossman (1979) summarize the life history based on reports from Great Slave Lake and British Columbia.

SPAWNING: Longnose suckers begin their spawning migration between mid-April and mid-May, at water temperatures of 5°C or higher. Where they occur together, longnose suckers spawn earlier than white suckers. Most commonly, they ascend streams and spawn over gravel in riffles with water velocities of 30–45 cm/s, but lake spawning is also known. The adhesive eggs are scattered over the gravel in small clusters.

GROWTH AND ADULT SIZE: Longnose suckers grow to a maximum of 642 mm fork length, and females have a larger average size than males (Scott and Crossman, 1979). The size at maturity varies greatly among locations, with lake-dwelling fish growing larger than stream dwellers. Ages up to 19 years are reported, but they are based on scales, which are unreliable for aging suckers (Scott and Crossman). Large longnose suckers in the University of Manitoba collection, from several locations in Manitoba, range from 403–488 mm total length.

SUCKERS, FAMILY CATOSTOMIDAE

FEEDING: Longnose suckers feed on bottom-dwelling invertebrates and some plant material. A variety of invertebrates, ranging in size from caddis fly larvae and small bivalve molluscs down to copepods, are eaten.

HABITAT: Longnose suckers live in both lakes and flowing water, but tend not to be found in smaller streams except when spawning.

ECOLOGICAL ROLE: Longnose suckers are first- and second-level benthic consumers. They are an important forage species for large piscivores such as northern pike and lake trout.

IMPORTANCE TO PEOPLE

Longnose suckers are of minor importance as commercial fish in Manitoba, being marketed, along with white sucker and the redhorse species, as "mullet." Spawning fish are also dipnetted and canned. Their flesh is firm, white, and flaky, and of good flavour. The intermuscular bones are mostly from the anal fin rearward, so nearly bone-free fillets can be prepared if the rear part of the body is not used.

Ecologically, like most suckers, they are first- and second-level consumers. As such, they are an important link in the aquatic food chain wherever they are found. Young longnose suckers can be abundant, and they remain small enough to be important as prey for larger predatory fish for at least their first one or two years.

COSEWIC Status as of January 1, 2004: Not Listed
MBESA Status as of January 1, 2004: Not Listed
MBCDC Status as of January 1, 2004: G5, S5

WHITE SUCKER; MEUNIER NOIR | *Catostomus commersoni*

5 CM   FRESH SPECIMEN

IDENTIFICATION

The white sucker is a **terete, small-scaled** sucker with a **short dorsal fin** and **fleshy, papillose lips**. It differs from the longnose sucker in having **fewer than 74 scales in the lateral line** and in having a **shorter snout**, which **projects beyond the upper lip only by a distance equal to or less than the thickness of the upper lip**.

DISTRIBUTION IN MANITOBA

The white sucker is found in all our streams, rivers, and lakes, except for the Seal and Thlewiaza watersheds. This species, the northern pike, the burbot, and the troutperch are our most widely distributed fishes.

BIOLOGICAL NOTES

SPAWNING: White suckers are usually stream spawners, but lake spawning also occurs. In southern Manitoba, they are among the early spawning species and begin running into streams in mid- to late April. White sucker spawning may be protracted, however. Derksen (pers. comm., 2003) found spawning white suckers in June in the Whitemud River. Where they occur with longnose suckers, they spawn a little later, at water temperatures of 10°C or above (Scott and Crossman, 1979). Spawning is usually over a gravel substrate, but can vary from sand to boulders. Water velocities can vary from still to rapids. The adhesive eggs are broadcast over the bottom and may drift with the current before adhering to the substrate.

SUCKERS, FAMILY CATOSTOMIDAE

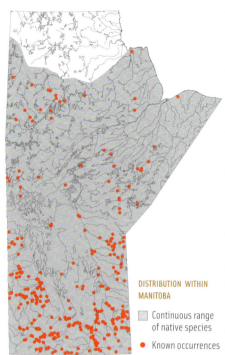

DISTRIBUTION WITHIN MANITOBA

☐ Continuous range of native species
● Known occurrences

GROWTH AND ADULT SIZE: The growth rate of white suckers varies widely, with lacustrine fish growing larger than riverine fish. In Manitoba, there appear to be slow-growing resident headwater populations of white suckers in some of our streams. We have observed these in the Brokenhead River, a Lake Winnipeg tributary, south of Provincial Highway 15; the Cypress River south of Provincial Highway 2; and Franzin (pers. comm., 2000) has observed them in Roseisle Creek, a tributary of the Red River. These fish retain throughout their life the three dark blotches on the sides that are characteristic of juvenile white suckers. Females with nearly mature eggs in these populations are only 200–250 mm long. These dwarfed white suckers are one of the eight species of fishes associated with bog habitats in headwater streams and ponds in Manitoba. See the pearl dace species account for a complete list and additional comments.

FEEDING: Like most other suckers, the white sucker feeds on benthic invertebrates.

HABITAT: White suckers are found in lakes, ponds, bogs, streams, and large rivers. They are benthic and can be found on a variety of substrates, but most commonly over sand, silt, and mud substrates. Valiant (1975) found the white sucker to be most strongly associated with pools located below riffles (0–15 cm/s water velocity, depth 35–100 cm, and gravel substrate) in five Manitoba Escarpment streams.

ECOLOGICAL ROLE: The white sucker is a first- and second-level, benthic consumer. Their abundance, wide distribution, and broad habitat usage make them probably the most important single species at this level in Manitoba. Because they are usually abundant, young white suckers are an important forage species for predatory fish.

IMPORTANCE TO PEOPLE

White suckers are the most common sucker in the commercial fishery and are marketed with other sucker species as "mullet." Since about 1960, the white sucker has been an important commercial fish in Lake Winnipegosis. The flesh is ground and formed into fish cakes (Derksen, pers. comm., 2002).

White suckers are dipnetted from spawning runs, and are canned or smoked. They are also a frequent, if usually unintentional, angler catch. The flesh is firm, white, and flaky, and of good flavour. Like the longnose sucker, the majority of intermuscular bones are concentrated in the caudal peduncle, making it practical to prepare relatively bone-free fillets from them.

Probably the greatest importance of the white sucker lies in its value as a forage species for game and commercial fish. This species, along with the emerald shiner and spottail shiner, is probably the most abundant forage fish in most of our lakes and streams.

COSEWIC Status as of January 1, 2004: Not Listed
MBESA Status as of January 1, 2004: Not Listed
MBCDC Status as of January 1, 2004: G5. S5

SUCKERS, FAMILY CATOSTOMIDAE

| NORTHERN HOG SUCKER; MEUNIER À TÊTE CARRÉE | *Hypentelium nigricans* |

NOTE: Not found in Manitoba; Red River watershed, Minnesota

2 CM   FRESH SPECIMEN

IDENTIFICATION
The northern hog sucker is the only sucker in the Hudson Bay Drainage that combines: (1) a **terete body** shape; (2) **fewer than 51 scales in the lateral line**; (3) **papillose lips**; and (4) the **top of the head between the eyes being concave**.

DISTRIBUTION IN MANITOBA
The northern hog sucker has not been found in Manitoba. It is found in the Ottertail River in Minnesota.

BIOLOGICAL NOTES
SPAWNING: Becker (1983) notes that northern hog suckers in Wisconsin spawn in April and May. Spawning is in riffles, and, although no nest is built, males clean an area of gravel and defend it against other males. This is the only evidence of territoriality among spawning suckers in the Hudson Bay Drainage. The eggs are not adhesive and are broadcast over the substrate.

GROWTH AND ADULT SIZE: The northern hog sucker is the smallest sucker species in the Hudson Bay Drainage. Females grow larger and live longer than males. Large adults seldom exceed 300 mm fork length.

FEEDING: Northern hog suckers feed on aquatic insect larvae and crustaceans. They are reported to feed in fast water, on rocky substrate, and use their head to push or roll stones aside to expose food beneath them (Scott and Crossman, 1979). Some mollusks and vegetation are also taken.

HABITAT: Northern hog suckers are strong swimmers and have streamlined bodies. They are found in fast water, often with brook lampreys, brook trout, stonerollers, and western blacknose dace.

ECOLOGICAL ROLE: The northern hog sucker is a second-level, benthic consumer. Because they remain small throughout life and can be abundant, they are important forage fish. Becker (1983) also notes that by turning over stones during feeding, they dislodge invertebrates that are then available to other fish as food.

IMPORTANCE TO PEOPLE
Where they occur, northern hog suckers are used as live bait for larger game fish such as northern pike and largemouth bass.

COSEWIC Status as of January 1, 2004: Not Listed
MBESA Status as of January 1, 2004: Not Listed
MBCDC Status as of January 1, 2004: G5, SP

SMALLMOUTH BUFFALO; BUFFALO À PETITE BOUCHE | *Ictiobus bubalus*

NOTE: Not found in Manitoba; Red River watershed, Minnesota

10 CM — FRESH SPECIMEN

IDENTIFICATION

The smallmouth buffalo is a **deep-bodied, robust, large-scaled** sucker with a **long dorsal fin**. It is distinguished from the quillback by **lacking any fleshy expansions of the lower lips** and by having the **longest anterior dorsal ray only about three times as long as the shortest dorsal rays**. It differs from the bigmouth buffalo in having the **mouth on the underside of the snout and not oblique**.

DISTRIBUTION IN MANITOBA

The smallmouth buffalo has not been found in Manitoba. It occurs in the Ottertail River in Minnesota.

BIOLOGICAL NOTES

SPAWNING: Becker (1983) reports that smallmouth buffalo in Wisconsin spawn from April to early June. Like the bigmouth buffalo, spawning is in vegetation in marshes or on flooded stream banks.

GROWTH AND ADULT SIZE: Smallmouth buffalo grow to a maximum reported age and size of 15 years and 15.9 kg.

FEEDING: As with the bigmouth buffalo, smallmouth buffalo are plankton feeders. The position of their mouth would suggest bottom feeding, but the food data reported by Becker (1983) do not support this.

HABITAT: The smallmouth buffalo prefers large rivers, where it is found in deeper waters, backwater ponds, and oxbow lakes. It prefers clear water.

ECOLOGICAL ROLE: The smallmouth buffalo is a benthic to midwater zooplanktivore.

IMPORTANCE TO PEOPLE

Where it occurs, the smallmouth buffalo is an important commercial species. It is also used in aquaculture in many areas of the United States. Like the bigmouth buffalo, its rapid early growth and robust shape apparently reduce its availability as prey for game fish.

COSEWIC Status as of January 1, 2002: Not Listed
MBESA Status as of January 1, 2002: Not Listed
MBCDC Status as of January 1, 2002: Not Listed

SUCKERS, FAMILY CATOSTOMIDAE

BIGMOUTH BUFFALO; BUFFALO À GRANDE BOUCHE | *Ictiobus cyprinellus*

FRESH SPECIMEN
10 CM

IDENTIFICATION

The bigmouth buffalo is a **robust, deep-bodied, large-scaled sucker** with a long dorsal fin, similar to the quillback, carp, and goldfish. It differs from the carp and goldfish by **lacking spines at the front of the dorsal and anal fins**, and from the carp in **lacking two barbels on each side of the upper jaw**. It differs from the quillback in having a **terminal mouth that lacks fleshy expansions of the lips**, and in having the **anterior dorsal rays three or fewer times longer than the posterior rays**. It differs from the smallmouth buffalo in having a **terminal, oblique mouth**.

DISTRIBUTION IN MANITOBA

The bigmouth buffalo is found mainly in the Red River and lowermost reaches of its tributaries and the Assiniboine River downstream of Portage la Prairie. Since the opening of the Assiniboine River Floodway, it has been collected occasionally in Delta Marsh, at the south end of Lake Manitoba (Stewart, Suthers, and Leavesley, 1985). There is an unconfirmed report of a bigmouth buffalo being caught in Lake Dauphin in 2002 (Derksen, pers. comm., 2003). A single specimen has been collected in the Icelandic River, which enters the south basin of Lake Winnipeg near Riverton. This species has either increased markedly in abundance since the mid-1980s, or the increasing use of electrofishing to sample our larger rivers has collected it more efficiently than the gillnets and seines used before.

DISTRIBUTION WITHIN MANITOBA
☐ Continuous range of native species
● Known occurrences

BIOLOGICAL NOTES

SPAWNING: Johnson (1963) reported that bigmouth buffalo in Saskatchewan spawn from mid-May to early June. Spawning occurs in shallow water, in marshes, or flooded riverbanks, or lakeshores. The adhesive eggs are scattered over vegetation. Apparently, high water events are required for spawning. In the Red River, underyearling bigmouth buffalo appear in early to mid-July.

GROWTH AND ADULT SIZE: Bigmouth buffalo grow to a larger size than any other sucker native to Canada. The largest individual in Johnson's (1963) age and growth series from Saskatchewan had a fork length of 696 mm and its scale age was 20 years. Scale ages older than ten years are not reliable in this species, however. Preserved specimens in the University of Manitoba collection, from Delta Marsh and the Red River, range from 358–690 mm total length.

FEEDING: The bigmouth buffalo will feed in midwater on plankton, which it filters from the water with its long, closely spaced gill rakers. It also can feed on the bottom, again using its gill rakers to filter minute organisms from the material it picks up. Planktonic and benthic cladocera and copepods, as well as chironomid larvae, are among the most frequent food items.

HABITAT: Bigmouth buffalo prefer still or slow-moving waters of large rivers or lakes.

ECOLOGICAL ROLE: The bigmouth buffalo is a second-level, benthic and pelagic consumer. Much of its diet consists of planktonic crustacea, but small benthic crustacea and insect larvae are also taken. Like the quillback, this species would be vulnerable to competition with bighead and silver carp, should either of these Asian carps reach Manitoba. Because their spawning habitat is used both for spawning and feeding by the common carp, the bigmouth buffalo may have been affected by that species already.

IMPORTANCE TO PEOPLE

The bigmouth buffalo is not common enough in Manitoba to sustain any economic exploitation. It is rarely caught by anglers and often misidentified as a carp when it is. There is a small commercial fishery for them in the Qu'Appelle Lakes in Saskatchewan, with the catch being exported to the United States.

COSEWIC Status as of January 1, 2004: Special Concern
MBESA Status as of January 1, 2004: Special Concern
MBCDC Status as of January 1, 2004: G5, S4

SILVER REDHORSE; CHEVALIER BLANC | *Moxostoma anisurum*

FRESH SPECIMEN

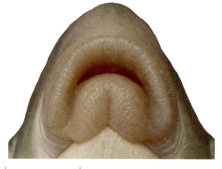

FRESH SPECIMEN, VENTRAL VIEW OF MOUTH

IDENTIFICATION

The silver redhorse is a **terete, large-scaled** sucker with a **short dorsal fin**. It can be distinguished from the longnose and white suckers by the **large scales, with fewer than 50 scales in the lateral line**, and by the **fleshy lips, which have only folds, not papillae**. It is distinguished from the golden and shorthead redhorses by the **thin lower lip, which forms a deep, forward-pointing V, and by the rounded margin of the dorsal fin, which has 15 or more dorsal fin rays**.

DISTRIBUTION IN MANITOBA

The silver redhorse is found in the larger streams of the Red, Assiniboine, Souris, and Winnipeg river watersheds

SUCKERS, FAMILY CATOSTOMIDAE

SILVER REDHORSE; CHEVALIER BLANC

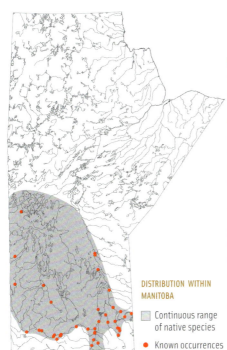

DISTRIBUTION WITHIN MANITOBA

▨ Continuous range of native species
● Known occurrences

in southern Manitoba, as well as all the Manitoba Great Lakes. It extends northwestward into the Saskatchewan River, but otherwise is not found north of Lake Winnipeg.

BIOLOGICAL NOTES

SPAWNING: We have no data on silver redhorse spawning in Manitoba. Becker (1983) notes that in Wisconsin, they spawn just after the spawning peak of the shorthead redhorse, which Harbicht (1990) reported to extend over most of May in the Ochre River, a tributary of Dauphin Lake. If the timing relationship holds true here, silver redhorse ought to spawn in late May or early June in southern Manitoba. Becker reports that they spawn over gravel to rubble substrates in 30–90 cm of water, in the main channel of the stream.

GROWTH AND ADULT SIZE: The silver redhorse grows to a larger size than our other two redhorse species. The only large adult silver redhorse in the University of Manitoba collection is from the Red River and is 518 mm total length. The largest specimen sampled in the Winnipeg River had a fork length of 548 mm.

FEEDING: The diet of the silver redhorse is similar to that of our other two redhorses. Aquatic insect larvae and small crustaceans are the most common foods. Small fish and crayfish are seen occasionally in the stomachs of larger fish.

HABITAT: Silver redhorse are primarily river fish in Manitoba, and typically are found in deeper, lower velocity water, over finer grained substrates, than shorthead redhorse.

ECOLOGICAL ROLE: The silver redhorse is a second- and third-level consumer, which, like other redhorses, takes some larger predatory invertebrates such as crayfish. Unlike the bigmouth buffalo, young silver redhorse remain small enough to be prey for larger predatory fish for at least their first year.

IMPORTANCE TO PEOPLE

The silver redhorse is of minor importance in the commercial fishery, being marketed collectively with other suckers as "mullet." Unlike the white and longnose suckers, spawners are not dipnetted for use as food. Its tendency to remain in deep water and avoid tributaries likely makes it inaccessible to dipnetters. It is a common but usually unintentional catch by anglers fishing on the bottom with natural baits in the rivers in which it occurs.

COSEWIC Status as of January 1, 2004: Not Listed
MBESA Status as of January 1, 2004: Not Listed
MBCDC Status as of January 1, 2004: G5, S5

SUCKERS, FAMILY CATOSTOMIDAE

GOLDEN REDHORSE; CHEVALIER DORÉ — *Moxostoma erythrurum*

FRESH SPECIMEN

FRESH SPECIMEN, VENTRAL VIEW OF MOUTH

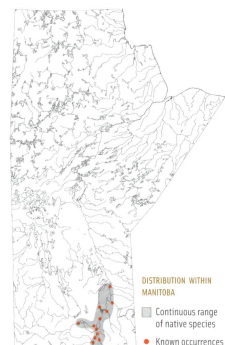

DISTRIBUTION WITHIN MANITOBA

- Continuous range of native species
- Known occurrences

IDENTIFICATION

The golden redhorse is a **terete, large-scaled** sucker with a **short dorsal fin**. Its overall appearance is more similar to the silver redhorse than the shorthead redhorse. It differs from the silver redhorse in having **14 or fewer rays in the dorsal fin**, the **margin of the dorsal fin being straight or falcate**, the **lower lip being more enlarged, with the rear margin forming a shallow, forward-pointing V**, and **the caudal fin being yellow in life**. It differs from the shorthead redhorse in having the **rear margin of the lower lip forming a shallow, forward-pointing V** instead of being straight, and in the **caudal fin being yellow**, not red, in life.

DISTRIBUTION IN MANITOBA

The golden redhorse was first found in Manitoba in 1985 (Franzin, Parker, and Harbicht, 1986). It is known from the Red River, the Roseau River upstream to Dominion City, the Brokenhead River downstream of Provincial Highway 12, the Rat River upstream to St. Pierre-Jolys, the Assiniboine River west to below the Assiniboine Floodway Control Structure at Portage la Prairie, the Winnipeg River below the Pine Falls Dam, one location on the west shore of the south basin of Lake Winnipeg, and the Manigotagan River on the east side of Lake Winnipeg.

BIOLOGICAL NOTES

SPAWNING: Nothing is known about the biology of the golden redhorse in Manitoba. Becker (1983) reported that they spawn in late May in Wisconsin. Spawning is in fast water (riffles and runs) in water between 30 cm–1 m deep, over coarse gravel. Usually spawning is in the main channel of the stream, as in the silver redhorse, but they sometimes ascend nearby tributaries.

GROWTH AND ADULT SIZE: Adult golden redhorse in Manitoba are between adult silver redhorse (larger) and adult shorthead redhorse (smaller) in size. Two large, preserved specimens from the Red River, in the University of Manitoba collection, are 362 and 413 mm total length.

FEEDING: As with the silver and shorthead redhorses, the food of the golden redhorse consists mainly of aquatic insect larvae, with some filamentous algae and occasional small bivalve molluscs. Becker (1983) does not report any crustaceans in the diet of the golden redhorse, unlike silver and shorthead redhorses.

HABITAT: Although the golden redhorse has a much more restricted distribution in Manitoba than the silver redhorse, it is found in closely similar habitat. It is most frequently collected in the mid-channel region of larger streams, in water over 1 m deep, over finer grained sediments ranging from fine sand to silt and clay.

ECOLOGICAL ROLE: The golden redhorse is a second-level consumer. Its low abundance, however, suggests that it has little importance as a prey species. It adds species and ecological diversity at a low level in the aquatic food chain, and this would enhance the resilience and stability of aquatic communities in which it is found.

IMPORTANCE TO PEOPLE

The golden redhorse is too uncommon and restricted in distribution to have any importance as a commercial, subsistence, or recreational fish in Manitoba.

COSEWIC Status as of January 1, 2004: Not at Risk
MBESA Status as of January 1, 2004: Not Listed
MBCDC Status as of January 1, 2004: G5, S4

SHORTHEAD REDHORSE; CHEVALIER ROUGE | *Moxostoma macrolepidotum*

5 CM — FRESH SPECIMEN

2 CM — FRESH SPECIMEN, VENTRAL VIEW OF MOUTH

IDENTIFICATION

The shorthead redhorse has a **terete body shape, large scales**, and a **short dorsal fin**. Unlike the other three redhorses in the Hudson Bay Drainage, the **rear margin of the lower lip is straight or slightly convex in life**, rather than indented into a forward-pointing V. The **caudal fin is red** in life.

DISTRIBUTION IN MANITOBA

The shorthead redhorse is found in lakes, larger streams, and rivers throughout southern and central Manitoba, north into the Nelson, Hayes, and Saskatchewan rivers. It has been taken in the Nelson River to just downstream from the Limestone Dam.

BIOLOGICAL NOTES

SPAWNING: Harbicht (1990) found that shorthead redhorse in Lake Dauphin began their upstream spawning migration into the Ochre River in late April or early May, when water temperatures had reached 8°–10°C. Both upstream and

SUCKERS, FAMILY CATOSTOMIDAE

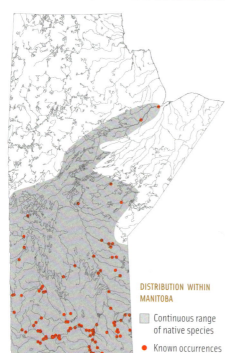

DISTRIBUTION WITHIN MANITOBA

☐ Continuous range of native species
● Known occurrences

downstream movements were positively correlated with stream discharge, and they moved up to 32 km upstream from Lake Dauphin. Spawning activity was first observed from May 1 to May 25 and ended from June 10 to June 20, at water temperatures from 10°–18°C. He reported that spawning was done in riffles with velocities from 30–70 cm/s, over substrates ranging from fine sand to cobble with scattered boulders. The eggs were broadcast over the substrate. Ripe and running male and female shorthead redhorse have been observed in the Winnipeg River above Pointe du Bois in early July.

GROWTH AND ADULT SIZE: Harbicht (1990) found that both sexes matured as young as Age III, and all individuals were mature by Age V. The mean fork length of mature female shorthead redhorse in Lake Dauphin varied from 353.5–375.6 mm, and for males it varied from 323.0–338.2 mm. The maximum age was 14 years for both sexes, and maximum fork length was 505 mm for a female and 474 mm for a male. A 510 mm fork length specimen has been collected from the Winnipeg River.

FEEDING: Shorthead redhorse feed mainly on aquatic insect larvae and also take bivalve molluscs.

HABITAT: In lakes, shorthead redhorse occupy nearshore areas at shallow depths. In streams, they are associated with shallow riffles and runs, over rocky substrate.

ECOLOGICAL ROLE: The shorthead redhorse is a second-level, benthic consumer. Unlike the large, robust bigmouth buffalo, young redhorses of all species are available as food to predatory fish and constitute a significant link in the food chain in their communities.

IMPORTANCE TO PEOPLE

The shorthead redhorse has minor importance as a commercial fish, being marketed collectively with other suckers as "mullet." It is a frequent but usually unintentional catch by anglers fishing on the bottom in streams, with worms or other small invertebrates as bait.

COSEWIC Status as of January 1, 2004: Not Listed
MBESA Status as of January 1, 2004: Not Listed
MBCDC Status as of January 1, 2004: G5, S5

SUCKERS, FAMILY CATOSTOMIDAE

GREATER REDHORSE; CHEVALIER JAUNE | *Moxostoma valenciennesi*

NOTE: Not found in Manitoba; Red River watershed, North Dakota

10 CM — FRESH SPECIMEN

IDENTIFICATION
The greater redhorse is a **terete, large-scaled** sucker with a **short dorsal fin**. It is most similar to the silver redhorse, from which it differs in having a **red caudal fin in life** (like the shorthead redhorse), **lacking transverse folds in the lips**, which are present on our other redhorses, and in **having 16 scales around the narrowest part of the caudal peduncle** instead of 11–14 as in our other redhorses.

DISTRIBUTION IN MANITOBA
The greater redhorse has not been found in Manitoba. It is known from the Sheyenne River in North Dakota.

BIOLOGICAL NOTES
Almost nothing is known of the biology of this species.

SPAWNING: The greater redhorse is reported to spawn from May to early July.

GROWTH AND ADULT SIZE: This is the largest redhorse, attaining weights up to 7.3 kg in Lake Ontario (Scott and Crossman, 1979).

FEEDING: There are no reports of feeding habits in this species.

HABITAT: The greater redhorse lives in both lakes and streams. It is said to prefer larger streams with clear water and sand, gravel, or boulder bottoms (Scott and Crossman, 1979).

ECOLOGICAL ROLE: The ecological role of the greater redhorse, although presumably similar to other suckers, is unknown.

IMPORTANCE TO PEOPLE
The greater redhorse is apparently never common. It has little or no commercial, subsistence, or recreational fishing importance.

COSEWIC Status as of January 1, 2004 : Not Listed
MBESA Status as of January 1, 2004 : Not Listed
MBCDC Status as of January 1, 2004: G3, SP

CATFISHES, ORDER SILURIFORMES
NORTH AMERICAN FRESHWATER CATFISHES, FAMILY ICTALURIDAE

ORDER SILURIFORMES

There are 34 families of catfishes in the world. Most catfish are tropical, but only two families are marine. Catfishes range in size from the 25 mm long, parasitic candiru (*Vandellia cirrhosa*) of South America to the 5 m long, 306 kg wels catfish, *Silurus glanis*, of Eurasia. All catfishes lack normal scales, although some may have an armour of bony plates covering the body instead of being naked. Catfishes also have spines at the leading edge of the dorsal (when present) and pectoral fins. There may be a potent venom produced by cells in the skin covering the spines. Most catfishes have barbels or "whiskers" around the mouth. Smell and taste receptors on the barbels help them locate food.

FAMILY ICTALURIDAE

The North American freshwater catfish are one of the most distinctive groups of fish in our area. They **lack scales** and there is a **strong spine at the leading edge of the dorsal fin and each pectoral fin**. There is an **adipose fin** between the dorsal fin and the tail, and there are **four pairs of barbels around the mouth**. There is a pair of **nasal barbels** on the top of the snout, a pair of **maxillary barbels** at the corners of the mouth, and two pairs of **mental barbels** on the chin. Catfish have considerable importance as recreational fish and are excellent food fish, although Manitobans usually do not eat them.

If catfish are not **handled carefully**, their **dorsal and pectoral spines can inflict a painful wound**. Spine pricks from juveniles of all our species except the tadpole madtom seem to be more painful than those inflicted by adults. **In the case of the tadpole madtom, the venom associated with the spines of all individuals causes intense pain and local irritation, comparable with a wasp sting, which may last for several hours.** This small catfish and the short-tailed shrew, a mammal, are the only venomous vertebrates in Manitoba.

CATFISHES, FAMILY ICTALURIDAE

KEY TO THE CATFISH FOUND IN MANITOBA AND ADJACENT AREAS OF THE HUDSON BAY DRAINAGE

1A Adipose fin forming a long, low ridge, either continuous with the dorsal edge of the caudal fin, or separated from it by a notch. Ten or fewer gill rakers.

genus *Noturus* / go to choice 2

1B Adipose fin shorter, forming a distinct tab with a free posterior end, and well separated from the caudal fin. Eleven or more gill rakers.

go to choice 3

2A (1A) Posterior margin of caudal fin nearly straight, and upper and lower edges of caudal fin light-coloured. Premaxillary tooth patch with posterior extensions at each end. A crescent-shaped pale patch on back just behind dorsal fin. Adipose fin separated from caudal fin by a notch.

stonecat, *Noturus flavus* page 140

2B Posterior margin of caudal fin rounded, and caudal fin uniformly dark-coloured. No posterior extensions at ends of premaxillary tooth patches. No pale patch on back. Adipose fin continuous with caudal fin.

tadpole madtom, *Noturus gyrinus* page 142

3A (1B) Caudal fin deeply forked. Colour in life grey above, fading to white or pinkish below. Fish up to about 45 cm usually have black spots scattered on back and sides, and have a bony ridge on the back between the back of the skull and the dorsal fin. Both these features become indistinct or are lost in larger fish.

channel catfish, *Ictalurus punctatus* page 137

3B Posterior margin of caudal fin slightly rounded, straight or slightly indented, but not deeply forked. Colour in life varies from dark olive or almost black above in young, to brownish or even yellowish brown above in adult fish, fading in all cases to yellowish or white below. Back and sides may be mottled, but no black spots.

genus *Ameiurus* / go to choice 4

4A (3B) Twenty-four to 27 anal rays. Chin barbels whitish. Posterior margin of caudal fin rounded.

yellow bullhead, *Ameiurus natalis* page 134
BOIS DE SIOUX, OTTERTAIL, AND ROSEAU WATERSHEDS, USA

4B Fifteen to 24 anal rays. Chin barbels grey to black. Posterior margin of caudal fin more or less straight to slightly indented.

go to choice 5

5A (4B) Fourteen or fewer short gill rakers on first arch. Median notch in anterior margin of supraethmoid bone about as deep as wide (see Diagram 1). Colour brown to yellowish brown, with darker mottling, especially in larger fish. Fin membranes between rays of caudal and anal fins about same colour as fin rays, and no indistinct pale bar at base of caudal fin.

brown bullhead, *Ameiurus nebulosus* page 135

5B Fifteen or more, longer gill rakers on first arch. Median notch in anterior margin of supraethmoid bone at least twice as wide as deep (see Diagram 2). Colour olive green to brown, usually without mottling. Fin membranes between rays of caudal and anal fins black, and notably contrasting with paler rays. An indistinct pale bar at base of caudal fin.

black bullhead, *Ameiurus melas* page 132

DIAGRAM 1   **DIAGRAM 2**

CATFISHES, FAMILY ICTALURIDAE

FRESH SPECIMEN

Note: The **flathead catfish**, *Pylodictis olivaris*, differs from the channel catfish and both bullheads by having the **lower jaw projecting beyond the upper jaw**, and the **head flattened**, so that the greatest depth at the back of the skull is less than 1/2 the head length. The flathead catfish has not been collected in the Hudson Bay Drainage, but it is included here because of persistent angler reports of large (over 5 kg) "bullheads" from the Red River. Most anglers in southern Manitoba can identify the channel catfish and would not confuse it with a bullhead. Flathead catfish resemble bullheads, but grow to large size.

BLACK BULLHEAD; BARBOTTE NOIRE | *Ameiurus melas*

FRESH SPECIMEN

IDENTIFICATION

The bullheads (*Ameiurus*) can be distinguished from the channel catfish by **not having a forked tail**. The bullheads in our area also **lack black spots**. They differ from the madtoms (*Noturus*) by the **rear margin of the adipose fin being free from the body** instead of the adipose fin continuing as a ridge to the anterior dorsal edge of the tail. The black bullhead has **black pigment on the fin membranes between the fin rays of the anal and caudal fins**. There is an **indistinct pale bar at the base of the caudal fin**. The **rear margin of the caudal fin is straight or slightly indented**. The black bullhead **almost always lacks dark mottling on the back and sides**, whereas most brown bullheads have mottling. **In cold water**, during early spring and late fall, **both species fade to brownish green above, greenish yellow on the sides, and yellow below**, and **mottling may disappear**. The anal fin has **15–19 rays**. The **barbels on the chin are black**. The black bullhead also has **15–20** relatively **long, slender, pointed gill rakers on the first arch**, and the **anterior margin of the supraethmoid has a shallow, median indentation at least twice as wide as deep**. *Note:* The presence or absence of barbs on the rear margin of the pectoral spines is not useful in identifying the bullhead species in our area.

CATFISHES, FAMILY ICTALURIDAE

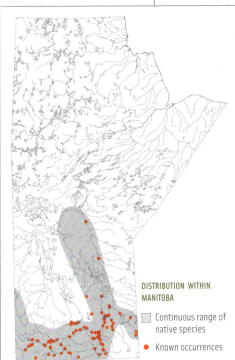

DISTRIBUTION WITHIN MANITOBA
- Continuous range of native species
- Known occurrences

DISTRIBUTION IN MANITOBA

The black bullhead is found throughout the Red and Assiniboine river watersheds; in the Winnipeg River mainstem at least upstream to Ryerson Creek, near the Ontario border; and in the Whiteshell River upstream to Lyons Lake. It is present in Lake Winnipeg north at least to the Mukutawa River and had reached Lake Manitoba by 1974, following the first operation of the Assiniboine River Floodway in the spring of 1970. Prior to 1970, there is only one record of a catfish from Lake Manitoba (Stewart, Suthers, and Leavesley, 1985). See the channel catfish species account for a discussion of the Fairford River/Lake St. Martin/Dauphin River as a possible route for catfish to reach Lake Manitoba from Lake Winnipeg. *Note*: Bullheads (species not identified) were reported in 2002 from Lake Winnipegosis and Lake Dauphin (Derksen, pers. comm., 2003).

BIOLOGICAL NOTES

SPAWNING: Black bullhead spawning has not been observed in Manitoba. The appearance of schools of underyearlings in tributaries and marginal waters in late June and early July suggests that spawning occurs in these areas during mid- to late June. Female bullheads excavate a nest in soft substrate under cut banks, in woody debris or other cover, and mating is with a single male, which shares nest guarding and egg fanning (Becker, 1983). The parents herd the young into a dense school and accompany them for a time after they have absorbed the yolk sac and begun to swim. These schools can be seen in quiet, protected backwaters and tributaries along the Red and Assiniboine rivers and the coastal marshes of lakes Winnipeg and Manitoba during most of July and early August. In years when cool weather persists into late June, spawning may be delayed and the schools of young will persist nearly to the end of August.

GROWTH AND ADULT SIZE: Underyearling black bullheads grow to a length of 40–45 mm by late August. Adult black bullheads from Netley Creek in the University of Manitoba collection range from 221–248 mm total length. There has not been an age and growth study of the black bullhead in Manitoba. Becker (1983) reports a maximum age of five in Wisconsin, and Carlander (1969) reports a maximum age of four and maximum length of 315 mm in North Dakota. The Manitoba angling record bullhead (species not determined) is a 45 cm fish caught in Netley Creek in 1996. This was probably a brown bullhead, *Ameiurus nebulosus*, however.

FEEDING: Black bullheads are opportunistic predators and scavengers that feed mostly on the bottom. In backwater habitats, snails, leeches, and crayfish are common in their stomachs, and tadpoles of wood and leopard frogs have also been found. They also take a variety of minnows, most commonly the fathead minnow, in the storm water retention ponds in Winnipeg. Pieces of larger fish (usually freshwater drum, carp, and goldeye), apparently taken as carrion, are also found. Some of these may be anglers' baits or fish that died after being caught and released by anglers.

HABITAT: The black bullhead is found in most of the same places as the brown bullhead, but is more common in tributaries and peripheral waters such as oxbow lakes and human-made ponds than the brown bullhead. It is less common than the brown bullhead in current and in deep water in river mainstems. It is mainly benthic, over fine substrates such as mud and silt in depths of 2 m or less.

ECOLOGICAL ROLE: The black bullhead is a benthopelagic, middle- to upper-level consumer and scavenger. It is eaten infrequently by northern pike, channel catfish, and freshwater drum. Its abundance in tributaries and peripheral waters makes it an important component of the food web in these habitats.

IMPORTANCE TO PEOPLE

The black bullhead is easily caught in numbers by anglers fishing with even the most basic tackle. It is readily accessible to anglers fishing from shore in our rivers, oxbow lakes, retention ponds, and tributary streams. This species, the brown bullhead, and the freshwater drum are probably the most frequent first fish caught by young anglers introduced to fishing in the Red and Assiniboine river systems. Unfortunately, bullheads are not highly regarded by the parents of young anglers, so they never get to discover that their flesh has excellent flavour and texture, and is free of bones when filleted. Both our bullheads have the potential to be popular recreational and food fish. We should follow the lead of anglers in the United States, who have recognized the value of bullheads for at least the last two centuries.

COSEWIC Status as of January 1, 2004: Not Listed
MBESA Status as of January 1, 2004: Not Listed
MBCDC Status as of January 1, 2004: G5, S5

YELLOW BULLHEAD; BARBOTTE JAUNE — *Amieurus natalis*

NOTE: Not found in Manitoba; Red River watershed, Minnesota, and North Dakota

PRESERVED SPECIMEN
5 CM

IDENTIFICATION

The bullheads (*Ameiurus*) can be distinguished from the channel catfish by **not having a forked tail**. The bullheads in our area also **lack black spots**. They differ from the madtoms (*Noturus*) by the **rear margin of the adipose fin being free from the body** instead of the adipose fin continuing as a ridge to the anterior, dorsal edge of the tail. **The fin membranes of the anal and caudal fins of the yellow bullhead are not darker than the rays** and there is **no indistinct pale bar along the base of the caudal fin**. The **rear margin of the caudal fin is rounded**. The **anal fin has 22–25 rays**. The **barbels on the chin are white**.

DISTRIBUTION IN MANITOBA

The yellow bullhead is not found in Manitoba. It occurs in the Bois de Sioux River and in the Ottertail and Roseau rivers in Minnesota (Koel, 1997).

BIOLOGICAL NOTES

SPAWNING: Spawning behaviour of the yellow bullhead is similar to the black bullhead. All the bullheads herd their young into tight schools, which can be seen in early to midsummer in quiet waters.

GROWTH AND ADULT SIZE: The yellow bullhead is the smallest of the three bullhead species in our area. Scott and Crossman (1979) report a maximum age of four years and a length of 295 mm for the yellow bullhead in northern United States waters. The largest reported yellow bullhead was a 465 mm, 1.65 kg specimen from Ohio (Trautman, 1957).

FEEDING: The yellow bullhead is a benthic invertebrate predator and scavenger, like the other bullheads.

CATFISHES, FAMILY ICTALURIDAE

HABITAT: The yellow bullhead is less tolerant of turbidity than either the black or brown bullheads. It is found most often in weedy waters with little or no current, in bays of lakes, ponds, or tributaries of larger rivers (Scott and Crossman, 1979). It is associated with sand to silt substrates (Becker, 1983). It is said to be more tolerant of chemical pollutants such as detergents than either the brown or black bullheads (Becker).

ECOLOGICAL ROLE: The yellow bullhead is a middle- to upper-level consumer, like the other bullheads. It is more closely limited to clear, weedy waters than the black and brown bullhead, which limits the range of aquatic communities it inhabits.

IMPORTANCE TO PEOPLE

The yellow bullhead is said to be the best eating of the three species of bullheads in our area. Like the black and brown bullhead, it is easily caught using only the most basic fishing tackle.

COSEWIC Status as of January 1, 2004: Not Listed
MBESA Status as of January 1, 2004: Not Listed
MBCDC Status as of January 1, 2004: G5, SP

BROWN BULLHEAD; BARBOTTE BRUNE *Ameiurus nebulosus*

FRESH SPECIMEN
5 CM

IDENTIFICATION

The bullheads (*Ameiurus*) can be distinguished from the channel catfish by **not having a forked tail**. The bullheads in our area also **lack black spots**. They differ from the madtoms (*Noturus*) by the **rear margin of the adipose fin being free from the body** instead of the adipose fin continuing as a ridge to the anterior, dorsal edge of the tail. The brown bullhead **lacks black pigment on the fin membranes between the fin rays of the anal and caudal fins**. There is **no pale bar at the base of the caudal fin**, and the **rear margin of the caudal fin is straight or slightly indented**. The anal fin has **18–21 rays**. The **barbels on the chin are black**. The brown bullhead frequently has **dark mottling on the back and sides**, unlike the black bullhead. **In cold water** during early spring and late fall, **both species fade to brownish green above, greenish yellow on the sides, and yellow below, and mottling may disappear**. The brown bullhead also has **12–14** relatively **short, stout, widely spaced and pointed gill rakers on the first arch**, and the **anterior margin of the supraethmoid has a forward-pointing, inverted omega (Ω)-shaped indentation at least twice as deep as wide**. *Note:* The presence or absence of barbs on the rear margin of the pectoral spines is not useful in identifying the bullhead species in our area.

DISTRIBUTION IN MANITOBA

The distribution of the brown bullhead in Manitoba is similar to that of the black bullhead. The brown bullhead has been collected from the Winnipeg River above the Point du Bois Dam. It has also been collected in Lyons Lake, Whiteshell Provincial Park, a headwater of the Whiteshell River. The brown bullhead also occurs in Lake Manitoba, but was first found there after the black bullhead. Unlike the black bullhead, the brown bullhead is absent from the Pembina River.

CATFISHES, FAMILY ICTALURIDAE

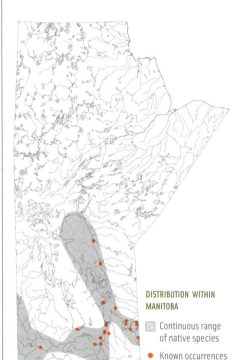

DISTRIBUTION WITHIN MANITOBA

▢ Continuous range of native species

● Known occurrences

BIOLOGICAL NOTES

SPAWNING: Spawning of the brown bullhead is similar to the black bullhead, except that the brown bullhead nests more commonly on sand or gravel substrates. As with the black bullhead, the parents herd the young into a tight school. Schools of underyearling brown bullheads are found in the same backwaters and tributaries of the Red and Assiniboine rivers as the black bullhead during most of July.

GROWTH AND ADULT SIZE: In Manitoba, the brown bullhead has a larger adult size than the black bullhead. Adult brown bullheads from Netley Creek in the University of Manitoba collection range from 230–295 mm total length. Becker (1983) reports a maximum age of five years for the brown bullhead in Wisconsin. The Manitoba angling record bullhead (species not determined, but probably a brown bullhead) is a 45 cm fish caught in Netley Creek in 1996.

FEEDING: The brown bullhead is a benthic predator and scavenger, like the black bullhead. Stomachs of brown bullheads contain the same array of species in their contents as black bullhead stomachs. Adult brown bullheads taken from mid-channel in our rivers have fish, including pieces of large fish probably consumed as carrion, in their stomachs.

HABITAT: The brown bullhead is mainly benthopelagic. Like the black bullhead, it is found in both tributaries and the mainstems of our rivers, but it is more common in mainstem habitats and in moderate current than the black bullhead. It is tolerant of turbid water and is found at depths ranging from less than 50 cm in tributaries and along shorelines to depths of 10 m in sections of the Red River. The brown bullhead, stonecat, and channel catfish are frequently collected together in mid-channel in the Red and Assiniboine rivers.

ECOLOGICAL ROLE: The brown bullhead is a benthopelagic, middle- and upper-level consumer and scavenger, ecologically similar to the black bullhead. It differs mainly in the adults more commonly being in river mainstems and in moderate current than the black bullhead.

IMPORTANCE TO PEOPLE

The brown bullhead, like the black bullhead, is easily caught in numbers by anglers fishing from shore with even the most basic tackle. It is readily accessible to anglers in almost all rivers, oxbow lakes, human-made ponds, and tributary streams in southern Manitoba. This species, the black bullhead, and the freshwater drum are probably the most frequent first fish caught by young anglers introduced to fishing in the Red and Assiniboine river systems. Unfortunately, bullheads are not highly regarded as food fish, but, contrary to the general opinion, their flesh has excellent flavour and texture, and is free of bones when filleted. Both our bullheads have the potential to be popular recreational and food fish.

COSEWIC Status as of January 1, 2004: Not Listed
MBESA Status as of January 1, 2004: Not Listed
MBCDC Status as of January 1, 2004: G5, S5

CHANNEL CATFISH; BARBUE DE RIVIÉRE | *Ictalurus punctatus*

FRESH SPECIMEN — 15 CM

FRESH SPECIMEN — 5 CM

IDENTIFICATION

The channel catfish differs from all our other catfish by having a **deeply forked tail** and being **grey above**, fading to white or pinkish on the underside. It is also unique in having **scattered black spots on the sides** in fish less than about 45 cm long. The spots are absent on large, mature fish.

DISTRIBUTION IN MANITOBA

The channel catfish occurs in the Red and Assiniboine river mainstems, Lake Winnipeg north to the Saskatchewan River at the Grand Rapids Dam, rarely in Playgreen Lake, the Winnipeg River below the Pine Falls Dam (native), and above the Pine Falls Dam up to the tailrace of the Seven Sisters Dam (possibly an illegal introduction) (Beyette, pers. comm., 1982). Channel catfish are also known from above impassable falls on the Bloodvein and Pigeon rivers (native) and at least the lower reaches of other tributaries to the east side of Lake Winnipeg north to the Poplar River (native).

Channel catfish were collected in Lake Manitoba in 1982 and 1983, 12 and 13 years after the first operation of the Assiniboine River Floodway, but they remain uncommon in Lake Manitoba (Stewart, Suthers, and Leavesley, 1985). There is one record of the channel catfish from the commercial fishery in Lake Manitoba in 1945, prior to the opening of the Assiniboine River Floodway. This may be erroneous, or, alternatively, the channel catfish may have been able to reach Lake Manitoba via the Fairford River, Lake St. Martin, and the Dauphin River, which flow from the north basin of Lake Manitoba into Sturgeon Bay, at the southwestern end of the north basin of Lake Winnipeg. Derksen (pers. comm., 2003) collected a channel catfish in the fishway of the Fairford Dam, just below where the Fairford River runs out of Lake Manitoba, in 1987. If transport by people was not involved, this fish must have ascended the Dauphin River from Lake Winnipeg and passed through Lake St. Martin and most of the Fairford River to reach the Fairford Dam. Prior to construction of the Fairford Dam, there were no impassable barriers to upstream fish movement from Lake Winnipeg to Lake Manitoba. Although the existence of channel catfish in Lake Manitoba prior to the opening of the Assiniboine River Floodway cannot be discounted, the occurrence in Lake Manitoba of

CATFISHES, FAMILY ICTALURIDAE

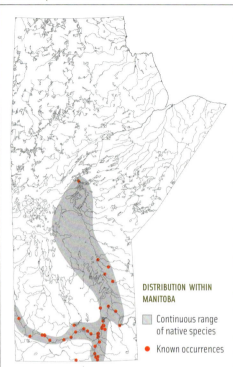

DISTRIBUTION WITHIN MANITOBA

☐ Continuous range of native species

● Known occurrences

four of the five species of catfish known from Manitoba, 12 years after the first operation of the floodway, demonstrates its effectiveness as a dispersal route.

There is one unequivocal record of a channel catfish being caught from the Saskatchewan River at Cumberland House, Saskatchewan (Hudson's Bay Company Archives, Cumberland House Post Journal 8, November 1797). This is an accurate and complete description of a channel catfish that eliminates all other possible species identifications. Peter Fidler, who reported the catch, also stated that this type of fish was caught rarely in that area ("This is the first fish of the Kind I have ever seen — now & then 1 is caught mostly every winter here as I am told."). This is the only clear-cut evidence of the native occurrence of channel catfish, or any catfish species, in the Saskatchewan River system above Grand Rapids.

BIOLOGICAL NOTES

SPAWNING: Channel catfish move to spawning areas in the Red River in early to mid-June, and spawning takes place from late June to early July, at water temperatures of 21°C or higher (Tyson, 1996). Radio (Tyson) and acoustic (MacDonald, 1992) telemetry studies show that they may move either upstream or downstream to spawning areas and it is not known whether they return to the same spawning area repeatedly. Known spawning areas in the Red River from downstream to upstream are: Netley Creek (MacDonald), Cook's Creek (Tyson), and the Red River mainstem south of St. Agathe and at Aubigny (Robert, 1990–1991). Underyearling channel catfish have also been taken in the Assiniboine River between Portage la Prairie and Winnipeg and above Portage la Prairie. All the main channel spawning areas and the Cook's Creek location have gravel to rubble substrates. The main channel locations also have higher water velocity than is typical for most of the length of the Red and Assiniboine rivers in Manitoba. In addition to the main channel spawning locations, Robert reported that channel catfish move into small tributaries and even drainage ditches in the Rat and Roseau river watersheds during the spring and early summer. It is not known whether they spawn in these areas.

Clemens and Sneed (1957) describe nesting and spawning behaviour of the channel catfish. A nest is excavated under cover, or a cavity, such as a hollow log, is cleaned by the male. A female pairs with a single male and spawns repeatedly until spent. The male cleans and fans the eggs until hatching, but does not herd the young like bullheads do.

In Manitoba, male channel catfish become emaciated and very dark-coloured during spawning and nesting. Open sores caused by *Columnaris* infection develop and erode down to the skeleton on the head, back, and sides. By late July, males appear to be recovering girth and weight, and the sores have scarred over. Completely recovered males can be found by mid-August.

In Manitoba, large channel catfish that have neither mature nor spent gonads can be taken along with mature or recovering spent fish throughout and after the spawning period. This suggests that adult channel catfish do not spawn every year. The interval between successive spawnings is unknown.

GROWTH AND ADULT SIZE: Most large, mature channel catfish in Manitoba are from 800–1000 mm total length and weigh 8–12 kg.

Three female channel catfish with enlarged eggs in their ovaries were found that were 501, 515, and 606 mm fork length, and 1754, 1865, and 3440 gm weight, respectively. They were taken in samples from the Red River at Emerson, near the international boundary, which were collected on October 9 and 10, 2003. These are the smallest mature channel catfish in our data. Their ages had not yet been determined at the time of writing. The sample also contained a number of larger mature fish, and young-of-the-year channel catfish.

The largest channel catfish known from Manitoba was angled from the Red River in 1992, and was 118 cm total length and weighed 20 kg.

Ages read from pectoral fin spine sections taken from specimens in the University of Manitoba collection indicate that Red River channel catfish mature at 10 years old, at a length of 600 mm. The largest specimen in the series was an 880 mm total length female that weighed 11.5 kg and had 27 annuli on its pectoral spine.

Underyearling channel catfish, up to now, have only been found in the Red and Assiniboine rivers. If these are the only significant spawning areas in the accessible reaches of the Red/Assiniboine/Lake Winnipeg system, then there is a large movement of juveniles at Age III and older from that area into the lower reaches of tributaries to the east shore of the north basin of Lake Winnipeg. These tributaries contain few channel catfish over 600 mm, however. Adult-sized fish are found in Lake Winnipeg, the lower Winnipeg River, and the Red and Assiniboine rivers. The channel catfish has a complex life history that makes use of all the accessible reaches of the Red/Assiniboine/Lake Winnipeg system. In addition, there are isolated, reproducing stocks upstream of impassable barriers in at least the Assiniboine, Winnipeg, Bloodvein, and Pigeon rivers.

FEEDING: Juvenile channel catfish feed mainly on benthic invertebrates. Crayfish, aquatic insects, and small freshwater mussels are found in their stomachs. They become increasingly piscivorous as they grow, and fish larger than about 800 mm have little other than fish in their stomachs.

Adult channel catfish sampled at Emerson on October 9 and 10, 2003 (see also Growth and Adult Size, above), contained mainly giant water bugs (Family Belostomatidae), water boatmen (Family Corixidae), and leopard frogs (*Rana pipiens*). The water temperature at that time was 11°C.

Stomach contents of large channel catfish sampled from the Red and Assiniboine rivers during the summer months include goldeye and mooneye, silver chub, emerald shiner, white sucker, shorthead redhorse, bullheads, and freshwater drum. Fragmentary remains of large fish may be either carrion or anglers' baits.

HABITAT: The channel catfish is mainly benthopelagic and prefers larger rivers and lakes. It is found in the mainstems of the larger rivers, offshore in Lake Winnipeg, and in the eastern tributaries of Lake Winnipeg. It is seldom seen in smaller streams. In rivers it prefers strong current and shear areas between strong current and eddies. It can be found near the surface or in shallow water, probably on feeding excursions. Although it can be found in depths of over 10 m in Lake Winnipeg and deep sections of the Red River, it is probably most common in a depth range from 2–5 m over substrates ranging from gravel to rubble in both Lake Winnipeg and the Red River. Clarke (1980), MacDonald (1992), Robert (1992), and Tyson (1996) tracked the movements of channel catfish by means of mark/recovery, acoustic telemetry, and radiotelemetry. Their results demonstrate that adult channel catfish move throughout all accessible reaches of at least the Red and Assiniboine rivers. Channel catfish tagged in the Red River between Selkirk and the Canada-US border have been recaptured as far away as Grafton, North Dakota, Brandon, Manitoba (before closure of the Assiniboine River Floodway Control Structure at Portage la Prairie), the mouth of the Sandy River in Lake Winnipeg, and in the Brokenhead River at Scanterbury. A few tagged fish have covered long distances in remarkably short times. Notably, a channel catfish tagged in the Red River at St. Jean Baptiste on June 25, 1991, was recaptured at the mouth of the Sandy River, on the east side of the south basin of Lake Winnipeg on July 8, 1991, having travelled a water distance of 350 km in 13 days (Robert). These studies also demonstrate that channel catfish tagged in the Red River enter Lake Winnipeg and then return to the Red River.

ECOLOGICAL ROLE: Adult channel catfish are one of the five species of apex predators in our fish fauna. They feed on or near the bottom, in midwater, and at the surface. They share the apex of the food web in their communities with walleyes, at least seasonally, the much less numerous northern pike (in that habitat), the burbot, and piscivorous birds.

IMPORTANCE TO PEOPLE

Over the last 20 years, channel catfish have gone from being regarded as a "coarse" fish to being a highly valued angling species. In the Red River, channel catfish and walleye are the two most valued recreational fishing species. On the lower Red River especially, there is an intensive recreational fishery for channel catfish that is pursued by both resident and non-resident anglers throughout the open-water season. If bullheads are the most likely first fish for young anglers, the channel catfish is the most likely "real monster" to be caught by beginning anglers in the Red and Assiniboine rivers. When hooked, even smaller channel catfish put up a good fight. Larger catfish make powerful runs and will even breach at the surface when hooked.

CATFISHES, FAMILY ICTALURIDAE

In addition to the sporting qualities of channel catfish, juvenile channel catfish, up to about 500 mm long, are also excellent eating fish. The recreational angling pressure, combined with the slow growth and long life of the channel catfish in our area, have led the Province of Manitoba to require release of all channel catfish over 600 mm long and to limit the catch of juveniles to four fish per angler.

COSEWIC Status as of January 1, 2004: Not Listed
MBESA Status as of January 1, 2004: Not Listed
MBCDC Status as of January 1, 2004: G5, S4

STONECAT; BARBOTTE DES RAPIDES *Noturus flavus*

2 CM   PRESERVED SPECIMEN

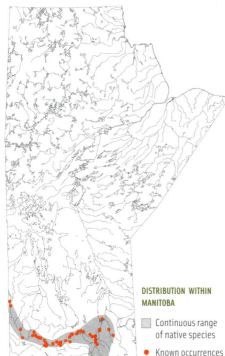

DISTRIBUTION WITHIN MANITOBA

▇ Continuous range of native species
● Known occurrences

IDENTIFICATION

The species of *Noturus* are all small, **seldom longer than 150 mm and never exceeding** a length of **300 mm** in our area. All have a **ridge-like adipose fin that extends to the anterior dorsal edge of the caudal fin**. The stonecat is distinguished from all other catfish in our area by the **subterminal mouth**, the **posterior extension of the tooth patch on each side of the upper jaw**, the **broad, flattened head**, a **pale saddle marking on the back, at the rear of the dorsal fin**, a **notch dividing the adipose fin from the caudal fin**, the **pale yellowish streak** along the **upper and lower margins of the caudal fin**, and the **square or slightly rounded posterior margin** of the caudal fin.

DISTRIBUTION IN MANITOBA

The first substantiated record of the stonecat in Manitoba was in 1969 (Stewart and Lindsey, 1970). The stonecat is found in the Red River, the Brokenhead River, the Assiniboine River upstream nearly to the Shellmouth Dam, and the tributaries of the Red and Assiniboine rivers, upstream to the bases of impassable dams (McCulloch and Stewart, 1998). The absence of stonecats above dams on Assiniboine River tributaries constructed as recently as 1960, and their presence up to the bases of those dams, and also in nearby tributaries not obstructed by dams, support the hypothesis that the entry of stonecats into Manitoba was not much earlier than their discovery here in 1969 (McCulloch, 1994). McCulloch; McCulloch and Stewart; and Stewart et al. (2001) discuss the probable routes of entry and dispersal of the stonecat in Manitoba. In the Lake Winnipeg watershed, it is known only from the

Brokenhead River. The stonecat is the only Manitoba species of catfish that has not been found in Lake Manitoba since the opening of the Assiniboine River Floodway.

BIOLOGICAL NOTES

SPAWNING: Spawning of the stonecat has not been observed in Manitoba. Like our other catfish, male stonecats excavate or clean a nest and tend it after spawning. Typically, a nest is located under a flat stone, but refuse deposited by people is also used. The only observations of nesting male stonecats in Manitoba are by McCulloch (pers. comm., 2003). He found a male stonecat with a nest inside an open and inverted abandoned toolbox in the Assiniboine River on June 28, 1989. Water temperature was 23°C, lowering the previously recorded low nesting temperature of the species by 2°C. Another male and a nest were observed in the Little Saskatchewan River at Rivers on July 9, 1991. The eggs were sitting in the bottom of a broken glass bottle. Again, the water temperature was 23°C. The apparent high dependence of stonecats on refuse discarded by people for nesting sites is likely an artifact of the limited number of observations and the greater likelihood of noticing something unusual, as opposed to finding a nesting male among boulders.

GROWTH AND ADULT SIZE: Stonecats attain larger sizes in the Red River than in the Assiniboine River and its tributaries. Adult stonecats from the Assiniboine River in the University of Manitoba collection range from 120–211 mm total length.

FEEDING: McCulloch (1994) showed that the stonecat was mainly a nocturnal feeder. It feeds mainly on aquatic insects, with caddis fly (*Hydropsyche* spp.) larvae being the most frequent food item at most locations. Amphipod crustaceans (*Gammarus* sp.) also are a significant part of the diet.

HABITAT: The stonecat lives in the interstitial spaces among stones in runs and riffles. It tolerates turbid water, and can be abundant both in the mainstems of large rivers and in their tributaries. It occurs in depths from 10 m in deep sections of the Red River to water as shallow as 30–50 cm along shorelines and in tributaries. The substrate size ranges from coarse gravel to boulders.

ECOLOGICAL ROLE: The stonecat is a benthic, nocturnal, middle-level predator. In tributary streams, its strong association with rocky, riffle habitat is shared only with the longnose dace, juvenile burbot, and the mudpuppy, a permanently aquatic salamander. McCulloch (1994) gives evidence that resource partitioning has occurred among the stonecat, burbot, and longnose dace. It is an example of a species that apparently reached Manitoba recently and dispersed and became established through the entire area of the Red and Assiniboine river watersheds accessible to it without human help. By these criteria, it would qualify as an invasive species.

IMPORTANCE TO PEOPLE

Anglers fishing on the bottom with natural bait in the Red and Assiniboine rivers commonly catch the stonecat. It is regarded as a nuisance and usually misidentified as a small bullhead. Larger stonecats caught in the Red River occasionally have been misidentified by anglers as young flathead catfish, a species that has never been found in the Hudson Bay Drainage. Although the flesh of the stonecat is quite tasty, they are seldom large enough to justify the effort of cleaning them. The main values of the stonecat lie in the diversity and interest it adds to our fish fauna and its usefulness as a model for studying the effects of invading species on our resident fishes.

COSEWIC Status as of January 1, 2004: Not Listed
MBESA Status as of January 1, 2004: Not Listed
MBCDC Status as of January 1, 2004: G5, S5

CATFISHES, FAMILY ICTALURIDAE

TADPOLE MADTOM; CHAT-FOU BRUN | *Noturus gyrinus*

1 CM — PRESERVED SPECIMEN

IDENTIFICATION

The species of *Noturus* are all small, **seldom longer than 150 mm and never exceeding** a length of **300 mm** in our area. All have a **ridge-like adipose fin** that extends to the anterior dorsal edge of the caudal fin. The tadpole madtom has a **terminal mouth** and there are **no posterior extensions on either end of the tooth patch on the upper jaw**. The **head is not flattened**. There are **no pale markings on the back or the edges of the tail**, and there is **no notch dividing the adipose fin from the caudal fin. The posterior margin of the tail is rounded**.

DISTRIBUTION IN MANITOBA

The tadpole madtom is found in tributaries and peripheral waters of the Red and Assiniboine river watersheds west to Brandon and Souris, Manitoba. It occurs in the Lake Winnipeg watershed north to the Etomami River (Berens River tributary) and in the Winnipeg River upstream to Seven Sisters. The tadpole madtom was first collected in Lake Manitoba in 1973, which makes it the first catfish species to be found in Lake Manitoba following the opening of the Assiniboine River Floodway (Stewart, Suthers, and Leavesley, 1985).

BIOLOGICAL NOTES

SPAWNING: Case (1970a) found underyearling tadpole madtoms in early August, suggesting a July spawning period. Becker (1983) summarizes reports of tadpole madtom spawning in Wisconsin. Like most of our catfish, the tadpole madtom nests under cover, and, where known, the male guards the nest. Unlike our other catfish, female madtoms may spawn several times, likely with different males, during the spawning period. There is no post-hatching parental care of young.

GROWTH AND ADULT SIZE: Case (1970a) used probability analysis of length frequency distributions to study the age and growth of the tadpole madtom in Manitoba. He found that underyearlings collected in August and September ranged from 28–40 mm, mode 33 mm in length. Age I madtoms collected in June were from 28–50 mm long, mode 40 mm. By September, they ranged from 56–70 mm long, mode 77 mm. Age II madtoms were from 56–85 mm long, with a broad mode from 55–75 mm. He identified Age II as the age at first sexual maturity. There were very few Age III+ fish, all over 85 mm, with the largest being 108 mm long.

DISTRIBUTION WITHIN MANITOBA
- Continuous range of native species
- Known occurrences

FEEDING: Case (1970a) analyzed the stomach contents of 61 tadpole madtoms collected in the Rat River, a Red River tributary, and in St. Malo reservoir, an impoundment on that river. He found that two groups, the amphipod crustacean *Hyalella azteca* and chironomid fly larvae, comprised most of the diet. *Hyalella* was the dominant food item in the reservoir and chironomids were dominant in the flowing portion of the stream.

HABITAT: The tadpole madtom lives in quiet, clear, weedy, protected water. It is most common in tributaries to the larger rivers. This is likely due to the clear water and the more abundant and dense growth of aquatic macrophytes in those habitats. The tadpole madtom is the most cryptophylic fish in our area. In both natural conditions and aquaria, they stay in the most dense stands of vegetation and are seldom seen in the open. Water depth is usually less than 1 m, and the substrate is usually mud or silt.

ECOLOGICAL ROLE: The tadpole madtom is a nocturnal, middle-level consumer. Unlike the stonecat, it is closely tied to weedbeds in quiet water.

Becker (1983) suggests that the tadpole madtom may be an important prey item for piscivorous fish. Case (1970a), however, found that food-deprived northern pike held in the laboratory and presented with several species of live minnows along with Age I and older tadpole madtoms would quickly consume the minnows, but not eat the madtoms. When the minnows were exhausted, the pike became cannibalistic, but still would not eat the madtoms, except for a single underyearling madtom. He also found that sauger and juvenile northern pike that were experimentally envenomated in the lateral musculature by a skin prick with the pectoral spine of a live tadpole madtom showed a slowed escape response to prodding and required about five hours for recovery. One 300 mm pike was paralyzed and had laboured breathing movements for 12 hours after experimental envenomation by a tadpole madtom pectoral spine. These observations suggest that the tadpole madtom is probably avoided by piscivores because of its venomous spines.

IMPORTANCE TO PEOPLE

People almost never see the tadpole madtom unless they are dipnetting or seining in weedbeds. As was stated in the introductory material about the catfishes, **the tadpole madtom has a potent venom associated with its dorsal and pectoral spines**. An invisible prick in the skin, even from a very small madtom, will cause intense, throbbing pain, similar to that of a wasp sting, almost instantly. The pain spreads and dulls over about an hour and is gone after about four or five hours in most cases. The surface irritation at the site of the sting disappears within about an hour.

COSEWIC Status as of January 1, 2004: Not Listed
MBESA Status as of January 1, 2004: Not Listed
MBCDC Status as of January 1, 2004: G5, S5

PIKE-LIKE FISHES, ORDER ESOCIFORMES
PIKE AND MUSKELLUNGE, FAMILY ESOCIDAE

ORDER ESOCIFORMES

The pike-like fishes all lack the adipose fin found in trout, salmon, and whitefish, and the dorsal and anal fins are displaced to the rear of the body, just in front of the tail. The order contains only two families, the pikes, Family Esocidae, and the mudminnows, Family Umbridae. Both groups contain freshwater fish living in cool temperate to Arctic climates in North America and Eurasia, and both are found in Manitoba.

FAMILY ESOCIDAE

Four of the five species of pikes are tolerant of salt water, especially cold water in Arctic and subarctic areas. The northern pike is found in the Baltic Sea, and has probably spread among coastal streams in the Arctic and on the east coast in North America by entering estuaries and coastal waters. This is apparently also true for the muskellunge and the two species of pickerel. Four of the five species of pikes occur in North America and two in Eurasia. Only one of the five species of pikes, *Esox reichertii*, the Amur pike, is restricted to Eurasia. Two species, the northern pike and the muskellunge, are found in Manitoba.

Pikes are **elongate, streamlined** fish with a **long head** and a **pointed, wedge-shaped, flattened snout. The tip of the lower jaw protrudes beyond the upper jaw**. The **lower jaw is armed with large fang-like teeth** and the **roof of the mouth has patches of smaller but strong teeth** on the palatines, and **larger, fang-like teeth on the head of the vomer**. There are **no teeth on the maxillae**. The body is **oval in cross-section** and the **dorsal and anal fins are set far back, just ahead of the tail**, and the **tail is deeply forked**. This family contains two of the six largest native fish species in Manitoba.

PIKE AND MUSKELLUNGE, FAMILY ESOCIDAE

KEY TO THE PIKE AND MUSKELLUNGE

1A Twelve or more mandibular pores (counting pores on both sides of the lower jaw). Lower 1/2 of cheek usually lacks scales. Colour pale with darker markings, irregular brownish blotches, or wavy diagonal bars. Young with a prominent mid-dorsal light stripe.

muskellunge, *Esox masquinongy* page 146

1B Eleven or fewer mandibular pores. Cheeks usually completely covered by scales. Colour dark with lighter markings, wavy diagonal bars in young, irregular series of oval spots in larger fish. No mid-dorsal light stripe, or only discontinuous portions of one in young.

northern pike, *Esox lucius* page 145

NORTHERN PIKE, GRAND BROCHET | *Esox lucius*

FRESH SPECIMEN
10 CM

IDENTIFICATION

The northern pike can be distinguished from the muskellunge by the **cheek being entirely covered with scales** and the **operculum having only the upper half scaled**, and by the presence of **five pores on the underside of each side of the lower jaw. There are 14–15 branchiostegal rays.** The colour in adults is greenish olive with pale yellowish oval spots (larger fish) or irregular diagonal bars, especially toward the rear (smaller fish). By contrast, the muskellunge has scales only on the upper half of the cheek and operculum, six or more pores on the underside of each side of the lower jaw, and a brownish olive colour marked with darker blotches, bars, or spots.

Note: At least three colour variants of the northern pike occur uncommonly or rarely in Manitoba. The most frequent variant is greenish blue on the back, with silver sides, and little or no evidence of spots or diagonal bars on the sides. This variant is sometimes referred to as a silver pike, and has been collected at scattered locations over much of southern and central Manitoba. One juvenile northern pike, about 350 mm total length, collected in Hemming Lake by the Manitoba Fisheries Branch, was yellowish brown above and golden yellow on the sides, and also lacked spots or bars on the sides. Another juvenile northern pike, about 400 mm total length, collected from Devonian Lake at the Fort Whyte Nature Centre in Winnipeg, was dark brown above, silvery laterally, and had diagonal rows of dark brown spots. All were unequivocally northern pike on the basis of cheek and opercular squamation, mandibular pore count, and branchiostegal ray count.

DISTRIBUTION WITHIN MANITOBA
☐ Continuous range of native species
● Known occurrences

THE FRESHWATER FISHES OF MANITOBA

PIKE AND MUSKELLUNGE, FAMILY ESOCIDAE

DISTRIBUTION IN MANITOBA
The northern pike is one of the three most widely distributed fish in Manitoba. It is found in nearly all permanent waters that support fish populations.

BIOLOGICAL NOTES
SPAWNING: Northern pike spawn in early April in southern Manitoba, just after the ice leaves rivers and streams, but while most lakes still have ice cover. They move upstream to shallow water with vegetation. One or more smaller males accompany a spawning female. Pike are broadcast spawners, and the adhesive eggs are scattered over the vegetation.

GROWTH AND ADULT SIZE: Female pike grow to larger size than males. The largest angler-caught pike from Manitoba was 150 cm from Max Lake in 1992. The largest specimen in the University of Manitoba collection is the skull of a 17.2 kg fish taken in a hoop net from the middle basin of Lake Athapapuskow in 1974.

FEEDING: Pike begin life feeding on zooplankton and aquatic insects. They grow rapidly, and shift to feeding on small fish within a week or two. They remain mainly piscivorous throughout life, although they also take leeches, dragonfly nymphs, mayflies, crayfish, frogs, and even mice, muskrats, and the young of aquatic birds.

HABITAT: Northern pike are most commonly found in cool, clear, quiet water with vegetation or other cover. They are most commonly found in lakes, but are also found in flowing water, ranging from headwater creeks to larger, turbid rivers, most often in areas where the water velocity is lowest, such as pools, eddies, and marginal waters.

ECOLOGICAL ROLE: Northern pike are one of the five top-level predators in our fish fauna. They share the top of the food web in their communities with the channel catfish, lake trout, walleye, burbot, some wading and diving birds, snapping turtles (at least north to Lake Athapapuskow), and the river otter.

IMPORTANCE TO PEOPLE
Pike are important commercial and game fish. Their greatest economic value is probably as game fish. They also carry parasites that can infect a variety of animals, including other fish and humans. The pike is the most common host of the adult stage of the tapeworm *Triaenophorus crassus*, whose larvae infect whitefish and ciscoes. The cysts formed by the larvae in the flesh of whitefish decreases their market value. Pike also carry infective cysts of the broad fish tapeworm *Diphyllobothrium latum*. **These cysts can infect humans with the adult stage of the worm, if incompletely cooked, infected pike meat is eaten.** Ecologically, because of its abundance and general distribution, the northern pike is probably the most important top-level predator in most aquatic communities in Manitoba.

COSEWIC Status as of January 1, 2004: Not Listed
MBESA Status as of January 1, 2004: Not Listed
MBCDC Status as of January 1, 2004: G5, S5

MUSKELLUNGE; MASKINONGÉ | *Esox masquinongy*

LIVE SPECIMEN
10 CM

IDENTIFICATION
The muskellunge is distinguished from the northern pike by having **scales only on the upper half of both the cheek and operculum, six or more pores on the underside of each side of the lower jaw, 16 or more branchiostegals on each side**, and **darker blotches, bars, or spots on a brownish olive, lighter background**. They also have a longer,

PIKE AND MUSKELLUNGE, FAMILY ESOCIDAE

more gently tapered head than the pike. Young-of-the-year muskellunge have a **mid-dorsal pale stripe**, which is incomplete, or, usually, absent in the pike.

DISTRIBUTION IN MANITOBA

Muskellunge are native to Manitoba only in the Winnipeg River in extreme eastern Manitoba. The only native Manitoba specimen we have seen was caught in Eaglenest Lake, which lies on the Manitoba-Ontario border. Muskellunge have also been introduced into a number of lakes in Riding Mountain National Park and Duck Mountain Provincial Park, in southwestern Manitoba. In April 1981, Derksen (pers. comm., 2003) examined a fish that he identified as a muskellunge, which was collected from Portage Bay in Lake Manitoba, near where the Fairford River runs out of Lake Manitoba. The mandibular pore and branchiostegal counts he gives support this identification. The Provincial Fisheries Branch has never planted muskellunge in Lake Manitoba or its tributaries. If it reached Lake Manitoba without human help, it would have had to traverse a complex and tortuous route either from Lake Audy in Riding Mountain National Park, via the Little Saskatchewan and Assiniboine rivers and the Assiniboine Floodway, or from Eaglenest Lake via the Winnipeg River, downstream over seven hydroelectric dams to Lake Winnipeg, and then upstream through the Dauphin River, Lake St. Martin, the Fairford River, and Fairford Dam Fishway into Lake Manitoba. Access via the Red River to the Assiniboine River is probably impossible because of the Assiniboine Floodway Control Structure at Portage la Prairie, which lacks a fishway. None of these routes is supported by the existence of muskellunge anywhere between the possible sources and Lake Manitoba.

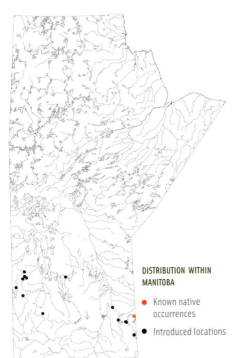

DISTRIBUTION WITHIN MANITOBA
● Known native occurrences
● Introduced locations

BIOLOGICAL NOTES

SPAWNING: The time of spawning of muskellunge in Manitoba is not known. Elsewhere, they spawn one or two weeks later than northern pike where the two occur together. The spawning habitat and process are about the same as described for the pike. The later spawning time means that the young muskellunge leave the spawning habitat at about the time that the young pike are beginning to feed on fish in the same areas. Predation on hatchling muskellunge by the somewhat more advanced pike fry often limits the abundance of muskellunge or prevents their establishment if they are introduced into waters with a large northern pike population.

GROWTH AND ADULT SIZE: Muskellunge can grow to a larger size than the pike, with a fish of about 45 kg being the largest ever reported. The Manitoba angling record muskellunge is a 106 cm muskellunge caught in 1999 from Line Lake.

FEEDING: Muskellunge, like northern pike, are top-level piscivores. The foods are nearly identical for the two species.

HABITAT: Muskellunge are narrower in their habitat preference than pike, being limited to lakes and larger streams with clear or brown-stained water and aquatic vegetation cover.

ECOLOGICAL ROLE: Muskellunge are top-level predators in their communities. Their scarcity in Manitoba limits their importance here.

IMPORTANCE TO PEOPLE

The muskellunge is one of the most highly valued game fish wherever it is found. In Manitoba, its importance is limited because of scarcity and the few areas where it is found.

COSEWIC Status as of January 1, 2004: Not Listed
MBESA Status as of January 1, 2004: Not Listed
MBCDC Status as of January 1, 2004: G5, S1

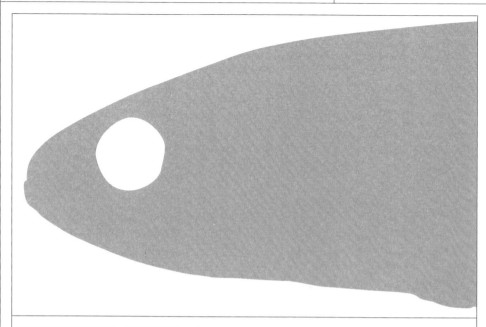

MUDMINNOWS, FAMILY UMBRIDAE

FAMILY UMBRIDAE

There are three genera and seven species of mudminnows. All the genera and four species occur in North America, and two genera and three species occur in Eurasia. One species, the central mudminnow, is found in Manitoba.

Mudminnows are **small fish** with a **robust, moderately elongate body** that is **nearly round in cross-section**. The **head is blunt** and the **dorsal and anal fins are set far back on the body, similar to those on a pike**, but the **tail is rounded**. They live in quiet, weedy waters along the margins of rivers and lakes, in tributaries, and in bogs, ponds, and marshes. They are one of a group of eight species of fish that constitute the distinctive fish fauna of bog habitats in Manitoba. Although they tolerate turbid water, mudminnows are most commonly found in clear or brown-stained water. Mudminnows feed mostly on benthic aquatic invertebrates. They have adapted to the oxygen deficiency that frequently develops during the summer in their heavily vegetated habitats by being able to breathe air, using their swim bladder to supplement the oxygen they get from the water.

MUDMINNOWS, FAMILY UMBRIDAE

CENTRAL MUDMINNOW; UMBRE DE VASE — *Umbra limi*

PRESERVED SPECIMEN
1 CM

IDENTIFICATION

The **moderately elongate, robust body**, with the **dorsal and anal fins set far back**, the **mottled, dark olive to brown colour**, and the **black vertical bar at the base of the rounded tail** are the best identifying characters for the central mudminnow.

DISTRIBUTION IN MANITOBA

The central mudminnow is found in southern Manitoba west to the Souris River, north to the Nelson River, and northwest to the Saskatchewan River near The Pas.

BIOLOGICAL NOTES

SPAWNING: Martin (1982) found that central mudminnows in the Bog River (Winnipeg River watershed) in southern Manitoba spawned during the first three weeks of May in 1978, but spawned in June in 1979. They move upstream or laterally to shorelines or into ponds or marshes to spawn. The eggs are adhesive and are deposited on submerged plants.

GROWTH AND ADULT SIZE: Martin (1982) showed that female central mudminnows grow more rapidly than males. Mean sizes at ages for males were: Age 0, 23.3 mm; Age I, 50.1 mm; Age II, 75.5 mm; Age III, 83.3 mm; and Age IV, 100.4 mm. For females, mean sizes were Age 0, 23.3 mm; Age I, 50.6 mm; Age II, 78.9 mm; Age III, 92.6 mm; and Age IV, 93.1 mm. She also found that males became sexually mature at Age II and females at Age III.

DISTRIBUTION WITHIN MANITOBA
- Continuous range of native species
- Known occurrences

Adult mudminnows in the University of Manitoba collection, from various locations in southern Manitoba, ranged from 90–127 mm total length. The largest mudminnow in the University of Manitoba collection was collected from the headwaters of the Manigotagan River in Nopiming Provincial Park and measured 148 mm long after preservation.

FEEDING: Martin (1982) found considerable seasonal variation in central mudminnow diets. In general, they took a wide variety of aquatic invertebrates. Benthic invertebrates were the most common items during most periods, but midwater and surface organisms were also taken. Fish became the most important diet item during the winter.

HABITAT: Mudminnows prefer beds of aquatic vegetation. Martin (1982) found significantly greater densities of central mudminnows in vegetation than in open water. She also demonstrated that mudminnows have a significant preference for vegetation in aquarium experiments, although it was more strongly expressed by groups of mudminnows than by single fish. Typically, the central mudminnow is found in streams and ponds in bogs. It is one of the eight species of fishes associated with bog habitats in headwater streams and ponds in Manitoba. See the pearl dace species account for a complete list and additional comments. The water in which mudminnows live is often oxygen-deficient by midsummer, and they are able to breathe air using their swim bladder to gain additional oxygen.

ECOLOGICAL ROLE: The central mudminnow is a benthopelagic to midwater, middle- to upper-level consumer. The ability of the mudminnow to occupy habitats that are often oxygen-deficient limits their availability as forage fish for larger piscivores. In their heavily vegetated bog habitats, they are near the top of the food web.

IMPORTANCE TO PEOPLE

The central mudminnow shows up infrequently in the live bait trade in Manitoba. Since commercial bait dealers collect mostly from boggy lakes and ponds, and apparently do not distinguish the mudminnow from the four cyprinid species that comprise the bulk of their catch, this should be expected. It is also used in native fish aquaria, although it may eat smaller fish in the tank. Beyond this, the central mudminnow is probably most ecologically significant as the top predator in the resident aquatic fauna of bogs.

COSEWIC Status as of January 1, 2004: Not Listed
MBESA Status as of January 1, 2004: Not Listed
MBCDC Status as of January 1, 2004: G5, S5

SMELT-LIKE FISHES, ORDER OSMERIFORMES

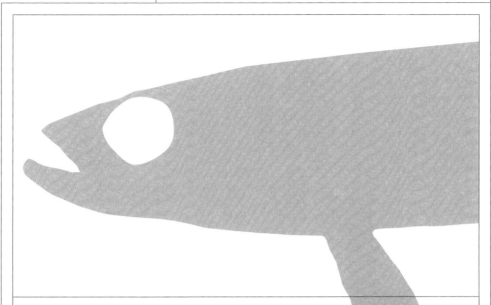

SMELTS, FAMILY OSMERIDAE

ORDER OSMERIFORMES

This group consists of 13 families, nine of which are marine, offshore fishes that live from the surface down to deep-sea habitats several kilometres below the surface. The smelt, along with five other related families, either have a mix of marine, diadromous, and freshwater species, or are strictly freshwater. Of all these families, only the Family Osmeridae is found in fresh water in the northern hemisphere.

FAMILY OSMERIDAE

The smelts are similar to the salmonids in appearance, but are smaller and have a **long, low anal fin, with 12–23 rays** in the two species in our area. **Smelt lack a pelvic axillary process**, which is present in all salmonids. There are two species of smelt in our area. The capelin is a marine fish that enters estuaries along the Hudson Bay coast, and the rainbow smelt is an introduced species that may live its entire life cycle in fresh water or have an anadromous life history. The recent discovery of rainbow smelt in the lower Churchill River in Manitoba suggests that this species has both freshwater and anadromous stocks in Manitoba.

SMELTS, FAMILY OSMERIDAE

KEY TO THE SMELTS FOUND IN MANITOBA

1A Strong fang-like teeth on the tongue, lower jaw, and palatines. Sixty-two to 72 scales in lateral series, with lateral line incomplete.

rainbow smelt, *Osmerus mordax* **page 153**

INTRODUCED

1B Tiny villiform teeth on tongue and lower jaw. No teeth on palatines. One hundred and seventy to 220 scales in complete lateral line.

capelin, *Mallotus villosus* **page 152**

MARINE, ENTERING ESTUARIES ON HUDSON BAY COAST

CAPELIN; CAPELAN | *Mallotus villosus*

NOTE: Marine species found near shore and in river mouths in Hudson Bay

FRESH SPECIMEN
2 CM

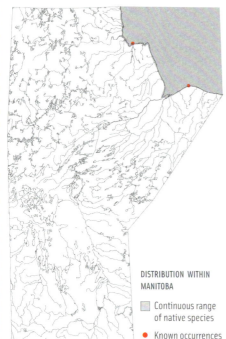

DISTRIBUTION WITHIN MANITOBA

▢ Continuous range of native species

● Known occurrences

IDENTIFICATION

The capelin superficially resembles a small trout or whitefish (Family Salmonidae). All osmerids differ from all salmonids in **lacking the pelvic axillary process**. The capelin differs from the rainbow smelt by having **minute villiform teeth on the jaws and tongue**. The **lateral line is complete, with 170–220 pored scales**. The base of the **adipose fin is longer than the diameter of the eye** and the **upper margin of the adipose fin is straight or nearly so**. **Spawning male capelin** have a band of hair-like villi on the sides of the body.

DISTRIBUTION IN MANITOBA

The capelin is a marine fish that spawns on beaches. It has been collected in the estuaries of the Churchill and Nelson rivers and probably enters the estuaries of other streams draining into Hudson Bay. It is included here because it enters fresh water in river mouths, and there are several records from the mouth of the Churchill River.

COSEWIC Status as of January 1, 2004: Not Listed
MBESA Status as of January 1, 2004: Not Listed
MBCDC Status as of January 1, 2004: G?, S5

SMELTS, FAMILY OSMERIDAE

RAINBOW SMELT; ÉPERLAN ARC-EN-CIEL | *Osmerus mordax*

NOTE: Introduced species

FRESH SPECIMEN
2 CM

IDENTIFICATION

The rainbow smelt resembles a small trout. It differs from all trout **by lacking the pelvic axillary process**. The rainbow smelt differs from the capelin in having **strong, fang-like teeth on the tongue and jaws**. The **lateral line is incomplete and has only 62–72 pored scales**. The **base of the adipose fin is shorter than the eye diameter** and the **upper margin of the adipose fin is rounded**. There are **no hair-like villi along the lateral line** in spawning male rainbow smelt.

DISTRIBUTION IN MANITOBA

The rainbow smelt is native to all three coasts of Canada, where it is anadromous. In addition, non-anadromous rainbow smelt occur in many lakes in eastern Canada and the northeastern United States. Non-anadromous rainbow smelt have also been widely introduced outside their native range, notably including the Great Lakes and Lake Sakakawea, a Missouri River reservoir in North Dakota. Rainbow smelt entered the Hudson Bay Drainage as a result of several unauthorized, illegal introductions into lakes in the Rainy and English/Wabigoon river systems in Minnesota and northwestern Ontario (Stewart et al., 2001). Campbell et al. (1991) recount the history of introduction and spread of the rainbow smelt in the Hudson Bay Drainage in northwestern Ontario and its first occurrences in Lake Winnipeg in 1991. At present, the rainbow smelt is found in the Winnipeg River, Lake Winnipeg, and the Nelson River downstream to its estuary in Hudson Bay (Remnant, Graveline, and Bretcher, 1997; Remnant, pers. comm., 2002). It has been observed in the Dauphin River (Lake Winnipeg watershed) by provincial fisheries officials (Derksen, pers. comm., 2003). In June of 2002, four rainbow smelt, three of which were mature males, were found in the stomach contents of a northern pike, which had been gillnetted upstream of the weir in the Churchill River at Churchill, Manitoba, by Warren Bernhart of North/South Consultants. This suggests that rainbow smelt may have spread northward along the Hudson Bay coastline from the Nelson River northward to at least the Churchill River. It also implies that there may now be anadromous rainbow smelt populations distributed along the west shore of Hudson Bay at least from the Nelson River to the Churchill River.

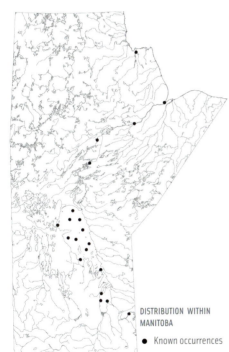

DISTRIBUTION WITHIN MANITOBA

● Known occurrences

BIOLOGICAL NOTES

SPAWNING: Spawning of rainbow smelt has not been observed in Manitoba. The rainbow smelt always spawns in fresh water and usually ascends streams to spawn, but they also spawn on reefs and along the shorelines of lakes (Scott and Crossman, 1979). Lacustrine rainbow smelt may spawn in inlet or outlet streams. O'Connor (pers. comm., 1989) observed rainbow smelt spawning in the Chukuni River, which is the outlet of Red Lake (English River system) in northwestern Ontario. Spawning in the Great Lakes takes place shortly after the ice has broken up, at water temperatures of 4.5°–15°C. The eggs are adhesive and sink to the bottom after spawning.

GROWTH AND ADULT SIZE: At least some of the rainbow smelt in the south basin of Lake Winnipeg grow to large size for the species. A sample of smelt caught incidentally in the commercial walleye fishery off Riverton in the late summer of 1995 all had otolith ages of two years and showed no enlargement of the gonads. They ranged from 189–211 mm total length. Smelt with maturing gonads have not been reported to date in Manitoba, likely because of inadequate sampling.

FEEDING: Rainbow smelt under about 150 mm total length are predatory on plankton. They become increasingly piscivorous as they grow larger. Becker (1983) notes that the planktonic crustaceans *Mysis relicta* and *Pontoporeia affinis* are the dominant prey species.

HABITAT: The rainbow smelt is a schooling, midwater fish that prefers cool lakes, reservoirs, or lake-like expansions of large rivers with water temperatures up to 15°C (Scott and Crossman, 1979). Becker (1983) reports that smelt in Lake Michigan become increasingly benthic as they approach maturity.

ECOLOGICAL ROLE: The rainbow smelt is a midwater to benthopelagic, middle- to upper-level consumer. It is an aggressive invading species wherever it has been introduced, and has been implicated in the decline of native species, including the lake whitefish, cisco, and emerald shiner (Franzin et al., 1994) in lakes in which smelt have become established.

In Lake Winnipeg, the rainbow smelt has become an important prey species for walleye and sauger. Feeding on smelt appears to be associated with large accumulations of mesenteric fat in these species (Derksen, pers. comm., 2002).

IMPORTANCE TO PEOPLE

The rainbow smelt is an invading exotic species in our area. It is not yet apparent what effects it will have on our native game, commercial, and forage fish species, but it has been shown to cause reductions in populations of pelagic and benthic planktivores elsewhere. It is also associated with increased growth, higher fat content, and sometimes reduced eating quality and increased mercury content of piscivorous game and commercial species that begin feeding on it.

The rainbow smelt is an excellent food fish in its own right, and it supports both commercial and recreational fisheries in the Great Lakes.

COSEWIC Status as of January 1, 2004: Not Listed
MBESA Status as of January 1, 2004: Not Listed
MBCDC Status as of January 1, 2004: G5, SE

TROUT-LIKE FISHES, ORDER SALMONIFORMES
WHITEFISH, GRAYLING, CHAR, TROUT, AND SALMON, FAMILY SALMONIDAE

ORDER SALMONIFORMES

The Order Salmoniformes contains only one family, the Salmonidae. The native distribution of the salmoniforms is restricted to temperate and Arctic regions of the northern hemisphere. They either live in fresh water or spawn in fresh water and move to the sea to feed.

FAMILY SALMONIDAE

The trout-like fishes comprise a single family of 11 or 12 genera and 66 species, most of which have anadromous or amphidromous populations, or are wholly anadromous or amphidromous. Their native range is restricted to the cooler regions of the northern hemisphere. The whitefishes and ciscoes are thought to have the most primitive body plan in the group, similar to the body plan of extinct fishes thought to be near the common ancestry of the modern bony fishes. The distinguishing characters for the order are the same as those given below for the family.

The salmonids have a **streamlined, terete body shape** and can be distinguished from all other fishes in our area by the following combination of characters. There are **no spines in the fins**, and the **scales are cycloid**. **The pectoral fins are low on the sides**, just behind the gill openings, and the **pelvic fins are about halfway between the pectoral fins and the anal fin**. There is a **narrow, triangular, fleshy tab, the pelvic axillary process**, just above the base of the pelvic fin on each side. There is an **adipose fin** on the back between the dorsal fin and the tail. The **dorsal and anal fins** are **not displaced to the rear** as they are in pike and mudminnows.

The salmonids are divided into three subfamilies, all of which are found in Manitoba.

1. The whitefish, ciscoes, and inconnu, **Subfamily Coregoninae**. The Manitoba species in this group all have **scales distinctly larger than those of trout**, with **fewer than 110 scales in the lateral line**. With the exception of the inconnu, which is not found in Manitoba, they have **no teeth as adults**, although young-of-the-year ciscoes can have minute teeth on the jaws, which they lose after their first year. The **mouth is small and inferior in whitefish**, but is **terminal and reaches back to below the middle of the eye in ciscoes**. The **maxillary is broad and flat, and is recurved**. The coregonines in our area also **lack spots or other markings on the body as adults**, although one species in our area, the round whitefish, *Prosopium cylindraceum*, has dark blotches (parr marks) on the sides when young. **Mature eggs are small** and **yellow** in colour. Whitefish are typically **fall spawners** that usually spawn under the ice in our area. Note, however, that the shortjaw cisco, *Coregonus zenithicus*, spawns in the spring in Lake Superior. The spawning time of Manitoba populations of this species is unknown.

WHITEFISH, GRAYLING, CHAR, TROUT, AND SALMON, FAMILY SALMONIDAE

2. **The graylings, Subfamily Thymallinae**. There is only one species of grayling, the Arctic grayling, in North America. **The grayling has large scales**, like a whitefish, with **less than 105 scales in the lateral line**. The mouth is always terminal and **armed with strong teeth**, and the **maxillary bone is slender, straight**, and **extends to below the eye**. There are **black spots on the sides of the body toward the front**, and **young grayling have parr marks**. The dorsal fin is long, high, and flag-like, with **17 or more rays**. The grayling has **small, yellow eggs**, like the whitefish and ciscoes, and is a **spring spawner**.

3. **The trout, char, and salmon, Subfamily Salmoninae**. Trout, char, and salmon have **small scales, with never less than 100 in the lateral line**, and **usually over 110**. The mouth is large, reaching to below or past the rear margin of the eye, and the **jaws, roof of the mouth, and tongue are armed with strong teeth**. The **maxillary is slender** and either **straight or decurved**. Most salmonines have **black spots, pale spots, or pale vermiculations** on the body. In our area, only the introduced kokanee salmon has very few or no spots. The **young of all salmonines in our area have parr marks**. The **dorsal fin has 14 or fewer rays**, and is **not high and flag-like** as in the grayling. All salmonines have **large eggs, which range from yellow-orange to bright red in colour**. All salmonines native to our area and all but two of the introduced species are **fall spawners**.

Within the Salmoninae, there are three genera in Manitoba. The genus *Oncorhynchus*, all of which are introduced in Manitoba, contains the western trout and Pacific salmon. Fish of this genus either **lack spots or have small black spots without light haloes, on a lighter background colour**. *Salmo*, represented in Manitoba only by the introduced brown trout, has **larger black spots, some with light haloes, and often some red spots, on a lighter background colour**. The genus *Salvelinus*, the chars, contains all our native salmonine species. Chars have **pale spots or vermiculations and some species have red or pink spots with bluish haloes against a darker background**. Chars also have a **white leading edge on the pectoral, pelvic, and anal fins**.

Most salmonids are tolerant of salt water, and many are anadromous. That is, they have a life history that is divided between a freshwater spawning and early development (parr) phase, and a marine phase in which they grow to maturity, after which they return to fresh water to spawn. In our area, the lake whitefish, cisco, round whitefish, Arctic char, and brook trout have all been collected in salt water along the Hudson Bay coastline. Among our native salmonids, only three, the Arctic grayling, shortjaw cisco, and lake trout, have not been found in Hudson Bay.

The salmonids contain the most economically valuable species of fishes in Canada. In Manitoba, two of our four most economically valuable species, the lake whitefish and lake trout, are salmonids. The popularity of trout for recreational fishing has led to the introduction of several species of trout far beyond their natural ranges. In our area, the brown trout, a Eurasian species, is widely introduced in streams, natural or human-made lakes, and small ponds in southern Manitoba. The rainbow trout, a species of the Pacific Ocean watersheds of North America and east Asia, is even more commonly stocked. The brook trout is native to Manitoba, but only in the northeastern reaches of the Churchill, Nelson, and Hayes river watersheds, and the Hudson Bay coastal watersheds south of the Churchill River. All the brook trout in southern Manitoba are the result of stocking programs, although some brook trout plantings in streams along the flanks of the Riding and Duck mountains have resulted in naturalized stocks, which spawn successfully in the wild. In addition, hatchery-produced hybrids between trout species are also stocked for recreational fishing. The "splake" is a hybrid between the brook trout and lake trout. It is stocked in lakes across southern Manitoba, mostly in Duck Mountain Provincial Park and Whiteshell Provincial Park. The "tiger trout" is a hybrid between the brook trout and brown trout. It was planted in One Lake, in Whiteshell Provincial Park, in 1990, but none survive at present. "Tiger trout" will be stocked in southern Manitoba in 2004.

WHITEFISH, GRAYLING, CHAR, TROUT, AND SALMON, FAMILY SALMONIDAE

KEY TO THE WHITEFISH, GRAYLING, CHAR, TROUT, AND SALMON FOUND IN MANITOBA

1A Well-developed teeth always present.

go to choice 2

1B Teeth absent except that minute teeth may occur in underyearlings.

whitefish, subfamily Coregoninae, go to choice 11

2A (1A) Dorsal fin with 17 or more rays. One hundred and three or fewer scales in the lateral line.

Arctic grayling, *Thymallus arcticus***, subfamily Thymallinae page 166**

2B Dorsal fin with 15 or fewer rays. One hundred and fifteen or more scales in the lateral line.

trout, salmon, and char, subfamily Salmoninae, go to choice 3

3A (2B) Thirteen or more anal rays. Few, or, usually no, black spots on body. *Note:* A series of dusky vertical bars (called parr marks) are seen on juveniles, but lost in adults.

kokanee salmon, *Oncorhynchus nerka* **page 171**
INTRODUCED

3B Twelve or fewer anal rays. Body marked with well-defined black spots, pale, or sometimes pink or red spots (whitish in preserved specimens) or pale vermiculations. *Note:* These markings may be masked by silvery pigment in lake- and sea-dwelling fish.

go to choice 4

4A (3B) Body with black spots on a lighter background. Vomerine teeth extending down midline of roof of mouth as far back as anterior margin of eye. Scales not tiny and embedded. Leading edges of pectoral, pelvic, and anal fins the same colour as the rest of the fin. (The dorsal and anal fin may have a pale tip.)

go to choice 5

4B Body with lighter spots or vermiculations on a darker background. Vomerine teeth confined to front of mouth and continuous with palatine teeth. Scales tiny and embedded. Pectoral, pelvic, and anal fins with a white leading edge.

genus *Salvelinus,* **go to choice 7**

5A (4A) Caudal fin usually unmarked or with a few indistinct dark markings. Some spots on sides are surrounded by light halos. A few red spots (white on preserved specimens) may be present on sides.

brown trout, *Salmo trutta* **page 173**
INTRODUCED

5B Caudal fin with black spots arranged along fin membrane between caudal rays. No light-coloured halos or red spots on body.

go to choice 6

6A (5B) Small teeth present at rear of tongue between bases of anterior gill arches. Underside of lower jaw with red or orange-red slash marking on each side in living or fresh specimens. *Note:* Red pigment is lost quickly after preservation in preserved specimens.

westslope cutthroat trout, *Oncorhynchus clarki lewisi* **page 168**
INTRODUCED

6B No teeth at rear of tongue between bases of anterior gill arches. Underside of lower jaw unmarked or with pale pinkish or yellowish mark on each side in living or fresh specimens. (See note in **6A**, above, about red pigment in preserved specimens.)

rainbow trout, *Oncorhynchus mykiss* **page 169**
INTRODUCED

WHITEFISH, GRAYLING, CHAR, TROUT, AND SALMON, FAMILY SALMONIDAE

7A (4B) Caudal fin distinctly forked, even when spread. Top and sides of head with distinct pale spots and/or vermiculations.

go to choice 8

7B Caudal fin square or only slightly indented when spread. No pale markings on sides of head.

go to choice 9

8A (7A) Pyloric caecae 93–208. Pale spots distributed profusely on body, top, and sides of head, and dorsal and caudal fins. Caudal fin deeply forked.

lake trout, *Salvelinus namaycush* page 179

8B Pyloric caecae 65–85. Pale spots and vermiculations on head and body, but less densely distributed than above. Few or no pale markings on dorsal or caudal fins. Caudal fin forked, but not deeply.

"splake," *Salvelinus namaycush X S. fontinalis* page 177

HUMAN-MADE HYBRID

9A (7B) Pectoral, pelvic, and anal fins with a distinct black streak posterior to white leading edge. Back and dorsal fin with pale vermiculations.

brook trout, *Salvelinus fontinalis* page 177

9B No dark streak, or only a weak one, behind white leading edges of pectoral, pelvic, and anal fins. Either has oval or round pale spots on back, but not on dorsal or caudal fins, or has a mix of reticulated (web-like) pale markings and spots on back, sides, dorsal, and caudal fins.

go to choice 10

10A (9B) No dark streak behind white leading edges of pectoral, pelvic, and anal fins. Oval or round pale and/or pink spots on back and sides, but not on dorsal or caudal fins.

Arctic char, *Salvelinus alpinus* page 175

FRESHWATER AND ANADROMOUS, CHURCHILL RIVER AND NORTHWARD

10B No, or only a weak, dark streak behind white leading edges of pectoral, pelvic, and anal fins. A mix of reticulate pale markings and spots on back, sides, dorsal, and caudal fins.

"tiger trout," *Salmo trutta X Salvelinus fontinalis* page 173

HUMAN-MADE HYBRID

11A (1B) Nostril divided by a single flap of skin. Twenty or fewer gill rakers on first arch.

round whitefish, *Prosopium cylindraceum* page 165

11B Nostril divided by double flap of skin. Twenty-two or more gill rakers on first arch.

genus *Coregonus*, go to choice 12

12A (11B) Mouth inferior, distinctly overhung by snout. Gill rakers usually fewer than 30, except in *C. artedi* X *C. clupeaformis* hybrids.

lake whitefish, *Coregonus clupeaformis* page 162

12B Mouth terminal, or nearly so. Gill rakers never less than 30, except in *C. artedi* X *C. clupeaformis* hybrids.

ciscoes, subgenus *(Leucichthys)*, go to choice 13

13A (12B) Forty-three or fewer short gill rakers on first arch. Lower jaw usually included. Premaxillae making a distinct, downturned angle in profile of the snout.

shortjaw cisco, *Coregonus zenithicus* page 164

13B Thirty-six or more (usually 40 or more) long gill rakers on first arch. Lower jaw usually the same length as, or projecting slightly beyond, the upper jaw. The snout profile is straight.

cisco, *Coregonus artedi* page 160

NOTE ON THE SPECIES DIFFERENTIATION OF CISCOES IN MANITOBA

Ciscoes are a group of species of the genus *Coregonus* that is characterized by having a terminal or nearly terminal mouth, which extends to well below the eye. The ciscoes of northeastern North America may be divided into two groups. The first consists of a single, widespread, surface or shallow water form, *Coregonus artedi*, the cisco, which occurs over most of northeastern North America, including Manitoba, northwest to the Mackenzie River Delta. The second group, containing the remaining eight species, is, or was, typically found in deep water in the Laurentide Great Lakes and/or Lake Nipigon. Three of them, *C. hoyi*, the bloater, *C. nigripinnis*, the blackfin cisco, and *C. zenithicus*, the shortjaw cisco, were reported by Hinks (1957) to occur in Manitoba on the basis of specimens collected in Lake Winnipeg. Clarke (1973) did not consider the Lake Winnipeg *C. hoyi* and *C. nigripinnis* to be different from *C. artedi*. He did, however, conclude that *C. zenithicus* was distinct, and that it occurred not only in Lake Winnipeg, but also in Lake of the Woods, Clearwater Lake, Lake Athapapuskow, and Reindeer Lake in Manitoba. It has also been found recently in George Lake (Winnipeg River watershed). Manitoba, then, has two types of ciscoes. (1) There is a variable, widely distributed, surface and shallow water, fall-spawning (but see note under Spawning in the *C. artedi* account) form with long gill rakers and a high gill raker count (*C. artedi*). (2) There is a form with fewer, short gill rakers that is found in deep lakes, generally near the bottom, and that may be a spring spawner (*C. zenithicus*).

The long-known ecological and morphological variability of ciscoes both within and between lakes (Todd and Smith, 1992), and the recently demonstrated high degree of genetic uniformity among all forms across their ranges (Reed et al., 1998; Snyder et al., 1992; and Todd, 1981) make their identification difficult. It is also doubtful in many cases whether cisco forms with similar characteristics and occupying similar habitats but found in different lakes are taxonomically equivalent to one another.

Recent studies of genetic, morphological, ecological, and geographic diversity of ciscoes (Turgeon and Bernatchez, 2001a, 2001b, and 2003; and Turgeon, Estoup, and Bernatchez, 1999) concluded that northeastern North America was colonized during deglaciation by two genetically distinguishable groups of *C. artedi*. One group came from the Atlantic Refugium to the southeast of the Laurentide Great Lakes, and one from the Mississippi Refugium to the southwest of the Laurentide Great Lakes. These forms mixed and interbred as their expanding ranges overlapped in the proglacial lakes along the retreating ice front. Following deglaciation and drainage of the proglacial lakes, cisco stocks were isolated in separated lake basins. In many cases, these isolated groups began to diverge ecologically into deep and shallow water forms and/or benthic and plankton feeders. In general, morphologically similar forms that are distributed over a wide area exhibit more genetic diversity than exists between morphologically different forms within a single lake. This implies that the morphologically different forms developed independently within the lakes in which they are found. It follows that similar forms in different lakes may neither share a common ancestor, nor necessarily be ecologically similar. It also implies that each morphologically and/or ecologically differentiated form in each lake constitutes an evolutionarily significant unit that is an important component of the biodiversity of the ciscoes of North America. This pattern of multiple independent origins of similar forms does not fit readily into our system of classification and naming of animals.

We have retained the traditional species names for the high gill raker, surface and shallow water form (cisco, *C. artedi*), and the low gill raker, deep water form (shortjaw cisco, *C. zenithicus*) in this book, even though they do not reflect the evolutionary complexity that apparently exists within the ciscoes. On the basis of this concept, the occurrence of the bloater, *C. hoyi*, and blackfin cisco, *C. nigripinnis*, in Manitoba as distinguishable eco/phenotypes should also be re-examined. If they exist here, they would add significantly to the cisco biodiversity in Manitoba.

WHITEFISH, GRAYLING, CHAR, TROUT, AND SALMON, FAMILY SALMONIDAE

CISCO; CISCO DE LAC | *Coregonus artedi*

3 CM — FRESH SPECIMEN

IDENTIFICATION

The cisco and shortjaw cisco differ from the lake and round whitefishes in having a **terminal mouth**, and the **maxillary reaching to below the pupil of the eye**. Ciscoes are variable in their morphology to the point where it is virtually impossible to distinguish species on the basis of single or simple combinations of morphological characters. Clarke (1973), using multivariate analysis, showed that Lake Winnipeg as well as several other lakes have two or more distinct types of the cisco. Schweitzer (1968) also gave evidence that Cedar Lake (Saskatchewan River system) contained slow-growing and more rapidly growing forms of the cisco. To further confound the problem, ciscoes also vary among lakes, so that it is difficult to decide whether a given type in one lake is equivalent to similar types in other lakes. As presently understood, the cisco and shortjaw cisco differ in the cisco's having **more and longer gill rakers**, the front of the premaxilla of the cisco **not being angled more steeply downward than the snout**, and the **lower jaw** usually being **terminal or projecting**, instead of included. The cisco **grows to a larger size**, and is found in **midwater, or on the bottom in shallower water**, than the shortjaw cisco.

DISTRIBUTION WITHIN MANITOBA

- Continuous range of native species
- Known occurrences

NATURALLY OCCURRING HYBRID

The cisco will hybridize with the lake whitefish. Hybrids show characters of both parents. Typically they have a **cisco-like mouth** that is **terminal or nearly so**, with a **longer snout and jaws** than the lake whitefish. The **gill rakers are longer, more slender**, and **more numerous** than is typical for lake whitefish.

DISTRIBUTION IN MANITOBA

The cisco is found in lakes throughout Manitoba, and also enters the lower reaches of streams to feed. Ciscoes are also found in salt water on the Hudson Bay coast (Hinks, 1957; Remnant, pers. comm., 2002).

BIOLOGICAL NOTES

SPAWNING: The cisco spawns in the fall, usually on reefs in lakes, at water temperatures below 5°C. The optimal spawning temperature range is 3°–4°C. In Manitoba, much of the spawning activity of both the cisco and lake whitefish takes place under ice cover. This makes the study of their spawning difficult, because the ice cover during the late fall/early winter period is often too thin to support vehicles, people, or equipment. Spawning occurs in water up to about 3 m deep, over a variety of substrates.

Note: In May 1972, ciscoes were collected (by W.G. Franzin and K.W. Stewart) at Pine Falls, below the Pine Falls Dam on the Winnipeg River. This area is accessible to fish from Traverse Bay, on the east side of the south basin of Lake Winnipeg. These fish appeared to be *C. artedi*, but had darkly pigmented fins. They also had fully developed gonads rather than recovering spent gonads. This suggests that they may have been spring spawners, and revives the question of whether there is more than one distinguishable form of *C. artedi* in Lake Winnipeg.

GROWTH AND ADULT SIZE: In Manitoba, the maximum length attained by ciscoes is 350–400 mm, and they reach an age of 10 years (Keleher, 1952). Sexual maturity is attained at three to four years old in Lake Winnipeg (Keleher) and probably older in northern Manitoba. Schweitzer (1968) showed that Cedar Lake contained two distinct forms of ciscoes, a dwarfed, slow-growing form and a faster growing form. That work was done before construction of the Grand Rapids Dam, and it is not known whether the dwarfed form persists, although large ciscoes are still taken in Cedar Lake. The Fisheries Branch of the Manitoba Department of Natural Resources also found dwarfed *C. artedi* in Lake Winnipegosis during the 1960s. Again, it is not known whether this form persists.

FEEDING: The cisco is usually a planktivore, although adults will often feed on benthic fauna, including insect larvae and small mollusks. They will also take insects from the surface.

HABITAT: The cisco is a midwater to benthopelagic fish in lakes, although it will enter the lower reaches of streams on feeding and, in a few cases, on spawning excursions. Ciscoes are tolerant of at least some turbidity, and are found in all the Manitoba Great Lakes. In the shallow, turbid, and eutrophic south basin of Lake Winnipeg, they are more common than lake whitefish. The habitat of the cisco includes shallower lakes than those in which the shortjaw cisco is found. In deep lakes, it usually lives at shallower depths than the shortjaw cisco.

ECOLOGICAL ROLE: The cisco is a midwater to benthopelagic, middle-level consumer. It is an important prey species for large piscivores including lake trout (Day, 1983), walleye, northern pike, burbot, and channel catfish (in Lake Winnipeg and the lower Red River). The cisco is also an important intermediate host for the parasitic tapeworm *Triaenophorus crassus*. With the establishment of the rainbow smelt in Lake Winnipeg and downstream in the Nelson River between 1990 and 1998, the cisco may begin to decline in affected waters. Ciscoes, lake whitefish, and emerald shiners have all declined in northwestern Ontario lakes in which smelt have become established (Franzin et al., 1994). Becker (1983) notes that the cisco has become rare in Lake Huron and is declining in lakes Michigan and Superior. By contrast, it remains abundant in inland lakes in Wisconsin in which smelt have not become established.

IMPORTANCE TO PEOPLE

The cisco is caught in commercial fisheries in Manitoba and marketed smoked as "tullibee." Anglers also catch it occasionally, either while ice fishing or while fishing for goldeyes near the mouths of streams entering Lake Winnipeg. Ciscoes are a common prey of lake trout, walleye, northern pike, burbot, and channel catfish. The cisco is also an important intermediate host of the tapeworm *Triaenophorus crassus*, which makes cysts in the flesh of infected ciscoes and lake whitefish. *Triaenophorus* will not infect people, but the cysts make the flesh very unattractive in appearance. They reduce the commercial value of the fish, and, if sufficiently numerous, can render the fish unacceptable as human food.

COSEWIC Status as of January 1, 2004: Not Listed
MBESA Status as of January 1, 2004: Not Listed
MBCDC Status as of January 1, 2004: G5, S5

WHITEFISH, GRAYLING, CHAR, TROUT, AND SALMON, FAMILY SALMONIDAE

LAKE WHITEFISH; GRAND CORÉGONE | *Coregonus clupeaformis*

FRESH SPECIMEN
10 CM

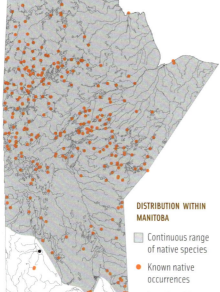

DISTRIBUTION WITHIN MANITOBA

- Continuous range of native species
- Known native occurrences
- Introduced locations

IDENTIFICATION

The lake whitefish can be distinguished from all other whitefishes in our area by the **inferior mouth, which does not reach to below the pupil of the eye**, the **double flap that separates the anterior and posterior nostrils**, and by having **more than 25 gill rakers on the first arch**. Lake whitefish are morphologically plastic (see notes in Feeding section below). Not only do they show variation between lakes, but more than one morphological type can occur in a single lake (Bodaly, 1977; Kristofferson, 1978).

NATURALLY OCCURRING HYBRID

To further complicate identification, lake whitefish and cisco will hybridize, producing fish with a combination of characters of both parents. See the cisco species account for a description of cisco X lake whitefish hybrids.

DISTRIBUTION IN MANITOBA

The lake whitefish is found in lakes and streams throughout the Canadian Shield portion of Manitoba, in the Manitoba Great Lakes except for Lake Dauphin, where there was a failed attempt to introduce it in 1982 (Matkowski, pers. comm., 2002), and lakes in Riding Mountain National Park and the Porcupine Mountains. From 1997 onward, it has been taken in the Red River in Winnipeg and the Assiniboine River between Portage la Prairie and its confluence with the Red River. These fish may have entered the Red and Assiniboine rivers from Lake Winnipeg, Lake Manitoba via the Assiniboine River Floodway, or possibly moved downstream in the Assiniboine River from lakes in the upper Assiniboine system in Saskatchewan. The lake whitefish has also been collected in salt water in river estuaries on the Hudson Bay coast (Hinks, 1957).

BIOLOGICAL NOTES

SPAWNING: Green and Derksen (1987) reported on studies of lake whitefish spawning in the area of Poplar River, on the east side of the north basin of Lake Winnipeg, from 1974 to 1977. They found that pre-spawning aggregation begins in mid-September, and fish in spawning condition first appeared between October 5 and October 15, at water temperatures of 9.4°C and 5.5°C, respectively. Spawning occurred in 1–3 m of water, over a mud or clay and detritus substrate, from which eggs were recovered. The earliest date on which they found spent whitefish was October 21, and the latest was October 31. Spent fish were found at water temperatures between 2.5°–4°C. Scott and

Crossman (1979) state that lake whitefish may ascend streams to spawn. They note that the spawning substrate is most frequently gravel, but spawning also occurs over sand. The eggs are broadcast over the bottom and sink. They also state that spawning lake whitefish in the Great Lakes have been observed thrashing at the surface and leaping clear of the water. Mavros (1992) demonstrated the existence of six, genetically distinct, lake whitefish stocks in the north basin of Lake Winnipeg, which could be differentiated on the basis of isozyme frequencies, morphometry, and carbon, nitrogen, and sulfur stable isotope ratios. This suggests that these stocks home to their respective spawning reefs, with limited interbreeding, and also have distinct feeding areas.

GROWTH AND ADULT SIZE: In Lake Winnipeg, lake whitefish attain an age of 17 years (Kennedy, 1954). The largest whitefish recorded in Manitoba was a 10.9 kg fish caught in Lake Winnipeg in 1924 (Keleher, 1961). The youngest age at maturity in Green and Derksen's (1987) study was three years for both males and females. They found that first spawning usually occurred at Age IV+ for males and V+ for females.

FEEDING: Lake whitefish feed mainly on benthic and planktonic invertebrates and small fish. They will also take insects from the water surface. Lake whitefish are very plastic in morphology, habits, and habitat. Kliewer (1970) showed that the morphology of lake whitefish varies with their habitat and feeding habits. In shallow lakes with a productive benthic community, they will be mainly benthic feeders, while those in deep lakes with steeply sloping bottoms and low benthic productivity tend to be plankton feeders. Plankton-feeding whitefish have longer, more numerous gill rakers, whereas benthic feeders have fewer, shorter gill rakers. Loch (1971) showed that the gill raker character will change when whitefish are transplanted from a lake with high benthic productivity to one with low benthic productivity. Bodaly (1977) showed that lake whitefish in a single lake can diverge into distinct groups with benthic- and plankton-feeding morphologies.

HABITAT: The lake whitefish is usually a schooling, benthic or benthopelagic fish that feeds on or near the bottom. It occurs in lakes and rivers. Coastal populations may be anadromous (or contain anadromous individuals). Lake whitefish living in rivers are more commonly found in the Canadian Shield region of Manitoba than in the prairies. In lakes, whitefish can occur over a wide depth range, but are more common in water less than 30 m deep.

ECOLOGICAL ROLE: The lake whitefish is a middle-level, benthic or benthopelagic consumer. It is an important component of the demersal community of lakes and larger rivers in the Canadian Shield. Juvenile lake whitefish are eaten by northern pike, walleye, and lake trout, while adults are only vulnerable to the largest size classes of piscivorous fish, large fish-eating birds such as ospreys and eagles, and probably only the river otter, among the piscivorous mammals.

IMPORTANCE TO PEOPLE

The lake whitefish is the third most valuable commercial fish in Manitoba, after the walleye and sauger. The flesh has excellent texture and a fine flavour. Among Aboriginals and European fur traders and settlers, whitefish was said to be a fish that could be eaten as a steady diet without growing tired of it.

Lake whitefish, like ciscoes, are intermediate hosts of the tapeworm *Triaenophorus crassus*. *Triaenophorus* cannot infect humans, but the cercariae of the worm form cysts in the flesh, which makes it unattractive and lowers its value. If the cysts are sufficiently numerous, they render the flesh unacceptable for eating. Since the northern pike is the host for the adult tapeworm, lakes with extensive weedy shorelines, which afford good habitat for pike, have the highest incidence of *Triaenophorus*-infected whitefish. Flooded timber along the shores of impoundments also increases pike habitat and, consequently, the rate of whitefish infestation by *Triaenophorus*.

The morphological and genetic variability of lake whitefish both within and among lakes (Franzin, 1974; Bodaly, 1977; Kristofferson, 1978) could be used as a management tool in identifying stocks and determining whether reproductive isolation exists among stocks in a given lake. Loch (1971) showed that, in addition to significant morphological differences, a change in gene frequency can occur in a transplanted lake whitefish population in less than ten years following transplantation, or about three generations of reproductive isolation. Although at least part of the present morphological and genetic diversity of lake whitefish may have existed before they colonized our area during deglaciation, much of it may have developed *in situ* during and after colonization. Morphological and genetic diversity seems to be characteristic of nearly all species of *Coregonus*. It may well be an important part of the ability of these species to survive environmental changes and its protection should be a priority in any plans for development that have an impact on their habitat.

COSEWIC Status as of January 1, 2004: Not Listed
MBESA Status as of January 1, 2004: Not Listed
MBCDC Status as of January 1, 2004: G5, S5

WHITEFISH, GRAYLING, CHAR, TROUT, AND SALMON, FAMILY SALMONIDAE

SHORTJAW CISCO; CISCO À MÂCHOIRES ÉGALES   *Coregonus zenithicus*

FRESH SPECIMEN
3 CM

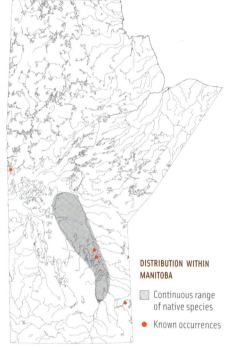

DISTRIBUTION WITHIN MANITOBA

- Continuous range of native species
- Known occurrences

IDENTIFICATION

The cisco and shortjaw cisco differ from the lake and round whitefishes in having a **terminal mouth** and the **maxillary reaching to below the eye**. The shortjaw cisco differs from the cisco in having **fewer** and **shorter gill rakers**, the **premaxilla angled more steeply downward than the snout**, and in having the **lower jaw usually included rather than terminal or projecting**. In Manitoba, the shortjaw cisco is **smaller than the cisco** and is found **near the bottom in deep water**.

Note: The status of the shortjaw cisco, as a distinct species from the cisco, and whether the shortjaw ciscoes of the Hudson Bay Drainage are the same species as the Lake Superior form, are still being studied.

DISTRIBUTION IN MANITOBA

The shortjaw cisco is found in large, usually deep lakes in Manitoba. It is known from Lake of the Woods, Lake Winnipeg, Lake Athapapuskow, and Reindeer Lake (Clarke, 1973), and most recently from George Lake, Whiteshell Provincial Park (Murray, pers. comm., 2003). It is likely that the full extent of its distribution in Manitoba has not been established. There are no records of this species in Manitoba from rivers or from estuaries on the Hudson Bay coast.

BIOLOGICAL NOTES

SPAWNING: Nothing is known about shortjaw cisco spawning in Manitoba. Most reports on the species' biology in the Great Lakes, up to at least Becker (1983), state that it is a fall spawner, like other coregonines. It now appears that the Lake Superior populations of shortjaw cisco are spring spawners (Canadian Wildlife Service 2001 Species at Risk Information Sheet). Spawning in Lake Superior occurs at depths of 30–70 m over a clay bottom (Scott and Crossman, 1979).

GROWTH AND ADULT SIZE: In Manitoba, the shortjaw cisco is smaller than the cisco. The few specimens in the University of Manitoba collection are all 100 mm or less in length (and are from burbot stomach contents from Lake Athapapuskow). In Lake Superior, the shortjaw cisco grows to 300–350 mm long and attains an age of nine years (Van Oosten, 1937).

FEEDING: Becker (1983) reported that *Mysis* and *Pontiporeia* comprise 95% of the food items in stomachs of shortjaw ciscoes from Lake Michigan. The mollusk *Pisidium* and debris and clay from the bottom made up the remainder.

HABITAT: Where data are available in Manitoba, the shortjaw cisco appears to be benthopelagic in deeper water than the cisco. Day (1983) found shortjaw ciscoes in the stomachs of lake trout caught near the floatline of gillnets set on the bottom in water over 40 m deep in Lake Athapapuskow, but near the leadline, burbot with shortjaw ciscoes and deepwater sculpins in their stomachs were caught. Murray (pers. comm., 2003) caught shortjaw ciscoes and deepwater sculpins in bottom-set gillnets at 40 m depth in George Lake.

ECOLOGICAL ROLE: The shortjaw cisco is a benthopelagic, deep-water, middle-level consumer. The Lake Athapapuskow data suggest it contributes significantly to the prey of burbot. It appears to co-occur with deepwater sculpin in at least Athapapuskow and George lakes. There is little information on the benthic fauna of other deep lakes in Manitoba, so the extent of this association is unknown.

IMPORTANCE TO PEOPLE

The shortjaw cisco is recognized by Lake Winnipeg commercial fishers as one of four types of ciscoes in their catch. Beyond that, few, if any, Manitobans ever see one, and the few that may be seen are simply considered to be ciscoes. It is apparently a significant component of the deep-water food web in Lake Athapapuskow. Because it has become rare in lakes Michigan and Huron, any populations of shortjaw ciscoes outside the Great Lakes may assume greater importance as surviving stocks of a declining species or eco-phenotype.

COSEWIC Status as of January 1, 2004: Threatened
MBESA Status as of January 1, 2004: Special Concern
MBCDC Status as of January 1, 2004: G2, S3

ROUND WHITEFISH; MÉNOMINI ROND | *Prosopium cylindraceum*

FRESH SPECIMEN
5 CM

IDENTIFICATION

The round whitefish can be distinguished from all other whitefishes in our area by the **inferior mouth, not reaching to below the eye**, the **single flap separating the anterior and posterior nostrils**, and by having **19–23 gill rakers on the first arch**.

DISTRIBUTION IN MANITOBA

The distribution of the round whitefish is disjunct or nearly so, with a northwestern/Arctic section that reaches its southeastern extreme in northern Manitoba, and a Great Lakes/eastern section that extends west to the head of Lake Superior. Round whitefish are uncommon in Manitoba. There are only three specimens from northern Manitoba in the Royal Ontario Museum records. Two of these were collected in the Churchill River at the coast, and a third in Putahow Lake in the Thlewiaza River watershed, inland in extreme northwestern Manitoba. Round whitefish also occur in Nueltin Lake (Thlewiaza River watershed), which straddles the Manitoba-Nunavut boundary (Scott and Crossman, 1979).

BIOLOGICAL NOTES

There are no studies of round whitefish biology in Manitoba. The information below is extracted from Scott and Crossman (1979). Where possible, information pertaining to the northwestern/Arctic section has been selected as being more likely to be representative of Manitoba fish.

SPAWNING: Round whitefish are fall spawners. In Nueltin Lake they begin an upstream spawning migration in late October. Spawning occurs over gravel substrate in shallows of lakes, river mouths, or upstream in rivers. The eggs are broadcast over the bottom and sink.

GROWTH AND ADULT SIZE: In Great Slave Lake, round whitefish attain an age of 14 years and a length of 513 mm (Scott and Crossman, 1979). By contrast, a maximum size of 394 mm and age of nine years is reported for Lake Superior round whitefish (Scott and Crossman). For the Lake Superior fish, sexually mature females ranged from

WHITEFISH, GRAYLING, CHAR, TROUT, AND SALMON, FAMILY SALMONIDAE

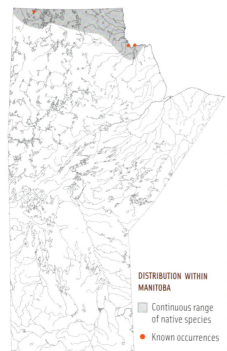

DISTRIBUTION WITHIN MANITOBA

☐ Continuous range of native species
● Known occurrences

305–394 mm, corresponding to an age range of five to nine years (Scott and Crossman).

FEEDING: Round whitefish feed on benthic invertebrates, and show less tendency to feed on plankton above the bottom than the lake whitefish. Larval insects, mollusks, the amphipod crustacean *Hyallela*, and occasionally small fish and fish eggs are taken.

HABITAT: The round whitefish is primarily a lake-dwelling, benthic fish. It can also be found in rivers, more commonly in the Arctic than in more southerly parts of its range.

ECOLOGICAL ROLE: The round whitefish is primarily a benthic, middle-level consumer at moderate depths in lakes. In Manitoba, it is too uncommon to be of great importance in the fish communities of our northern lakes.

IMPORTANCE TO PEOPLE

The round whitefish is an excellent food fish, but it is not used extensively because of its small size and restricted availability in comparison to lake whitefish, lake trout, and Arctic char in northern lakes. Round whitefish have been implicated as potential egg predators on commercially valuable species such as lake whitefish. Although fish eggs have been found in their stomachs, they have not been shown to be significant egg predators.

COSEWIC Status as of January 1, 2004: Not Listed
MBESA Status as of January 1, 2004: Not Listed
MBCDC Status as of January 1, 2004: G5, S3S4

ARCTIC GRAYLING; OMBRE ARCTIQUE | *Thymallus articus*

FRESH SPECIMEN
5 CM

IDENTIFICATION

The Arctic grayling is our only salmonid with the combination of **large scales, strong teeth, black spots on the body**, and a **long, high, flag-like dorsal fin**.

DISTRIBUTION IN MANITOBA

The Arctic grayling is found in coastal streams north of the Nelson River system and in the lower Churchill River, then northward throughout the Hudson Bay coastal drainages and inland from the Seal River northward. The Arctic grayling does not enter sea water in Hudson Bay. It was introduced into a human-made pond at the Fort Whyte Centre for

WHITEFISH, GRAYLING, CHAR, TROUT, AND SALMON, FAMILY SALMONIDAE

DISTRIBUTION WITHIN MANITOBA

- Continuous range of native species
- Known native occurrences
- Introduced locations

Outdoor Education in Winnipeg during the late 1980s. None have been taken there since the late 1980s, so it is unlikely that any survive.

BIOLOGICAL NOTES

Gillies (1975) reported his studies of the growth of Arctic grayling in Manitoba and reviewed the literature and other reports on its biology. Much of the information below is extracted from his report.

SPAWNING: Unlike all other native salmonids in Manitoba, the Arctic grayling is a spring spawner. Grayling spawning has not been observed in Manitoba, but Johnson (1971) reported that Arctic grayling in Black Lake, Saskatchewan (Churchill River watershed, 59° 10'N, 105° 20'W), spawned between May 18 and June 12, at water temperatures ranging from 3°–10°C over a 10-year period. Spawning fish migrate from ice-covered lakes into streams in which the ice is breaking up. Spawning is done over gravel substrate, and males defend a territory, although no nest is constructed (Scott and Crossman, 1979).

GROWTH AND ADULT SIZE: Gillies (1975) combined grayling growth data from seven sites in Manitoba and reported a maximum age of seven years. The mean maximum size was 436 mm at Age VI. By comparison, in Lake Athabasca, the Arctic grayling attains an age of seven years and a mean fork length of 375 mm at that age (Scott and Crossman, 1979). The Manitoba record for the Arctic grayling is a 57 cm total length fish caught in Nueltin Lake in 1998. Sexual maturity is at four to five years over the range of grayling in Canada (Gillies).

FEEDING: Adult grayling feed mainly on aquatic and terrestrial insects, but will also take small fish, including grayling fry, fish eggs, and even a lemming has been recorded.

HABITAT: The Arctic grayling lives in clear water in rivers and streams and along the shorelines of lakes. It is found most often over rocky substrates in water less than 3 m deep.

ECOLOGICAL ROLE: The Arctic grayling is a middle-level consumer in streams and the littoral zones of lakes. In many respects, it is ecologically similar to trout. In Manitoba streams, the grayling is probably a significant prey species for northern pike, but farther north, it is likely to be the only large fish in many streams and smaller lakes. In larger lakes, it is eaten by lake trout and northern pike, but whitefish, ciscoes, and suckers are all much more abundant prey species. Like the lake whitefish, grayling have been accused of being predators on the eggs of lake trout, Pacific salmon, and lake whitefish.

IMPORTANCE TO PEOPLE

The Arctic grayling is a superb angling species. It has a striking appearance and beautiful colours. It rises readily to flies and also takes spinners and other small baits. The flesh has excellent flavour and texture. It has also been used by the Dene and Inuit as food for dogs (and for themselves when whitefish or Arctic char are scarce). The requirement of grayling for clear, cold water makes them vulnerable to human encroachment on their habitat. Historically, there were isolated areas of grayling distribution in northern and southern Michigan, and in Missouri River headwaters in the Rocky Mountains in Montana. The Michigan populations have been extirpated and the Montana populations also are nearly gone. Montana is planting Arctic grayling in some headwaters in which it was formerly found, as is Parks Canada, in the headwaters of the Waterton River in Waterton Lakes National Park. Northern Canada and Alaska are the remaining sanctuaries for this beautiful and distinctively Arctic fish.

COSEWIC Status as of January 1, 2004: Not Listed
MBESA Status as of January 1, 2004: Not Listed
MBCDC Status as of January 1, 2004: G5, S4

WHITEFISH, GRAYLING, CHAR, TROUT, AND SALMON, FAMILY SALMONIDAE

WESTSLOPE CUTTHROAT TROUT; TRUITE FARDÉE | *Oncorhynchus clarki lewisi*

NOTE: Introduced species

5 CM — FRESH SPECIMEN

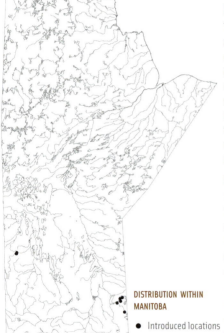

DISTRIBUTION WITHIN MANITOBA

● Introduced locations

IDENTIFICATION

The westslope cutthroat trout can be distinguished from all other trout in our area by the following combination of characters: (1) there are **small black spots without light-coloured halos on the body, dorsal fin, and tail;** (2) there are **no red spots;** (3) there is a **red slash marking on each side of the lower jaw;** (4) there is **no pinkish or reddish band on each side of the body;** (5) there may be **reddish to violet colour on the gill covers and along each side of the abdomen;** and (6) there are **teeth on the rear of the tongue between the bases of the gill arches (basihyal teeth).**

DISTRIBUTION IN MANITOBA

In Manitoba, the westslope cutthroat trout was introduced into lakes in Duck Mountain Provincial Park, and, in southeastern Manitoba, in Whiteshell Provincial Park in 1989 (Matkowski, pers. comm., 2001). Probably none of these survive at present.

The westslope cutthroat is native to the headwaters of the Kootenay and Fraser rivers in British Columbia, Kootenay River headwaters in Idaho and Montana, the headwaters of the South Saskatchewan and Missouri rivers in Alberta, and the northern headwaters of the Missouri River in Montana.

BIOLOGICAL NOTES

SPAWNING: The westslope cutthroat is not known to spawn in Manitoba. It is a spring spawner that ascends into small tributaries to spawn. The female excavates a depression, or redd, in the gravel in which the eggs are deposited and then covered with gravel. Spawning habitat typically is shallow riffles.

GROWTH AND ADULT SIZE: In their native range, westslope cutthroat in larger streams and rivers can grow to about 500 mm total length, and most adults are from 200–300 mm long. In small headwater streams at high elevations, they often are dwarfed, and mature individuals 150 mm long, still retaining parr marks, are found.

FEEDING: The westslope cutthroat is primarily an invertebrate predator that feeds on aquatic and terrestrial insects. In lakes, they are plankton feeders. Of all the native and introduced trout in North America, they are the least inclined to piscivory (Behnke, 1992).

WHITEFISH, GRAYLING, CHAR, TROUT, AND SALMON, FAMILY SALMONIDAE

HABITAT: The westslope cutthroat trout today mainly is a stream-dwelling fish in the headwater sections of mountain streams, usually above impassable falls and rapids. It prefers pools and runs, and will move into riffles and rapids to feed. Where it coexists with introduced trout such as brook and rainbow trout, the westslope cutthroat is found in faster water than the others. Historically, westslope cutthroat also lived in lakes and in the foothill and western prairie reaches of their native streams. The introduction of exotic trout species has resulted in the extirpation of westslope cutthroats from most lakes in their native range. Similarly, introduction of exotic trout species into downstream sections of their native range virtually confines the westslope cutthroat to high-elevation headwaters above impassable falls.

ECOLOGICAL ROLE: The westslope cutthroat is a middle-level consumer adapted to clear, cold mountain streams and lakes. Of all the trout that have been introduced into Manitoba, it seems to be the least likely to be able to adapt to our conditions.

IMPORTANCE TO PEOPLE

In its native range, the westslope cutthroat is a popular game fish that can provide excellent fly fishing. Limited stocking in Manitoba, combined with the narrow environmental and ecological tolerances of the westslope cutthroat, makes it unlikely to be more than a curiosity in Manitoba.

COSEWIC Status as of January 1, 2004: Not Listed
MBESA Status as of January 1, 2004: Not Listed
MBCDC Status as of January 1, 2004: G4, SE

RAINBOW TROUT; TRUITE ARC-EN-CIEL | *Oncorhynchus mykiss*

NOTE: Introduced species

FRESH SPECIMEN
5 CM

IDENTIFICATION

The rainbow trout can be distinguished from all other trout in our area by the following combination of characters: (1) there are **small black spots without light-coloured halos on the body, dorsal fin, and tail**; (2) there are **no red spots**; (3) there are **no red slash markings on each side of the lower jaw**; (4) there is a **pinkish or reddish band on each side of the body, which runs forward onto the gill cover, but no red or violet pigment along each side of the abdomen**; and (5) there are **no teeth on the tongue between the bases of the gill arches**.

DISTRIBUTION IN MANITOBA

In Manitoba, the rainbow trout is the most frequently stocked trout species. It has been stocked in many prairie potholes, small lakes, ponds, artificial impoundments, flooded quarries and gravel pits, and some streams across southern Manitoba northward into the Churchill River system.

The native range of the rainbow trout includes coastal watersheds of the Pacific Rim from Baja California to the Kamchatka Peninsula in Russia. Non-migratory coastal stocks of these fish are called "rainbow trout," and migratory fish are called "steelhead." Inland, non-migratory races of this species in North America are usually referred to as "redband trout." The hatchery strain of rainbow trout originates from cross-breeding of migratory coastal rainbow trout and non-migratory redband trout from the McCloud River in California (Behnke, 1992). This is the strain

WHITEFISH, GRAYLING, CHAR, TROUT, AND SALMON, FAMILY SALMONIDAE

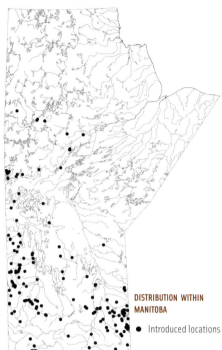

DISTRIBUTION WITHIN MANITOBA

• Introduced locations

that is also used in aquaculture. It has become adapted to hatchery rearing and propagation. It has been introduced to every continent except Antarctica. Hatchery rainbow trout qualify as domestic animals, and, together with carp and goldfish, are among the first domesticated fish.

BIOLOGICAL NOTES

SPAWNING: Rainbow trout apparently do not spawn successfully in the wild in Manitoba. In their native range, they are spring spawners. Lake-dwelling rainbows may spawn either in inlet or outlet streams, and river fish ascend tributaries. The spawning temperature ranges from 10°–15°C. Like most trout and salmon, the female excavates a nest, or redd, in gravel, in a riffle. The eggs are covered after being deposited.

GROWTH AND ADULT SIZE: Hatchery rainbow trout can grow to a length of 180-200 mm in their first year. The largest angler-caught rainbow trout in Manitoba was caught in East Blue Lake in 2001, and was 83 cm total length.

FEEDING: Rainbow/redband trout feed mostly on invertebrates, including benthic insects, crustaceans and mollusks, midwater planktonic animals, and surface insects. Larger individuals may become fish predators, which further accelerates their growth.

HABITAT: Non-migratory rainbow/redband trout live in both lakes and streams, but are more commonly lake dwellers. In lakes, they are schooling, midwater fish, and in streams, they inhabit pools and runs, often entering faster water to feed. They have low tolerance of turbidity, and require well-oxygenated water of 21°C or lower.

ECOLOGICAL ROLE: The rainbow trout is a middle-level consumer that is pelagic and schooling in lakes, and benthic in streams. Unlike the cutthroat, large rainbows may become piscivorous. Rainbow trout tolerate warmer water for limited periods of time than cutthroat or brook trout.

IMPORTANCE TO PEOPLE

The hatchery strain of rainbow trout is the preferred trout for put-and-take planting of fish to extend angling opportunities throughout southern Manitoba. This is due to a combination of availability of hatchery rainbow trout eggs, fry, and fingerlings; their adaptation to growth and reproduction under hatchery conditions; and their tolerance of at least short-term exposure to water temperatures over 20°C. Although rainbow trout in Manitoba are maintained only by stocking, they have been planted in so many areas for so long that people are often surprised to learn they are not native here. They provide angling opportunities in many areas of southern Manitoba where there are no nearby waters that support fishable stocks of native species. The attraction of rainbow trout fishing also contributes significantly to the income from tourism, especially in western Manitoba northward to about Lake Athapapuskow.

It should be noted that there are negative aspects to introduction of trout. They add to the numbers of consumers that the food base in the host community supports. Introduction of large numbers of trout can significantly reduce the abundance and diversity of invertebrates, native fishes, and sometimes amphibians (tadpoles and larval salamanders). This suggests that trout introductions should not be done where there is an economically valuable stock of a native species or a native species that is rare and/or of limited distribution with which they might compete.

COSEWIC Status as of January 1, 2004: Not Listed
MBESA Status as of January 1, 2004: Not Listed
MBCDC Status as of January 1, 2004: G5, SE

KOKANEE; KOKANI *Oncorhynchus nerka*

NOTE: Introduced species

FRESH SPECIMEN, IMMATURE FISH
3 CM

FRESH SPECIMEN, SPAWNING MALE
3 CM

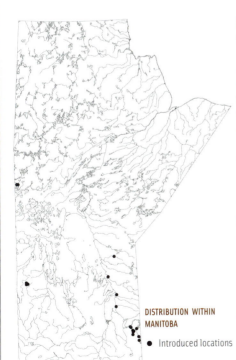

DISTRIBUTION WITHIN MANITOBA
● Introduced locations

IDENTIFICATION

The kokanee is a dwarfed, non-migratory form of the sockeye salmon. It is distinguished from all other salmonids in our area by the following. The **anal fin is long and low, with 13 or more rays**. The **body is steel blue to green above and the sides are bright silver in immature fish. Sexually mature males become bright red to maroon on the body, with a green head**. Mature females may show red colour or remain silvery, but are usually less colourful than males. There are **no spots on the head or sides of the body**. *Note:* There may be a few scattered black spots on the top of the back, which are hard to see on live or unpreserved specimens unless viewed looking straight down on the back in good light.

DISTRIBUTION IN MANITOBA

The kokanee has been introduced into lakes in Duck Mountain and Whiteshell provincial parks. There was also one failed attempt to introduce it into tributaries to the east side of the south basin of Lake Winnipeg in 1969. Kokanee salmon mature and die at four years of age, and none are present in Manitoba at the time of this writing.

The native range of the kokanee includes all the range of the sockeye, which is the Pacific Rim from northern California to Hokkaido, Japan, and the Arctic Ocean from Bathurst Inlet, NT, to the Anadyr River, Russia. It also extends inland to above the present limit of migration for the sockeye in the Fraser and Columbia river watersheds.

WHITEFISH, GRAYLING, CHAR, TROUT, AND SALMON, FAMILY SALMONIDAE

BIOLOGICAL NOTES

Most of the following information is extracted from Scott and Crossman (1979).

SPAWNING: Kokanees do not spawn in Manitoba. The kokanee is a fall spawner. It usually ascends tributary streams and spawns in gravel, in riffles and runs, but beach spawning also occurs. Kokanees, like all Pacific salmon, die after spawning. Although spawning is unknown in Manitoba, mature male kokanees have been caught in midwinter by anglers fishing through the ice in Duck Mountain Provincial Park.

GROWTH AND ADULT SIZE: Kokanees, like the sockeye, have a fixed life history and die after they spawn. Usually kokanees mature at four years old, but the age at maturity can vary from as little as two years for precocial males to as many as eight years. In their native lakes, kokanees seldom grow larger than 300 mm total length. Larger size at maturity is often seen in kokanees introduced into impoundments. The Manitoba angling record for the kokanee is a 55 cm individual caught in Gull Lake, Duck Mountain Provincial Park, in 1997.

FEEDING: Kokanees are mainly plankton feeders, but will also take insects from the water surface.

HABITAT: The kokanee is a schooling, midwater, lacustrine fish. In its native range, it is found in clear, cold montane lakes. It also requires cold, clear tributary streams with riffles and gravel substrates for spawning.

ECOLOGICAL ROLE: The kokanee is a pelagic, lacustrine, middle-level consumer. It is possible that the kokanee may compete with the cisco if it were introduced into a lake containing ciscoes. This has not been investigated, however.

IMPORTANCE TO PEOPLE

In its native range, the kokanee is probably more intensively sought by anglers than the rainbow trout that often shares its lakes. Its main value is its bright red, flavourful flesh, rather than its sporting qualities. While it can make leaps and fast runs when caught on light tackle, and will take flies or small spinning lures, it is most commonly caught with heavy rods and lines with large "gang trolls" fished from boats well offshore. In Manitoba, kokanees are said to be very difficult to catch, except for mature or post-mature, moribund individuals caught in the winter after they should have spawned.

COSEWIC Status as of January 1, 2004: Not Listed
MBESA Status as of January 1, 2004: Not Listed
MBCDC Status as of January 1, 2004: G5, SE

WHITEFISH, GRAYLING, CHAR, TROUT, AND SALMON, FAMILY SALMONIDAE

BROWN TROUT; TRUITE BRUNE *Salmo trutta*

NOTE: Introduced species

PRESERVED SPECIMEN, BROWN TROUT
5 CM

PRESERVED SPECIMEN, "TIGER TROUT"
3 CM

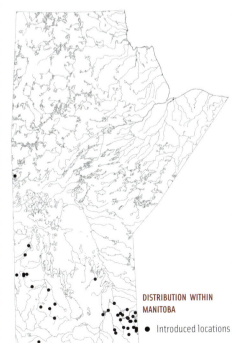

DISTRIBUTION WITHIN MANITOBA
● Introduced locations

IDENTIFICATION

The brown trout can be distinguished from the rainbow and cutthroat trout by the **large black spots on the body**. Some of the **spots on the sides are surrounded by light halos**. There may also be **a few red spots on the sides**. Unlike the rainbow and cutthroat trout, the **spots do not extend onto the caudal fin**.

HUMAN-MADE HYBRID

"tiger trout"; truite tigre; brook trout X brown trout (either reciprocal cross). The "tiger trout" is a sterile hybrid between the brook trout and brown trout. "Tiger trout" may have either a normal diploid chromosome number, or fertilized eggs may be temperature-shocked to produce a triploid chromosome number (McKay, Issen, and McMillan, 1992a, b). The "tiger trout" has **char-like markings**, consisting of a **reticulate pattern of whitish and olive to bluish markings**, which extend onto the dorsal and caudal fins, as in the brook trout. There may be a few **scattered red spots on the sides**. In sexually mature males, **the body colour becomes yellow-orange toward the abdomen, and the pectoral, pelvic, and anal fins become reddish orange with white leading edges**, as in char.

DISTRIBUTION IN MANITOBA

In Manitoba, the brown trout is stocked less frequently and in smaller numbers than the rainbow trout. Most brown trout stocking locations are in southern Manitoba as far north as Duck Mountain Provincial Park. The brown trout is native to Iceland and Eurasia east to the Aral Sea.

The "tiger trout" was planted only in One Lake, Whiteshell Provincial Park, in 1990.

BIOLOGICAL NOTES

SPAWNING: So far as known, brown trout do not spawn in the wild in Manitoba. Elsewhere, the brown trout is a fall spawner. Typically, they ascend into headwaters and spawn on riffles, as do most other trout. In Lake Superior, however, brown trout have been observed spawning on rocky reefs along the lakeshore (Scott and Crossman, 1979).

GROWTH AND ADULT SIZE: Most commonly, adult brown trout are from 400–600 mm long and 1–2 kg in weight, but the species can grow to very large size. The largest brown trout caught in Manitoba was a 73 cm fish caught in West Blue Lake, Duck Mountain Provincial Park, in 1997. Both anadromous and lake-dwelling brown trout elsewhere can exceed 850 mm long and weights of 10 kg.

FEEDING: Juvenile and smaller adult brown trout feed mainly on invertebrates. They consume a wide variety of aquatic and terrestrial insects, benthic mollusks, and crustaceans. Juvenile brown trout in lakes also feed on plankton (Becker, 1983). Adult brown trout tend to be more piscivorous than most other trout, and this contributes to the large size they can attain. It has also led to extirpation of stocks of native trout such as brook, cutthroat, and rainbow trout in waters in which introduced brown trout have become established. Brown trout also prey on adult frogs, tadpoles, and larval salamanders.

HABITAT: Brown trout live in lakes and streams. They are more tolerant of turbidity than most trout, and do well in a temperature range of 18°–24°C. This makes them attractive to use in stocking waters that other trout species likely would not survive in over the summer. Although brown trout can live in a wide range of water velocities, large individuals are almost always in lakes or deep pools and runs in streams. In lakes, they tend to stay close to the shore in water less than 15 m deep.

ECOLOGICAL ROLE: The brown trout is a benthopelagic, middle- to high-level consumer. Its tendency to piscivory can have a significant effect on, or even cause extirpation of, native fish and amphibians in waters in which it has been introduced.

IMPORTANCE TO PEOPLE

In Manitoba, the brown trout is stocked in some waters as part of a program of maintaining put-and-take trout-fishing opportunities. Its tolerance of warm and turbid water makes it more likely to survive through a southern Manitoba summer in a small stream or lake than other trout. Brown trout, especially larger adults, are notoriously hard to catch. This makes them more of a challenge for anglers than rainbow or brook trout, and they are not as popular with anglers for that reason. Because of their piscivorous habits, natural waters in which they are to be introduced should be evaluated for the presence of native species that are rare or have restricted distribution before brown trout are stocked.

COSEWIC Status as of January 1, 2004: Not Listed
MBESA Status as of January 1, 2004: Not Listed
MBCDC Status as of January 1, 2004: G5, SE

WHITEFISH, GRAYLING, CHAR, TROUT, AND SALMON, FAMILY SALMONIDAE

ARCTIC CHAR; OMBLE CHEVALIER | *Salvelinus alpinus*

FRESH SPECIMEN, AMPHIDROMOUS
10 CM

FRESH SPECIMEN, AMPHIDROMOUS, SPAWNING
10 CM

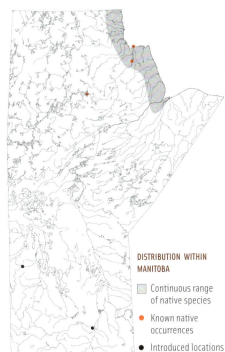

DISTRIBUTION WITHIN MANITOBA

- Continuous range of native species
- Known native occurrences
- Introduced locations

IDENTIFICATION

Species of the genus *Salvelinus* (chars) are distinguished by having **pale and/or pink spots against a darker background colour** of the body. **Black spots are never present**. They also have a **white streak at the leading edges of the pectoral, pelvic, and anal fins**. The Arctic char is distinguished by the **lack of pale markings on the dorsal and caudal fins**. It also **lacks a black streak behind the white streak at the leading edges of the pectoral and pelvic fins**. It has only **spots, not vermiculations** like the brook trout and lake trout, and **lacks red spots on the sides**, although it **often has pink spots**.

DISTRIBUTION IN MANITOBA

The Arctic char is native in northern Manitoba. Probable amphidromous Arctic char are recorded as far south as the Churchill River. The records of the Fisheries Branch of the Manitoba Department of Water Stewardship contain a single record of an angler-caught Arctic char from the Nelson River, below the Kettle Rapids Dam, which was caught before closure of the Long Spruce Dam. Amphidromous Arctic char become common north of the Churchill River. We have no records of native, non-migratory Arctic char from Manitoba. The Arctic char has also been stocked in lakes in Duck Mountain Provincial Park, and in human-made ponds at the Fort Whyte Centre for Outdoor Education in Winnipeg.

BIOLOGICAL NOTES

SPAWNING: The Arctic char is an amphidromous fall spawner. Amphidromous Arctic char may spawn either on reefs in lakes or in deep pools in rivers. In either case, the water must be deep enough that it does not freeze to the bottom over the winter while the eggs are developing. In its native range in Manitoba, the Arctic char spawns under ice cover. Spawning has not been observed in Manitoba, but is similar to the spawning of other trout elsewhere. The female excavates a redd in gravel, the eggs are deposited in several separate spawning acts, and the female covers the eggs with gravel when egg deposition is complete (Scott and Crossman, 1979).

GROWTH AND ADULT SIZE: Arctic char in northern Canada are very slow growing. On the Arctic Ocean coast, young amphidromous char first go to sea at an age of five to seven years and a length of 150–200 mm. First sexual maturity ranges from seven to ten years after the young first go to sea, and adults do not spawn every year. The oldest fish may be up to 30 years old, with a tendency for longer lifespans in more northerly populations. Mature amphidromous char have been taken at a length of 820 mm and a weight of 7.17 kg on the west coast of Hudson Bay in Nunavut (Sprules, 1952). The Manitoba angling record for Arctic char is a 71 cm fish caught in 1994 from a human-made pond at the Fort Whyte Centre for Outdoor Education.

FEEDING: At sea, Arctic char feed on a wide variety of benthic and midwater invertebrates and, sometimes, small fishes. In fresh water, juvenile and non-migratory char feed on benthic and planktonic insects and crustaceans.

HABITAT: Arctic char may be either amphidromous or non-migratory. Amphidromous char in Canada's Arctic return to fresh water to overwinter every fall, whether they are sexually mature or not. In fresh water, the Arctic char must live in lakes or rivers that are deep enough that they do not freeze to the bottom during winter. Most commonly, they are lake-dwellers in fresh water, but some stocks of amphidromous fish overwinter in rivers.

ECOLOGICAL ROLE: The Arctic char is a middle- to high-level consumer in one of the least productive and most rigorous environments inhabited by fish. In Arctic marine communities, it is one level below the top of the food web, since it is eaten by seals. Non-migratory Arctic char occur farther north than any other freshwater fish in the world.

IMPORTANCE TO PEOPLE

The Arctic char is an important food source for the Inuit over the entire Canadian Arctic and Hudson Bay coastline. It is also important to the Inuit as prey for seals, which are one of their most important resources. It is also fished for export to the south as a source of cash in the northern communities. In addition, it is a source of tourism from anglers who come to the Arctic. The Arctic char is one of the best food fish. Amphidromous char have firm, bright red flesh with a high fat content and excellent flavour.

COSEWIC Status as of January 1, 2004: Not Listed
MBESA Status as of January 1, 2004: Not Listed
MBCDC Status as of January 1, 2004: G5, S3

WHITEFISH, GRAYLING, CHAR, TROUT, AND SALMON, FAMILY SALMONIDAE

BROOK TROUT; OMBLE DE FONTAINE | *Salvelinus fontinalis*

3 CM — PRESERVED SPECIMEN, NON-MIGRATORY, IMMATURE

5 CM — FRESH SPECIMEN, AMPHIDROMOUS, IMMATURE

5 CM — FRESH SPECIMEN, "SPLAKE"

IDENTIFICATION

The brook trout has **pale spots and vermiculations ("worm tracks") on a darker background**. There are **scattered red spots with bluish halos on the sides**, and the **pectoral, pelvic, and anal fins have white leading edges with a black streak just behind the white**. The pale and dark **vermiculation pattern extends onto the dorsal and caudal fins but not onto the sides of the head**. The **rear margin of the tail has little or no indentation when the tail is spread ("square tail")**.

HUMAN-MADE HYBRIDS

(1) **"splake"; truite moulac; female lake trout X male brook trout**. The "splake" ("splake" = **sp**eckled + **lake** trout) is a human-made hybrid that grows more rapidly than brook trout, but can survive in lakes that are too shallow and/or warm for lake trout. Only the cross of male brook trout to female lake trout is used, because the hybrid embryo is too large to develop inside a brook trout egg. Externally, "splake" look more like lake trout than brook trout. Unlike the "tiger trout," the "splake" is capable of back-crossing at least to the lake trout. The **vermiculations and scattered red spots of the brook trout are absent**, replaced by the **pale yellowish spots of the lake trout**. The **pale markings extend onto the sides of the head**, as in the lake trout, but they are more scattered. The **tail is**

WHITEFISH, GRAYLING, CHAR, TROUT, AND SALMON, FAMILY SALMONIDAE

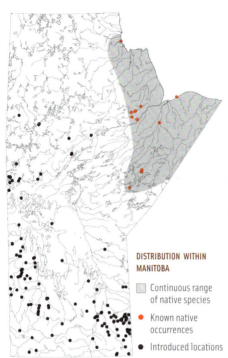

DISTRIBUTION WITHIN MANITOBA
- Continuous range of native species
- Known native occurrences
- Introduced locations

moderately forked when spread instead of square as in the brook trout or deeply forked as in the lake trout, and there is **no black streak behind the leading edge of the pectoral, pelvic, and anal fins**. The best diagnostic character is the pyloric caecae count. Brook trout have from 23–55 pyloric caecae, lake trout have 93–208, and the **"splake" has 65–85 pyloric caecae**. "Splake" are stocked in a number of lakes in southern Manitoba, mainly in Duck Mountain and Whiteshell provincial parks.

(2) "tiger trout"; brook trout X brown trout (either reciprocal cross). See the brown trout species account.

DISTRIBUTION IN MANITOBA

The brook trout is native in Manitoba in the lowermost portion of the Churchill River and its tributaries, the Nelson River system from the Limestone River downstream to the coast, the Hayes River system, and in Hudson Bay coastal streams south of the Churchill River. The Nelson and Hayes river systems have both amphidromous and non-migratory brook trout, but the migratory status of the Churchill River and some other populations is not known. Brook trout have also been stocked in many locations in southern Manitoba, from Whiteshell Provincial Park in the southeast to Footprint Lake in the northwest. Stocked brook trout in Stony Creek, near Neepawa, the upper Birdtail River, and in several streams in the northeastern portion of Duck Mountain Provincial Park, spawn successfully in the wild.

BIOLOGICAL NOTES

SPAWNING: Brook trout are fall spawners. The time of spawning may be as early as August in northern parts of their range to as late as December in the southern part of their range. They usually spawn in streams, using gravel substrate in riffles, in the headwaters. Lake spawning on a gravel bottom with spring water percolating through it is also known (Becker, 1983). As with other trout, the female excavates a redd in which the eggs are deposited and covers the eggs following spawning.

GROWTH AND ADULT SIZE: Scott and Crossman (1979) reported that brook trout in the Nelson and Hayes rivers lived to an age of six years and grew to 531 mm. First maturity was usually at three years, but some matured at Age II. The Manitoba angling record is a 71 cm brook trout caught in the Churchill River in 1994.

FEEDING: Brook trout are mainly predators on a wide variety of invertebrates, fish, fish eggs, and even small amphibians, reptiles, and mammals. Young brook trout feed mainly on invertebrates, and larger fish are more likely to take fish or other vertebrates. Amphidromous brook trout at sea eat a similarly wide range of marine prey (Scott and Crossman, 1979).

HABITAT: The brook trout is mainly a stream fish, but will also live in lakes. In its native range in Manitoba, it seems to be in larger streams, such as the Hayes, Nelson, and Limestone rivers. The lack of records from small streams may reflect lack of collecting effort more than lack of fish, however. The reproducing stocks of introduced brook trout in streams on the flanks of the Riding and Duck mountains live in headwater habitats.

ECOLOGICAL ROLE: The brook trout is a middle-level consumer, with larger adults feeding at a somewhat higher level. Schlick (1966) found that underyearling brook trout grew more slowly in an experimental section of the North Pine River (Lake Winnipegosis watershed) with high densities of longnose and western blacknose dace than in sections lacking these species. This is the only study in Manitoba of interaction between introduced salmonids and native fish species. Like studies done elsewhere, it shows that such interactions do occur where salmonids are introduced, and underscores the importance of assessing waters targeted for salmonid introductions for the presence of rare or ecologically important species, which may be affected by such introductions.

WHITEFISH, GRAYLING, CHAR, TROUT, AND SALMON, FAMILY SALMONIDAE

IMPORTANCE TO PEOPLE

The brook trout is a popular game fish. It rises to flies readily, and also takes spinning lures and natural baits. In Manitoba, the native amphidromous and non-migratory brook trout of northeastern Manitoba are a tourism attraction, as are the introduced brook trout in Duck Mountain Provincial Park. Elsewhere, introduced brook trout provide angling opportunities on small streams, and in natural and human-made lakes and ponds that otherwise support few or no other game fish.

COSEWIC Status as of January 1, 2004: Not Listed
MBESA Status as of January 1, 2004: Not Listed
MBCDC Status as of January 1, 2004: G5, S4

LAKE TROUT; TOULADI — *Salvelinus namaycush*

FRESH SPECIMEN
10 CM

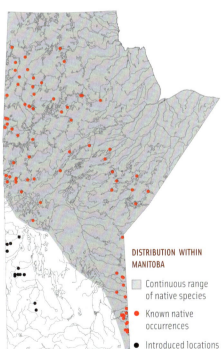

DISTRIBUTION WITHIN MANITOBA

☐ Continuous range of native species
● Known native occurrences
● Introduced locations

IDENTIFICATION

The lake trout has **profuse yellowish spots on an olive to green background**. The spots **extend onto the dorsal and caudal fin and the top and sides of the head**. There are **no red or pink spots** on the body. The lake trout has a **deeply forked tail**, and the **pectoral, pelvic, and caudal fins do not have a black streak behind the white leading edge**.

HUMAN-MADE HYBRID

"splake"; **female lake trout X male brook trout**. See the brook trout species account.

DISTRIBUTION IN MANITOBA

The lake trout is found in deep, cold lakes throughout the Canadian Shield region of Manitoba. In addition, it has been stocked in Clear Lake, Riding Mountain National Park, and in East and West Blue lakes, Duck Mountain Provincial Park, in the prairie region of the province. In addition, they have also been stocked in some lakes with native lake trout in efforts to enhance the stock.

The "splake" is stocked mainly in lakes in Duck Mountain and Whiteshell provincial parks.

BIOLOGICAL NOTES

SPAWNING: In Manitoba, lake trout spawn during October and November, with the timing being earlier toward the north. Spawning is done over bedrock, boulder, or rubble substrate on reefs in lakes at depths of 0.3–35 m in most lakes. Unlike other trout, lake trout do not excavate a redd, but the males arrive at the spawning grounds before the females and clean the substrate by brushing with their fins (Becker, 1983). The eggs sink into crevices between stones in the substrate.

WHITEFISH, GRAYLING, CHAR, TROUT, AND SALMON, FAMILY SALMONIDAE

GROWTH AND ADULT SIZE: The growth rate of lake trout varies, becoming slower toward the north. Age at maturity is usually six to seven years, but can be 12 years or more in Arctic lakes. The lake trout is the second-largest North American salmonine, and the largest non-anadromous North American salmonine. Most angler-caught lake trout weigh from 4–6 kg, but anglers have caught lake trout up to about 29 kg. The largest lake trout caught by any method was taken from Lake Athabasca in 1961 and weighed 46 kg. The Manitoba angler record is a 126 cm lake trout caught in God's Lake in 1998.

FEEDING: Juvenile lake trout are invertebrate predators. Early juveniles feed mainly on plankton. This shifts to larger benthic invertebrates as they grow, and they become increasingly piscivorous at larger sizes. Unlike other large piscivores, the lake trout is restricted to feeding below the thermocline in the summer months. Because of this, ciscoes, longnose and white suckers, and lake chubs are the most common fish eaten. Rainbow smelt are also taken, but smelt predation by lake trout in Manitoba has not been observed up to now.

HABITAT: Over most of Manitoba, the lake trout lives in deep, cold lakes, which do not become anoxic below the thermocline during the summer. They require access to well-oxygenated water 10°C or colder, and they can be found in smaller, shallower lakes and occasionally in rivers in extreme northern Manitoba and Nunavut. Lake trout are midwater to benthopelagic, and, over most of Manitoba, descend below the thermocline when the lake warms and stratifies during the summer months. Lake trout are never anadromous.

ECOLOGICAL ROLE: Adult lake trout are one of the five large apex predators in our fish fauna. They are one of the two that inhabit the deepest water in our deepest lakes, the other being the burbot. Day (1983) found that burbot abundance increased in Lake Athapapuskow in response to depletion of the lake trout. This suggests that, where there is a healthy population of lake trout, they are the dominant piscivores in deep-water lacustrine communities.

IMPORTANCE TO PEOPLE

Lake trout are valuable both as commercial and game fish. They have firm flesh, with excellent texture and flavour, that varies from white to reddish orange in colour. In Manitoba, lake trout and walleye are the two most important species in attracting tourist anglers to the province. The slow growth and long life of lake trout make them susceptible to depletion by overfishing, and even low to moderate angling pressure may deplete stocks in Arctic lakes. Since many of the valuable sport fisheries for lake trout are in remote northern lakes, which are expensive and logistically difficult to study, these fisheries should be regulated very conservatively to assure sustainability of the resource.

COSEWIC Status as of January 1, 2004: Not Listed
MBESA Status as of January 1, 2004: Not Listed
MBCDC Status as of January 1, 2004: G5, S4

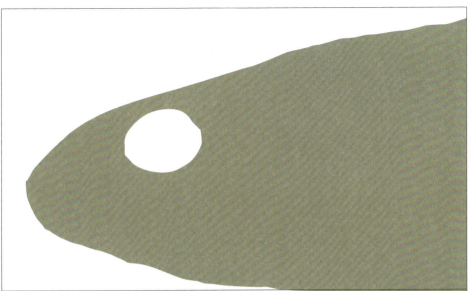

TROUTPERCHES, PIRATE PERCH, AND CAVEFISHES, ORDER PERCOPSIFORMES

TROUTPERCHES, FAMILY PERCOPSIDAE

ORDER PERCOPSIFORMES

This order contains the troutperches, Family Percopsidae, of North America and Eurasia, the pirate perch, Family Aphredoderidae, of eastern North America, and the cavefishes, Family Amblyopsidae, which lack eyes and pigment in their skin, of the southeastern United States. These families are surviving primitive representatives of the lineage of fishes that also contains the codfishes (represented in fresh water in Manitoba by the burbot) and marine families, which contain the bizarre-looking frogfishes and deep-sea anglerfishes.

FAMILY PERCOPSIDAE

The troutperch family is a unique and interesting group of North American freshwater fishes. Troutperch are small, streamlined fish, which resemble juvenile trout or minnows. They have **robust, silvery bodies** that may appear to be **translucent or partially transparent**, especially dorsally and toward the tail. They are marked with **two rows of diffuse, sometimes indistinct, greyish to nearly black blotches** along the sides of the body, similar in appearance to the parr marks of a trout, char, or grayling. The **mouth is small**, not reaching to below the eye, and **inferior**. The **teeth are weak** and not apparent without magnification. There are **two weak spines at the leading edge of the dorsal fin** and **one weak spine at the leading edge of the anal fin**. There is also a **small adipose fin**. The **pelvic fins are placed forward on the abdomen**, with the **pectoral fins extending well behind their base**. The **scales are ctenoid**, and thin.

TROUTPERCHES, FAMILY PERCOPSIDAE

TROUTPERCH; OMISCO — *Percopsis omiscomaycus*

1 CM — PRESERVED SPECIMEN

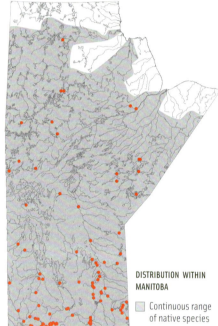
DISTRIBUTION WITHIN MANITOBA
☐ Continuous range of native species
● Known occurrences

IDENTIFICATION

The troutperch can be distinguished from the rainbow smelt, all juvenile trout and char, the grayling, and ciscoes by the combination of the **small, inferior mouth** with **weak teeth**, the **pectoral fins reaching well behind the base of the pelvic fins**, the **ctenoid scales**, and the **weak spines at the leading edge of the dorsal and anal fins**. They differ from juvenile round whitefish, lake whitefish, and all minnows in all of the above except the small, inferior mouth.

DISTRIBUTION IN MANITOBA

Troutperch are one of the three most widely distributed fish in Manitoba. They are found in rivers, larger streams, and lakes over almost the entire province.

BIOLOGICAL NOTES

SPAWNING: There are only a few reports of probable spawning of troutperch in Manitoba. In the Red Lakes, Minnesota, as well as elsewhere, spawning runs have been observed in May, and Lawler (1954) reported aggregations at this time in north-central Manitoba.

We observed a large aggregation of troutperch in Mud Turtle lake, Whiteshell Provincial Park, in May 2001. The fish were in a dense group over a bedrock substrate in a depth of about 30 cm. Although spawning was not observed, this midday aggregation contrasts with the known nocturnal onshore feeding movement of the troutperch and may have been a spawning aggregation.

Spawning has not been observed in Manitoba, but elsewhere, it occurs in April to June (Wisconsin) or May to August, with spawning periods in lakes being protracted (Scott and Crossman, 1979; Becker, 1983). Troutperch are broadcast spawners, which deposit the non-adhesive eggs over rocky substrate. The eggs fall into crevices among the rocks.

GROWTH AND ADULT SIZE: Although troutperch can grow to a maximum of about 150 mm, a sample of Manitoba specimens from the Assiniboine River ranged from 88–101 mm total length.

FEEDING: Troutperch feed on or near the bottom, mostly on aquatic invertebrates, but very large individuals may take the fry and eggs of other fish. Ratynski (1978) reported that troutperch sampled at Grand Rapids had mainly amphipods (65%) and chironomid fly larvae (30%) in their stomach contents. In lake-dwelling populations, there is a marked inshore migration at night, presumably for feeding (Scott and Crossman, 1979).

HABITAT: Troutperch are tolerant of turbid water, and occur in both lakes and flowing water. They are associated with rocky substrates. In the south basin of Lake Winnipeg, troutperch are one of the most abundant fish in the nearshore benthic habitat.

ECOLOGICAL ROLE: Troutperch are a benthic, middle-level consumer. They are probably prey for piscivores in their communities. We have identified troutperch in the stomach contents of walleye from Lake Winnipeg. They may be an important food source where they are very abundant, such as in the nearshore waters of the south basin of Lake Winnipeg.

IMPORTANCE TO PEOPLE

Troutperch show up infrequently in the bait fish trade, in tubs of frozen or salted minnows. They are common in southern Manitoba, especially in shallow, higher velocity reaches of somewhat turbid streams, like the Assiniboine River. They are also common in the nearshore waters of the Manitoba Great Lakes. As one of our most unique and distinctive fish, they contribute to the diversity and interest of our fish fauna.

COSEWIC Status as of January 1, 2004: Not Listed
MBESA Status as of January 1, 2004: Not Listed
MBCDC Status as of January 1, 2004: G5, S5

COD-LIKE FISHES, ORDER GADIFORMES

COD-LIKE FISHES, ORDER GADIFORMES
CODFISHES, FAMILY GADIDAE

ORDER GADIFORMES
The Order Gadiformes consists of 12 families, 11 of which are exclusively marine fishes, some living in the deepest parts of the ocean. The 12th family, the Gadidae, contains about 24 marine species and one freshwater species, the burbot, which is found in Manitoba. All gadiforms live in cool to cold water. Those living at shallow depths are found in the cool temperate to polar seas of the northern and southern hemispheres, and those that live at lower latitudes are found in the deep sea. The gadiforms are related to the troutperch and to the bizarre-looking marine frogfishes and deep-sea anglerfishes.

FAMILY GADIDAE
Codfishes range from **robust, terete shapes** to **elongate, eel-like** shapes like the burbot. There are **never any spines in the fins** and the **scales are small to very small, cycloid**, and, in the burbot, **deeply imbedded in the skin**. Many members of the family, including the burbot, have a **single barbel at the tip of the chin**. The **pelvic fins are set very far forward on the abdomen, their base being in advance of the base of the pectoral fins**.

CODFISHES, FAMILY GADIDAE

BURBOT; LOTTE *Lota lota*

5 CM — FRESH SPECIMEN

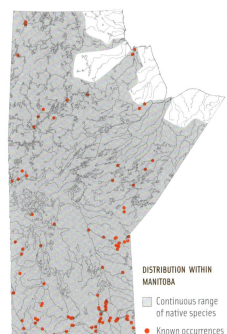

DISTRIBUTION WITHIN MANITOBA

☐ Continuous range of native species
● Known occurrences

IDENTIFICATION

The **elongate, eel-like shape**, the **single barbel at the tip of the chin**, and the **pelvic fins being inserted in front of the pectoral fins** distinguish the burbot from all other freshwater fishes in the province.

DISTRIBUTION IN MANITOBA

The burbot, northern pike, and troutperch are the three most widely distributed fish in Manitoba. The burbot is found in most streams and lakes, in all watersheds in the province.

BIOLOGICAL NOTES

SPAWNING: Burbot spawn in midwinter. Although spawning in deep water has been reported, mature and spent burbot in the Red and Winnipeg rivers are found in 2–4 m of water. Female burbot with nearly mature eggs have been sampled in late December and mid-January, and both sexes have been found with spent gonads in mid-February. Spawning is nocturnal, and the non-adhesive, semipelagic eggs are broadcast over sand or gravel substrate.

GROWTH AND ADULT SIZE: Burbot can grow to large size. Burbot reach sexual maturity at three to four years of age and sizes of 280–480 mm (Scott and Crossman, 1979). The angling record for Manitoba is a 99 cm fish caught in Lake Athapapuskow in 1991.

FEEDING: Juvenile burbot feed mainly on benthic and planktonic crustaceans (Becker, 1983). Invertebrates, especially crayfish, remain significant and fish also become a significant part of the diet of adults. Specimens of shortjaw cisco and deepwater sculpin have been found in burbot stomachs (Day, 1983). These prey species are found near the bottom in our deepest lakes.

HABITAT: Burbot are benthic at all life-history stages. Although they can be found in both rivers and lakes, over a wide range of depths, they can live at greater depth than most of our fish, being found at the bottom of our deepest lakes. Juvenile burbot are often collected among boulders in riffles, the tails of rapids, or lakeshores, while adults are found in the main channels of rivers and offshore in lakes. In Manitoba, the largest burbot are from larger, deeper lakes.

ECOLOGICAL ROLE: The burbot qualifies as one of the five species of apex predators in our fish fauna, even though it feeds at a range of trophic levels. They are probably most similar to the catfishes in being broadly adapted benthic predators. Although they occur with catfishes, they differ from catfishes in preferring cooler and often deeper water, and in occupying the benthic offshore habitat in large lakes. Burbot and lake trout are the largest benthic predators in the deepest waters in our lakes. Day (1983) suggested that burbot in Lake Athapapuskow increased in abundance as a result of a decline in lake trout populations due to overfishing. Examining the stomach contents of

CODFISHES, FAMILY GADIDAE

burbot caught in deep water may be the best way to detect the presence of deepwater sculpins. This emphasizes the importance of burbot as one of the most important predators in the benthic, deep-water habitat in lakes.

IMPORTANCE TO PEOPLE

Burbot are of secondary importance to both anglers and commercial fishers. Most burbot caught by anglers are taken while ice fishing, and, regrettably and illegally, wasted by throwing them out on the ice to die. In fact, the burbot is one of the highest quality food fish in Manitoba. Their flesh is firm, white, and of excellent flavour, resembling fresh codfish in eating qualities. Aboriginal people eat the liver of burbot. Burbot livers are large, with a high oil content and a mild flavour. They are an excellent high-energy food.

Note: Burbot have suffered a severe decline in abundance in the Kootenay River and its tributary lakes in British Columbia, Montana, and Idaho. This has apparently resulted from the development of hydroelectric dams on the river and the resulting management of water flows to accommodate electricity-generating needs. Burbot also declined in the Great Lakes as the sea lamprey spread into the upper Great Lakes, but seem to have recovered with the control of the sea lamprey.

COSEWIC Status as of January 1, 2004: Not Listed
MBESA Status as of January 1, 2004: Not Listed
MBCDC Status as of January 1, 2004: G5, S5

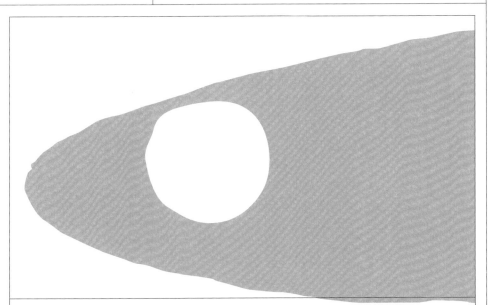

TOPMINNOWS, ORDER CYPRINODONTIFORMES
KILLIFISHES, FAMILY FUNDULIDAE

ORDER CYPRINODONTIFORMES

Topminnows are part of a diverse group of small- to medium-sized, mostly surface-living, marine, brackish, and freshwater fishes that live in temperate to tropical waters. Most species of this order are found in the Americas, but members of this order also occur in Europe and south Asia. This group also contains the live-bearing tropical guppies, mollies, platys, and swordtails of the aquarium trade. This order is related to the flying fishes, needlefishes, and halfbeaks, as well as the silversides.

FAMILY FUNDULIDAE

Killifishes are small, surface-living fish that superficially resemble the mudminnow (see Family Umbridae). They differ from the mudminnow in having the **dorsal fin base above the tips of the pelvic fins** instead of behind them, a **small mouth, which does not reach the anterior margin of the eye**, the **premaxillae being moveably joined to the snout**, and the **tip of the lower jaw projecting beyond the upper jaw**. Topminnows and killifishes are a diverse family, with many species in the southeastern United States. The family reaches its northwestern limit of distribution in Manitoba.

BANDED KILLIFISH; FONDULE BARRÉE | *Fundulus diaphanus*

FRESH SPECIMEN
0.5 CM

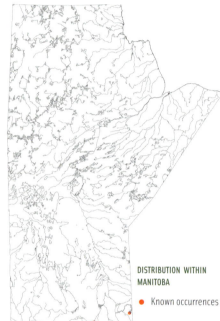

DISTRIBUTION WITHIN MANITOBA

● Known occurrences

IDENTIFICATION

This is our only small fish with a **small, oblique mouth**, the **lower jaw projecting beyond the upper jaw**, and **12–20 narrow, dark, vertical bars on the sides**. It is most similar to the mudminnow, but differs from it in all the above. The logperch has 15–25 dark vertical bars, but its mouth is horizontal and overhung by its pointed snout, and it has a spiny first dorsal fin and spines at the leading edges of the anal and pelvic fins.

DISTRIBUTION IN MANITOBA

The banded killifish is probably the rarest fish in Manitoba. Only three specimens are known from Manitoba, two from the Red River at the University of Manitoba campus in Winnipeg (Stewart-Hay, 1954) and one from Crowduck Lake, in Whiteshell Provincial Park in 1986 (Parker, pers. comm., 1986). Additional specimens have been found in Lake of the Woods in Ontario, and it is also known from the Red River in the United States (Koel, 1997).

BIOLOGICAL NOTES

Nothing is known of the biology of this species in Manitoba.

SPAWNING: Becker (1984) and Scott and Crossman (1979) state that the banded killifish spawns in late May (Québec) and from June to August (Wisconsin). Spawning takes place in quiet, heavily vegetated water, with a single male defending a territory and mating with a single female. The eggs stick to the vegetation by means of adhesive threads.

GROWTH AND ADULT SIZE: Banded killifish are reported to attain a length of 76 mm (Scott and Crossman, 1979).

FEEDING: Banded killifish feed from surface to bottom, and their main foods are reported to be aquatic insect larvae and planktonic crustaceans.

HABITAT: The preferred non-spawning habitat of banded killifish is shallow, clear, quiet water, over sand or gravel bottom with patches of vegetation. This can range from marginal waters of streams, rivers, or lakes, to small ponds. The Crowduck Lake specimen came from the edge of a wild-rice bed in the south arm of the lake (Parker, pers. comm., 1986). They are surface to midwater dwellers.

ECOLOGICAL ROLE: Banded killifish are low-level consumers that feed in the upper part of the water column. This would make them comparable to the sticklebacks. If they were more numerous, they might be preferred over sticklebacks by piscivores because they lack fin spines. The banded killifish is probably of little ecological importance in our area because of its rarity.

IMPORTANCE TO PEOPLE

In Manitoba, this species is so rare that it has no importance to people and probably is not significant in our aquatic communities. Being a warm-water species, should an increase in its abundance and/or distribution occur, it might be seen as additional evidence of climate warming.

COSEWIC Status as of January 1, 2004: Not at Risk
MBESA Status as of January 1, 2004: Not Listed
MBCDC Status as of January 1, 2004: G5, S1

STICKLEBACKS, PIPEFISHES, SEAHORSES, AND RELATED FAMILIES, ORDER GASTEROSTEIFORMES

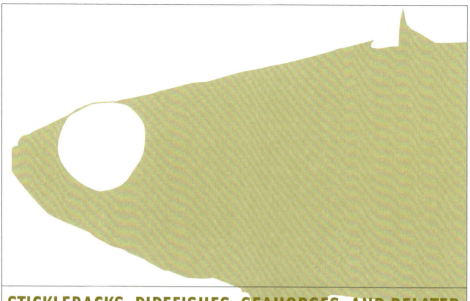

STICKLEBACKS, FAMILY GASTEROSTEIDAE

ORDER GASTEROSTEIFORMES

The diverse members of this order are tied together by an elongated snout with small jaws at its end, the body either naked or with bony plates instead of scales, and an ability to swim by sculling with the dorsal or pectoral fins. The group contains 11 families ranging from the mostly "normal-looking" sticklebacks to the bizarre sea moths, seahorses, and shrimpfishes. Many of the species are adapted for living in dense growths of aquatic vegetation.

FAMILY GASTEROSTEIDAE

The sticklebacks are a group of small marine, anadromous, and freshwater fishes distributed from the cool temperate to Arctic climate zones in North America and Eurasia. They are related to the marine tubesnouts, pipefishes, and seahorses. Sticklebacks are found in nearshore habitats in lakes and the sea, and streams and ponds, including bog habitats, in fresh water. Four of the five genera of sticklebacks are found in Canada and three of those occur in Manitoba.

Sticklebacks can be distinguished from all other fish in our area by the **row of separate spines on the back in front of the soft dorsal fin**. The **pelvic fins consist of a single spine or are absent**. There are **no normal scales on the body**, but some may have a **row of plates on the sides**. The base of the tail is slender and may be expanded into a laterally projecting caudal keel on each side.

STICKLEBACKS, FAMILY GASTEROSTEIDAE

KEY TO THE STICKLEBACKS FOUND IN MANITOBA

1A Three dorsal spines. Gill membranes joined to isthmus. Bony plates on sides of body and a caudal keel on either side at the base of the tail.
threespine stickleback, *Gasterosteus aculeatus* page 193
FRESHWATER AND ANADROMOUS ON THE HUDSON BAY COAST
1B At least 4, usually 5 or more, dorsal spines. Gill membranes free from isthmus. No scales or plates on body.
go to choice 2

2A (1B) Seven or more dorsal spines, alternately slanted to right and left of dorsal midline. A laterally projecting keel on each side of the narrow caudal peduncle at the base of the tail.
ninespine stickleback, *Pungitius pungitius* page 194
2B Usually 6 or fewer dorsal spines, all vertical, not slanted. No keels on caudal peduncle, and caudal peduncle deeper, about equal in depth to the eye diameter.
brook stickleback, *Culaea inconstans* page 191

BROOK STICKLEBACK; ÉPINOCHE À CINQ ÉPINES | *Culaea inconstans*

1 CM — PRESERVED SPECIMEN

IDENTIFICATION

The first dorsal fin of the brook stickleback has **four to seven separate spines**, which are **vertical, not alternately inclined to the right and left**. The body is naked, the **caudal peduncle is deeper than wide, being about as deep as the eye diameter**, and there is **no caudal keel** on each side of the base of the tail.

DISTRIBUTION IN MANITOBA

The brook stickleback is generally distributed in Manitoba northward into the Churchill River watershed.

BIOLOGICAL NOTES

SPAWNING: In southern Manitoba, the brook stickleback spawns in June. Males become nearly black, with scattered, irregular, lighter spots. The male builds a hollow, more or less spherical, nest with a single opening. The nest is made of organic detritus and filamentous algae, and anchored on vegetation just above the bottom. The male attracts females to enter the nest where they deposit eggs, which he then fertilizes. When spawning is complete, the nest will contain the eggs of several females. The male guards the nest and cleans and ventilates the eggs. The male remains with the young until they disperse after hatching (Scott and Crossman, 1979).

GROWTH AND ADULT SIZE: In southern Manitoba, sexually mature brook sticklebacks are usually 36–47 mm long. The uniformity in size of spawning adults and size increase of underyearlings during the summer suggest that brook sticklebacks in southern Manitoba mature at Age I and seldom, if ever, survive their second winter.

FEEDING: Brook sticklebacks feed on or near the bottom, on aquatic insects, crustaceans, filamentous algae, and the eggs and hatchlings of fish. Salfert (1984) found that brook sticklebacks cannibalized eggs from their own nests and raided the nests of neighbouring males. The likelihood and frequency of cannibalism were correlated with availability of food to nesting males.

STICKLEBACKS, FAMILY GASTEROSTEIDAE

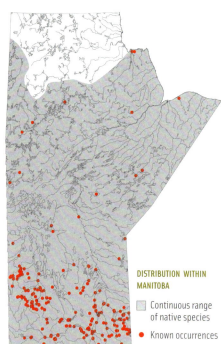

DISTRIBUTION WITHIN MANITOBA

- Continuous range of native species
- Known occurrences

HABITAT: The brook stickleback lives in quiet, weedy water in stream headwaters, ponds, prairie pothole lakes, and human-made impoundments. Valiant (1975) found the brook stickleback to be most strongly associated with pools (0–10 cm/s water velocity, depth 35–100 cm, and variable substrate) in five Manitoba Escarpment streams. Brook sticklebacks move from the mainstems of streams into tributaries and human-made drainage ditches and water retention ponds during April and May. Since many of these habitats dry out as summer progresses, there must be a return movement of adults and young by early August in most years. Brook sticklebacks are common in bog ponds and streams. This species is one of eight species that are typical of headwater bog habitats in Manitoba. See the pearl dace species account for a list and additional comments. There are a few reports from the southern Interlake region of brook sticklebacks in groundwater-supplied ponds that are not connected to other surface water. Connection during flooding and/or transport of fish by people cannot be ruled out in these cases, however.

ECOLOGICAL ROLE: The brook stickleback is a low- to middle-level consumer. Because of its tendency to disperse into headwater locations in the spring, brook sticklebacks can be one of the dominant fish species in natural and human-made ponds and bogs. Although it is eaten by other fish, it is often found in habitats that are devoid of larger piscivores.

IMPORTANCE TO PEOPLE

The brook stickleback has no direct economic importance. It is sometimes used as an aquarium fish in native fish aquaria by individuals and in classrooms, but requires live or frozen foods. It is also used in research and teaching of fish behaviour.

COSEWIC Status as of January 1, 2004: Not Listed
MBESA Status as of January 1, 2004: Not Listed
MBCDC Status as of January 1, 2004: G5, S5

STICKLEBACKS, FAMILY GASTEROSTEIDAE

THREESPINE STICKLEBACK; ÉPINOCHE À TROIS ÉPINES | *Gasterosteus aculeatus* species complex

FRESH SPECIMEN
0.5 CM

IDENTIFICATION

The threespine stickleback has **three large, vertical, separate dorsal spines**. In our area, there is a **row of vertically elongated bony plates on the sides**. The **plates overlap and project laterally on the caudal peduncle** to form **a caudal keel on each side of the base of the tail**. *Note:* The threespine stickleback includes an unknown but large number of reproductively isolated stocks. This is a complex of an unknown number of similar-appearing but distinct species. We follow Nelson (1994) and Scott and Crossman (1979) in referring to it as the *Gasterosteus aculeatus* species complex.

DISTRIBUTION IN MANITOBA

The threespine stickleback is rare in Manitoba. It has been found along the Hudson Bay coast, in river estuaries along the coast, and inland. McKillop and McKillop (1997) found a single specimen in the Caribou River, the inlet of Nueltin Lake (Thlewiaza River watershed). The site is far removed from any fishing lodge and lies above impassable falls. This suggests that the specimen was part of an inland, non-migratory freshwater population of threespine sticklebacks. If that is true, it would be the only known non-migratory population of threespine sticklebacks in the Hudson Bay Drainage. The specimen agrees with the morphology of the marine type of *G. aculeatus* (McKillop and McKillop), which is also unusual, since freshwater forms typically have reduced numbers of plates and lack the caudal keel.

DISTRIBUTION WITHIN MANITOBA
☐ Continuous range of native species
● Known occurrences

BIOLOGICAL NOTES

SPAWNING: Spawning of threespine sticklebacks in Manitoba has not been observed. Elsewhere, they spawn in late spring to early summer. Male threespine sticklebacks build a barrel-shaped nest in aquatic vegetation. Females are courted and enticed to enter the nest and deposit eggs, which are then fertilized by the male. The male guards the nest, and cleans and ventilates the eggs by fanning them with his fins and water expelled from his mouth. The hatchlings are also tended by the male until they are swimming and feeding on their own. Reproductive isolation among anadromous, freshwater littoral, and freshwater pelagic stocks of threespine sticklebacks has been demonstrated.

GROWTH AND ADULT SIZE: Adult threespine sticklebacks live to three or three and a half years old and grow to a length of 50–55 mm. Sexual maturity is attained at Age I. A few individuals as long as 75 mm have been reported (Scott and Crossman, 1979).

FEEDING: Threespine sticklebacks feed on invertebrates in midwater and on the bottom. Crustaceans, aquatic insects, worms, and the eggs and fry of fish, including other threespine sticklebacks, are taken.

HABITAT: The threespine stickleback exists as both anadromous and freshwater populations. Spawning is always done in fresh water, in quiet, weedy water. Non-migratory threespine sticklebacks usually live in quiet, weedy headwater habitats in streams or along lakeshores. In some Pacific coastal drainages, there are also pelagic populations in offshore surface waters in lakes. The habitat used by the probable freshwater population in the Caribou River was reported as "a quiet, sandy-bottomed backwater, approximately one-half meter in depth" (McKillop and McKillop, 1997). Anadromous threespine sticklebacks are pelagic, schooling fish at sea. They are found in coastal and open-ocean environments.

ECOLOGICAL ROLE: The threespine stickleback is a middle-level consumer. It is eaten by a variety of larger piscivorous fish, and birds. In Manitoba, there is no evidence that it is abundant enough to be a significant link in the food web.

IMPORTANCE TO PEOPLE

In Manitoba, the threespine stickleback is too rare to be of any importance to people. Its small size, short life cycle, adaptability to aquarium conditions, and capacity to become adapted quickly to local conditions have made it an invaluable scientific resource for the study of the genetic basis of ecological adaptation, reproductive isolation, and the evolution of species. It is kept by aquarium hobbyists occasionally, and has been introduced and become established in several small lakes and retention ponds in the Edmonton, Alberta, area, probably from illegal aquarium releases. This illustrates the invasive potential of this species and the hazard of releasing any aquarium fish into natural waters.

COSEWIC Status as of January 1, 2004: 1 subspecies, the Charlotte unarmoured stickleback, is listed in the Special Concern category
MBESA Status as of January 1, 2004: Not Listed
MBCDC Status as of January 1, 2004: G5, S1

Note: This classification predates the discovery by McKillop and McKillop (1997) of a non-anadromous threespine stickleback in the inlet of Nueltin Lake (Thlewiaza River system). This is the only evidence of non-migratory threespine sticklebacks in the Hudson Bay watershed. If the existence of a population of freshwater threespine sticklebacks in that area can be demonstrated, its biological uniqueness may qualify it for protection.

NINESPINE STICKLEBACK; ÉPINOCHE À NEUF ÉPINES | *Pungitius pungitius*

PRESERVED SPECIMEN
1 CM

IDENTIFICATION

The first dorsal fin of the ninespine stickleback has **eight or more separate dorsal spines**, which are **alternately inclined to the right and left**. There are **minute plates on the sides of the body**, visible with magnification. The **caudal peduncle is long and slender**, being **wider than deep**, and there are **caudal keels**.

DISTRIBUTION IN MANITOBA

The ninespine stickleback is found in larger rivers, except the Red River above Winnipeg, and lakes and streams throughout Manitoba. An anadromous, coastal form is found in river mouths along the Hudson Bay coast.

STICKLEBACKS, FAMILY GASTEROSTEIDAE

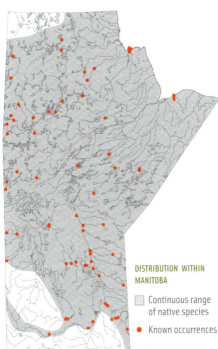

DISTRIBUTION WITHIN MANITOBA

☐ Continuous range of native species
● Known occurrences

BIOLOGICAL NOTES

SPAWNING: In southern Manitoba spawning occurs in June. Like the other sticklebacks, the male builds a hollow, tube-like nest, which is anchored in vegetation near the bottom. Males spawn with more than one female and guard the nest and tend the eggs and young as in other sticklebacks. Narita (1970) found that coastal-form ninespine sticklebacks in the Churchill, Manitoba, area spawned from late June to mid-July. He found that non-migratory ninespine sticklebacks in the Churchill area had a much shorter spawning period, from late June to early July. He also found that inland ninespine sticklebacks, at Lake Athapapuskow, spawned from early June to late July. Narita found the migratory and non-migratory forms both constructed nests that rested on the bottom, in areas with less than 5 cm/s current. Becker (1983) describes ninespine sticklebacks nesting in tunnel-like nests in mud substrate and nests constructed of plant material in crevices in rocky substrate in the Apostle Islands in Lake Superior.

GROWTH AND ADULT SIZE: Adult inland-form ninespine sticklebacks from Lake Manitoba in the University of Manitoba collection range from 47–56 mm total length. Narita (1970) found that most spawning ninespine sticklebacks of all forms were Age I+. He found none over Age II+. A maximum age of three and a half years is reported (Scott and Crossman, 1979).

FEEDING: Narita (1970) found that all forms of the ninespine stickleback feed mainly on benthic crustaceans and aquatic insects. Planktonic organisms comprised a minor portion of their diets. He noted that the migratory coastal form appeared to be emaciated on entry into fresh water in the spring and fed vigorously until they spawned. Underyearlings also fed vigorously and grew rapidly until they migrated downstream in the fall. He concluded that migratory ninespine sticklebacks fed little, if at all, during overwintering in salt water. The inland form has been observed to be cannibalistic on eggs and fry during the spawning and nesting phase (Becker, 1983).

HABITAT: The ninespine stickleback exists as anadromous populations along the Hudson Bay coast and as non-migratory freshwater populations. Unlike the brook stickleback, it prefers open water in the mainstems of rivers and in lakes.

ECOLOGICAL ROLE: The ninespine stickleback is a middle-level consumer, like the threespine stickleback. Because of its open-water habitat, it is more accessible to predators than the brook stickleback. They can be a significant part of the prey of our larger piscivores, including lake trout, northern pike, burbot, yellow perch, and walleye.

IMPORTANCE TO PEOPLE

The ninespine stickleback has no direct economic importance. It can be a significant source of prey for game fish. It is also an incidental species in the frozen bait minnow trade.

COSEWIC Status as of January 1, 2004: Not Listed
MBESA Status as of January 1, 2004: Not Listed
MBCDC Status as of January 1, 2004: G5, S5

SCORPIONFISHES AND RELATED FAMILIES, ORDER SCORPAENIFORMES

SCULPINS, FAMILY COTTIDAE

ORDER SCORPAENIFORMES

Most of the 25 families and over 1200 species in this order are marine and tropical. Members of this order resemble perch-like fishes, but differ from the Order Perciformes by having the gill slit behind the last gill arch either closed or only partly open, and having a bony strut across the cheek, running from below the eye to the preopercular bone at the rear of the cheek. There are often venom cells in the skin covering the dorsal fin spines, and the spines of the stonefish of the Indian Ocean and western tropical Pacific can be lethal to people. Fortunately, our sculpins all have blunt, weak spines without venom. Although there are exceptions, scorpaeniforms are typically bottom-dwelling fish that live on coral reefs or rocky bottoms in coastal waters. Our sculpins carry the preference for rocky habitat into fresh water.

FAMILY COTTIDAE

The sculpins are a diverse family of mostly marine fishes. Except for a group of four deep-sea species, the sculpins are coastal and freshwater fishes of temperate and Arctic climates in the northern hemisphere. The greatest diversity of sculpins is in the coastal waters of the North Pacific. All but a few species of freshwater sculpins are in the genus *Cottus*.

The sculpins are among the least-studied fishes in our area. They are never common in samples and often do not show up in repeat samples from sites in which they were collected previously. For the three *Cottus* species, at least some of this may be due to the inefficiency of seining and electrofishing for collecting fish that lack a swim bladder and live in cover on the bottom.

Sculpins can be distinguished by either **lacking scales** or having **rows of prickles** instead of scales, usually above the lateral line. The dorsal, anal, and pelvic **fin spines are weak and flexible**. The **pectoral fins are large and have rounded margins**. The **lower pectoral rays are unbranched, thickened, and have blunt, rounded tips**.

SCULPINS, FAMILY COTTIDAE

KEY TO THE FRESHWATER SCULPINS AND MARINE SCULPINS OF THE GENUS *MYOXOCEPHALUS* FOUND IN MANITOBA

1A Posterior margin of gill membranes free from isthmus. Three or 4 preopercular spines. Second preopercular spine protrudes through skin and points rearward. A pair of nasal spines on top of snout, behind upper jaw. Anterior and posterior dorsal fins separated by a distinct gap.

genus *Myoxocephalus*, go to choice 2

1B Posterior margin of gill membranes joined to isthmus. Second preopercular spine covered by skin and pointing downward. Usually 3 preopercular spines (occasionally 4 preopercular spines in *Cottus ricei*). No nasal spines. Anterior and posterior dorsal fins touching, or nearly so.

genus *Cottus*, go to choice 5

2A (1A) Three preopercular spines, 1 directed downward or forward, 2 directed rearward. Top of head decorated with sharp, bony spines and/or fleshy cirri, not 4 rough-topped bony knobs.

go to choice 3

2B Four preopercular spines. Two directed rearward, 2 directed forward or downward. An irregular row of distinct, prickle-like scales on each side above lateral line.

go to choice 4

3A (2A) Fourteen to 16 pectoral fin rays. Fleshy cirri over eyes, not sharp, bony spines.

shorthorn sculpin, *Myoxocephalus scorpius* page 204
MARINE, ENTERING ESTUARIES ON HUDSON BAY COAST

3B Seventeen to 18 pectoral fin rays. Sharp, bony spines over the eyes, not fleshy cirri.

Arctic sculpin, *Myoxocephalus scorpioides* page 203
MARINE, ENTERING ESTUARIES ON HUDSON BAY COAST

4A (2B) Four rough, bony, knob-like projections on top of head, 2 just behind eyes, and 2 at rear corners of head. An irregular row of prickles running along each side below dorsal fin.

fourhorn sculpin, *Myoxocephalus quadricornis* page 202
MARINE, ENTERING ESTUARIES ON HUDSON BAY COAST

4B No bony, knob-like projections on head. Prickles on sides small, more easily felt than seen.

deepwater sculpin, *Myoxocephalus thompsoni* page 205

5A (1B) Upper preopercular spine long and curved upward. A single pore at midline on tip of chin. Lateral line pores extend to base of caudal fin.

spoonhead sculpin, *Cottus ricei* page 200

5B Upper preopercular spine shorter, and straight, or nearly so. Two pores at tip of chin, one on either side of midline. Lateral line pores do not reach base of caudal fin.

go to choice 6

6A (5B) Pelvic fins with 4 fully developed rays. Palatine teeth present. Lateral line pores extend to below posterior half of second dorsal fin, with 23–36 pores. Anal fin with 12–14 rays.

mottled sculpin, *Cottus bairdi* page 198

6B Pelvic fins with 3 fully developed rays. Palatine teeth absent. Lateral line pores stop before middle of second dorsal, with 12–25 pores. Anal fin with 10–12 rays.

slimy sculpin, *Cottus cognatus* page 199

MOTTLED SCULPIN; CHABOT TACHETÉ | *Cottus bairdi*

PRESERVED SPECIMEN
0.5 CM

DISTRIBUTION WITHIN MANITOBA

☐ Continuous range of native species
● Known occurrences

IDENTIFICATION

The mottled and slimy sculpins can be distinguished from other sculpins in our area by having a combination of the following characters: (1) the **gill membrane is attached to the isthmus**; (2) the **lateral line does not reach the base of the tail**; (3) the **upper preopercular spine is straight, not curved**; (4) the **lower preopercular spine is covered by skin**; and (5) there is **no lateral line pore on the midline of the chin**. The mottled sculpin differs from the slimy sculpin by **having palatine teeth** as well as vomerine teeth on the roof of the mouth, **four fully developed pelvic fin rays, 12–14 anal rays**, and **23–36 lateral line pores**, with the **lateral line pores extending to below the rear half of the second dorsal fin**.

DISTRIBUTION IN MANITOBA

The mottled sculpin is found in the Winnipeg River system, and the watersheds of lakes Winnipeg, Manitoba, and Winnipegosis.

BIOLOGICAL NOTES

SPAWNING: Spawning of the mottled sculpin has not been studied in Manitoba. In southern Ontario, mottled sculpins have been observed spawning in late May. In all species of *Cottus*, the male selects a nest site under a ledge or boulder, and entices a female to enter it. The eggs are deposited on the roof of the chamber, and are tended and ventilated by the male (Scott and Crossman, 1979).

GROWTH AND ADULT SIZE: Adult mottled sculpins in the University of Manitoba collection range from 61–117 mm total length. Scott and Crossman (1979) and Becker (1983) give two (rarely) to three years as the age at maturity, and Becker reports a maximum age of four years.

FEEDING: Mottled sculpins are reported to feed mostly on aquatic insect larvae, but large individuals may also take crayfish (Scott and Crossman, 1979). They have been accused of eating brook trout eggs, but the low numbers of mottled sculpins, combined with the rarity of fish eggs in their stomachs, makes them insignificant as egg predators where this has been investigated.

HABITAT: The mottled sculpin lives in cool streams and lakes. In our area, it seems to be associated with smaller and shallower bodies of water than the slimy sculpin. It is also more commonly collected than the slimy sculpin in our area. Most of the specimens in the University of Manitoba collection were taken from quiet water with aquatic vegetation, gravel, boulders, or bedrock as cover. It varies from frequent to sporadic in occurrence and is never abundant in our samples. This may reflect sampling efficiency (seining and electrofishing) more than the abundance and distribution of the species.

ECOLOGICAL ROLE: The mottled sculpin is a middle-level consumer. It is eaten occasionally by benthic piscivores such as walleye and burbot, although species identification of sculpin remains is often not possible, and these specimens are likely a mix of mottled and slimy sculpins. If its apparent uncommon occurrence is not a sampling artifact, its importance in aquatic communities is small.

IMPORTANCE TO PEOPLE

The mottled sculpin has no direct economic importance. It shows up rarely in native fish aquaria and adds interest and diversity to our native fish fauna.

COSEWIC Status as of January 1, 2004: Not Listed
MBESA Status as of January 1, 2004: Not Listed
MBCDC Status as of January 1, 2004: G5, S5

SLIMY SCULPIN; CHABOT VISQUEUX | *Cottus cognatus*

PRESERVED SPECIMEN
1 CM

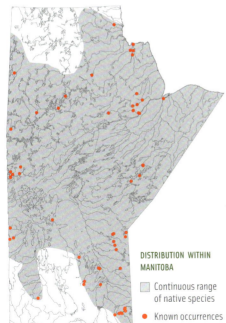

DISTRIBUTION WITHIN MANITOBA

- Continuous range of native species
- Known occurrences

IDENTIFICATION

The mottled and slimy sculpins can be distinguished from other sculpins in our area by having a combination of the following characters: (1) the **gill membrane is attached to the isthmus**; (2) the **lateral line does not reach the base of the tail**; (3) the **upper preopercular spine is straight, not curved**; (4) the **lower preopercular spine is covered by skin**; and (5) there is **no lateral line pore on the midline of the chin**. The slimy sculpin differs from the mottled sculpin by **lacking palatine teeth**, having **three, fully developed pelvic fin rays, 10–12 anal rays**, and **12–25 lateral line pores**, with the **lateral line pores extending to below the front half of the second dorsal fin**.

DISTRIBUTION IN MANITOBA

The slimy sculpin is found in the Winnipeg River watershed to the south, Lake Winnipeg, the watersheds of lakes Dauphin and Winnipegosis, and the Saskatchewan, Nelson, Hayes, and Churchill river watersheds.

BIOLOGICAL NOTES

SPAWNING: Spawning of the slimy sculpin has not been observed in Manitoba. Elsewhere, its spawning habits and habitat are similar to those of the mottled sculpin.

SCULPINS, FAMILY COTTIDAE

GROWTH AND ADULT SIZE: Adult slimy sculpins in the University of Manitoba collection range from 70–119 mm total length. Most are between 70–85 mm long. As with the mottled sculpin, most slimy sculpins are sexually mature at Age III. Becker (1983) reports a maximum age of seven years.

FEEDING: Aquatic insects are the most common food of the slimy sculpin. Some crustaceans, fish eggs, and small fish are also found. As with the mottled sculpin, the slimy sculpin has been implicated as a predator on brook trout eggs. Again, this is not supported by the rate of occurrence of trout eggs in sculpin stomachs or by the relatively low abundance of slimy sculpins.

HABITAT: In Manitoba, the slimy sculpin seems to be more commonly found in deeper water, and larger streams and lakes, than the mottled sculpin. It is also collected less often. Where it is found, it is associated with quiet water and usually rocky cover. As with the mottled sculpin, sampling efficiency and possibly lack of sampling effort in the right habitat may affect our idea of its distribution and abundance in Manitoba. Slimy sculpins have been collected with deepwater sculpins from water over 100 m deep in West Hawk Lake.

ECOLOGICAL ROLE: The slimy sculpin is a middle-level consumer. It appears to be more common in deeper water and in larger lakes and rivers than the mottled sculpin. Sculpins other than the deepwater sculpin are found occasionally in the stomach contents of walleye, burbot, and lake trout. Species identification is often not possible, but it seems reasonable to presume that some of these are slimy sculpins, especially those in lake trout stomach contents.

IMPORTANCE TO PEOPLE

The slimy sculpin is of no economic importance. It is seldom encountered by people except when accidentally caught by young anglers fishing for yellow perch around human-made cover such as breakwaters and boat docks.

COSEWIC Status as of January 1, 2004: Not Listed
MBESA Status as of January 1, 2004: Not Listed
MBCDC Status as of January 1, 2004: G5, S4

SPOONHEAD SCULPIN; CHABOT À TÊTE PLATE | *Cottus ricei*

PRESERVED SPECIMEN
1 CM

IDENTIFICATION

The spoonhead sculpin differs from all other sculpins in our area by having the **upper preopercular spine curved upward**, a **lateral line pore on the midline of the chin**, and the **lateral line pores extending to the base of the tail**.

DISTRIBUTION IN MANITOBA

The spoonhead sculpin is found in Lake Winnipeg, and the Saskatchewan, Hayes, and Churchill river watersheds. The lack of records from the Nelson River watershed may reflect sampling error, rather than absence of the spoonhead sculpin.

BIOLOGICAL NOTES

SPAWNING: Nothing is known of the spawning of the spoonhead sculpin in Manitoba. Deslisle and Van Vliet (1968) give evidence for a late-summer spawning period. There are no observations of spawning itself for this species.

SCULPINS, FAMILY COTTIDAE

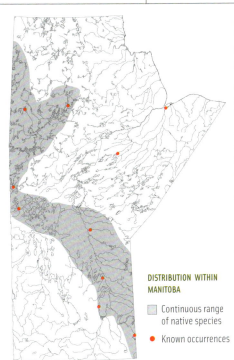

DISTRIBUTION WITHIN MANITOBA

▢ Continuous range of native species
● Known occurrences

GROWTH AND ADULT SIZE: Spoonhead sculpins from Lake Winnipeg in the University of Manitoba collection range from 54–85 mm long. Age at maturity and maximum age and size are unknown.

FEEDING: The food of the spoonhead sculpin has not been studied in Manitoba. Becker (1983) reports a study of the stomach contents of spoonhead sculpins from the Apostle Islands in Lake Superior. Amphipods and mysid crustaceans dominated the food taken, with aquatic insects and fish eggs also being present. Nothing is known about the food of this species in stream habitats.

HABITAT: The habitat of the spoonhead sculpin is poorly known everywhere. In the Great Lakes, it is found from the littoral zone to depths up to 130 m (Becker, 1983). In the north, it tends to be found in shallower water and shows up in small lakes and fast-moving streams as well as larger waters. All the spoonhead sculpins in the University of Manitoba collection were collected in lakes. The largest single collection came from a beach seine haul on a coarse gravel bottom in Lake Winnipeg near Hnausa in 1982. Subsequent collections in the same area have yielded no additional specimens.

ECOLOGICAL ROLE: The spoonhead sculpin appears to be a benthic middle-level consumer, as are other *Cottus* species. In Lake Michigan, it was demonstrated to have been a common food of lake trout and burbot. It may now be extirpated from Lake Michigan (Becker, 1983). Nothing is known of its ecological role in Manitoba.

IMPORTANCE TO PEOPLE

The spoonhead sculpin has no direct economic importance. It is rarely, if ever, seen by anyone other than biologists and is not likely to be recognized as different from the slimy or mottled sculpins without close examination. Becker (1983) states that the spoonhead sculpin is preyed on by lake trout and burbot in Lake Michigan. In Manitoba, not enough is known about its distribution or abundance to assess its importance as prey for other species.

COSEWIC Status as of January 1, 2004: Not at Risk
MBESA Status as of January 1, 2004: Not Listed
MBCDC Status as of January 1, 2004: G5, S3

SCULPINS, FAMILY COTTIDAE

FOURHORN SCULPIN; CHABOISSEAU À QUATRE CORNES | *Myoxocephalus quadricornis*

NOTE: Marine sculpin, restricted to coastal waters and river mouths on Hudson Bay

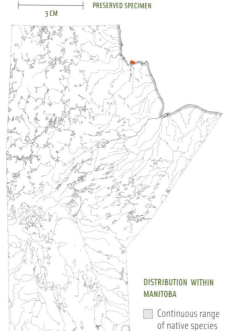

PRESERVED SPECIMEN
3 CM

DISTRIBUTION WITHIN MANITOBA

▢ Continuous range of native species

● Known occurrences

IDENTIFICATION

The fourhorn sculpin is very similar to the deepwater sculpin, but differs in **having four large, rough-topped, bony knobs on top of the head**, and in having an **irregular row of large, easily visible prickles above the lateral line**. These two characters are less well-developed in juvenile fourhorn sculpins than in adults. So far as known, there are no Manitoba records of deepwater sculpins anywhere near the Hudson Bay coast. An estuarine or Hudson Bay coastal sculpin that is identified as the deepwater sculpin is most likely a juvenile fourhorn sculpin. The fourhorn sculpin differs from the shorthorn and Arctic sculpins, which are also found in estuaries on the Hudson Bay coast, by having the **four rough, bony knobs or spines on the head** and by having **four preopercular spines, instead of three**.

DISTRIBUTION IN MANITOBA

The fourhorn sculpin is a marine and estuarine fish found along our Hudson Bay coast. It is included here because there are a number of records of this species from the mouth of the Churchill River.

COSEWIC Status as of January 1, 2004: Not at Risk
MBESA Status as of January 1, 2004: Not Listed
MBCDC Status as of January 1, 2004: G5, S4S5

ARCTIC SCULPIN; CHABOISSEAU ARCTIQUE | *Myoxocephalus scorpioides*

NOTE: Marine sculpin, restricted to coastal waters and river mouths on Hudson Bay

PRESERVED SPECIMEN
2 CM

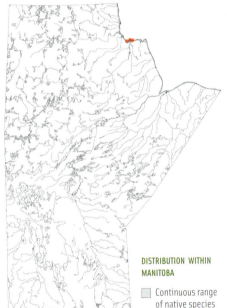

DISTRIBUTION WITHIN MANITOBA

- Continuous range of native species
- Known occurrences

IDENTIFICATION

The Arctic sculpin differs from the fourhorn sculpin by **lacking the four rough, bony knobs on top of the head**, having **three preopercular spines**, instead of four, and **not having a row of prickles above the lateral line**. It differs from the shorthorn sculpin by having **cirri over the eyes**, and having **14–16 pectoral fin rays, instead of 17 or 18**.

DISTRIBUTION IN MANITOBA

The Arctic sculpin is a coastal and estuarine marine sculpin. It is included here because it enters fresh water in river mouths, and there are several records from the mouth of the Churchill River.

COSEWIC Status as of January 1, 2004: Not Listed
MBESA Status as of January 1, 2004: Not Listed
MBCDC Status as of January 1, 2004: G?, S4S5

SHORTHORN SCULPIN; CHABOISSEAU À ÉPINES COURTES | *Myoxocephalus scorpius*

NOTE: Marine sculpin, restricted to coastal waters and river mouths on Hudson Bay

PRESERVED SPECIMEN
2 CM

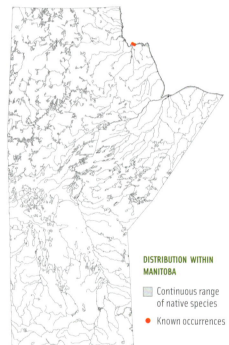

DISTRIBUTION WITHIN MANITOBA

☐ Continuous range of native species
● Known occurrences

IDENTIFICATION

The shorthorn sculpin differs from the fourhorn sculpin by **lacking the four rough, bony knobs on top of the head**, having **three preopercular spines** instead of four, and **having two rows of prickles, one above and the other below the lateral line**. It differs from the Arctic sculpin by **lacking cirri over the eyes**, and having **17 or 18 pectoral fin rays** instead of 14–16.

DISTRIBUTION IN MANITOBA

The shorthorn sculpin is a coastal fish that is included here because it has been found in the mouth of the Churchill River. Of the three marine sculpins included here, the shorthorn sculpin lives in deeper water and is the least likely to be found in estuaries.

COSEWIC Status as of January 1, 2004: Not Listed
MBESA Status as of January 1, 2004: Not Listed
MBCDC Status as of January 1, 2004: G?, S3

DEEPWATER SCULPIN; CHABOT DE PROFONDEUR | *Myoxocephalus thompsoni*

PRESERVED SPECIMEN
2 CM

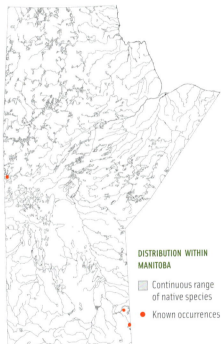

DISTRIBUTION WITHIN MANITOBA

☐ Continuous range of native species
● Known occurrences

IDENTIFICATION

The deepwater sculpin differs from all other freshwater sculpins in our area by having the **gill membrane free from the isthmus**, the **first and second dorsal fins being separated by a gap**, and having **four preopercular spines** instead of three, with the **second not covered by skin** and **pointing to the rear** instead of downward. It is distinguished from the closely related marine and estuarine fourhorn sculpin by **lacking four rough, bony spines on top of the head** and having only **minute prickles above the lateral line** instead of large, easily visible prickles. So far as known, there are no Manitoba records of deepwater sculpins anywhere near the Hudson Bay coast. An estuarine or Hudson Bay coastal sculpin that is identified as the deepwater sculpin is most likely a juvenile fourhorn sculpin.

DISTRIBUTION IN MANITOBA

The deepwater sculpin has been found in West Hawk and George lakes in Whiteshell Provincial Park, and Lake Athapapuskow, and Reindeer Lake in northwestern Manitoba. It was discovered in George Lake in 2000 (Murray, pers. comm., 2002), which suggests that sampling on the bottom in other deep lakes in Manitoba may increase its known distribution. The deepwater sculpin is referred to as a marine glacial relict. It is thought to have descended from marine fourhorn sculpins, which were trapped in proglacial lakes in front of the advancing Laurentide Ice Sheet at the beginning of the last major advance of glaciers across northern North America. As the ice receded, the now freshwater-adapted descendants, the deepwater sculpin, moved north in proglacial lakes along the retreating ice edge. As the climate warmed, after melting of the last glaciers, the deepwater sculpin died out in all but the deepest, coldest lakes, leaving it with its present distribution.

BIOLOGICAL NOTES

SPAWNING: There are no reports of spawning of deepwater sculpins in Manitoba. In the Great Lakes, eggs have been found in females in August. In Great Bear Lake, NWT, females with eggs have been taken in July (Scott and Crossman, 1979).

GROWTH AND ADULT SIZE: Two of the three deepwater sculpins in the University of Manitoba collection are from burbot stomach contents. They both are about 65 mm total length. Nothing is known of size at maturity. The largest known specimen is from Lake Ontario and measured 235 mm total length (Scott and Crossman, 1979).

FEEDING: The deepwater sculpin feeds on benthic crustaceans, including the glacial relict crustaceans *Mysis relicta* and *Pontiporeia affinis*. It also feeds on other deep-water crustaceans and chironomid fly larvae (Scott and Crossman, 1979).

HABITAT: The deepwater sculpin lives on the bottom of our deepest lakes. Little else is known about its habitat.

ECOLOGICAL ROLE: The deepwater sculpin is a benthic, deep-water, middle-level consumer. In the Great Lakes, it was abundant enough historically to have been an important food source for lake trout and burbot, the only large fishes that occurred at the depths it lived in. Day (1983) found deepwater sculpins more commonly in burbot stomachs than in lake trout from Lake Athapapuskow. The deepwater sculpin may be a significant food resource for piscivores in our deepest lakes.

IMPORTANCE TO PEOPLE

The deepwater sculpin has no direct economic importance and is virtually never seen by the public. Its main importance lies in its ecological role in the waters of our deepest lakes.

COSEWIC Status as of January 1, 2004: Threatened (Great Lakes)
MBESA Status as of January 1, 2004: Not Listed
MBCDC Status as of January 1, 2004: G5, S2, S3

PERCH-LIKE FISHES, ORDER PERCIFORMES
TEMPERATE BASSES, FAMILY MORONIDAE

ORDER PERCIFORMES

The temperate bass family is one of 148 families in the Order Perciformes (perch-like fishes). The minnow family (Cyprinidae) is the most species-diverse family of vertebrates, but the perch-like fishes are by far the most diverse order of vertebrates. They encompass the widest range of body plans of any major group of fish, ranging from the familiar shape of our yellow perch or walleye to the eel-like pricklebacks and eelpouts of our Hudson Bay coast, the ultra-streamlined, fast-swimming, marine tunas and billfishes, and the distinctively shaped and strikingly coloured butterflyfishes and surgeonfishes of tropical coral reefs.

The vast majority of perch-like fishes are marine and tropical, but four families—the temperate basses (Family Moronidae), the basses, crappies, and sunfishes (Family Centrarchidae), the perch family (Family Percidae), and the drum family (Family Sciaenidae)—are found in fresh water in Manitoba.

FAMILY MORONIDAE

Temperate basses comprise six species of mostly coastal marine fish, some of which spawn in fresh water. In North America, the white perch, yellow bass, and white bass of the Mississippi River system are freshwater members of this family. The white bass has been introduced into the Hudson Bay Drainage and is found in southern Manitoba. Moronids are **streamlined, deep-bodied, compressed** fishes with **large eyes** that are schooling, surface-living, open-water fish predators. They differ from members of the perch, sunfish, and drum families in having a **spine at the rear upper corner of the opercular bone**, **falcate margins of the posterior dorsal fin and anal fin**, and often a **series of stripes** on the sides.

TEMPERATE BASSES, FAMILY MORONIDAE

WHITE BASS; BAR BLANC *Morone chrysops*

NOTE: Introduced species

FRESH SPECIMEN
5 CM

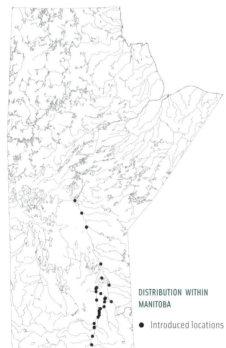

DISTRIBUTION WITHIN MANITOBA
● Introduced locations

IDENTIFICATION

The white bass has a **spine at the upper rear corner of the opercular bone, stripes on the sides**, and **falcate margins of the posterior dorsal and anal fins**.

DISTRIBUTION IN MANITOBA

White bass were introduced into Lake Ashtabula, a reservoir on the Sheyenne River in North Dakota, in 1953. In 1963, they appeared in a commercial fisher's gillnet catch off Riverton. Sampling from 1991 to 1993 revealed young-of-the-year white bass north to the mouth of the Belanger River on the east side of the north basin of Lake Winnipeg, and by 1996, they had become the most numerous perch-like fish in samples from the south basin of the lake. White bass are found in the Red River, the Assiniboine River close to its confluence with the Red, Lake Winnipeg, the Winnipeg River below the Pine Falls Dam, and Playgreen Lake. They are abundant only in Lake Winnipeg and the Winnipeg River below the Pine Falls Dam, however.

BIOLOGICAL NOTES

SPAWNING: White bass in Lake Winnipeg spawn in early to mid-June. Spawning runs have been observed in the lower Red and Winnipeg rivers, the Icelandic River, and the Manigotagan River. In addition, young-of-the-year white bass have been collected from the mouths of the Pigeon, Berens, Poplar, Mukutawa, and Belanger rivers on the east side of the north basin of Lake Winnipeg. Spawning occurs in 1–2 m of water, over hard bottoms ranging from sand to boulders and bedrock outcrops. Females scatter the eggs, which sink and are adhesive.

GROWTH AND ADULT SIZE: White bass in Manitoba apparently live longer and grow larger than they do in their native range. Becker (1983) reported a four-year-old, 376 mm total length white bass from Lake Pepin on the Mississippi River. We have found six annuli on the scales of a 450 mm mature female white bass from the Winnipeg River below Pine Falls. The Manitoba angling record white bass is a 49 cm fish caught from the Manigotagan River in 1994.

FEEDING: The main prey of young-of-the-year white bass in Lake Winnipeg is zooplankton (Hanke, 1996). At all stages beyond young-of-the-year, the emerald shiner is the most common prey item (Hanke). They are voracious feeders, and schools of white bass have been observed driving emerald shiners to the surface while feeding, using similar tactics to those used by some marine, schooling, predatory fish.

HABITAT: White bass are tolerant of turbidity and prefer shallow, highly productive lakes and larger, slow-flowing rivers.

ECOLOGICAL ROLE: Adult white bass are schooling, surface-living, daytime-feeding, pelagic fish predators (Hanke, 1996). No other fish in Manitoba has these characteristics. White bass have the potential to expand explosively in all the Manitoba Great Lakes if and when they reach them.

IMPORTANCE TO PEOPLE

White bass are of minor importance in the Lake Winnipeg commercial fishery. They are rapidly gaining importance as game fish as anglers discover the spawning runs in the south basin tributaries of Lake Winnipeg. They grow to a good size, are readily caught in large numbers, and put up a good fight, characterized by fast runs. They have firm, white flesh of excellent texture and flavour. Angling other than in spawning runs is much more restricted because few anglers venture onto the offshore waters of Lake Winnipeg. Spawning male white bass have been collected from the Winnipeg River spawning run by American fish hatchery operators for hybridizing with female striped bass. The hybrids, called "wipers" or "sunshine bass," are used to stock reservoirs and private lakes that cannot support fishable populations of striped bass.

COSEWIC Status as of January 1, 2004: Not Listed
MBESA Status as of January 1, 2004: Not Listed
MBCDC Status as of January 1, 2004: G5, SE4

BASS, CRAPPIES, AND SUNFISHES, FAMILY CENTRARCHIDAE

BASS, CRAPPIES, AND SUNFISHES, FAMILY CENTRARCHIDAE

FAMILY CENTRARCHIDAE

The bass, crappies, and sunfish are endemic to fresh waters in North America. All but one species are native only east of the Rocky Mountains, although several have been widely introduced, including west of the Rocky Mountains and in Europe. Except for the single centrarchid species that is native west of the Continental Divide, the family reaches the northwestern limit of its native distribution in Manitoba, with the rock bass extending the farthest north, in Lake Winnipeg, and west, in the Assiniboine River watershed.

Of the seven species of centrarchids found in Manitoba at present, the rock bass, pumpkinseed, black crappie, and probably the bluegill and white crappie (Koel, 1997; Henry and Thompson, 1897) are native. An additional six species—the green sunfish, orangespotted sunfish, longear sunfish, smallmouth bass, and largemouth bass—are native to the Hudson Bay Drainage (Koel). Of those, the smallmouth bass and largemouth bass have been introduced into Manitoba.

At least some of the distribution of our centrarchid species seems to have been the result of non-target species being present as contaminants in stocks being planted. Manitoba government stocking records include only the largemouth and smallmouth basses and the black crappie (Matkowski, pers. comm., 2003). This implies that the occurrence of the pumpkinseed and possibly bluegill in Lake Minnewasta, and the bluegill in Whiteshell Provincial Park are the result of contamination of largemouth and smallmouth bass plantings with these species (Matkowski, pers. comm., 2003; Butler, Internal Memoranda of Fisheries Branch, 1942–1953). Any further planting of centrarchids that originate outside Manitoba should be carefully examined to ensure that only the intended species is present. Some centrarchids, notably the green sunfish, are invasive, and their introduction has led to the extirpation of native fish elsewhere.

All centrarchids build nests, which are tended by the male, and successful hatching of the eggs is dependent on the male's guarding the nest against predators, and cleaning and fanning the eggs. Nesting behaviour is temperature-dependent in centrarchids, and males will abandon a nest if the water temperature drops too low. The increased likelihood of late spring/early summer cold snaps to the north and west in the prairies, and the disruption of nesting they cause, likely limits reproductive success of centrarchids in our area. Also, the shorter growing season and long winters probably limit growth, increase the age at maturity, and reduce the winter survival of underyearlings. If climate warming continues, further range expansion of centrarchids seems likely.

Centrarchids are distinguished by having **three or more strong spines in the anal fin**, having the **base of the second dorsal fin shorter than the length of the head**, and having the **margins of the second dorsal and anal fins rounded**.

BASS, CRAPPIES, AND SUNFISHES, FAMILY CENTRARCHIDAE

KEY TO THE BASS, CRAPPIES, AND SUNFISHES FOUND IN MANITOBA AND ADJACENT AREAS OF THE HUDSON BAY DRAINAGE

1A Three anal spines.

go to choice 2

1B More than 3 anal spines.

go to choice 8

2A (1A) Anterior and posterior dorsal fins divided by a distinct notch. Mouth large, the posterior tip of the maxilla reaching to or beyond middle of eye. Fifty-five or more lateral line scales. Maximum body depth 1/3 or less the length to the base of the caudal fin.

genus *Micropterus*, go to choice 3

2B Anterior and posterior dorsal fins not divided by a notch. Mouth smaller, the posterior tip of the maxilla reaching, at most, to below middle of eye, and usually only to anterior margin of eye. Fifty or fewer lateral line scales. Maximum body depth more than 1/3 the length to the base of the caudal fin.

genus *Lepomis*, go to choice 4

3A (2A) Posterior tip of maxilla not extending beyond posterior margin of eye. Anterior and posterior dorsal fins broadly connected, the shortest spine in the notch dividing the two being 1/2 or more the length of the longest dorsal spine. Three dark bands on cheek, radiating rearward from eye. Sides of body with a series of 8 or more indistinct vertical bars, which become very difficult to see on large fish.

smallmouth bass, *Micropterus dolomieu* page 221
INTRODUCED

3B Posterior tip of maxilla extending beyond rear margin of eye. Anterior and posterior dorsal fins narrowly connected, the shortest spine in the notch dividing the two less than 1/2 as long as the longest dorsal spine. No radiating bands on cheek or vertical bars on sides, but a broad, dark, lateral band extends from tip of snout to base of tail. This band becomes indistinct on large fish.

largemouth bass, *Micropterus salmoides* page 223
INTRODUCED

4A (2B) Mouth reaches past anterior margin of eye. Posterior margin of pectoral fin convex, and its tip rounded to bluntly pointed.

go to choice 5

4B Mouth reaches no farther back than anterior margin of eye. Posterior margin of pectoral fin straight or somewhat concave (falcate), and its tip sharply pointed.

go to choice 7

5A (4A) Sides light metallic blue and marked with brilliant orange spots in life. Cheeks with both orange spots and longitudinal orange streaks. Pectoral fin length about 1/3 the body length to base of tail.

orangespotted sunfish, *Lepomis humilis* page 217
RED RIVER DRAINAGE, USA

5B No orange spots or streaks on cheeks or sides. Pectoral fin length less than 1/3 the body length to base of tail.

go to choice 6

BASS, CRAPPIES, AND SUNFISHES, FAMILY CENTRARCHIDAE

6A (5B) Fourteen long, slender gill rakers on lower limb of first arch. Eight to 10 scale rows between lateral line and origin of dorsal fin.

green sunfish, *Lepomis cyanellus* **page 214**
RED RIVER DRAINAGE, USA, AND RAINY RIVER, ONTARIO

6B Twelve short, stumpy gill rakers on lower limb of first arch. Four to 6 scale rows between lateral line and origin of dorsal fin.

longear sunfish, *Lepomis megalotis* **page 220**
RED RIVER DRAINAGE, USA, AND RAINY RIVER, ONTARIO

7A (4B) Black opercular flap with a pale posterior margin, which usually has a bright orange or red spot in it in life. Eight short gill rakers on lower limb of first arch. No black blotch on lower rear corner of posterior dorsal fin.

pumpkinseed, *Lepomis gibbosus* **page 215**

7B Opercular flap black to posterior margin, no pale edge or orange spot. Twelve longer, more slender gill rakers on lower limb of first arch. A large black blotch on lower rear corner of posterior dorsal fin.

bluegill, *Lepomis macrochirus* **page 218**

8A (1B) Ten or more dorsal spines. Base of anal fin distinctly shorter than base of dorsal fin.

rock bass, *Ambloplites rupestris* **page 213**

8B Eight or fewer dorsal spines. Base of anal fin about as long as or slightly longer than base of dorsal fin.

genus *Pomoxis,* **go to choice 9**

9A (8B) Six dorsal spines. Distance from snout to dorsal origin about equal to distance from dorsal origin to middle of base of caudal fin. Body silvery, with 5–10 indistinct vertical bars, which may be very hard to see on small fish.

white crappie, *Pomoxis annularis* **page 225**

9B Seven or 8 dorsal spines. Distance from snout to dorsal origin less than the distance from dorsal origin to middle of base of tail. Body silvery, with an irregular network of black markings, which extend onto dorsal, caudal, and anal fins. This is faded and indistinct on small fish, which may resemble white crappies in colour and markings.

black crappie, *Pomoxis nigromaculatus* **page 226**

BASS, CRAPPIES, AND SUNFISHES, FAMILY CENTRARCHIDAE

ROCK BASS; CRAPET DE ROCHE | *Ambloplites rupestris*

FRESH SPECIMEN
2 CM

IDENTIFICATION

The rock bass can be distinguished from all other centrarchids by having **five to seven anal spines, ten to 12 dorsal spines**, and having the **base of the dorsal fin longer than the base of the anal fin**. The body is deep, and robust, but **not almost circular in outline** and **notably less compressed** than sunfishes or crappies.

DISTRIBUTION IN MANITOBA

The rock bass has the widest native distribution of any centrarchid in Manitoba. It is found in the watersheds of the Winnipeg, Red, and Assiniboine rivers and the tributaries of Lake Winnipeg.

BIOLOGICAL NOTES

SPAWNING: Spawning of rock bass has not been studied in Manitoba. Scott and Crossman (1979) state that rock bass spawn in June, at water temperatures between 16°–21°C. The spawning behaviour of rock bass is similar to other centrarchids. The male excavates a shallow nest depression, which he defends against other males. A female is driven into the nest and deposits eggs in several separate spawning acts. The male guards the nest and fans the eggs during development, and nest tending ceases as the hatched young disperse from the nest.

DISTRIBUTION WITHIN MANITOBA
☐ Continuous range of native species
● Known occurrences

GROWTH AND ADULT SIZE: Most rock bass collected in Manitoba are under 100 mm total length. The largest specimen we have measured was a 210 mm individual angled from the Red River north of Selkirk. The maximum reported age in Wisconsin is 13 years for a 227 mm fish (Becker, 1983).

FEEDING: Rock bass are predators mainly on crayfish, other aquatic crustacea, and aquatic insects. Minnows and juvenile fish are also taken. Becker (1983) states that the most common prey is crayfish.

HABITAT: The rock bass is found in rocky habitats in the littoral zone of lakes, and pools and runs in streams and in rivers. Within this habitat, it prefers areas with submerged wood or aquatic plants as additional cover. It tolerates turbidity sufficiently to be found in reaches of both the Red and Assiniboine rivers with reduced current and rocky substrates.

ECOLOGICAL ROLE: The rock bass is a benthopelagic, middle- to upper-level consumer. Small rock bass are eaten by pike, walleye, and smallmouth bass.

IMPORTANCE TO PEOPLE

The rock bass is a common incidental catch by anglers fishing for walleye and smallmouth bass. They readily take bait and small lures fished in cover near the bottom. The flesh has good texture and flavour. Rock bass are also used in native fish aquaria and in classroom aquaria.

COSEWIC Status as of January 1, 2004: Not Listed
MBESA Status as of January 1, 2004: Not Listed
MBCDC Status as of January 1, 2004: G5, S5

GREEN SUNFISH; CRAPET VERT — *Lepomis cyanellus*

NOTE: Not found in Manitoba; Red and Winnipeg river watersheds, Minnesota, North Dakota, and Ontario

1 CM — FRESH SPECIMEN

IDENTIFICATION

The green sunfish is distinguished by having a **deep, compressed body, and three spines in the anal fin**. The **mouth reaches past the anterior margin of the eye**, there are **no orange spots on the body nor orange streaks on the gill covers**, and there are **14 long, slender gill rakers on the lower limb of the first gill arch**.

DISTRIBUTION IN MANITOBA

The green sunfish is not found in Manitoba. It is found in Red River tributaries in Minnesota and North Dakota, and in the Rainy River system in Minnesota and northwestern Ontario.

BIOLOGICAL NOTES

SPAWNING: Spawning of green sunfish is similar to other centrarchids. In Wisconsin, spawning begins in May and continues into August (Becker, 1983). See the rock bass account for a summary of spawning habits.

GROWTH AND ADULT SIZE: Green sunfish in Wisconsin may be sexually mature as early as Age I, and may live to 10 years. They attain a length up to 190 mm, although most are much smaller (Becker, 1983). In common with some other *Lepomis* species, green sunfish can become stunted in ponds where there is not enough predation to keep their abundance in check.

FEEDING: Green sunfish feed on a wide variety of aquatic invertebrates and will also take terrestrial insects. They may also be significant predators on the eggs and young of largemouth bass (Becker, 1983).

HABITAT: The green sunfish lives in quiet water in ponds, lakes, streams, and rivers. It prefers cover such as submerged wood and weedbeds. It tolerates turbid water.

BASS, CRAPPIES, AND SUNFISHES, FAMILY CENTRARCHIDAE

ECOLOGICAL ROLE: The green sunfish is a middle-level consumer. It has a larger mouth than many other sunfish, and can take larger prey items. It probably occupies a similar ecological position to that of the rock bass.

IMPORTANCE TO PEOPLE

The green sunfish is an incidental catch of anglers where it is found. Because of its tendency to become overcrowded and stunted, it is regarded as a nuisance species in human-made ponds that are being managed for largemouth bass and bluegills. When introduced outside its range, it has caused declines or extirpation of populations of native species (Moyle, 1976). This species is seen occasionally in the tropical aquarium trade in Manitoba, misidentified as a Central or South American cichlid, or as a contaminant in shipments of goldfish (Stewart et al., 2001). Because of its invasiveness, the possibility of the green sunfish's reaching Manitoba should be of concern. A large part of the risk of importation of green sunfish could be eliminated by careful examination of goldfish shipments.

COSEWIC Status as of January 1, 2004: Not at Risk
MBESA Status as of January 1, 2004: Not Listed
MBCDC Status as of January 1, 2004: G5, SP

PUMPKINSEED; CRAPET-SOLEIL | *Lepomis gibbosus*

PRESERVED SPECIMEN
1 CM

IDENTIFICATION

The pumpkinseed is distinguished by having a **deep, compressed, nearly circular body outline, three anal spines**, the **mouth reaching only to below or in front of the anterior margin of the eye, eight short gill rakers on the lower limb of the first arch**, and a **bright red spot on the rear edge of the opercular flap**. In preserved specimens, the red spot shows as a well-marked whitish spot. The pumpkinseed also **either lacks dark bars on the sides or has indistinct bars**, and there is **no dark spot just ahead of the rear margin of the dorsal fin**.

DISTRIBUTION IN MANITOBA

The native range of the pumpkinseed in Manitoba is restricted to Lake of the Woods and its tributaries, and the Winnipeg River system in Whiteshell Provincial Park. Collections made in Falcon Lake during the last 20 years have yielded bluegills instead of the pumpkinseeds reported there in the 1950s and 1960s. The bluegill may be replacing the pumpkinseed in that area. The pumpkinseed is also found in Lake Minnewasta, a reservoir on Dead Horse Creek near Morden (Red River watershed). This is almost certainly an introduction, but there are no records of plantings of pumpkinseeds in Lake Minnewasta. This points out the need for rigorous inspection and identification of centrarchids intended for planting in Manitoba. (See also the discussion of the distribution of the bluegill.) Historically, stocks for planting have been obtained from the wild in locations where species other than the target species occur (Matkowski, pers. comm., 2003).

BASS, CRAPPIES, AND SUNFISHES, FAMILY CENTRARCHIDAE

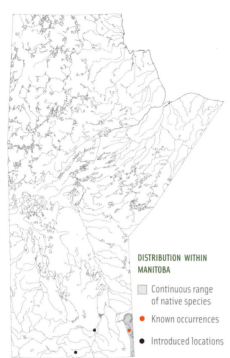

DISTRIBUTION WITHIN MANITOBA

☐ Continuous range of native species
● Known occurrences
● Introduced locations

BIOLOGICAL NOTES

SPAWNING: Spawning of the pumpkinseed has not been reported in Manitoba. Its spawning habits are similar to other centrarchids, with the male excavating and guarding a nest. See the rock bass account for a summary of spawning habits. The eggs and hatchlings are tended until the hatchlings disperse from the nest.

GROWTH AND ADULT SIZE: All the pumpkinseeds in the University of Manitoba collection are juveniles up to 45 mm total length. In Ontario, they reach an age of nine years and a fork length of 241 mm (Scott and Crossman, 1979).

FEEDING: Aquatic insects are the dominant food of adult pumpkinseeds, but a variety of other invertebrates are also eaten. Small fish may be significant diet items seasonally.

HABITAT: The pumpkinseed prefers quiet, clear to slightly turbid water. It is usually found in weedbeds or submerged wood cover. It is found in lakes, ponds, and slow-moving areas of rivers.

ECOLOGICAL ROLE: The pumpkinseed is a benthic to midwater, middle-level consumer. It is eaten by larger piscivorous fish, but its limited distribution and low abundance in Manitoba limit its importance in our aquatic communities.

IMPORTANCE TO PEOPLE

The pumpkinseed is a popular pan fish in the United States and southern Ontario. In Manitoba, it is seldom, if ever, caught by anglers. Its vivid colours and intricate markings make it an attractive aquarium species, but, like all centrarchids, it is aggressive toward other fish.

COSEWIC Status as of January 1, 2004: Not Listed
MBESA Status as of January 1, 2004: Not Listed
MBCDC Status as of January 1, 2004: G5, S1

ORANGESPOTTED SUNFISH; CRAPET MENU — *Lepomis humilis*

NOTE: Not found in Manitoba; Red River tributaries in Minnesota

FRESH SPECIMEN
1 CM

IDENTIFICATION
The orangespotted sunfish is one of the most strikingly and brightly coloured freshwater fish in North America. It is distinguished by having a **deep, compressed body** and **three anal spines**. The **mouth reaches past the anterior margin of the eye**, the **pectoral fins are long, about one-third the body length to the base of the tail**, and live or fresh specimens have **brilliant orange spots on the body and streaks on the gill covers**, against a **light, metallic blue background colour**. Preserved specimens lose the bright colours, but the spots and streaks can be seen as lighter and/or darker markings.

DISTRIBUTION IN MANITOBA
The orangespotted sunfish is not found in Manitoba. It is found in the headwaters of Red River tributaries in Minnesota.

BIOLOGICAL NOTES
SPAWNING: In Wisconsin, the orangespotted sunfish spawns from May to August. Nesting and spawning behaviour are similar to that of other centrarchids (Becker, 1983). See the rock bass account for a summary of spawning habits.

GROWTH AND ADULT SIZE: The orangespotted sunfish is the smallest species of the genus *Lepomis*. It lives to four years of age and attains a length up to 100 mm in Iowa. Most are half or less of this size (Becker, 1983).

FEEDING: Like most sunfish, the orangespotted sunfish feeds on a variety of aquatic insects and crustacea. It occasionally takes small fish (Becker, 1983).

HABITAT: The orangespotted sunfish prefers quiet, shallow, usually turbid water, with a soft substrate such as mud or sand. It can also tolerate low dissolved oxygen and large, rapid changes in water pH (Becker, 1983). It is usually in marginal waters such as stream mouths, oxbow lakes, and sloughs along large rivers (Becker). Degradation, such as siltation and pollution of marginal water habitats in the United States, has allowed it to increase its range there in recent years.

ECOLOGICAL ROLE: The orangespotted sunfish is a middle-level consumer. It is eaten by larger predators such as largemouth bass. It can live in degraded habitats that receive limited use by most other fish. This suggests that it may have a significant impact on habitats such as the peripheral marshes at the south ends of lakes Winnipeg and Manitoba, and in oxbow lakes along the Red and Assiniboine rivers, if it reaches Manitoba.

IMPORTANCE TO PEOPLE
In its native range, the orangespotted sunfish is a significant food of largemouth bass. It is also an attractive

BASS, CRAPPIES, AND SUNFISHES, FAMILY CENTRARCHIDAE

aquarium fish. Although it has not appeared in the aquarium trade in Winnipeg up to now, its importation should be prevented because of the high risk that it could establish in Manitoba if released into the wild here.

COSEWIC Status as of January 1, 2004: Special Concern (Ontario)
MBESA Status as of January 1, 2004: Not Listed
MBCDC Status as of January 1, 2004: G5, SP

BLUEGILL; CRAPET ARLEQUIN *Lepomis macrochirus*

PRESERVED SPECIMEN
5 CM

DISTRIBUTION WITHIN MANITOBA

- Continuous range of native species
- Known occurrences
- Introduced locations

IDENTIFICATION

The bluegill is distinguished by having a **deep, compressed, nearly circular body outline, three anal spines**, the **mouth reaching only to below or in front of the anterior margin of the eye**, having **12 long, slender gill rakers on the lower limb of the first arch**, and the **opercular flap being black with no red spot or white edge**. The bluegill also has **dark bars on the sides**, which may become indistinct in fish taken from cold water, such as during late fall, and a **dark spot just in front of the rear edge of the dorsal fin**.

DISTRIBUTION IN MANITOBA

The bluegill is restricted to the Red River, Winnipeg River, and Lake of the Woods watersheds in Manitoba. There are no recorded introductions of the bluegill in Manitoba. It may be native in the Red River watershed in Manitoba. Koel (1997) lists the bluegill as native to the Red River watershed in Minnesota, and Henry's accounts of his journeys on the Red River between 1802 and 1804 refer to "brim," which is identified in editor Elliot Coues's notes attached to Henry's narrative as *Lepomis pallidus* (Henry and Thompson, 1897). *L. pallidus* is included in the synonymy of the bluegill, but not the pumpkinseed (Scott and Crossman, 1979). This supports the suggestion that the bluegill was present in Manitoba prior to any introductions.

The present distribution of the bluegill in Manitoba, however, probably reflects a combination of unintentional introductions of bluegills, most likely in Whiteshell Provincial Park, as contaminants in largemouth and smallmouth bass plantings; and native bluegills, most likely in the Red River watershed.

Bluegills may also have been unintentionally introduced into Lake Minnewasta, a reservoir on Dead Horse Creek (Red River watershed), as contaminants in intentional plantings of largemouth bass (Matkowski, pers. comm., 2002 and 2003). In the early 1950s, about 10 years after largemouth bass were first introduced into Lake Minnewasta, in 1942, the bluegill became abundant there (G.E. Butler, Fisheries Branch Internal Memoranda, 1942–1953). Recent collections from Lake Minnewasta have contained only the pumpkinseed, however. There are no records of planting of any centrarchid but largemouth bass in the reservoir.

During the 1980s, the bluegill increased in abundance in lakes in Whiteshell Provincial Park (Lake of the Woods and Winnipeg River watersheds). Collections made in Falcon Lake during the last 20 years have yielded bluegills instead of the pumpkinseeds reported in the 1950s and 1960s by Kooyman and Keleher (Manitoba Fisheries Branch records and ROM Accession Records). The bluegill may be replacing the pumpkinseed in that area.

Bluegills in the Red River watershed in Manitoba may be native, but the close association of most of the recorded occurrences with plantings of bass or black crappies suggests that there may also have been bluegills introduced as contaminants in plantings of largemouth or smallmouth bass, or black crappies.

BIOLOGICAL NOTES

SPAWNING: Spawning of the bluegill has not been observed in Manitoba. Scott and Crossman (1979) state that the bluegill spawns in early to midsummer in Canada, with peak spawning probably in early July. Nesting and spawning behaviour are similar to other centrarchids, with substrates ranging from gravel to mud being used for nests (Scott and Crossman). See the rock bass account for a summary of spawning habits.

GROWTH AND ADULT SIZE: All the bluegills in the University of Manitoba collection are juveniles up to 55 mm total length. The largest bluegill recorded from Manitoba is a 235 mm total length fish caught in the La Salle River at La Barriere Park, St. Norbert, on October 20, 2003, by Fisheries and Oceans Canada. There were eight annuli on the scales, and it was a female with small, apparently spent, ovaries. (See species illustration, previous page.) Becker (1983) reported a maximum size of 184 mm total length and a maximum age of 11 years for bluegills in Wisconsin. He reported the age at maturity to be two or three years. Like some other centrarchids, the bluegill will become stunted when populations become overcrowded due to lack of predation (Becker).

FEEDING: Like other sunfish, the bluegill feeds on aquatic insects, small crayfish and other crustaceans, other aquatic invertebrates, and small fish. Plant material can also make up a significant proportion of stomach contents (Becker, 1983).

HABITAT: The bluegill lives in lakes, streams, and rivers, usually in areas of slow or no current. It can tolerate turbid water and prefers cover such as weedbeds, submerged wood, or boulders. It also does well in small human-made impoundments, provided the dissolved oxygen concentration remains above about 0.8 mg/l^{-1} throughout the winter (Becker, 1983).

ECOLOGICAL ROLE: The bluegill is a middle-level consumer. It is a significant prey species for most piscivores in its communities.

IMPORTANCE TO PEOPLE

At this time in Manitoba, the bluegill is neither common nor widespread enough to be significant as either an angling species or a prey species for other game fish. In southern Ontario and the United States, it is a valuable pan fish. It has been widely introduced outside its native range. It has also been used in human-made ponds as a pan fish and forage fish for largemouth bass.

COSEWIC Status as of January 1, 2004: Not Listed
MBESA Status as of January 1, 2004: Not Listed
MBCDC Status as of January 1, 2004: G5, S1

LONGEAR SUNFISH; CRAPET À LONGUES OREILLES   *Lepomis megalotis*

NOTE: Not found in Manitoba; headwaters of Red River tributaries in Minnesota and Rainy River watershed in northwestern Ontario

FRESH SPECIMEN
2 CM

IDENTIFICATION

The longear sunfish is distinguished by having a **deep, compressed, nearly circular body outline, three anal spines,** the **mouth reaching past the anterior margin of the eye,** and **12 short, stumpy gill rakers on the lower limb of the first arch**.

Note: There are two subspecies of the longear sunfish. *L. megalotis peltastes*, the northern longear sunfish, is the form that occurs in Canadian waters.

DISTRIBUTION IN MANITOBA

The longear sunfish is not found in Manitoba. It is found in Red River tributaries in Minnesota and in the Rainy River system in Minnesota and northwestern Ontario. Its distribution becomes discontinuous in the upper Mississippi and Hudson Bay drainages, and it probably reaches its northern limit in northwestern Ontario.

BIOLOGICAL NOTES

SPAWNING: In Wisconsin, the longear sunfish spawns from late June to August (Becker, 1983). Nesting and spawning habits are similar to those of other centrarchids. See the rock bass account for a summary of spawning habits.

GROWTH AND ADULT SIZE: Becker (1983) reported sizes up to 102 mm total length and a maximum age of four years for the longear sunfish in Wisconsin.

FEEDING: As in other sunfish, the main food of the longear sunfish is aquatic insects. Large individuals may also prey on fish, including the fry of other sunfish (Becker, 1983).

HABITAT: The longear sunfish prefers the clear, quiet water of streams and, less commonly, lakes. It is usually found over sand to rubble substrates with moderate growth of aquatic plants. Its habitat requirements are more stringent than those of other sunfish, and it has been classified as threatened in Wisconsin (Becker, 1983).

ECOLOGICAL ROLE: The longear sunfish is a middle-level consumer. It is not abundant or widespread enough in the Hudson Bay Drainage to be a significant food source for other fish.

IMPORTANCE TO PEOPLE

Anglers in northwestern Ontario almost never catch the longear sunfish. When it is caught, it may be mistaken for the pumpkinseed. Its discontinuous distribution and low abundance in the Hudson Bay Drainage suggest it is unlikely to be able to establish in Manitoba. Longear sunfish were first noted in the aquarium trade in Winnipeg in the spring of 2003 (Hanke, pers. comm., 2003). This illustrates yet again the risk of introduction of exotic species from this source and the need for more careful monitoring by the industry and provincial and federal government agencies.

COSEWIC Status as of January 1, 2004: Not at Risk
MBESA Status as of January 1, 2004: Not Listed
MBCDC Status as of January 1, 2004: G5, SP

SMALLMOUTH BASS; ACHIGAN À PETITE BOUCHE | *Micropterus dolomieu*

NOTE: Introduced species

FRESH SPECIMEN
5 CM

IDENTIFICATION

The **basses are less deep-bodied and compressed than all other centrarchids, and the first and second dorsal fins have at least a distinct notch between them.** The smallmouth bass is distinguished from the largemouth bass by having the **mouth reaching only to below the eye, a broad connection between the first and second dorsal fins, the cheeks having three, radiating, dark bands behind the eye**, and the **body having indistinct vertical bars**.

Note: Underyearling smallmouth bass have **narrow, distinct vertical bars. The caudal fin is yellow from the base out to a black crescent just ahead of its rear margin. The fin margin, including the tips of the upper and lower lobes, is transparent**. At first sight, they appear to be **small fish with vertical bars and a rounded, yellow caudal fin with a black border**.

DISTRIBUTION IN MANITOBA

The smallmouth bass was first introduced into Manitoba in 1900, and introductions have continued since then. By virtue of these introductions and one accidental escape from an impoundment, it is more widespread in Manitoba than the rock bass. It is found throughout the Winnipeg

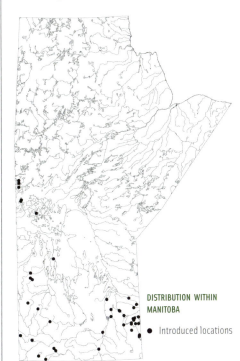

DISTRIBUTION WITHIN MANITOBA

● Introduced locations

River system, in Lake Winnipeg tributaries north to the Wanipigow River, in Dauphin Lake (via a failed dam), the Valley River, and in the Saskatchewan River watershed north to Lake Athapapuskow. In October 2002, specimens were collected from Hecla Island, Lake Winnipeg (Hanke, pers. comm., 2002), and the Red River at the mouth of the Morris River, in Winnipeg and below the St. Andrews Dam. These records are the first evidence that the smallmouth bass is spreading into the main body of Lake Winnipeg and into the Red River.

BIOLOGICAL NOTES

SPAWNING: Male smallmouth bass begin nest building at water temperatures as low as 12°C, and spawning takes place at water temperatures between 16°–18°C (Scott and Crossman, 1979). Like other centrarchids, the male smallmouth bass excavates a nest in gravel or rubble substrate. The nest is circular and has a diameter about twice the body length of the male (Becker, 1983). In addition to excavation, the male cleans the substrate in the nest.

GROWTH AND ADULT SIZE: Smallmouth bass are reported to live to an age of 13 years (Green Bay, Lake Michigan, Wisconsin) (Becker, 1983), to 15 years (Lake Huron, Ontario) (Scott and Crossman, 1979). The largest sizes reported in these sources range from 450–500 mm total length. The angling record for this species in Manitoba is a 56 cm long fish caught from Tooth Lake, Nopiming Provincial Park, in 1998.

FEEDING: Smallmouth bass start life as invertebrate predators, feeding on small crustaceans and insects. Before the end of their first summer, they begin feeding on small fish, and they remain predators on fish and crayfish throughout their lives. Aquatic and terrestrial insects, mollusks, and amphipods are also eaten.

HABITAT: In Manitoba, the smallmouth bass is found mostly in lakes and lake-like, usually impounded, reaches of rivers (mainly the Winnipeg River). It is most often associated with rocky substrates, using boulders and bedrock ledges for cover. It also can be found near submerged wood or, least commonly, aquatic vegetation. It tolerates some turbidity.

ECOLOGICAL ROLE: The smallmouth bass is a top-level consumer. Unlike the walleye and northern pike, however, its diet is varied enough that it does somewhat better in lakes with low populations of forage fish. Fedoruk (1961) studied the interactions between introduced smallmouth bass and native walleye in Falcon Lake, Whiteshell Provincial Park (Winnipeg River watershed), 10 to 12 years after smallmouth bass had been introduced. He found evidence that both species consumed some of the same types of food items, but little other evidence for competitive interaction. The only significant difference in diet was the dominance of crayfish in the diet of smallmouth bass. He suggested that any further increase in smallmouth bass abundance could have a negative effect on the walleye stock in the lake. The greater abundance of crayfish in warmer, shallower lakes may be the means by which the smallmouth bass increases in abundance to the point where it becomes the dominant species in those lakes. Smallmouth bass are probably limited more by cooler water temperatures and a short growing season in much of Manitoba than by lack of suitable habitat or prey. If this is the case, further expansion of the smallmouth bass in Manitoba may be expected if climate warming continues.

IMPORTANCE TO PEOPLE

The smallmouth bass is a highly valued game fish everywhere it is found. Its abundance, distribution, and, consequently, its popularity, have increased sharply in Manitoba over the last 20 years. It remains less popular than the walleye, however. Because its habitat and feeding are similar to those of the walleye, it may compete with walleye in some lakes, as noted above. The smallmouth bass is an excellent food fish, but it is not as highly regarded by Manitobans as the walleye and sauger.

COSEWIC Status as of January 1, 2004: Not Listed
MBESA Status as of January 1, 2004: Not Listed
MBCDC Status as of January 1, 2004: G5, SE4

BASS, CRAPPIES, AND SUNFISHES, FAMILY CENTRARCHIDAE

| LARGEMOUTH BASS; ACHIGAN À GRANDE BOUCHE | *Micropterus salmoides* |

NOTE: Introduced species

FRESH SPECIMEN
5 CM

DISTRIBUTION WITHIN MANITOBA
● Introduced locations

IDENTIFICATION

The **basses are less deep-bodied and compressed than all other centrarchids and the first and second dorsal fins have at least a distinct notch between them**. The largemouth bass is distinguished from the smallmouth bass by having the **mouth reaching past the eye**, a **narrow connection between the first and second dorsal fins, no radiating dark bands behind the eye**, and the **body having a longitudinal dark band**, which becomes less distinct in large fish.

DISTRIBUTION IN MANITOBA

The largemouth bass has been planted in many locations across southern Manitoba. It has survived in some of the lakes where it was introduced, and recently shows evidence of spreading beyond the waters into which it was introduced. The largemouth bass is found in Buffalo Bay, Lake of the Woods, Lake Minnewasta, a reservoir on Dead Horse Creek near Morden (Red River watershed), where it was introduced in 1942, and a human-made pond at the Fort Whyte Centre for Outdoor Education, in Winnipeg, where it was introduced in 1948.

The largemouth bass may now be spreading in Manitoba. Several underyearling largemouth bass were caught from the tailrace of the dam on the La Salle River (Red River watershed) at La Barriere Park in the fall of 2001 (Franzin, pers. comm., 2001). In July 2002, juvenile largemouth bass were taken in the La Salle River above the dam at La Barriere Park (Manitoba Fisheries Branch records), and in October 2002, two largemouth bass were collected from the lower Roseau River. With the exception of the occurrence above the dam at La Barriere Park, these are the first collections of largemouth bass from areas where access by fish to the Red River is possible at normal summer water levels.

BIOLOGICAL NOTES

SPAWNING: The largemouth bass spawns between early June and August, at water temperatures between 16°–18°C (Scott and Crossman, 1979). This is about the same range of temperatures as the smallmouth bass, but a longer time period. Male largemouth bass excavate larger and deeper nests (up to 1 m in diameter and 30 cm deep) than smallmouth bass do. They will spawn on finer substrates if there are hard surfaces available for the eggs to adhere to (Becker, 1983). Spawning and nest guarding are similar to that of the smallmouth bass. Hatchling largemouth bass form a dense swarm accompanied by the male. Unlike other centrarchids, the male remains with his young for a time after feeding begins (Becker).

GROWTH AND ADULT SIZE: The largemouth bass can grow to larger size than the smallmouth. In our area, however, they are usually smaller. Scott and Crossman (1979) give a maximum age of 15 years and a total length of 544 mm for southern Ontario fish. The angling record largemouth bass in Manitoba is a 53 cm long individual caught in 1998 in a pond at the Fort Whyte Centre for Outdoor Education in Winnipeg.

FEEDING: Hatchling largemouth bass begin feeding on plankton, but shift to fish during their first summer. They are more committed piscivores than the smallmouth bass, and largemouth bass that begin feeding on fish earlier in life gain a growth advantage over those that continue to feed on invertebrates. In addition to fish, adult largemouth bass also feed on frogs, snakes, small rodents, and ducklings that they take from the surface. They are apparently also able to take prey flying close to the water surface. A 2.25 kg largemouth bass caught in 1973 from a small impoundment in northeastern Iowa had a fresh, undigested barn swallow in its stomach.

HABITAT: The largemouth bass is found in lakes and larger rivers, usually in quiet marginal waters. It is somewhat more tolerant of turbidity than the smallmouth bass. It prefers cover such as submerged wood or weedbeds. It differs from the smallmouth bass in being in shallower, warmer, sometimes more turbid water, usually with finer grained substrates such as mud or sand.

ECOLOGICAL ROLE: The largemouth bass is a top-level consumer. Its limited distribution and low abundance in Manitoba decrease its significance in our aquatic communities.

IMPORTANCE TO PEOPLE

The largemouth bass is the most important game fish in the United States east of the Rocky Mountains. It is also a highly valued game fish in southern Ontario. In Manitoba, it is seldom caught by anglers.

COSEWIC Status as of January 1, 2004: Not Listed
MBESA Status as of January 1, 2004: Not Listed
MBCDC Status as of January 1, 2004: G5, SE

WHITE CRAPPIE; MARIGANE BLANCHE *Pomoxis annularis*

PRESERVED SPECIMEN
2 CM

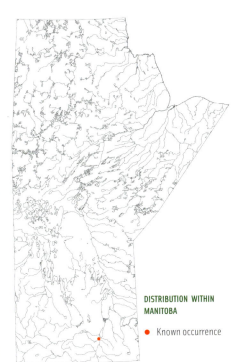

DISTRIBUTION WITHIN MANITOBA
● Known occurrence

IDENTIFICATION

Crappies have **six or seven spines in the anal fin**, and the dorsal and anal spines increase in length from front to rear, so that the **spiny portion of the fin slopes upward to join the rayed portion**. The **body is extremely compressed**, being **thinner in cross-section than in any other group of fish in our area**. The white crappie differs from the black crappie by having **six dorsal spines**. The **base of the dorsal fin is distinctly shorter than the base of the anal fin**. The white crappie also has **five to seven dark bars on the sides**, but these are often very indistinct on underyearlings, and underyearling black crappies have very similar markings.

DISTRIBUTION IN MANITOBA

There are six records of white crappies from Manitoba. All are underyearlings and all came from the Red River, within about 200 m of the mouth of the La Salle River, south of Winnipeg. There have been no collections of the white crappie in Manitoba in the last 10 years. This may be a native occurrence. Koel (1997) lists the white crappie as native, but scattered and uncommon in the Red River watershed in the United States. Its most northerly occurrence there is in the Mustinka River, North Dakota, just south of the International Boundry. Non-native occurrences of centrarchid species resulting from contamination of largemouth and smallmouth bass plantings are found with one or the other of these species. This is not the case for white crappies in Manitoba.

BIOLOGICAL NOTES

SPAWNING: In Wisconsin, the white crappie spawns in May and June, at water temperatures between 16°–20°C (Becker, 1983). Nests are cleaned or excavated in finer grained substrates than most centrarchids use. Spawning

BASS, CRAPPIES, AND SUNFISHES, FAMILY CENTRARCHIDAE

habits are similar to other centrarchids, except that the male does not abandon the nest when the water temperature drops (Becker). See the rock bass account for a summary of spawning habits.

GROWTH AND ADULT SIZE: All the white crappies collected in Manitoba are underyearlings 25–35 mm total length. In Wisconsin, white crappies live to nine years old and grow to 363 mm total length (Becker, 1983). In the southern United States, this species can reach weights of over 2.5 kg.

FEEDING: Juvenile white crappies feed on plankton, but shift to mainly aquatic insects and fish as they grow.

HABITAT: The white crappie lives in lakes and rivers. It prefers turbid water and can be found over a variety of substrates from mud or silt to gravel. Most often, it is found in or near cover such as submerged wood. They are schooling fish, and spend more time at midwater depths than most centrarchids.

ECOLOGICAL ROLE: The white crappie is a middle- to upper-level consumer. Where it is abundant, it can be a significant predator on minnows. In Manitoba, it is so rare that it is not significant. It differs from the black crappie in being more tolerant of turbidity and being more common in the mainstems of rivers than in lakes and marginal waters of rivers.

IMPORTANCE TO PEOPLE

The white crappie is a valued pan fish in its native range. Its eating qualities are considered to be among the best of all centrarchids. In Manitoba, it is probably never caught by anglers.

COSEWIC Status as of January 1, 2004: Not Listed
MBESA Status as of January 1, 2004: Not Listed
MBCDC Status as of January 1, 2004: G5, SE

BLACK CRAPPIE; MARIGANE NOIRE *Pomoxis nigromaculatus*

FRESH SPECIMEN
2 CM

IDENTIFICATION

Crappies have **six or seven spines in the anal fin**, and the **dorsal and anal spines increase in length from front to rear**, so that the **spiny portion of the fin slopes upward to join the rayed portion**. The **body is extremely compressed, being thinner in cross-section than in any other group of fish in our area**. The black crappie differs from the white crappie by having **seven or eight dorsal spines and the base of the dorsal fin being nearly the same length as the base of the anal fin**. The black crappie also is **mottled with black pigment on the sides and the dorsal and anal fins, and lacks dark bars**. *Note:* Underyearling black crappies are often very pale, and their markings may be difficult to distinguish from those of underyearling white crappies.

BASS, CRAPPIES, AND SUNFISHES, FAMILY CENTRARCHIDAE

DISTRIBUTION IN MANITOBA

The native range of the black crappie in Manitoba probably included the Winnipeg and Red river watersheds and Lake Winnipeg and its tributaries north to the Berens River. In addition to probable native occurrences of black crappies in the Winnipeg River watershed, there is at least one probable illegal introduction of black crappies into Brereton Lake, from which they were unknown. The lake drains via a marsh and lacked crappies until they were found there in 2001 (Bayette, pers. comm., 2003). The black crappie has also been introduced into some Red River tributaries, such as Lake Minnewasta.

BIOLOGICAL NOTES

SPAWNING: Spawning of the black crappie has not been observed in Manitoba. Becker (1983) describes spawning of this species in Wisconsin, where spawning takes place in June and July, at water temperatures between 18°–20°C. The male excavates or cleans a nest on substrate ranging from clay to fine gravel. Spawning is similar to that described for other centrarchids. See the rock bass account for a summary of spawning habits.

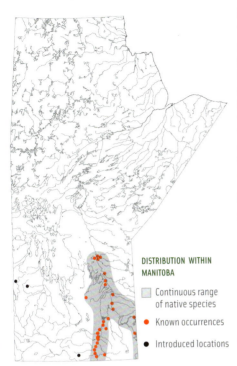

DISTRIBUTION WITHIN MANITOBA
- Continuous range of native species
- Known occurrences
- Introduced locations

GROWTH AND ADULT SIZE: Scott and Crossman (1979) give age and growth data for the black crappie from Lake of the Woods. In that lake, they live to nine years and grow to a fork length of 318 mm. Adult black crappies in the University of Manitoba collection are 120–150 mm total length. The Manitoba angling record for the black crappie is a 43 cm long individual taken from Lake Winnipeg in 1999.

FEEDING: Hatchling black crappies begin feeding on plankton. As they grow, they shift to a diet of fish and aquatic insects, but also continue to feed on planktonic crustacea (Becker, 1983).

HABITAT: The black crappie is found in clear, quiet waters of lakes and rivers. It is usually associated with cover such as weedbeds or submerged wood. It can tolerate slightly turbid water. Like the white crappie, it is a schooling, midwater fish. It differs from the white crappie in being less tolerant of turbidity and being more common in lakes and the marginal waters of rivers, such as oxbow lakes and sloughs.

ECOLOGICAL ROLE: The black crappie is a middle- to upper-level consumer. It can be one of the most important predators on minnows in small lakes, sloughs, and oxbow lakes.

IMPORTANCE TO PEOPLE

The black crappie is a valued pan fish in the United States and southern Ontario. Like the white crappie, it is an excellent food fish. It is more tolerant of low oxygen than most pan fish species, and has been used in stocking small lakes and impoundments that are affected by winterkill. It has been increasing in distribution and abundance in Manitoba over the last 20 years, and is gaining increasing recognition as an angling species.

COSEWIC Status as of January 1, 2004: Not Listed
MBESA Status as of January 1, 2004: Not Listed
MBCDC Status as of January 1, 2004: G5, SE

DARTERS, PERCH, SAUGER, AND WALLEYE, FAMILY PERCIDAE

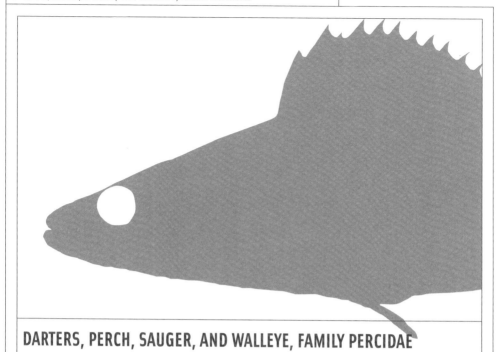

DARTERS, PERCH, SAUGER, AND WALLEYE, FAMILY PERCIDAE

FAMILY PERCIDAE

Members of the perch family are found in fresh water in temperate and subarctic North America and Eurasia. Percids can be distinguished from all other families in our area by the following combination of characters: (1) the **spines in the dorsal, anal, and pelvic fins are strong and sharp**; (2) the **spiny and soft-rayed dorsal fins are separated**; (3) the **anal fin has only one or two spines**; and (4) the **second anal spine, when present, is slender and about the same length as the first**.

There are two subfamilies of percids in our area.

1. Subfamily Percinae, yellow perch and darters. **Small to medium-sized fish with small to medium-sized mouths and small teeth**. Percines have **one or two strong anal spines**, and **small teeth**, and the **lateral line does not extend onto the tail**. They are represented by the yellow perch and five species of darters in Manitoba.

A. Tribe Percini, yellow perch. Medium-sized fish with a medium-sized mouth. The **margin of the preopercular bone is serrated**, the **body is relatively deep and compressed**, there is a **well-developed swim bladder**, and **adults are 150–400 mm long in our area**. In North America, there is one native species, the yellow perch, and the introduced river ruffe, a Eurasian percine.

B. Tribe Etheostomatini, darters. **Small fish with small mouths**. The **margin of the preopercular bone is smooth**, the **body is slender and round in cross-section**, the **swim bladder is reduced or absent**, and **adults range from 25–100 mm long**, depending on species, in our area. There are four genera and about 145 species of darters, making them one of the most diverse groups of freshwater fish in North America.

2. Subfamily Luciopercinae, sauger, and walleye. **Medium to large fish with large mouths and large teeth**. The North American luciopercines grow to a much larger size than percines, **adults always being longer than 200 mm in our area**. They are **slender, with a round cross-section**, have **two thin, weak anal spines**, and **strong, fang-like teeth**, and the **lateral line extends onto the base of the tail**. There are two native species, the sauger and walleye, in North America, and both are found in our area.

Note: The zander, *Sander luciopercus*, a Eurasian luciopercine, was introduced into Spiritwood Lake (Missouri River basin, James River watershed), North Dakota, in 1989. The capture of three, two-year-old zander in Spiritwood Lake in the spring of 2001 demonstrates that the species has survived and reproduced (Wright, pers. comm., 2001).

DARTERS, PERCH, SAUGER, AND WALLEYE, FAMILY PERCIDAE

KEY TO THE DARTERS, PERCH, SAUGER, AND WALLEYE FOUND IN MANITOBA AND ADJACENT AREAS OF THE HUDSON BAY DRAINAGE

1A Maxilla reaching to below or beyond middle of eye. Lower edge of preopercular bone with serrate (sawtooth) edge.

go to choice 2

1B Maxilla reaching only to, or a little past, anterior margin of eye. Lower edge of preopercular bone smooth.

go to choice 4

2A (1A) Teeth small, not strong and fang-like. Posterior dorsal fin with 15 or fewer soft rays. Anal fin with 8 or fewer soft rays.

yellow perch, *Perca flavescens* page 235

2B Large, fang-like teeth on lower jaw and roof of mouth. Posterior dorsal fin with 17 or more soft rays, and anal fin with 12 or more soft rays. Lateral line extending onto the base of the caudal fin.

genus *Sander*, go to choice 3

3A (2B) Membrane of first dorsal fin dusky anteriorly, with the pigment concentrated into a black blotch posteriorly. Three pyloric caecae, each about as long as the stomach. Cheek scaleless. Lower rear corner of caudal fin white.

walleye, *Sander vitreus* page 242

3B Membrane of first dorsal fin pale, marked with 3–4 rows of black spots. Usually 5 or more pyloric caecae, none as long as the stomach. Cheek scaled. Lower edge of caudal fin with a pale streak, but no white patch in lower rear corner.

sauger, *Sander canadensis* page 240

4A (1B) Belly covered by normal scales. Anal fin smaller than the posterior dorsal fin.

genus *Etheostoma*, go to choice 5

4B One or 2 enlarged, modified scales between the bases of the pelvic fins, and belly either naked or with a median row of enlarged scales. Anal fin nearly the same size or larger than the posterior dorsal fin.

genus *Percina*, go to choice 8

5A (4A) Lateral line complete to base of caudal fin.

go to choice 6

5B Lateral line incomplete, extending no farther than to below anterior half of posterior dorsal fin.

go to choice 7

6A (5A) Only 1 anal spine. Anterior dorsal fin with 7–9 spines. Upper lip separated from snout by a continuous groove. A series of w-shaped black markings on sides.

johnny darter, *Etheostoma nigrum* page 233

6B Two anal spines. Anterior dorsal fin with 8–13 spines. Groove separating upper lip from snout is not continuous across the midline. Sides with dusky vertical bars, but never w-shaped markings.

rainbow darter, *Etheostoma caeruleum* page 230

OTTER TAIL RIVER (RED RIVER DRAINAGE), MINNESOTA

7A (5B) Anterior dorsal fin with 8–12 spines. Posterior dorsal fin with 1 spine and 10–12 soft rays. Cheeks scaled. Lateral line extends to below posterior dorsal fin.

Iowa darter, *Etheostoma exile* page 231

7B Anterior dorsal fin with 5–7 spines. Posterior dorsal fin with 1 spine and 8 or 9 soft rays. Cheeks scaleless. Lateral line absent, or, at most, only 8 or so scales with pores just behind head.

least darter, *Etheostoma microperca* page 232

RED RIVER TRIBUTARIES, USA

DARTERS, PERCH, SAUGER, AND WALLEYE, FAMILY PERCIDAE

8A (4B) Tip of snout conical, pointed, and projecting beyond upper jaw. A series of 9 or more narrow, vertical, somewhat irregular dark bars on sides.

logperch, *Percina caprodes* page 236

8B Tip of snout does not project beyond upper jaw. Various dark markings on sides, but never narrow vertical bars.

go to choice 9

9A (8B) Cheeks scaled. A series of dusky blotches, sometimes indistinct, on sides. Anterior dorsal fin with a dark blotch at upper anterior and lower posterior corners.

river darter, *Percina shumardi* page 239

9B Cheeks scaleless. A series of large, oval, black blotches on sides, which may be so broadly connected as to form a dark lateral band. Anterior dorsal fin uniformly dusky, no dark blotches.

blackside darter, *Percina maculata* page 238

RAINBOW DARTER; DARD ARC-EN-CIEL | *Etheostoma caeruleum*

NOTE: Not found in Manitoba; Ottertail River, Minnesota

1 CM PRESERVED SPECIMEN

IDENTIFICATION

The rainbow darter can be distinguished by the combination of: (1) having a **complete lateral line**; (2) having **two anal spines** and **8–13 dorsal spines**; and (3) having **vertical bars on the sides**.

DISTRIBUTION IN MANITOBA

The rainbow darter has not been found in Manitoba. It is found in the Ottertail River (Red River Drainage) in Minnesota.

BIOLOGICAL NOTES

SPAWNING: Becker (1983) states that rainbow darters in Wisconsin spawn in April to June, at water temperatures over 15°C. Spawning habitat is fast riffles with fine gravel to rubble substrate. Males defend a territory around a female they are following. The eggs are released into spaces between stones and fertilized as they are released (Winn, 1958).

GROWTH AND ADULT SIZE: The rainbow darter grows to 63 mm total length and lives to four years old. Sexual maturity is attained at two or three years (Becker, 1983).

FEEDING: Underyearling rainbow darters feed mostly on copepods. As they grow, the diet shifts to aquatic insects, amphipods, crayfish, and fish eggs (Becker, 1983).

HABITAT: The rainbow darter lives in pools and riffles in clear streams. It does not tolerate turbidity. It is found on a variety of substrates, most commonly on sand or rocky bottoms (Becker, 1983). Scott and Crossman (1979) state that shallow riffle habitat with gravel or rocky bottom is required for spawning.

ECOLOGICAL ROLE: The rainbow darter is a middle-level consumer. There are apparently no data on its use as food by larger piscivores (Scott and Crossman, 1979).

DARTERS, PERCH, SAUGER, AND WALLEYE, FAMILY PERCIDAE

IMPORTANCE TO PEOPLE

The rainbow darter is intolerant of pollution (Becker, 1983), and its presence is considered to be an indicator of good water quality.

COSEWIC Status as of January 1, 2004: Not Listed
MBESA Status as of January 1, 2004: Not Listed
MBCDC Status as of January 1, 2004: Not Listed

IOWA DARTER; DARD À VENTRE JAUNE | *Etheostoma exile*

PRESERVED SPECIMEN, MATURE MALE
0.5 CM

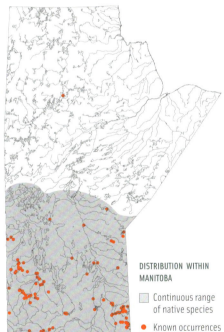

DISTRIBUTION WITHIN MANITOBA

- Continuous range of native species
- Known occurrences

IDENTIFICATION

The Iowa darter is distinguished by having an **incomplete lateral line, scales on the cheeks, 8–12 dorsal spines,** and **10–12 dorsal rays**.

DISTRIBUTION IN MANITOBA

The Iowa darter is found throughout southern Manitoba and the Manitoba Great Lakes. We have no records of it from the Saskatchewan or Nelson rivers, but it has been collected in the Churchill River at Southern Indian Lake. Collecting in suitable habitats in the Saskatchewan and Nelson river watersheds would probably fill this gap in its distribution.

BIOLOGICAL NOTES

SPAWNING: Balesic (1971) collected aggregations of ripe Iowa darters from early May to early July in Lake Dauphin and the Valley River. The apparent spawning aggregations were found in protected water, either in aquatic vegetation or on pebble-rubble substrate. In Michigan, the Iowa darter spawns from late April to mid-June, at water temperatures above 13°C. Males defend a territory in shallow water along a shoreline, on a substrate of exposed fibrous tree roots (Winn, 1958). As with other *Etheostoma* species, the male positions himself on the female's back during mating and the eggs are deposited. The male continues to guard the nest site, but provides no other care for the eggs (Winn).

GROWTH AND ADULT SIZE: The Iowa darter is the smallest native species of darter in Manitoba. Large specimens in the University of Manitoba collection are 35–40 mm total length, but most are 30 mm or less. It shares the distinction, with the blacknose shiner and mimic shiner, of being our smallest native fish. Becker (1983) states that Iowa darters live to Age IV, but his largest specimens are almost twice the size of large individuals in Manitoba.

FEEDING: The Iowa darter feeds on a variety of aquatic insect larvae and crustaceans. Balesic (1971) found that Iowa darters of all sizes consumed midge fly larvae, amphipods, and small planktonic crustacea as the bulk of their diet. Fish eggs appeared seasonally in the stomach contents of larger individuals. Becker (1983) notes that a significant part of its food consists of midwater, rather than benthic, species.

HABITAT: Balesic (1971) found that the Iowa darter prefers water with aquatic vegetation at all ages and over the entire open-water season. In our experience, it is found in weedbeds along the shores of lakes and rivers, in oxbow lakes, and in headwater streams and ponds including bog habitats. It is the only darter in the group of fish species associated with bogs in Manitoba. See the pearl dace species account for a list and additional comments.

ECOLOGICAL ROLE: The Iowa darter is a middle-level consumer. The appearance of planktonic animals among its prey is unusual for a darter. Iowa darters live in heavy growths of aquatic plants, however, and likely spend much of their time well above the bottom, swimming and resting among the vegetation. In Manitoba, the Iowa darter, brook stickleback, central mudminnow, and tadpole madtom are often found together in (as opposed to above or around) dense growths of aquatic plants. This habitat is occupied transiently by the young and/or feeding adults of piscivores such as northern pike and yellow perch. This habitat and species association should be studied to evaluate their significance in production of larger piscivores.

IMPORTANCE TO PEOPLE

The Iowa darter has no direct economic importance. Male Iowa darters in Manitoba retain the red and blue spawning colours on the body and dorsal fin throughout the year. This makes them attractive in native fish aquaria.

COSEWIC Status as of January 1, 2004: Not Listed
MBESA Status as of January 1, 2004: Not Listed
MBCDC Status as of January 1, 2004: G5, S5

LEAST DARTER; PETIT DARD | *Etheostoma microperca*

NOTE: Not found in Manitoba; Red River tributaries in Minnesota

FRESH SPECIMEN
0.5 CM

IDENTIFICATION

The least darter can be distinguished by the **incomplete lateral line**, having **no scales on the cheeks**, and having **five to seven dorsal spines** and **eight to nine dorsal rays**.

DISTRIBUTION IN MANITOBA

The least darter is not found in Manitoba. It occurs in the headwaters of Red River tributaries in Minnesota.

BIOLOGICAL NOTES

SPAWNING: The least darter spawns in May and June (Scott and Crossman, 1979) among aquatic plants. The eggs are deposited on the stems of plants, with the male and female oriented vertically along a stem during mating (Winn, 1958).

GROWTH AND ADULT SIZE: Least darters attain a total length up to 38 mm and an age of two. They become sexually mature at Age I, and most do not survive beyond their first spawning (Becker, 1983). Scott and Crossman (1979) consider the least darter to be the smallest freshwater fish in Canada.

FEEDING: The least darter feeds mainly on copepod and entomostracan crustaceans, but also takes some aquatic insect larvae (Becker, 1983).

HABITAT: The least darter prefers similar habitat to the Iowa darter, being found in quiet, clear, weedy waters of slow-moving streams and small lakes (Scott and Crossman, 1979).

ECOLOGICAL ROLE: The least darter is a middle-level consumer. There are no reports of its importance as prey of larger piscivores.

IMPORTANCE TO PEOPLE

The least darter has no economic importance. It is probably almost never seen by people other than aquatic biologists.

COSEWIC Status as of January 1, 2004: Not at Risk
MBESA Status as of January 1, 2004: Not Listed
MBCDC Status as of January 1, 2004: G5, SP

| JOHNNY DARTER; RASEUX-DE-TERRE | *Etheostoma nigrum* |

PRESERVED SPECIMEN
0.5 CM

IDENTIFICATION

The johnny darter can be distinguished by having a **complete lateral line**, only **one anal spine**, **seven to nine dorsal spines**, and **w-shaped markings along the sides**.

DISTRIBUTION IN MANITOBA

The johnny darter is the most common darter in Manitoba. It is found in streams, rivers, and along lakeshores throughout southern and central Manitoba north into the Churchill River Drainage.

BIOLOGICAL NOTES

SPAWNING: Balesic (1971) found ripe johnny darters in the Valley River and in Lake Dauphin from early May through June. Winn (1958) found that, in Ontario and Quebec, spawning also occurs during May and June, with the timing being later in cooler environments. Spawning occurs in quiet water, in pools in streams and along lakeshores. Nests are established by males under objects ranging from rocks or freshwater mussel shells to human-made artifacts like empty metal cans. Eggs are deposited on the roof of the nest.

GROWTH AND ADULT SIZE: Johnny darters in the University of Manitoba collection are up to 50 mm total length, but most are less than 35 mm. Smart (1979) found a few johnny darters in the Whitemouth River that were up to 60–65 mm total length. Becker (1983) states that johnny darters in southern Wisconsin grow to 68 mm total length and reach an age of three years.

FEEDING: Like most darters, the johnny darter feeds on aquatic insects and crustaceans. Balesic (1971), in Lake Dauphin and the Valley River, and Smart (1979), in the Whitemouth River, found chironomid fly larvae were the

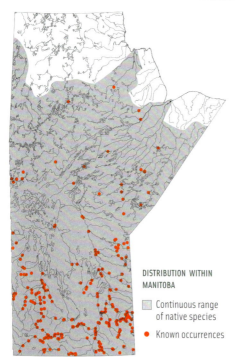

DISTRIBUTION WITHIN MANITOBA

☐ Continuous range of native species
● Known occurrences

most common food item of johnny darters. Smart found that mayfly naiads become numerous during the summer and amphipods increase in importance in autumn. By contrast, Balesic found mayfly naiads were significant only in the Valley River, among smaller individuals. In Lake Dauphin, they appeared in the stomach contents of johnny darters only in late summer, and only in darters collected from protected rubble habitats.

HABITAT: The johnny darter lives in the littoral zone of most rivers, streams, and lakes. Balesic (1971) compared habitats used by four darter species—the johnny darter, Iowa darter, river darter, and logperch—in Lake Dauphin and the Valley River. He found that the johnny darter was the only one of the four species to remain in the Valley River during the entire open-water season. It was also the only species to occur on sand or gravel substrates devoid of cover. Valiant (1975) found the johnny darter to be most strongly associated with pools located below riffles (0–15 cm/s water velocity, depth 35–100 cm, and gravel substrate) in five Manitoba Escarpment streams. Smart (1979) found that it was more commonly found in current-exposed conditions than sheltered from the current. It prefers sand and gravel substrates, devoid of vegetation or other cover, often in very shallow water. This species is often the only fish present in clean sand beach habitats of lakes.

ECOLOGICAL ROLE: The johnny darter is a benthic, middle-level consumer. In the open, shallow-water habitats in which it is found, it is one of the few fish species present. It is eaten by a variety of larger piscivores such as burbot, smallmouth bass, yellow perch, and walleye (Scott and Crossman, 1979).

IMPORTANCE TO PEOPLE

The johnny darter has no direct economic importance. Scott and Crossman (1979) point to its importance in making food production available to larger piscivores. The johnny darter also is used in native fish aquaria, although it does not adapt well to commercial dry aquarium fish foods.

COSEWIC Status as of January 1, 2004: Not Listed
MBESA Status as of January 1, 2004: Not Listed
MBCDC Status as of January 1, 2004: G5, S5

YELLOW PERCH; PERCHAUDE — *Perca flavescens*

4 CM — FRESH SPECIMEN

IDENTIFICATION

The yellow perch can be distinguished from all other percids in our area by the combination of: (1) the **body being deep and compressed** but **robust and oval in cross-section**; (2) the **mouth reaching to below the middle of the eye**, and the **jaws having pads of minute villiform teeth**; and (3) having **six or seven bars on the sides that become narrower toward the lower part of the body**.

DISTRIBUTION IN MANITOBA

The yellow perch is found in rivers, streams, and lakes throughout southern and central Manitoba northward into the Churchill River watershed.

DISTRIBUTION WITHIN MANITOBA
- Continuous range of native species
- Known occurrences

BIOLOGICAL NOTES

SPAWNING: In southern Manitoba, yellow perch spawn in May or early June, at water temperatures above 6°C. Rowes (1994) collected larval yellow perch in Lake Dauphin during almost all of June, with a strong peak in catches in early June. Female yellow perch have a median ovary and oviduct, and the eggs are expelled in a thick, pleated strand, which is bound together by a gelatinous mucous tube secreted in the oviduct of the female. The egg strand of a female, after the eggs have taken up water, may be up to 2 m long and weigh about 2 kg (Scott and Crossman, 1979). Most commonly, the egg strand will break up after deposition, due to wave action. During spawning, a female, attended by several males, expels her eggs above the bottom. The egg strands are slightly buoyant, and usually become entangled in vegetation.

GROWTH AND ADULT SIZE: In Hemming Lake, Lawler (1953) found that yellow perch grow to 302 mm fork length and live to Age IX. Yellow perch can adapt to overpopulation or low productivity in lakes by stunting. In such cases, adult perch may be 150 mm or less in total length. The largest yellow perch caught by anglers in Manitoba are 41 cm long. They were caught in 1991, 1996, and 1999, in the Winnipeg River, Lake of the Prairies, and Oak Lake, respectively.

FEEDING: The yellow perch is an opportunistic feeder, taking a wide variety of invertebrates and fish from midwater to near the bottom. Hanke (1996) found that underyearling yellow perch in Lake Winnipeg begin feeding on plankton and switch to insect larvae by midsummer. By late summer, they begin to feed on other fish. He suggested that the feeding habits and habitat of underyearling yellow perch and white bass in Lake Winnipeg are similar enough that there is a possibility of competition between them. Johnson (2001) showed that the foods taken by yellow perch varied among lakes, depending on the productivity and faunal diversity of the lake.

HABITAT: The yellow perch is found in waters with slow or no current. It is most often found around cover, which may be vegetation, submerged wood, or human-made structures such as boat docks or breakwaters. It is tolerant of moderate turbidity. In southern Manitoba, the yellow perch is uncommon only in the mainstems of the Red River (probably too much turbidity) and the Assiniboine River (probably both too turbid and too fast).

ECOLOGICAL ROLE: The yellow perch is a schooling, benthic to midwater, upper-level consumer. It is eaten by apex predators such as walleye, northern pike, and lake trout. Its abundance in a wide variety of habitats makes it an important component of most aquatic communities in Manitoba.

IMPORTANCE TO PEOPLE

Yellow perch are valued as food fish by commercial fishers and anglers. Their abundance around shorelines and human-made structures makes them readily accessible to anglers fishing from shore. They are one of the most common first catches of young anglers fishing in any of our lakes and in Canadian Shield rivers.

COSEWIC Status as of January 1, 2004: Not Listed
MBESA Status as of January 1, 2004: Not Listed
MBCDC Status as of January 1, 2004: G5, S5

LOGPERCH; FOUILLE-ROCHE | *Percina caprodes*

FRESH SPECIMEN
2 CM

IDENTIFICATION

The logperch can be distinguished by the **long, pointed snout that projects beyond the upper jaw and the series of nine or more dark bars on the sides.**

DISTRIBUTION IN MANITOBA

The logperch is found in the Red and Winnipeg river watersheds, the Manitoba Great Lakes and their tributaries, and the Saskatchewan River watershed.

BIOLOGICAL NOTES

SPAWNING: Rowes (1994) found that logperch in Lake Dauphin spawn from early May to late June, at water temperatures of 16°–23°C. Balesic (1971) found aggregations of ripe logperch in the Valley River from late May through early August in 1968 and 1969. The largest numbers were found in late May and June. He did not find ripe logperch in Lake Dauphin. Spawning of logperch has not been observed in Manitoba. Winn (1958) found that lake-spawning logperch behave differently from those in flowing water. Lake-spawning males are non-territorial, and form a dense school over gravel substrate in water up to 2 m deep. Male logperch in streams defend moving territories around a ripe female. The male mounts the female, as in most darters, and the eggs are deposited in gravel substrate. Vibrating movements of the male and female during spawning help to bury the eggs. The eggs are abandoned after spawning.

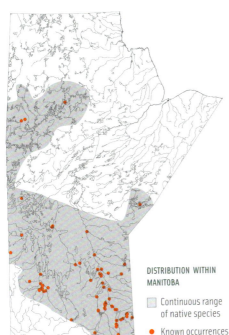

DISTRIBUTION WITHIN MANITOBA

☐ Continuous range of native species
● Known occurrences

GROWTH AND ADULT SIZE: The logperch and blackside darter are the two largest darters in Manitoba. Large adults of both reach 90 mm total length in southern Manitoba, but most are from 40–50 mm. In Wisconsin, logperch reach an age of four years (Becker, 1983).

FEEDING: Underyearling logperch feed on planktonic crustaceans. The diet shifts to predominantly aquatic insects as they grow. Fish eggs, notably logperch eggs, are also eaten by adult logperch (Scott and Crossman, 1979). Hanke (1996) found the same feeding habits in underyearling logperch in Lake Winnipeg.

HABITAT: Balesic (1971) compared habitats used by four darter species—the johnny darter, Iowa darter, river darter, and logperch—in Lake Dauphin and the Valley River. The logperch is found along the shorelines of lakes, rivers, and larger streams. It prefers rocky substrate with sparse or no aquatic vegetation. He found that the logperch preferred pebble-rubble substrates that were protected from wave action, but was also found in wave-exposed habitats. Hanke (1996) also found logperch in nearshore habitat, on coarse gravel substrate, in Lake Winnipeg. It is tolerant of turbid water and is found (uncommonly) even in the mainstem of the Red River. Scott and Crossman (1979) state that it is typically offshore, in water 1 m or more deep, and thus may escape capture by beach seining. In Manitoba, it is never a common or dominant species in samples, but seining offshore by using a boat to set the beach seine or setting a small mesh gillnet offshore do not seem to produce more logperch than does seining within wading depth.

ECOLOGICAL ROLE: The logperch is a benthic, middle-level consumer. It is eaten by walleye and northern pike in our area, although it is far less abundant than the cyprinids and catostomids that have a similar trophic position in the same aquatic communities.

IMPORTANCE TO PEOPLE

The logperch has no direct economic importance. As one of several intermediate species in the trophic structure of our aquatic communities, it contributes diversity and, hence, stability, to the communities of which it is a part. The logperch is also used in native fish aquaria. It adapts well to aquarium conditions and is not as aggressive toward other fish as most centrarchids are.

COSEWIC Status as of January 1, 2004: Not Listed
MBESA Status as of January 1, 2004: Not Listed
MBCDC Status as of January 1, 2004: G5, S5

DARTERS, PERCH, SAUGER, AND WALLEYE, FAMILY PERCIDAE

BLACKSIDE DARTER; DARD NOIR *Percina maculata*

PRESERVED SPECIMEN
1 CM

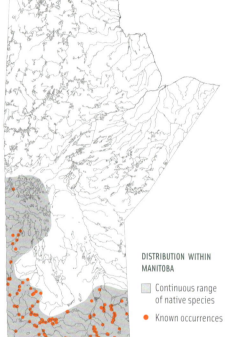

DISTRIBUTION WITHIN MANITOBA

☐ Continuous range of native species
● Known occurrences

IDENTIFICATION

The blackside darter is distinguished by the series of five to seven, oval-shaped, dusky to black blotches on the sides. These may be so broadly connected that they make an irregular dark band down the sides. In addition, the mouth is terminal, the cheeks are scaleless, and the dorsal fin is uniformly dusky in colour, lacking distinct dark markings.

DISTRIBUTION IN MANITOBA

The blackside darter is found in the Red, Winnipeg, and Assiniboine river watersheds, the south basin of Lake Winnipeg, the Lake Winnipegosis watershed, and the Saskatchewan River watershed.

BIOLOGICAL NOTES

SPAWNING: Smart (1979) observed male blackside darters defending spawning territories in riffles in the Whitemouth River, at water velocities up to 10 cm/s. She did not give the time or water temperature at which this was observed. Winn (1958) found that they spawn in early May in southern Michigan, and Becker (1983) gives April to June as the spawning time in Wisconsin. A May–June spawning period seems likely for Manitoba. Winn stated that the blackside darter spawns in gravel or coarse sand, in slow-moving water of pools and runs in streams. The males defend a moving territory around a ripe female and mount the female during spawning, as do most other darters. The eggs are extruded into interstitial spaces in the substrate or are covered with sand stirred up by vibration of the bodies of the male and female during egg deposition. The eggs are abandoned after laying (Winn).

GROWTH AND ADULT SIZE: The blackside darter and logperch are the two largest darter species in Manitoba. Large adults of both reach 90 mm total length in southern Manitoba, but most are from 40–50 mm. In Wisconsin, blackside darters reach an age of four years (Becker, 1983).

FEEDING: Hatchling blackside darters feed near the surface, but become benthic feeders as they grow. The diet consists of planktonic crustaceans initially, but shifts to aquatic insects and some fish eggs in adults (Becker, 1983).

HABITAT: The blackside darter lives in flowing water ranging from small streams to large rivers, and, less commonly, in the littoral zone of lakes. Valiant (1975) found the blackside darter to be most strongly associated with pools located below riffles (0–15 cm/s water velocity, depth 35–100 cm, and gravel substrate) in five Manitoba Escarpment streams. It prefers clear to slightly turbid water, and rocky substrates, and is often found around vegetation. It is found rarely in the mainstems of the Red and Assiniboine rivers, but commonly in their tributaries.

ECOLOGICAL ROLE: Like other darters, the blackside darter is a middle-level consumer. It is more common overall than the logperch, and is more common in streams than lakes. McCulloch (1994) noted that blackside darters were rare in a study site on the Little Saskatchewan River at which stonecats were present, but were abundant at a site above an impassable dam that did not have stonecats.

IMPORTANCE TO PEOPLE

The blackside darter has no direct economic importance. Like other darters, it is a link between low trophic levels and higher level piscivores. Because of its abundance in medium-sized streams, it may be a significant part of the trophic structure of these systems. The blackside darter is also used in native fish aquaria.

COSEWIC Status as of January 1, 2004: Not Listed
MBESA Status as of January 1, 2004: Not Listed
MBCDC Status as of January 1, 2004: G5, S5

RIVER DARTER; DARD DE RIVIÈRE | *Percina shumardi*

PRESERVED SPECIMEN
1 CM

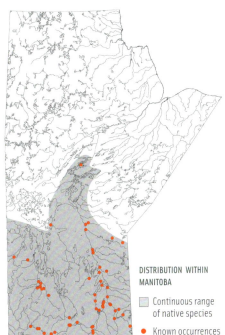

DISTRIBUTION WITHIN MANITOBA

☐ Continuous range of native species
● Known occurrences

IDENTIFICATION

The river darter has a **terminal mouth**. The **colour pattern is more faded** than it is in either the logperch or the blackside darter, with a **series of eight to 11 often indistinct, dusky blotches on the sides**. The spiny dorsal fin has a well-marked dark spot on the upper anterior and lower posterior corners.

DISTRIBUTION IN MANITOBA

The river darter is found in the Red, Winnipeg, Assiniboine, and Nelson rivers, and the Manitoba Great Lakes.

BIOLOGICAL NOTES

SPAWNING: Balesic (1971) found ripe river darters in the Valley River between late May and early July, with the largest concentrations being in June of 1968 and 1969. He also found smaller numbers of ripe river darters in Lake Dauphin during the same period. Hanke (pers. comm., 2003) found large numbers of river darters below the falls in the Manigotagan River (Lake Winnipeg watershed) in late May and early June of 1994 and 1995. He speculated that this may have been a spawning aggregation. Spawning of the river darter has not been observed in Manitoba, and the spawning habitat is unknown.

GROWTH AND ADULT SIZE: In Manitoba, the river darter is smaller than the logperch and blackside darter. Most adults in the University of Manitoba collection are 40 mm or less total length. Hanke (1996) found a length range of 28–56 mm in river darters collected from the shoreline of Lake Winnipeg. Becker (1983) found that they become sexually mature at Age I and live to two years in Wisconsin.

FEEDING: Hanke (1996) found that aquatic insects were the dominant food of river darters. Zooplankton and fish eggs were taken in smaller quantities. Balesic (1971) found corixids to be significant or the dominant food type, in all but the smaller individuals, throughout the summer, in Lake Dauphin.

HABITAT: Balesic (1971) compared habitats used by four darter species—the johnny darter, Iowa darter, river darter, and logperch—in Lake Dauphin and the Valley River. He found that river darters preferred pebble-rubble substrates, either in protected or exposed locations. It was the most abundant darter by a wide margin in both protected and wave-exposed pebble-rubble habitats. The river darter is found in the littoral areas of the Manitoba Great Lakes and our larger rivers. In our experience, it prefers flowing water or wave action to quiet, protected water. It is usually found on rocky substrates with little or no vegetation. It tolerates turbidity and is the only *Percina* species that has its greatest abundance in the mainstems of the Red and Assiniboine rivers.

ECOLOGICAL ROLE: Like the other *Percina* species, the river darter is a benthic, middle-level consumer. It is vastly outnumbered by several species of minnows and suckers that occupy the same trophic position in the mainstems of the Red and Assiniboine rivers, so it is of minor importance in these communities.

IMPORTANCE TO PEOPLE

The river darter is of no direct economic importance. So little is known about it that it is difficult to assess its importance in the communities of which it is a part. The river darter is classified as endangered in Michigan. It adapts well to aquaria and will take commercial dry aquarium foods.

COSEWIC Status as of January 1, 2004: Not at Risk
MBESA Status as of January 1, 2004: Not Listed
MBCDC Status as of January 1, 2004: G5, S5

SAUGER; DORÉ NOIR | *Sander canadensis*

NOTE: This species was formerly known as *Stizostedion canadense*, sauger, doré noir

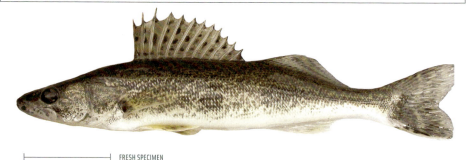

FRESH SPECIMEN
5 CM

IDENTIFICATION

The sauger and walleye are our only two spiny-rayed fish with **large, fang-like teeth**. The sauger differs from the walleye by the following characters: (1) there are **three to four rows of black spots on the spiny dorsal fin**; (2) there are **scales on the cheeks**; (3) there may be a **white streak along the anterior edge of the anal fin and lower edge of the caudal fin**; and (4) there is a **brownish colouration** with **two or three large, irregular blotches on the sides**. Internally, the sauger usually has **five pyloric caecae, none of which are as long as the stomach**.

NATURALLY OCCURRING HYBRID

Hybrids between the sauger and walleye are seen infrequently. They are often first spotted by having **partially scaled cheeks**. They are often **more yellowish in colour than either the walleye or sauger**, and they **have rows of**

DARTERS, PERCH, SAUGER, AND WALLEYE, FAMILY PERCIDAE

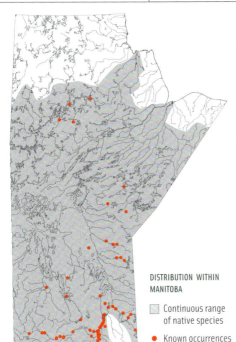

DISTRIBUTION WITHIN MANITOBA

☐ Continuous range of native species

● Known occurrences

spots on the dorsal fin like a sauger. The best way to identify them with certainty is to examine the pyloric caecae. There will be more than three, as in the sauger, but they will be **as long as the stomach, as in the walleye**. The University of Manitoba collection has walleye X sauger hybrids from the Assiniboine River and Southern Indian Lake (Churchill River watershed).

DISTRIBUTION IN MANITOBA

The sauger is found in rivers, lakes, and streams throughout Manitoba north into the Churchill River watershed. Curiously, there are no records of sauger from the Whitemouth River, a Winnipeg River tributary. The absence of catfish and the sauger, along with the presence of the northern brook lamprey and the rosyface shiner, which have restricted distributions centred on the Whitemouth River, make the Whitemouth River biologically unique.

BIOLOGICAL NOTES

SPAWNING: Saugers may spawn in streams or lakes. In lakes, saugers spawn on shoals or reefs with gravel to rubble substrates. In the lower Red River, the sauger spawns in late May and early June, a little later than peak walleye spawning. Male saugers with running milt have been collected in the Red River below the St. Andrews Dam in about the same locations as mature walleyes have been collected. The substrate in this area is limestone rubble, and the water depth is between 2.5–4 m. Water velocities at this time are high for the Red River, from 1–1.5 m/s at the surface. Saugers may use even faster and more turbulent water for spawning, since a few individual males with running milt have been taken within a few metres of the face of the St. Andrews Dam, and at the base of the spillway at the outlet of the Red River Floodway. Sauger spawning is not described for Manitoba, but elsewhere, they have been observed to scatter the eggs over rocky substrate. No nest is built and the eggs are abandoned after spawning.

GROWTH AND ADULT SIZE: The sauger is smaller than the walleye. In the Red and Assiniboine rivers, large adults are 400 mm or less in total length and most adults are from 250–350 mm long. Saugers up to 500 mm total length have also been caught by commercial fishers in the north basin of Lake Winnipeg (Derksen, pers. comm., 2003). Carlander (1950) found a maximum age of seven years and a fork length of 399 mm for saugers in Lake of the Woods.

FEEDING: Juvenile saugers feed on zooplankton and aquatic insects, but become piscivorous by the end of their first summer. In addition to fish, adult saugers also eat crayfish, leeches, and aquatic insects.

HABITAT: In Manitoba, the sauger prefers shallower, more turbid water than the walleye, and is more common in our turbid rivers than the walleye. In the mainstem of the Red River, above the St. Andrews Dam, the sauger typically outnumbers the walleye by about 50:1 in both gillnet and angling catches. The sauger is also markedly more abundant than the walleye in the Assiniboine River upstream to Portage la Prairie. Above Portage la Prairie, the sauger declines in abundance upstream, and is rare to absent at St. Lazare. Both species are common to abundant in the Manitoba Great Lakes, with the sauger more common than the walleye in samples from nearshore areas. The sauger is found on substrates ranging from clay or silt to rubble and boulders. It is more common over rocky substrates.

ECOLOGICAL ROLE: The sauger is a top-level consumer. It is probably the most abundant piscivore in the mainstems of the Red and Assiniboine rivers. It is frequently found in the stomach contents of large channel catfish.

IMPORTANCE TO PEOPLE

The sauger is an important commercial and game fish. In the commercial fish trade, sauger and walleye are both marketed as "pickerel," with sauger and smaller walleye being distinguished as "baby pickerel." The sauger is the second most valuable commercial fish species in Lake Winnipeg, after the walleye, although its harvest has been controversial. Legalization of commercial gillnets with a mesh size small enough to catch sauger effectively exposes immature walleye to harvest. This may have two results over time. First, it may lead to earlier maturation in walleyes (depensation), which will reduce the average size of mature adults. This may, in itself, decrease the yield of the stock, and it may also decrease its rate of reproduction, further decreasing the ability of the stock to withstand exploitation. Second, unless depensation occurs quickly, the increased harvest of immature fish will decrease the number of fish surviving to reproduce, which will also decrease the ability of the stock to withstand exploitation.

A possible remedy to this problem would be to use a method of harvesting sauger that allowed walleyes to be released alive from the gear. The use of hoop nets or similar types of trap nets should be examined for feasibility.

Anglers distinguish between sauger and walleye, but regard the sauger as equally high in eating quality as the walleye. In the mainstems of the Red and Assiniboine rivers, the sauger is the most commonly caught of the two species. The walleye replaces it in lakes and reservoirs on the prairies and in the less turbid water of our Canadian Shield rivers and lakes.

COSEWIC Status as of January 1, 2004: Not Listed
MBESA Status as of January 1, 2004: Not Listed
MBCDC Status as of January 1, 2004: G5, S5

WALLEYE; DORÉ JAUNE	*Sander vitreus*
NOTE: This species was formerly known as *Stizostedion vitreum*, walleye, doré jaune	

FRESH SPECIMEN, "YELLOW FORM"
5 CM

FRESH SPECIMEN, "GREENBACK FORM"
10 CM

IDENTIFICATION

The sauger and walleye are our only two spiny-rayed fish with **large, fang-like teeth**. The walleye differs from the sauger by the following characters: (1) there are **no black spots on the spiny dorsal fin**; (2) the **cheeks are scaleless or have only a few scales**; (3) the **lower corners of the anal and caudal fins are white**; and (4) the walleye is usually **olive green above**, often with **indistinct, broad, darker bars** fading to **brassy yellow on the sides**. The walleye

DARTERS, PERCH, SAUGER, AND WALLEYE, FAMILY PERCIDAE

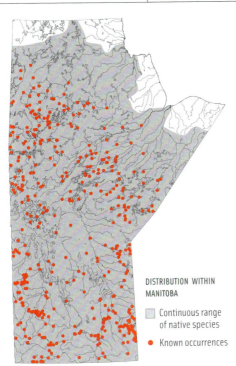

DISTRIBUTION WITHIN MANITOBA

- Continuous range of native species
- Known occurrences

usually has **three pyloric caecae, which are as long as the stomach.**

COLOUR VARIANT: Some of the walleyes in Lake Winnipeg and virtually all the walleyes entering the lower Winnipeg and Red rivers from Lake Winnipeg in the late summer and fall are jade green above, fading to brassy yellow or silvery on the sides. There are rare individuals that apparently lack yellow pigment and are blue above and silvery on the sides, among these fish. Fish with this green colour are recognized as distinct by anglers, who call them "greenbacks." Eighty-two males of this colour variant, all with running milt, were collected in a single two-hour gillnet set in early May 1986, about 1 km below the St. Andrews Dam at Lockport. This raises the possibility that walleyes with this colour pattern may not spawn with normally coloured walleyes. This colour variant probably explains Hinks's (1943) reference to the blue walleye, *Sander vitreus glaucus* (formerly *Stizostedion vitreum glaucum*), as being in Lake Winnipeg. *S. v. glaucus* was known only from Lake Erie, and is now extinct.

NATURALLY OCCURRING HYBRID

Walleye X sauger hybrids are found occasionally. See the note in the sauger species account.

DISTRIBUTION IN MANITOBA

The walleye is found throughout Manitoba north into the Seal River watershed.

BIOLOGICAL NOTES

SPAWNING: The walleye will spawn in lakes or streams. Spawning begins shortly after the ice cover breaks up, at water temperatures of 4°C. In time, this can range from mid- to late April to late May in most of Manitoba. Mature walleyes may also ascend from still-frozen lakes into the warmer waters of tributaries. The eggs are broadcast over rocky substrate and abandoned by the parents. Male walleyes with running milt have been collected in early to mid-May in the Red River between St. Andrews Dam and the mouth of Cook's Creek, north of Selkirk. At least some mature fish also run into Red River tributaries, and ripe male walleyes have been taken in Cook's Creek and in the lower reaches of the Rat and Roseau rivers, which enter the Red River south of Winnipeg. Mature walleyes seem to be found more frequently in Red River tributaries than saugers, even though saugers outnumber walleyes in the mainstem of the river. This may be due to the lower turbidity of the tributaries.

GROWTH AND ADULT SIZE: The walleye grows to substantially larger size than the sauger. Adult walleyes from the Red River are commonly from 350–500 mm total length. The Manitoba angling record for walleye is a 99 cm total length fish caught in the Red River in 1997. The growth rate of the walleye varies, depending at least in part on the productivity of the system.

FEEDING: Like the sauger, underyearling walleyes start feeding as planktivores and shift first to larger invertebrates and then to fish. Beyond the first year, walleyes are mainly piscivorous. Since the first appearance of the rainbow smelt in Lake Winnipeg in 1991, smelt have become established and spread throughout the lake. In recent years, the stomach contents of walleyes caught in the north basin of the lake indicate they have begun feeding on smelt (Derksen, pers. comm., 2002). The commercial and angling catches of Lake Winnipeg walleye should be monitored to determine whether the growth rate and length-to-weight ratio of Lake Winnipeg walleyes are changing in response to the diet shift. Casual observation of the total length and weight, and of mesenteric fat content of angler-caught walleyes in the Red River below the St. Andrews Dam, suggests that such a shift is occurring.

HABITAT: The walleye is typically found in deeper, less turbid water than the sauger. It is more common than the sauger in the Winnipeg River, our Canadian Shield lakes and streams, and in the deeper, offshore areas of the

Manitoba Great Lakes. In our turbid rivers, walleye abundance becomes nearly equal to sauger abundance only in the lower Red River, below the St. Andrews Dam at Lockport, during the fall, when walleyes move into the river from Lake Winnipeg.

ECOLOGICAL ROLE: The walleye is one of the five species of apex predators in our fish fauna. In Canadian Shield lakes and rivers, it shares the top of the food web with the northern pike and, where they are found, with the lake trout and the introduced smallmouth bass. Fedoruk (1961) studied the interactions of walleye and smallmouth bass in Falcon Lake, Whiteshell Provincial Park (Winnipeg River watershed), 12 to 13 years after smallmouth bass had been introduced into the lake. By that time smallmouth bass had increased in abundance to about equal to walleye abundance. He found evidence that both species consumed some of the same types of food items, but little other evidence for competitive interaction. The only significant difference in diet was the dominance of crayfish in the diet of smallmouth bass. He suggested that any further increase in smallmouth bass abundance could have a negative effect on the walleye stock in the lake. The walleye is apparently less tolerant of warm, shallow water than the smallmouth bass, and can be displaced by smallmouth bass in lakes that are marginal because of high temperatures and shallow water. From Fedoruk's study, the greater abundance of crayfish in warmer, shallower lakes may be the means by which the smallmouth bass increases in abundance to the point where it becomes the dominant species in those lakes. Juvenile walleyes may be eaten by larger predatory fish such as northern pike and channel catfish.

IMPORTANCE TO PEOPLE

The walleye is the most valuable and intensively utilized fishery resource in Manitoba. The commercial walleye fisheries in the Manitoba Great Lakes constitute the second-largest and second most valuable commercial inland fishery in Canada, after the commercial fisheries of the Laurentide Great Lakes. The walleye is also the primary target of most of the subsistence fisheries in Manitoba. In addition, the walleye is also the premier game fish in Manitoba. Walleye angling probably accounts for more time and money spent in Manitoba by both resident and non-resident anglers than angling for all other species combined. As a predator at the top of the food web, our walleye stocks do not just depend on regulating the catch. Stable, healthy, and productive walleye stocks also depend on maintaining their habitat, and the health and species diversity of the aquatic communities on which the walleye depends.

COSEWIC Status as of January 1, 2004: Not Listed
MBESA Status as of January 1, 2004: Not Listed
MBCDC Status as of January 1, 2004: G5, S5

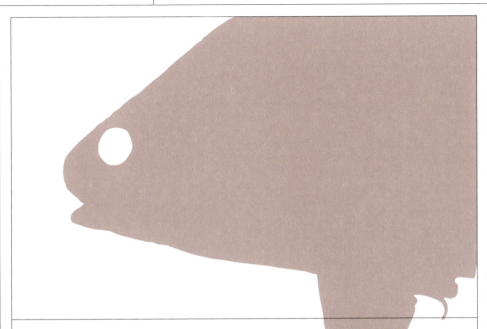

DRUMS, FAMILY SCIAENIDAE

FAMILY SCIAENIDAE

Drums are temperate to tropical, marine coastal fish, many of which enter estuaries to feed and some to spawn. The freshwater drum is the only strictly freshwater member of the family. All members of the family have a **well-developed lateral line that runs to the end of the tail**. There are **only two anal spines** and the **second anal spine is longer and thicker than the first**. The **second dorsal fin is longer than the head**. In addition, the **swim bladder**, which is used to produce sounds, has **two chambers and thick walls with body-wall muscles attached to it**. Most drums are bottom feeders, with the **mouth overhung by the snout**. The **jaws have pads of tiny, villiform teeth**, but the **pharyngeal bones, at the top and bottom of the throat, are massive and armed with a pavement of blunt, rounded teeth**, which are used to crush the shelled animals that are the food of many species of drums.

FRESHWATER DRUM; MALACHIGAN *Aplodinotus grunniens*

FRESH SPECIMEN
5 CM

IDENTIFICATION

The freshwater drum differs from all other perch-like fishes in our area by having an **inferior mouth overhung by a blunt, rounded snout**, the **lateral line extending to the rear margin of the tail**, and a **blue or purplish-silver colouration, lacking any darker or lighter markings**.

DISTRIBUTION IN MANITOBA

Freshwater drum are found in the Red River and Assiniboine River west to Brandon, the Manitoba Great Lakes, and the Nelson River downstream to about 50 km above its estuary (Remnant, pers. comm., 2004). There are unconfirmed angler reports of freshwater drum being caught in Lake Dauphin. With a north-south range from the mouth of the Nelson River in Manitoba to the Rio Usumacinta Basin in Guatemala (Burr and Mayden, 1992), the freshwater drum has the greatest latitudinal range of any North American freshwater fish.

DISTRIBUTION WITHIN MANITOBA
- Continuous range of native species
- Known occurrences

BIOLOGICAL NOTES

SPAWNING: Sexually mature freshwater drum are found in the Red River in mid- to late June, at water temperatures from 20°–23°C. At this time, the croaking sound the males make with their swim bladder (which may function as a mating call to attract females) can be heard with increasing intensity during the evening as the light level drops before and after sunset. At its greatest intensity, the calls merge into a continuous rumbling noise, which is often mistaken for the sound of distant traffic of heavy trucks on a highway. Even experienced anglers and guides are often surprised to learn that the noise they hear is coming from the water through the hulls of their boats, and is being made by fish. Although spawning has not been observed, it is likely that it occurs at this time. Spawning is done in midwater, and the eggs float to the surface (Becker 1983). In the Red River in Manitoba, croaking males can be heard and caught in current, in water from 3–4 m deep, over substrates ranging from silt and clay to rubble.

GROWTH AND ADULT SIZE: Female freshwater drum grow larger than males. Growth rates and age at maturity have not been studied in Manitoba. Becker (1983) reported that freshwater drum in the Mississippi River first mature at Age II or III. Both Becker, and Scott and Crossman (1979) note that growth rate decreases and longevity increases markedly with increasing latitude. The largest reported angler-caught freshwater drum in Manitoba was an 89 cm fish, caught from the Fairford River in 1998. This is considerably larger than the maximum sizes reported by either Becker or Scott and Crossman.

FEEDING: The adult freshwater drum we have examined (from the Red and Assiniboine rivers) feed mostly on benthic invertebrates, especially crayfish, snails, and mussels, which they crush with their massive, fused pharyngeal bones and molar-like pharyngeal teeth. They will also take fish. Becker (1983) and Scott and Crossman (1979) suggest that only river-dwelling drum feed extensively on mollusks, with lake-dwellers eating fish, leeches, and aquatic insects.

HABITAT: Freshwater drum live in the mainstems of large rivers and in the Manitoba Great Lakes.

ECOLOGICAL ROLE: Freshwater drum are broadly adapted, benthic invertebrate and fish predators. They are also important as hosts for the glochidia larvae of several species of freshwater mussels, on which they also feed. The abundance and size of freshwater drum, along with their benthic feeding specialization and role in the life history of some of our freshwater mussels, make them one of the most important benthic-feeding predators in the riverine and lacustrine communities in southern Manitoba.

IMPORTANCE TO PEOPLE

Freshwater drum are of minor and mainly local importance in the Lake Winnipeg commercial fishery, where they are marketed as "sunfish." They are commonly caught by anglers throughout their range in the province, but most of the angling activity for them is on the Red and Assiniboine rivers. Although many anglers do not eat drum, the flesh is firm and has good flavour if the red muscle along the midline of the fillet and the thin layer of subcutaneous fat on the skin side of the fillet are removed after the fillet is skinned. They are also delicious when smoked.

COSEWIC Status as of January 1, 2004: Not Listed
MBESA Status as of January 1, 2004: Not Listed
MBCDC Status as of January 1, 2004: G5, S5

APPENDIX

LIST OF ABBREVIATIONS AND EXPLANATION OF TERMS USED IN THE DISTRIBUTION TABLE

?	Indicated occurrence or status in that watershed is questionable (for example, N?, I?, I Failed?, Anadromous?).
Anadromous or Amphidromous	The term we have used in the table to designate the freshwater spawning fish species that are also found in salt water in Hudson Bay. Because so little is known of the life histories of these fish on the Hudson Bay coast, we have not used any more specific terms to describe their life histories.
E	East or eastern
I	Introduced. A species whose occurrence in that watershed is the result of introduction, or which has dispersed into the watershed from an introduction in an adjacent area. We have not made any distinction between species that do not reproduce successfully in the wild and those that do. Especially in the case of some of the introduced salmonid species and introductions of centrarchids into central Manitoba locations, this means they may not be present in a given water body at a particular time, although there are recurring introductions made.
I failed	A species that has been introduced into a watershed but failed to reproduce there and that has not been reintroduced (for example, lake whitefish into Lake Dauphin).
MN	Minnesota
N	Native. A species that occurs in that watershed in the absence of any evidence of introduction by humans, or has been known there since before any introductions were made. Most commonly, these species also have more extensive distributions contiguous with that watershed and with Manitoba, but Manitoba is often at the northwestern limit of those distributions. In the case of recently discovered species, the following additional criteria are assessed for evidence of native status: (1) Does the species occur in Hudson Bay Drainage areas adjacent to and upstream from Manitoba? (2) Does the species have a distribution in Manitoba that is too broad to be the result of dispersal from (a) recent point introduction(s)? (3) Is the species similar to other previously known species in that watershed with which it may have been confused in the past?
ND	North Dakota
O	Unknown from that watershed.
ON	Ontario
RECENT	First collection from that watershed was made within the last about 20 years.
RI	Reintroduced to former native habitat after having been extirpated there in the past.
SD	South Dakota
T	Transplanted. A species native to Manitoba that has been transplanted outside its native range in that watershed.
T failed	As for T, but the transplant failed.

APPENDIX

DISTRIBUTION OF MANITOBA FRESHWATER FISHES BY WATERSHED

SPECIES / WATERSHED	Red R.	Winnipeg R.	Assiniboine R.	Lk. Winnipeg	Lk. Manitoba	Lk. Dauphin
1. LAMPREYS, FAMILY PETROMYZONTIDAE						
chestnut lamprey *Ichthyomyzon castaneus*	N	N	N	N	0	0
northern brook lamprey *Ichthyomyzon fossor*	0	N Whitemouth & Winnipeg Rivers	0	0	0	0
silver lamprey *Ichthyomyzon unicuspis*	N	N	N Rare	N	0	0
2. STURGEON, FAMILY ACIPENSERIDAE						
lake sturgeon *Acipenser fulvescens*	N Rare	N	N Extirpated, RI Recent	N	0	0
3. MOONEYES, FAMILY HIODONTIDAE						
goldeye *Hiodon alosoides*	N	N to Pine Falls	N	N	N	N
mooneye *Hiodon tergisus*	N	N	N	N	N	0
4. MINNOWS, FAMILY CYPRINIDAE						
goldfish *Carassius auratus*	I	0	I Urban	0	0	0
lake chub *Couesius plumbeus*	0	N	0	N	0	0
spotfin shiner *Cyprinella spiloptera*	N	0	N Lower	0	0	0
carp *Cyprinus carpio*	I	I	I	I	I	I
brassy minnow *Hybognathus hankinsoni*	N Pembina River	0	N Duck Mtn. Prov. Park	0	0	N
common shiner *Luxilus cornutus*	N Tributaries	N	N Mostly Tributaries	N Tributaries	0	N
silver chub *Macrhybopsis storeriana*	N	0	N	N South Basin	0	0
pearl dace *Margariscus margarita*	N Pembina & Rat Rivers	N	N Tributaries	N Tributaries	N	N
hornyhead chub *Nocomis biguttatus*	N Erroneous Record?	N Whitemouth River	0	N Brokenhead River	0	0
golden shiner *Notemigonus crysoleucas*	N Rare	N	N Oxbow Lakes	N Tributaries	N	N
emerald shiner *Notropis atherinoides*	N	N	N	N	N	N
river shiner *Notropis blennius*	N	0	N Lower	N South Basin	0	0
bigmouth shiner *Notropis dorsalis*	N Roseau & Pembina Rivers	0	N Mostly Tributaries	0	0	0
blackchin shiner *Notropis heterodon*	0	N	N Oxbow Lakes	0	0	0
blacknose shiner *Notropis heterolepis*	0	N	N Oxbow Lakes	N Mostly Tributaries	N	N
spottail shiner *Notropis hudsonius*	N	N	N	N	N	N
carmine shiner *Notropis percobromus*	0	N	0	0	0	0
sand shiner *Notropis stramineus*	N Mostly Tributaries	0	N	0	0	0
weed shiner *Notropis texanus*	0	N	N Oxbow Lakes	N Tributaries	0	N
mimic shiner *Notropis volucellus*	0	N	0	N Tributaries	0	0
northern redbelly dace *Phoxinus eos*	N Rat River	N	N Tributaries	N Tributaries	N Rare, Tributaries	N Tributaries
finescale dace *Phoxinus neogaeus*	N Rat River	N	N Tributaries, Upper	N Tributaries	N Whitemud & Big Grassy Rivers	N Tributaries
bluntnose minnow *Pimephales notatus*	N 1 Record	N Above McArthur Falls	0	0	0	0
fathead minnow *Pimephales promelas*	N	N	N Mostly Tributaries	N Mostly Tributaries	N	N
flathead chub *Platygobio gracilis*	N Lower	0	N	N	0	0

Lk. Winnipegosis	Saskatchewan R.	Nelson R.	Hayes R.	Churchill R.	Seal R.	Thlewiaza R.	Coastal
0	0	0	0	0	0	0	0
0	0	0	0	0	0	0	0
0	0	N	N	N	0	0	0
0	N	N	N	N	0	0	0
N	N	0	0	0	0	0	0
N	N	N	0	0	0	0	0
0	I	0	0	0	0	0	0
0	N	N	N	N	N?	N	N
0	0	0	0	0	0	0	0
I	I	I	0	0	0	0	0
0	0	0	0	0	0	0	0
N	0	0	0	0	0	0	0
0	0	0	0	0	0	0	0
N	N Erroneous Record?	N	N	0	0	0	0
0	0	0	0	0	0	0	0
N	0	0	0	0	0	0	0
N	N	N	N	N	0	0	0
0	N	0	0	0	0	0	0
N Tributaries	0	0	0	0	0	0	0
N Mossy River	0	0	0	0	0	0	0
N	0	N	N	0	0	0	0
N	N	N	N	N	0	0	0
0	0	0	0	0	0	0	0
0	0	0	0	0	0	0	0
0	0	0	0	0	0	0	0
0	0	0	0	0	0	0	0
0	0	0	0	0	0	0	0
N	0	0	0	0	0	0	0
0	0	0	0	0	0	0	0
N	N	N	N	0	0	0	0
N Tributaries	N	0	0	0	0	0	0

APPENDIX

SPECIES / WATERSHED	Red R.	Winnipeg R.	Assiniboine R.	Lk. Winnipeg	Lk. Manitoba	Lk. Dauphin
4. MINNOWS, FAMILY CYPRINIDAE (CONT'D)						
longnose dace *Rhinichthys cataractae*	N	N	N	N	O	N
western blacknose dace *Rhinichthys obtusus*	N	O	N	N	O	N
creek chub *Semotilus atromaculatus*	N	N 1 Record	N Mostly Tributaries	N Tributaries	O	N
5. SUCKERS, FAMILY CATOSTOMIDAE						
quillback *Carpiodes cyprinus*	N	N Lower	N	N	N	N
longnose sucker *Catostomus catostomus*	O	N	O	N	O	O
white sucker *Catostomus commersoni*	N	N	N	N	N	N
bigmouth buffalo *Ictiobus cyprinellus*	N	O	N Rare, Mostly Lower	N South Basin	N Rare, Delta Marsh	O
silver redhorse *Moxostoma anisurum*	N	N	N	N	O	N
golden redhorse *Moxostoma erythrurum*	N	N Lower	N Lower	N South Basin Tributaries	O	O
shorthead redhorse *Moxostoma macrolepidotum*	N	N	N	N	N	N
6. CATFISHES, FAMILY ICTALURIDAE						
black bullhead *Ameiurus melas*	N	N	N	N	N Recent	O
brown bullhead *Ameiurus nebulosus*	N	N	N	N	N Recent	O
channel catfish *Ictalurus punctatus*	N	N to Pine Falls; T in Lac du Bonnet	N	N	N Recent	O
stonecat *Noturus flavus*	N	O	N	N Brokenhead River	O	O
tadpole madtom *Noturus gyrinus*	N	N	N Tributaries & Oxbow Lakes	N Tributaries	N Recent	O
7. PIKES, FAMILY ESOCIDAE						
northern pike *Esox lucius*	N	N	N	N	N	N
muskellunge *Esox masquinongy*	O	N Rare	T Duck Mtn. Prov. Park	O	T	O
8. MUDMINNOWS, FAMILY UMBRIDAE						
central mudminnow *Umbra limi*	N	N	N Tributaries & Oxbow Lakes	N Tributaries	N Recent	O
9. SMELTS, FAMILY OSMERIDAE						
capelin *Mallotus villosus*	O	O	O	O	O	O
rainbow smelt *Osmerus mordax*	I Lower, 1 Record	I Recent	O	I Recent	O	O
10. TROUT AND WHITEFISH, FAMILY SALMONIDAE						
cisco *Coregonus artedi*	N Lower	N	N Riding Mtn. Nat. Park	N	N	N
lake whitefish *Coregonus clupeaformis*	N Recent	N	N	N	N	T Failed
shortjaw cisco *Coregonus zenithicus*	O	N George Lake	O	N	O	O
round whitefish *Prosopium cylindraceum*	O	O	O	O	O	O
arctic grayling *Thymallus arcticus*	T Fort Whyte Nature Centre	O	O	O	O	O
westslope cutthroat trout *Oncorhynchus clarki lewisi*	I Clandeboye Ponds	I Whiteshell Prov. Park	O	O	O	O
rainbow trout *Oncorhynchus mykiss*	I	I	I	I	I	I
kokanee salmon *Oncorhynchus nerka*	O	I	O	I Failed	O	I Duck Mtn. Prov. Park
brown trout *Salmo trutta*	I	I	I	I	I	I

THE FRESHWATER FISHES OF MANITOBA

APPENDIX

Lk. Winnipegosis	Saskatchewan R.	Nelson R.	Hayes R.	Churchill R.	Seal R.	Thlewiaza R.	Coastal
N	N	N	N	N	0	0	0
N	0	0	0	0	0	0	0
N	0	0	0	0	0	0	0
N	N	0	0	0	0	0	0
0	N	N	N	N	N	0	N
N	N	N	N	N	0	0	N
0	0	0	0	0	0	0	0
N	N	0	0	0	0	0	0
0	0	0	0	0	0	0	0
N	N	N	N	0	0	0	0
0	0	0	0	0	0	0	0
0	0	0	0	0	0	0	0
0	N Grand Rapids Historical, Cumberland House	N Rare	0	0	0	0	0
0	0	0	0	0	0	0	0
0	0	0	0	0	0	0	0
N	N	N	N	N	N	N	N?
0	0	0	0	0	0	0	0
N	N	0	0	0	0	0	0
0	0	N Estuarine	0	N Estuarine	N Estuarine	0	N Estuarine
0	0	I Recent Anadromous?	0	I Anadromous? Lower Only, Recent	0	0	0
N	N	N Resident & Anadromous	N Resident & Anadromous	N Resident & Anadromous	N?	N	N
N	N	N	N	N Resident & Anadromous	N?	N?	N?
0	N	0	0	N	0	0	0
0	0	0	0	N Rare	0	N 1 Record	N Knife River
0	0	0	0	N Lower	N	N	N Nelson River Northward
I Duck Mtn. Prov. Park	0	0	0	0	0	0	0
I	I	I	0	I	0	0	0
I Duck Mtn. Prov. Park	0	0	0	0	0	0	0
I	I	0	0	0	0	0	0

THE FRESHWATER FISHES OF MANITOBA

APPENDIX

SPECIES / WATERSHED	Red R.	Winnipeg R.	Assiniboine R.	Lk. Winnipeg	Lk. Manitoba	Lk. Dauphin
10. TROUT AND WHITEFISH, FAMILY SALMONIDAE (CONT'D)						
"tiger trout" brown X brook trout hybrid	0	I One Lake	0	0	0	0
arctic char *Salvelinus alpinus*	T Ft. Whyte & Hatchery Escapees	0	0	0	0	T Failed Duck Mtn. Prov. Park
brook trout *Salvelinus fontinalis*	T	T	T Riding Mtn. Nat. Park & Duck Mtn. Prov. Park	T	T	T Duck Mtn. Prov. Park
"splake" brook X lake trout hybrid	0	I	I Riding Mtn. Nat. Park	I	0	I Duck Mtn. Prov. Park
lake trout *Salvelinus namaycush*	0	N	T Riding Mtn. Nat. Park & Duck Mtn. Prov. Park	N Historically in Lake, Still in Eastern Tributaries	0	I Duck Mtn. Prov. Park
11. TROUTPERCH, FAMILY PERCOPSIDAE						
troutperch *Percopsis omiscomaycus*	N	N	N	N	N	N
12. CODFISHES, FAMILY GADIDAE						
burbot *Lota lota*	N	N	N	N	N	N
13. KILLIFISHES, FAMILY FUNDULIDAE						
banded killifish *Fundulus diaphanus*	N 1 Record	N 1 Record, Crowduck Lake	0	0	0	0
14. STICKLEBACKS, FAMILY GASTEROSTEIDAE						
brook stickleback *Culaea inconstans*	N	N	N	N Mostly Tributaries	N	N
threespine stickleback *Gasterosteus aculeatus*	0	0	0	0	0	0
ninespine stickleback *Pungitius pungitius*	0	N	N	N	N	0
15. SCULPINS, FAMILY COTTIDAE						
mottled sculpin *Cottus bairdi*	0	N	0	N	N	0
slimy sculpin *Cottus cognatus*	0	N	N	N	0	0
spoonhead sculpin *Cottus ricei*	0	0	0	N	0	0
fourhorn sculpin *Myoxocephalus quadricornis*	0	0	0	0	0	0
arctic sculpin *Myoxocephalus scorpioides*	0	0	0	0	0	0
shorthorn sculpin *Myoxocephalus scorpius*	0	0	0	0	0	0
deepwater sculpin *Myoxocephalus thompsoni*	0	N West Hawk Lake & George Lake	0	0	0	0
16. TEMPERATE BASSES, FAMILY MORONIDAE						
white bass *Morone chrysops*	I	I	0	I	0	0
17. SUNFISHES, FAMILY CENTRARCHIDAE						
rock bass *Ambloplites rupestris*	N	N	N	N Mostly Tributaries	0	0
pumpkinseed *Lepomis gibbosus*	T Lake Minnewasta	N Whiteshell Prov. Park	0	0	0	0
bluegill *Lepomis macrochirus*	N Tributaries	T Rare, Whiteshell Prov. Park	0	0	0	0
smallmouth bass *Micropterus dolomieu*	I Recent	I	0	I South Basin	0	I
largemouth bass *Micropterus salmoides*	I	I Lake of the Woods	I Failed?	I Failed?	0	I Failed?
white crappie *Pomoxis annularis*	N Rare	0	0	0	0	0
black crappie *Pomoxis nigromaculatus*	N	N	0	N Mostly Tributaries	0	T Failed

APPENDIX

Lk. Winnipegosis	Saskatchewan R.	Nelson R.	Hayes R.	Churchill R.	Seal R.	Thlewiaza R.	Coastal
0	0	0	0	0	0	0	0
0	0	0	0	N Amphidromous Rare	N Amphidromous	0	N Resident?, Amphidromous Churchill R. Northward
T	T	N Resident & Amphidromous	N Resident & Amphidromous	N Resident & Amphidromous?	N Amphidromous	0	N Resident & Amphidromous Nelson R. Southward
0	I	0	0	0	0	0	0
I Duck Mtn. Prov. Park	N	N	N	N	N	N	N?
N	N	N	N	N	N	0	0
N	N	N	N	N	N	N	N
0	0	0	0	0	0	0	0
N	N	N	N	N	0	0	0
0	0	0	0	0	0	N	N Estuarine, Anadromous
N	N	N	N	N Resident & Anadromous	N	0	N
N	0	0	0	0	0	0	0
N	N	N	N	N	0	0	0
0	N	0	N	N	0	0	0
0	0	N Estuarine	0	N Estuarine	N Estuarine	0	N Estuarine
0	0	N Estuarine	0	N Estuarine	N Estuarine	0	N Estuarine
0	0	N Estuarine	0	N Estuarine	N Estuarine	0	N Estuarine
0	N Lake Athapapuskow	0	0	N Reindeer Lake	0	0	0
0	0	0	0	0	0	0	0
0	0	0	0	0	0	0	0
0	0	0	0	0	0	0	0
0	0	0	0	0	0	0	0
0	I Lake Athapapuskow	0	0	0	0	0	0
I Failed?	I Failed?	0	0	0	0	0	0
0	0	0	0	0	0	0	0
0	0	0	0	0	0	0	0

THE FRESHWATER FISHES OF MANITOBA

APPENDIX

SPECIES / WATERSHED	Red R.	Winnipeg R.	Assiniboine R.	Lk. Winnipeg	Lk. Manitoba	Lk. Dauphin
18. PERCH, FAMILY PERCIDAE						
Iowa darter *Etheostoma exile*	N Mostly Tributaries	N	N Tributaries & Oxbow Lakes	N Tributaries	N	N
johnny darter *Etheostoma nigrum*	N	N	N	N	N	N
yellow perch *Perca flavescens*	N	N	N	N	N	N
logperch *Percina caprodes*	N	N	0	N Mostly Tributaries	N	N
blackside darter *Percina maculata*	N	N	N	N Tributaries	0	0
river darter *Percina shumardi*	N	N	N	N	N	N
sauger *Sander canadensis*	N	N	N	N	N	N
walleye *Sander vitreus*	N	N	N	N	N	N
19. DRUMS, FAMILY SCIAENIDAE						
freshwater drum *Aplodinotus grunniens*	N	N to Pine Falls	N	N	N	N

PROVINCE-WIDE TOTALS / TOTALS BY WATERSHED	Red R.	Winnipeg R.	Assiniboine R.	Lk. Winnipeg	Lk. Manitoba	Lk. Dauphin
NATIVE FRESHWATER SPECIES **MANITOBA TOTAL: 79**	57	61	55	60	35	33
NATIVE FRESHWATER SPECIES RE-INTRODUCED AFTER EXTIRPATION IN THAT WATERSHED *****MANITOBA TOTAL: 1**	0	0	1	0	0	0
NATIVE FRESHWATER SPECIES TRANSPLANTED OUTSIDE NATIVE RANGE IN MANITOBA ****** MANITOBA TOTAL: 8**	4	2	3	1	2	4
INTRODUCED FRESHWATER SPECIES **MANITOBA TOTAL: 10**	9	9	5	8	3	7
HUMAN-MADE FRESHWATER HYBRIDS **MANITOBA TOTAL: 2**	0	2	1	1	0	1
ESTUARINE SPECIES IN DATABASE **MANITOBA TOTAL: 4**	0	0	0	0	0	0
COMBINED NATIVE, TRANSPLANTED NATIVE, INTRODUCED AND ESTUARINE SPECIES, AND HUMAN-MADE HYBRIDS: *****, ****** MANITOBA TOTAL: 95**	70	74	65	70	40	45

* Reintroduced native species have already been counted as native species for Manitoba, so they are not added into the total for Manitoba. They are, however, added into the totals for the watersheds into which they were reintroduced.

** Transplanted native species have already been counted as native species for Manitoba, so they are not added into the total for Manitoba. They are, however, added into the totals for the watersheds into which they were transplanted.

SPECIES IN HUDSON BAY DRAINAGE AREAS UPSTREAM FROM MANITOBA

SPECIES / WATERSHED	Red R.	Winnipeg R.
GARS, FAMILY LEPISOSTEIDAE		
longnose gar *Lepisosteus osseus*	N 1 Record Lake Traverse, MN&SD	0
BOWFIN, FAMILY AMIIDAE		
bowfin *Amia calva*	N MN Tributaries	I Lake of the Woods
MINNOWS, FAMILY CYPRINIDAE		
central stoneroller *Campostoma anomalum*	N MN&ND	0
largecale stoneroller *Campostoma oligolepis*	N (?) Forest River, ND	0
pugnose shiner *Notropis anogenus*	N MN Tributaries	0
bullhead minnow *Pimephales vigilax*	N MN Tributaries	0

SPECIES / WATERSHED	Red R.	Winnipeg R.
SUCKERS, FAMILY CATOSTOMIDAE		
northern hog sucker *Hypentelium nigricans*	N Ottertail River, MN	0
smallmouth buffalo *Ictiobus bubalus*	N (?) ND	0
greater redhorse *Moxostoma valenciennesi*	N Sheyenne River, ND	0
CATFISHES, FAMILY ICTALURIDAE		
yellow bullhead *Ameiurus natalis*	N	0

Lk. Winnipegosis	Saskatchewan R.	Nelson R.	Hayes R.	Churchill R.	Seal R.	Thlewiaza R.	Coastal
N	0	0	0	N	0	0	0
N	N	N	N	N	0	0	0
N	N	N	N	N	0	0	0
N	N	0	0	0	0	0	0
N	N	0	0	0	0	0	0
N	0	N	0	0	0	0	0
N	N	N	N	N	0	0	0
N	N	N	N	N	0	0	0
0	0	N	0	0	0	0	0

Lk. Winnipegosis	Saskatchewan R.	Nelson R.	Hayes R.	Churchill R.	Seal R.	Thlewiaza R.	Coastal
39	34	31	27	29	12	9	14
0	0	0	0	0	0	0	0
1	1	0	0	0	0	0	0
7	6	3	0	1	0	0	0
0	1	0	0	0	0	0	0
0	0	4	0	4	4	0	4
47	42	38	27	34	16	9	18

SPECIES IN HUDSON BAY DRAINAGE AREAS UPSTREAM FROM MANITOBA (CONT'D)

SPECIES	WATERSHED	Red R.	Winnipeg R.
SUNFISHES, FAMILY CENTRARCHIDAE			
green sunfish *Lepomis cyanellus*		N MN & ND	N Rainy River, ON
orangespotted sunfish *Lepomis humilis*		N MN Tributaries	0
longear sunfish *Lepomis megalotis*		N MN Tributaries	N Rainy River, ON
PERCH, FAMILY PERCIDAE			
rainbow darter *Etheostoma caeruleum*		N Ottertail River, MN	0
least darter *Etheostoma microperca*		N MN Tributaries	0

GLOSSARY

abdomen - The portion of the lower body bounded above by the **lateral** midline running down the side, **anteriorly** by the back of the gill cavity, and **posteriorly** by the **origin** of the **anal fin**. The internal organs or viscera are contained in the abdomen.

abdominal - Pertaining to the **abdomen**, or located in or on the surface of the abdomen, such as abdominal **pelvic fins**.

adipose fin - A fleshy tab or ridge-like **median** fin on the back, between the back of the **dorsal fin** and the base of the tail.

algivorous - Feeding on algae.

ammocoetes larva - The larval stage of lampreys (Family Petromyzontidae). Ammocoetes larvae burrow in sand or silt in the bottom of streams, and feed by pumping a current of water through their gill chambers and filtering organic **detritus** and minute plants and animals from the water. They have a hood-like covering over the mouth opening (the **oral hood**), and the eyes are undeveloped.

amphidromous - Fish that move between the sea and fresh water for reasons other than, or in addition to, spawning. Also see **anadromous** and **diadromous**. *Note:* The salmonid species on our Hudson Bay coast that are listed as anadromous in the Appendix are probably actually amphidromous, and return to fresh water to overwinter, whether they are going to **spawn** or not.

anadromous - Fish that live in the sea and migrate into fresh water to **spawn**. Also see **amphidromous** and **diadromous**.

anal fin - The **median** fin on the underside of the fish between the base of the tail and the **vent**.

annulus - A growth ring or marking on a **scale** or other bony structure, or an **otolith** of a fish, that is made once each year.

anoxic - Absence of oxygen.

anterior(ly) - Toward the front or head of the fish.

anus - The posterior opening of the digestive system. Often used as a synonym for **vent**.

apex - The highest point, such as the **distal** corner of a **fin**.

aquatic - Found in or living in water.

arthropod(a) - A **phylum** of animals characterized by having an external skeleton and jointed legs. It includes the insects and **crustaceans**.

axil(lary) - The area in the angle between the base of a **paired fin** and the side of the body (pertaining to or located in the axil).

back-cross - As used in this book, the offspring of an **interspecific hybrid** mating with one of its parent **species**. As a verb, the process of mating by an **interspecific hybrid** with one of its parent **species**.

band - A relatively broad, sometimes indistinct, **longitudinal** marking. (Compare with **stripe**.)

bar - A vertical marking.

barbel(s) - "Whisker"-like structures on the head of a fish, located in the area of the mouth or nostrils, which usually serve a touch, taste, or smell function.

basicaudal (spot) - A black spot at the base of the **caudal fin**. The spot is often at the posterior end of a **lateral stripe**, but may not be associated with a lateral stripe.

basin - The **watershed** of a major river system that may, but does not necessarily, end at the sea. Also see **drainage** and **watershed**.

benthic - Living on the bottom.

GLOSSARY

benthivor(e) (ous) - An animal that feeds on **benthos** (feeding on **benthos**).

benthopelagic - A fish that lives just above the bottom.

benthos - The **community** of organisms living on and in the bottom.

bog - A wetland underlain by peat. Bogs may be forested, typically with black spruce, *Picea mariana*, or more open, with a mix of sedges, *Carex*, Labrador tea, *Ledum*, willow, *Salix*, and alder, *Alnus*, as plant cover. Open water in bogs may be small lakes, ponds, or streams, typically with beds of aquatic plants.

branchiostegals – Thin, bony supports in the lower part of the **gill membrane**, below the bony part of the **operculum**.

breeding (or nuptial) tubercles - Horny structures developing on the skin of the head, and sometimes the **fins**, and body surface, at breeding time, in male fish, especially minnows, suckers, and whitefish. Also called pearl organs.

buccal funnel - In adult lampreys, the round, funnel-like mouth cavity.

cannibalism - Feeding on other individuals of the same species.

carnivor(e) (ous) - An animal that eats other animals; the same as **predator** (flesh eating).

carrion - Animals used as food (by fish, in this case) that are already dead and possibly also partly decomposed.

caudal fin - The tail fin.

caudal peduncle - The part of the body between the **posterior** end (**insertion**) of the **anal fin** and the base of the **caudal fin**.

cheek - A region of the side of the head of a fish, located behind the eye, above the upper jaw and in front of the **preopercular bone**.

chemoreceptor(s) - Sensory nerve(s) that detect chemical stimuli (smell and taste).

cirri - Fleshy tabs or projections of skin, often found on the heads of marine sculpins.

commensial - A **symbiotic** association in which one organism benefits and the other is not affected.

community - The association of all organisms in a specific area (for example, the community of a particular body of water). This may be further subdivided into **benthic**, **pelagic**, and **littoral** communities.

copepod - Small, **planktonic crustacean**.

crepuscular - Active during dawn and dusk. Also see **diel**, **diurnal**, and **nocturnal**.

crustacea(n) - A group of **arthropods** that contains many important species of **plankton**, as well as larger aquatic animals such as crayfish and (in sea water) lobsters. The group also contains some terrestrial animals, such as wood lice.

cryptophylic - Loving concealment. A fish that seeks cover or concealment.

cteni (pronounced "teen eye") - Small, bristle-like projections on the exposed **posterior field** of a **ctenoid scale**.

ctenoid scales (pronounced "teen oid") - Thin, flexible, overlapping **scales** with small teeth (or **cteni**) on the exposed **posterior fields** of the **scales**.

cusp - The projecting, often pointed, part of a tooth.

cycloid scales - Thin, flexible, overlapping **scales** that lack **cteni** on the exposed **posterior fields**.

decurved - Curved downward, as in a decurved **maxilla** or **lateral line**.

demersal - Living on or near the bottom. Also see **benthic**.

depensation - A reduction in size at first sexual maturity that may occur in fish populations exposed to harvest at a size smaller than their normal size at first maturation.

depressed - Flattened from top to bottom, rather than side to side.

detritivor(e) (ous) - An animal that eats **detritus** (feeding on **detritus**).

GLOSSARY

detritus - Decomposed organic matter.

diadromous - A fish that migrates between fresh water and salt water. Also see **amphidromous** and **anadromous**.

diel - Pertaining to the daily pattern of activity. Also see **crepuscular**, **diurnal**, and **nocturnal**.

distal - The point on a **fin** or other structure that is farthest away from the axis of the body.

diurnal - Active during daylight hours. Also see **crepuscular**, **diel**, and **nocturnal**.

dorsal - Pertaining to the upper surface or back.

dorsal fin - Any of the one to three **ray**- and/or **spine**-supported **median fins** on the back. (The **adipose fin** does not have supporting rays or spines.)

dorsoventral - The body axis or direction from the back to the belly.

drainage - A major system named for its main river or receiving area of the sea, from the uppermost headwaters to the sea (for example, the Mississippi River Drainage or the Hudson Bay Drainage). Also see **basin** or **watershed**.

eddy - In a stream, a circular flow, often where water flows past a projecting point or into a wider area, such as a **pool**.

elongate - A fish or structure that is longer, and usually more slender, than normal. Pike or burbot, for example, are elongate.

endemic - A species or higher group that evolved in, and whose natural distribution is limited to, a specific area. For example, the brook trout is endemic to northeastern North America.

entomostraca(n) - A group (or member of that group) of **planktonic crustaceans** commonly called water fleas.

established - An introduced stock or population of a species that maintains itself by reproducing in the wild. Also see **naturalized**.

eutrophic (lake) - A body of water with a high level of nutrients (mainly nitrates and phosphates) in the water, that usually also has a heavy growth of algae and higher plants, and may be subject to winter- or summer-kills due to oxygen depletion.

exotic - An organism that is not **native** to the area.

extinct - A distinct group of organisms that no longer exists.

extirpated - Eliminated from a specific part of the range of a group of organisms.

falcate fin - A fin with a concave, sickle-shaped, margin.

family - In classification, a group of related organisms between an **order** and a **genus**, which share all the characters of their **order** and also have a distinctive set of adaptations of the family; for example, lack of **scales**, presence of **barbels**, and **spines** in the **dorsal** and **pectoral fins** in the Family Ictaluridae, the North American freshwater catfishes. Three of the families in this book are subdivided into subfamilies and two of the subfamilies are subdivided into tribes.

fauna - All the kinds of animals living in an area or **community**.

feral - A domestic animal that lives in the wild.

fin - An appendage of a fish that helps it to swim or control its swimming.

first-level consumers - Animals that feed on plants (the first or lowest level of the **food web** of a **community**). The same as a **primary consumer**.

food web - The feeding relationships among the organisms of a **community**.

fork length - The length of a fish from the tip of the **snout** to the tip of the shortest **ray** in the centre of the **caudal fin**.

frenum - A fleshy bridge on the **dorsal** midline, joining the upper lip and the **snout**.

ganoid scales - Thick, **rhombic**, very hard scales, which appear to join edge-to-edge, rather than overlapping. They have a shiny outer covering of enamel-like material (ganoine).

GLOSSARY

genus - In classification, a group of related organisms ranked between a **family** and a **species**. Members of a genus share all the characters of their family and also share a set of characters unique to that genus.

gill arch - The bony arch supporting a gill, together with the soft gill filaments, on its **posterior** side, and the bony, tooth-like **gill rakers** on its **anterior** side.

gill membrane - The membrane on the rear edge of the **operculum** that helps seal the gill opening when the fish is taking water or food into its mouth. It often continues across the throat and joins the gill membrane on the opposite side. The thin, rod-like, bony **branchiostegals** support the gill membrane below the **operculum**.

gillnet - A fishing net that hangs vertically and catches fish by entangling them in the meshes, which are made of fine thread.

gill rakers - The tooth-, bristle-, or comb-like structures on the **anterior** surface of a **gill arch**. They help the fish in feeding and also protect the gill filaments from large or hard objects that might injure them.

glochidi(um) (a) - The **larval** stage of freshwater mussels of the Family Unionidae. Glochidia are parasitic on fish. After they are shed by the parent mussel, they enter the gill chamber of a fish and attach to the gill filaments. When ready to transform, they drop off and are expelled by the water current caused by the breathing of the host fish and settle to the bottom.

gonad - An **ovary** or a **testis**. A general term for the sex organs of an organism.

gonadosomatic index - The ratio of **gonad** weight to body weight. A measure of the degree of sexual maturity of a fish.

gradient - A continuous change. For example, the gradient of a stream is its change in elevation with distance. A temperature gradient would be a change in temperature with depth or distance.

headwater(s) - The uppermost **tributaries** of a **watershed**.

hermaphrodit(e) (ism) - An individual that functions as both male and female, either at the same time or at different times during its life history.

heterocercal tail (also may be called an **epicercal** tail) - A **caudal fin** in which the body extends into at least the base of the upper lobe. Usually, the tail is externally asymmetrical, with the upper lobe longer than the lower lobe, like a sturgeon or shark tail.

homocercal tail - A **caudal fin** in which the body does not extend into the upper lobe. A homocercal tail is almost always externally symmetrical, with the upper and lower lobes being equal in size.

hybrid - An organism that is the result of interbreeding between members of different genetic stocks (usually **species**, in the sense used in this book) or between hybrids.

hypoxi(a)(c) - A lower than normal level of oxygen in the body of an organism.

impassable - In the sense used in this book, a barrier that fish cannot pass.

included lower jaw - The margin of the lower jaw is inside the margin of the upper jaw. In this case, the mouth is also **subterminal**, and may be **inferior**, at least to a small degree.

inferior mouth - A mouth in which the upper jaw and/or **snout** overhang the lower jaw. In this case, the lower jaw is also **included**.

infraoral lamina - In lampreys, the horny tooth plate just **posterior** to the mouth opening in the centre of the **buccal funnel**.

insertion - The point where the **posterior** end of a **fin** joins the body.

interopercular - The lowermost and smallest of the enlarged, plate-like bones forming the **operculum**.

interspecific hybrid - A hybrid individual, either natural or human-made, produced by the mating of parents that are different **species**.

interstitial - The (water-filled) spaces in the **substrate** of a water body. These spaces may be used as habitat by organisms.

GLOSSARY

introduced - An organism that has been released into an area in which it is not **native**. (Also see **exotic**.)

invasive - Used in reference to an **introduced** species that is able to establish and spread quickly in new areas. It may also displace or cause **extirpation** of **native** species.

isthmus - The narrow bridge of tissue connecting the **ventral** surface of the **abdomen** with the underside of the head.

jugular (**pelvic fins**) - Pelvic fins with bases located **anterior** to the bases of the **pectoral fins**.

lacustrine - Living in lakes.

larva(e) - The early developmental stage(s) of an organism. Larvae are different in form, habitat, and ecology from adults of their species.

lateral - Toward either side of the body.

lateral line - A system of canals running through superficial bones on the head and under the skin, through the **scales** (if present) on the sides of the body of a fish. It opens to the surface through a series of pores, typically one pore in each lateral line scale along the sides of the body. On the head, pores can be seen around the eye socket (**supraorbital and suborbital** pores), along the lower surface of the lower jaw (**mandibular** pores), and down the side of the head, behind the cheek (**preopercular** pores).

littoral - The habitat along the shore of a body of water.

livebear(er) (ing) - An organism that gives birth to living young rather than depositing eggs in which embryos complete development and hatch after the eggs have been deposited.

low-level consumer - An animal that feeds near the bottom of the **food web** of a **community**, although its diet may not be restricted entirely to plants. Also see **first-level consumer**.

mandibular pores - (Of the **lateral line**) are on the underside of the lower jaw. The location and number of these pores are useful in identifying some species of fish.

maxilla(e) = maxillar(y) (ies) - The bones forming the **lateral** margins of the upper jaw in primitive fish such as mooneye and goldeye, trout, smelt, mudminnows, and pike. In more advanced fish, they are usually located just above the margin of the upper jaw, although in catfish they are hidden within the base of the **maxillary barbel**.

maxillary barbel(s) – In catfishes, a barbel at the rear corner of the mouth on each side, supported by the **maxillae**.

median fins - Located on the midline of the body (such as **dorsal, adipose, caudal,** and **anal fins**).

melanin - Black or brown pigment in the skin or **peritoneum**.

melanophore(s) - Cells in the skin that contain the black or brown pigment **melanin**.

mental barbel(s) - Any **barbel** located on the chin. In catfishes, there are four barbels arranged in a **transverse** row across the chin. In the burbot, there is a single, **median** barbel on the chin.

middle-level consumer - An animal that feeds on **first-** or **low-level consumers**. Essentially the same as **second-level consumer**.

midwater - A depth range below the surface but above the bottom of a water body.

migrat(e) (ion) - Movement of a group of organisms during a particular span of time, which starts in a particular area and ends in another area.

milt - The seminal fluid produced by the **testes** of a fish.

moribund - About to die.

nape - The area of the back of a fish between the back of the head and the **origin** of the **dorsal fin**. Also see **predorsal**.

nasal barbel(s) - In catfishes, a barbel located just **anterior** to the **posterior nostril** on each side of the **snout**.

natal - Pertaining to birth or hatching, as in natal stream.

native - An organism that occurs naturally in an area. Not **introduced** by humans.

GLOSSARY

naturalized - A self-maintaining introduced stock or species that reproduces in the wild. Equivalent to **established**.

nocturnal - Active mainly at night. Also see **diurnal** and **crepuscular**.

oblique mouth - An upwardly angled mouth.

omnivor(e) (ous) - An animal that eats plants and animals as well as **detritus**. Also see **carnivore**, **detritivore**, and **predator**.

opercular bone - The uppermost and largest of the broad, plate-like bones in the **operculum**.

opercular flap - A fleshy flap or tab at the upper, **posterior** corner of the **operculum**. It is part of the **gill membrane**.

operculum - The gill cover, consisting of four bones: the **preopercular**, **anteriorly**, just behind the **cheek**; and behind it, from top to bottom, the **opercular**, **subopercular**, **interopercular**; and **branchiostegals**, together with the **gill membrane**.

oral disc - In lampreys, another term for the **buccal funnel**.

oral hood - In the **ammocoetes larvae** of lampreys, the hood-like structure forming most of the front of the head, which surrounds the mouth cavity.

order - In classification, a group of related organisms that share a set of general adaptations; for example the presence of a bony strut across the cheek, a reduced or closed slit behind the fourth **gill arch**, and thickened, unbranched **rays** on the lower part of the **pectoral fins**, which define the Order Scorpaeniformes, which contains the sculpins, Family Cottidae. The order is the highest level of classification used in this book.

origin - The point where the **anterior** end of a **fin** joins the body.

otolith - "Ear stone." A dense, mineralized body in the inner ear of a fish that grows with the fish and has growth rings. Otoliths are often used for age determination.

ovar(y) (ies) - Female sex organ(s).

paired fins - Fins that are in pairs, with one member of the pair on each side of the body. The **pectoral** and **pelvic fins** of fish.

palatine(s) - The paired bones that, together with the **vomer**, a **median** bone, form the **anterior** part of the roof of the mouth in fish. The palatine bones often have rows or pads of **palatine teeth**.

palatine teeth – Pads or rows of teeth borne on the **palatine bones**, on either side of the front of the roof of the mouth.

papilla(e) - Small, fleshy bumps, as on the lips of some suckers.

papillose lips - Lips with with small bumps or **papillae** on their surface.

parr - The juvenile stage of a salmonid, after the yolk sac is absorbed. Parr are often marked with a series of dark **bars** or blotches on the sides and, usually, the back (**parr marks**). Similar blotches on the sides of juveniles of other groups of fishes, notably the white sucker, may also be referred to as **parr marks**.

parr marks - Dark **bars** or blotches on the sides, and usually, the back of juvenile salmonids (**parr**), and juvenile white suckers.

pectoral fin(s) - **Paired fins** located just behind the head.

pelagic - Living in open water.

pelvic axillary process - A slender, fleshy tab in the **axil** of the **pelvic fin**, lying between the upper side of the base of the pelvic fin and the surface of the body.

pelvic fin(s) - **Paired fins** located on either side of the **abdomen** of a fish. They may be located about halfway between the head and the **vent** (**abdominal**), beneath or slightly behind the bases of the **pectoral fins** (**thoracic**), or in advance of the bases of the **pectoral fins** (jugular).

peritoneum - The membrane lining the inside of the body cavity.

GLOSSARY

pharyngeal teeth - Teeth located on the bony arch imbedded in the rear wall of the gill chamber, which project into the esophagus, and help fish break up and/or manipulate food when swallowed. They may be in pads or in one to three rows, and may be pointed, hooked, blunt, or even molar-like. In most cyprinids, they are in one or two rows: an outer (main) row and an inner (lesser) row. In identifying some cyprinid species, the counts are given in the order of left arch inner row, outer row-right arch outer row, inner row; for example, 2,4-4,2.

phylu(m) (a) - A large group of organisms that share a body plan that differs fundamentally from that of all other phyla.

phytoplankton - **Planktonic** plants.

piscivor(e) (ous) - An animal that feeds on fish (feeding on fish).

planktivor(e) (ous) - An animal that eats **plankton**. Such animals are **low-** or **middle-level consumers** (feeding on **plankton**).

plankton(ic) - The small, often microscopic, plants (**phytoplankton**), animals, and protozoans (**zooplankton**) that live in open water, usually in lakes or the sea, but plankton is also found in large, slow-moving streams.

plicate lips - Lips with longitudinal and/or **transverse** folds on their surface.

pool - In a stream, a wide, deep area with reduced current, and often with a circular flow (**eddy**).

posterior(ly) - The rear end, or toward the rear, of the fish.

posterior field of a scale - The rear portion of a **cycloid** or **ctenoid scale**, which is not overlapped by adjacent scales.

precocial - An animal (usually a male, in fish) that becomes sexually mature earlier than normal for the species.

predat(or) (ory) (ion) - An animal that eats other animals; a **carnivore** (the act of eating other animals).

predorsal - The area of the body above the **lateral line** and between the **origin** of the **dorsal fin** and the back of the head. Also see **nape**.

premaxill(a) (ae) - The bones forming the front of the upper jaw in all fish, and extending to form the **lateral** margins in advanced fish, such as perch, bass, and walleye.

preopercular bone - The narrow, vertical, crescent-shaped bone at the front of the **operculum**, just behind the **cheek**. It often has pores of the **lateral line** in it.

prickles - Modified **scales**, which consist of one or a few tiny spines protruding through the skin.

primary consumer - An animal that feeds on plants. The same as a **first-level consumer**.

projecting lower jaw - The tip of the lower jaw extends beyond the tip of the upper jaw.

protozoa(n) - Eukaryotic, single-celled organism(s). Many types of protozoa are found in **plankton**.

protracted - Extended; for example, a protracted spawning period is one that is extended over a long period of time.

protractile (or protrusible) (mouth) - A fish's mouth in which the upper jaws can slide forward as the mouth opens, allowing the fish to suck in food particles. The presence of a **frenum** prevents protrusibility by binding the **premaxillae** closely to the **snout**.

pyloric caecae - Slender, finger-like outgrowths from the gut wall at the **posterior** end of the stomach.

rapid - In a stream, an area of very fast flowing water, usually over boulders or bedrock outcrops, which is turbulent enough to make breaking waves on the surface (white water). Also see **riffle**.

ray - A flexible, bony **fin** support, which is branched and consists of a series of small, bony segments movably jointed to one another.

recurved maxillary - The maxillary is curved upward toward the rear.

reticulate(d) - A net-like or web-like pattern of markings (or marked with such a pattern).

GLOSSARY

rhombic - Diamond-shaped (such as **ganoid scales**).

riffle - In a stream, an area of shallow, medium- to fast-flowing water, usually flowing over gravel or rubble, with enough turbulence to make the surface appear roughened. Also see **rapid**.

ripe - A fish that is sexually mature and ready to **spawn**. Mature eggs or **milt** may be expressed from the genital pores or **vent** by pressing on the **abdomen**.

riverine - Living in streams or rivers.

run (or slick) - In a stream, an area of moderately fast-flowing, usually deep, water that is not turbulent and has a smooth surface.

scale(s) - Bony plates in the skin of a fish. Scales form the body covering of most fish.

second-level consumer - An animal that feeds on other animals that feed on plants. Also see **middle-level consumer**.

seine - A fishing net that hangs vertically in the water and is pulled through the water and onto shore to catch fish.

serrate(d) - Saw-toothed, referring to the edge of a bone or **scale**.

snout - The portion of the head **anterior** to the eyes and above the mouth.

spawn(ing) - The fertilized eggs of fish and other aquatic animals; the act of mating and deposition of eggs by aquatic animals.

species - In classification, a group of related organisms that share all the characters of their **genus** and also have a unique set of adaptations of their own. Species maintain their distinctness by either, or a combination of, having barriers to interbreeding with related species, and/or having **hybrids** selected against if they are produced.

spent - A fish that has recently completed **spawning**.

spine - A bony **fin** support that is neither branched nor jointed. They are usually stiff and sharply pointed, but may be weak and flexible in some fish, such as sculpins.

squamation - The covering of **scales** on the body or a part of the body. Often used in reference to the pattern of scale coverage.

stagnant - In small bodies of water, not flowing and usually **hypoxic** or **anoxic**.

standard length - The straight-line distance from the tip of the **snout** to the base of the **caudal fin**.

stripe - A narrow marking running lengthwise on a fish's body (or **fins**). (Compare with **bar** and **band**.)

subopercular bone - The plate-like bone of the **operculum** located beneath the **opercular** and above the **interopercular** bones.

suborbital - Located below the eye (as bones, pores, markings, etc.).

subspecies - In classification, a distinguishable, interbreeding, usually geographically isolated population of a **species**.

substrate - The materials comprising the bottom of a water body.

subterminal mouth - The upper jaw, but not the **snout**, projects beyond the lower jaw. (See also **included lower jaw**.)

superior mouth - The lower jaw projects beyond the upper jaw, and the mouth is also **oblique**.

supraorbital - Located above the eye (as bones, pores, spines, markings, etc.).

symbiosis (symbiotic) - An association between (usually) two organisms.

talus - A sloping surface of boulders and smaller rock fragments at the foot of a cliff.

terete - A streamlined, cylindrical body shape, tapered at both ends.

terminal (mouth) - A mouth located at the anteriormost point of the head, in which neither the upper nor lower jaw projects beyond the other, and the **snout** does not project **anterior** to the mouth.

GLOSSARY

terrestrial - Living on land.

test(is) (es) - Male sex organ(s).

thermocline - In most lakes during the summer, the layer of water beginning at the depth where mixing of surface water by the wind and wave action no longer occurs, and extending downward through the depth range where the temperature declines rapidly. This layer is often only about a metre thick. Below the thermocline, the rate of temperature decline is gradual.

thoracic (pelvic fins) - **Pelvic fins** with bases located below or slightly behind the bases of the **pectoral fins**.

transverse - Running from side to side of the body.

tributar(y) (ies) - Streams that flow into a larger water body.

trophic level - A level in the **food web** of a **community**.

turbid(ity) - Water made cloudy with suspended clay, silt, mud, or other particulate matter in it.

turbulent - Water with disorderly flow, such as in a **rapid** or **riffle**.

underyearling - An animal in its first year of life. Also called young-of-the-year or YOY.

upper-level consumer - An animal that eats other **predatory** animals. Often a **piscivore**.

vent - The posterior opening of the digestive and urogenital systems. Also called the **anus**.

ventral - Toward the underside; the underside.

ventral mouth - A mouth on the underside of the head, well behind the tip of the **snout**.

vermiculations - Irregular, "worm track"-like markings on the body and/or some **fins** of a fish.

villiform teeth - Minute teeth in pads or patches, usually on the jaws, but may also be on the roof of the mouth or tongue.

vomer - The **median** bone at the front of the roof of the mouth. It may bear a patch and/or row of **vomerine teeth**.

vomerine teeth - A **median** patch or row of teeth on the **vomer** bone, at the front of the roof of the mouth.

watershed - A water body together with all its tributaries. Also see **drainage** or **basin**.

zoogeography - The study of the geographical distribution of animals, which attempts to discover when and by what routes animals dispersed over an area and to explain the causes of patterns of distributions.

zooplankton - **Planktonic** animals.

REFERENCES

Bailey, R. M. and Allum, M. O. 1962. *Fishes of South Dakota. Miscellaneous Publications of the Museum of Zoology, University of Michigan* 119: 131.

Balesic, H. 1971. Comparative ecology of four species of darters (Etheostomatinae) in Lake Dauphin and its tributary, the Valley River. Unpublished M.Sc. Thesis, University of Manitoba, Department of Zoology: 77.

Bartnick, V. G. 1970. Reproductive isolation between two sympatric species of dace, *Rhinichthys cataractae* and *Rhinichthys atratulus*, in the Mink and Valley Rivers, Manitoba. Unpublished M.Sc. Thesis, University of Manitoba, Department of Zoology: 84.

Becker, G. C. 1983. *Fishes of Wisconsin*. University of Wisconsin Press, Madison, WI: 1052.

Behnke, R. J. 1992. *Native trout of western North America. American Fisheries Society Monograph* 6. American Fisheries Society, Bethesda, MD: 273.

Block, D. 2001. Growth estimates, habitat use and ecology of the lake sturgeon, *Acipenser fulvescens* Rafinesque, from Round Lake and Mature Reservoirs in the Winnipeg River. Unpublished M.Sc. Thesis, University of Manitoba, Department of Zoology: 171.

Bodaly, R. A. 1977. Evolutionary divergence between sympatric lake whitefish, *Coregonus clupeaformis*, in the Yukon Territory. Unpublished Ph.D. Thesis, University of Manitoba, Department of Zoology: 119.

Breder, C. M. and Rosen, D. E. 1966. *Modes of reproduction in fishes*. Natural History Press, New York, NY: 941.

Brown, J. H., Hammer, U. T., and Koshinsky, G. D. 1970. Breeding biology of the lake chub, *Couesius plumbeus*, at Lac la Ronge, Saskatchewan. *Journal of the Fisheries Research Board of Canada* 27 (6): 1005-1015.

Burr, B. M. and Mayden, R. L. 1992. Phylogenetics and North American freshwater fishes. In R. L. Mayden (Ed.), *Systematics, historical ecology & North American freshwater fishes*. Stanford University Press, Stanford, CA: 18-75.

Butler, G. E. 1953. Lake Minnewashta-largemouth black bass. Internal Memorandum of Manitoba Department of Mines and Natural Resources, Game and Fisheries Branch, July 22, 1953. (First reference to bluegill in Lake Minnewasta.)

Butler, G. E. 1952. Lake Minnewashta. Internal Memorandum of Manitoba Department of Mines and Natural Resources, Game and Fisheries Branch, August 19, 1952.

Butler, G. E. 1946. Largemouth black bass. Internal Memorandum of Manitoba Department of Mines and Natural Resources, Game and Fisheries Branch, July 3, 1946.

Butler, G. E. 1945. Lake Minnewashta near Morden. Internal Memorandum of Manitoba Department of Mines and Natural Resources, Game and Fisheries Branch, July 10, 1945.

Butler, G. E. 1942. Lake Minnewashta. Internal Memorandum of Manitoba Department of Mines and Natural Resources, Game and Fisheries Branch, August 19, 1942. (First reference to possible contamination of largemouth bass plantings with crappies [species not stated].)

Campbell, K. B., Derksen, A. J., Remnant, R. A., and Stewart, K. W. 1991. First specimens of the rainbow smelt, *Osmerus mordax* from Lake Winnipeg, Manitoba. *Canadian Field-Naturalist* 105 (4): 568-570.

Carlander, K. D. 1969. *Handbook of freshwater fishery biology. Vol. 1. Life history data on the freshwater fishes of the United States and Canada, exclusive of the perciformes*. Iowa State University Press, Ames, IA: 752.

Carlander, K. D. 1950. Growth rate studies of saugers, *Stizostedion canadense* (Smith), and yellow perch, *Perca flavescens* (Mitchill), from Lake of the Woods, Minnesota. *Transactions of the American Fisheries Society* 79 (1949): 30-42.

Case, B. E. 1970a. An ecological study of the tadpole madtom *Noturus gyrinus* (Mitchill), with special reference to movements and population fluctuations. Unpublished M.Sc. Thesis, University of Manitoba, Department of Zoology: 90.

REFERENCES

Case, B. E. 1970b. Spawning behaviour of the chestnut lamprey (*Ichthyomyzon castaneus*). *Journal of the Fisheries Research Board of Canada* 27 (10): 1872-1874.

Clarke, A.H. 1981. *The freshwater mollusks of Canada*. National Museum of Natural Sciences, National Museums of Canada, Ottawa: 446.

Clarke, R. McV. 1973. The systematics of ciscoes (Coregonidae) in central Canada. Unpublished Ph.D. Thesis, University of Manitoba, Department of Zoology: 260.

Clarke, R. McV., Boychuck, R. W., and Hodgins, D. A. 1980. Fishes of the Red River at Winnipeg, Manitoba. Unpublished Manuscript Report, Western Region, Department of Fisheries and Oceans: 42.

Clemens, H. P. and Sneed, K. E. 1957. The spawning behaviour of the channel catfish *Ictalurus punctatus*. U. S. Fish and Wildlife Service Special Scientific Report-Fisheries #219: 11.

Crossman, E. J. and McAllister, D. E. 1986. Zoogeography of freshwater fishes of the Hudson Bay Drainage, Ungava Bay and the Arctic Archipelago. In C.H. Hocutt and E.O. Wiley (Eds.), *The zoogeography of North American freshwater fishes*. John Wiley and Sons, New York: 53-104.

Cunningham, A. G. 1944. Exchange of pickerel eggs for largemouth black bass. Internal Memorandum of Manitoba Department of Mines and Natural Resources, Game and Fisheries Branch, October 14, 1944.

Cvancara, A. M., Bickley, W. B., Jr., Jacob, A. F., Ashworth, A. C., Brephy, J. A., Shay, C. T., Delorme, L. D., and Lammers, G. 1971. Paleolimnology of Late Quaternary Deposits: Siebold Site, ND. *Science* 171: 172-174.

Day, A. C. 1983. Biological population characteristics, and interactions between an unexploited burbot (*Lota lota*) population and an exploited lake trout (*Salvelinus namaycush*) population from Lake Athapapuskow, Manitoba. Unpublished M.Sc. Thesis, University of Manitoba, Department of Zoology: 177.

Deslisle, C. and Van Vliet, W. 1968. First records of the sculpins *Myoxocephalus thompsoni* and *Cottus ricei* from the Ottawa Valley, Southwestern Québec. *Journal of the Fisheries Research Board of Canada* 25 (12): 2733-2737.

Fedoruk, A. N. 1971. *Freshwater fishes of Manitoba: checklist and keys*. Manitoba Department of Renewable Resources and Transportation Services: 127.

Fedoruk, A. N. 1961. Interrelationships of smallmouth bass (*Micropterus dolomieui*) and walleyed pike (*Stizostedion vitreum*) in Falcon Lake, Manitoba. Unpublished M.Sc. Thesis, Department of Zoology, University of Manitoba: 75.

Franzin, W. G. 1974. Genetic studies of protein variants and their use in a zoogeographic study of lake whitefish, *Coregonus clupeaformis* (Mitchill) in Western Canada. Unpublished Ph.D. Thesis, University of Manitoba, Department of Zoology: 178.

Franzin, W. G., Barton, B. A., Remnant, R. A., Wain, D. B., and Pagel, S. J. 1994. Range extension, present and potential distribution, and possible effects of rainbow smelt (*Osmerus mordax*) in Hudson Bay Drainage waters of Northwestern Ontario, Manitoba and Minnesota. *North American Journal of Fisheries Management* 14: 65-76.

Franzin, W. G., Parker, B. R., and Harbicht, S. M. 1986. A First Record of the Golden Redhorse *Moxostoma erythrurum* (Rafinesque), Family Catostomidae, from the Red River in Manitoba, Canada. *Canadian Field-Naturalist* 100: 270-271.

Franzin, W. G., Stewart, K. W., Hanke, G. F., and Heuring, L. 2003. The fish and fisheries of Lake Winnipeg: The first 100 years. *Canadian Technical Report of Fisheries and Aquatic Science* 2398: 53.

Gilbert, C. R. 1978. *Notropis anogenus* Forbes pugnose shiner. In Lee, et al. (Eds.), *Atlas of North American Freshwater Fishes*. Publication 1980-12, North Carolina Biological Survey. North Carolina State Museum of Natural History, Raleigh, NC: 227.

Gilbert, C. R. and Burgess, G. H. 1979. *Notropis dorsalis* (Agassiz) bigmouth shiner. In Lee, et al. (Eds.), *Atlas of North American Freshwater Fishes*. Publication 1980-12, North Carolina Biological Survey. North Carolina State Museum of Natural History, Raleigh, NC: 260.

Gillies, D. G. 1975. The arctic grayling (*Thymallus arcticus*) in Manitoba and a literature review. Manitoba Department of Mines, Resources and Environmental Management, Research Branch Report 75-13: 51.

REFERENCES

Green, D. J. and Derksen, A. J. 1987. Observations on the spawning of lake whitefish (*Coregonus clupeaformis*) in the Poplar River area of Lake Winnipeg, 1974-1977. Manitoba Department of Natural Resources, Fisheries Branch Manuscript Report 87-24: 86.

Hanke, G. F. 1996. A survey of the fishes of Lake Winnipeg and interactions of the introduced white bass with the native ichthyofauna of the Hudson Bay Drainage: with emphasis on young-of-the-year fishes in nearshore environments. Unpublished M.Sc. Thesis, University of Manitoba, Department of Zoology: 318.

Harbicht, S. 1990. Ecology of the shorthead redhorse, *Moxostoma macrolepidotum* (LeSeur) 1817 in Dauphin Lake, Manitoba. Unpublished M.Sc. Thesis, University of Manitoba, Department of Zoology: 116.

Harbicht, S. M., Franzin, W. G., and Stewart, K. W. 1988. New distribution records for the minnows *Hybognathus hankinsoni*, *Phoxinus eos* and *Phoxinus neogaeus* in Manitoba. *Canadian Field-Naturalist* 102, (3): 475-484.

Harkness, W. J. K. 1936. Report on the sturgeon situation in Manitoba. Manitoba Department of Natural Resources Manuscript Report 80-31980: 18

Henry, A. and Thompson, D. 1897. *The manuscript journals of Alexander Henry and David Thompson 1799-1814, exploration and adventure among the Indians on the Red, Saskatchewan, Missouri and Columbia Rivers. Edited with copious comments by Elliott Coues*. Ross & Haines, Inc., Minneapolis, MN, Vol. I: 1-446, Vol. II: 447-1027.

Hinks, D. 1957. *The fishes of Manitoba*. Department of Mines and Natural Resources, Province of Manitoba. Second printing, 1962: 102.

Horn, B. M. 1993. Geographic variation of populations of mimic shiners, *Notropis volucellus* and sand shiners, *N. stramineus stramineus* (Cyprinidae) in Manitoba and Southern Ontario. Unpublished M.Sc. Thesis, University of Manitoba, Department of Zoology: 89.

Hubbs, C. L. and Cooper, G. P. 1936. *Minnows of Michigan*. Cranbrook Institute of Science Bulletin #8: 95.

Hudson's Bay Company Archives, Cumberland House Post Journal, 1797-98, B.49/a/28, November 8, 1797.

Johnson, M. 2001. Indicators (parasites and stable isotopes) of trophic status of yellow perch (*Perca flavescens*, Mitchill) in nutrient poor Canadian Shield lakes. Unpublished M.Sc. Thesis, University of Manitoba, Department of Zoology: 409.

Johnson, R. P. 1971. Limnology and fishery biology of Black Lake, Saskatchewan. Fisheries Report #9, Saskatchewan Department of Natural Resources.

Johnson, R. P. 1963. Studies on the life history and ecology of the bigmouth buffalo, *Ictiobus cyprinellus* (Valenciennes). *Journal of the Fisheries Research Board of Canada* 20 (6): 1397-1429.

Kallemeyn, L. W., Holmberg, K. L., Perry, J. A., and Odde, B. Y. 2003. Aquatic synthesis for voyageurs national park. *Information and Technology Report USGS/BRD/ITR*–2003–0001, May 2003: 96.

Keleher, J. J. 1961. Comparison of largest Great Slave Lake fish with North American records. *Journal of the Fisheries Research Board of Canada* 18 (3): 417-421.

Keleher, J. J. 1952. Growth, and *Triaenophorus* parasitism in relation to taxonomy in Lake Winnipeg ciscoes (*Leucichthys*). *Journal of the Fisheries Research Board of Canada* 8 (7): 469-478.

Keleher, J. J. and Kooyman, A. 1957. Supplement to Hinks, "The fishes of Manitoba." Department of Mines and Natural Resources, Province of Manitoba. In Hinks, D. 1957. *The Fishes of Manitoba*. Department of Mines and Natural Resources, Province of Manitoba: 103-117.

Kennedy, W. A. 1954. Tagging returns, age studies and fluctuations in abundance of Lake Winnipeg whitefish 1931-1951. *Journal of the Fisheries Research Board of Canada* 11 (3): 284-309.

Kliewer, E. V. 1970. Gill raker variation and diet in lake whitefish *Coregonus clupeaformis* in Northern Manitoba. In C. C. Lindsey and C. S. Woods (Eds.), *Biology of Coregonid Fishes*. University of Manitoba Press, Winnipeg, Manitoba: 560.

REFERENCES

Koel, T. M. 1997. Distribution of fishes in the Red River of the North Basin on multivariate environmental gradients. Ph.D. Thesis, North Dakota State University, Fargo, North Dakota. Northern Prairie Wildlife Research Center Home Page. http://www.npwrc.usgs.gov/resource/1998/norbasin/norbasin.htm (Version 03JUN98).

Kramer, R. H. and Smith, L. L. 1960. Utilization of nests of largemouth bass, *Micropterus salmoides*, by golden shiners, *Notemigonus crysoleucas*. *Copeia* 1 (1960): 73-74.

Kristofferson, A. 1978. Evidence for the existence of subpopulations of lake whitefish, *Coregonus clupeaformis* (Mitchill) in Lake Winnipeg. Unpublished M.Sc. Thesis, University of Manitoba, Department of Zoology: 94.

Langlois, T. H. 1929. Breeding habits of the northern dace. *Ecology* 10 (1): 161-163.

Lanteigne, J. 1988. Identification of lamprey larvae of the genus *Ichthyomyzon* (Petromyzontidae). *Environmental Biology of Fishes* 23 (1-2): 55-63.

Lawler, G. H. 1954. Observations on the trout-perch *Percopsis omiscomaycus* (Walbaum), at Hemming Lake, Manitoba. *Journal of the Fisheries Research Board of Canada* 11 (1): 1-4.

Lawler, G. H. 1953. Age, growth, production and infection with *Triaenophorus nodulosus* of the yellow perch, *Perca flavescens* (Mitchill) of Manitoba. *Fisheries Research Board of Canada, Manuscript Report of the Biological Station* 151: 19.

Loch, J. S. 1971. Phenotypic variation in the lake whitefish as induced by introduction into a new environment. Unpublished M.Sc. Thesis, University of Manitoba, Department of Zoology: 96.

MacDonald, D. A. 1992. The channel catfish sport fishery of the lower Red River. Unpublished Master of Natural Resource Management Practicum, University of Manitoba, Natural Resources Institute: 160.

Malaher, G. W. 1946. Special fishery regulations Lake Minnewashta. Internal Memorandum of Manitoba Department of Mines and Natural Resources, Game and Fisheries Branch, June 17, 1946.

Martin, K. A. 1982. Adaptive strategies of the central mudminnow, *Umbra limi* (Kirtland) in Southern Manitoba. Unpublished M. Sc. Thesis, University of Manitoba, Department of Zoology: 72.

Mavros, W. V. 1992. Genetic, morphological and isotopic population structure of lake whitefish (*Coregonus clupeaformis*) in northern Lake Winnipeg and Playgreen Lake. Unpublished M.Sc. Thesis, University of Manitoba, Department of Zoology: 97.

McCulloch, B. R. 1994. Dispersal of the stonecat (*Noturus flavus*) in Manitoba and its interactions with resident fish species. Unpublished M.Sc. Thesis, University of Manitoba, Department of Zoology: 108.

McCulloch, B. R. and Franzin, W. G. 1996. Fishes of the Canadian portion of the Assiniboine River Drainage. *Canadian Technical Reports of Fisheries and Aquatic Sciences* 2087: 62.

McCulloch, B. R. and Stewart, K. W. 1998. Range extensions and new locality records for the stonecat, *Noturus flavus* in Manitoba: Evidence for a Recent Natural Invasion. *Canadian Field-Naturalist* 112 (2): 217-224.

McKay, L. R., Issen, P. E., and McMillan, I. 1992a. Early mortality of tiger trout (*Salvelinus fontinalis X Salmo trutta*) and the effects of triploidy. *Aquaculture* 102 (1992): 43-54.

McKay, L. R., Issen, P. E., and McMillan, I. 1992b. Growth and mortality of diploid and triploid tiger trout (*Salmo trutta X Salvelinus fontinalis*). *Aquaculture* 106 (1992): 239-251.

McKillop, W. B. and McKillop, W. M. 1997. Distribution records for the threespine stickleback, *Gasterosteus aculeatus* Linnaeus (Pisces: Gasterosteidae), in Manitoba. *Canadian Field-Naturalist* 111 (4): 662-663.

McPhail, J. D. and Lindsey, C. C. 1970. *Freshwater fishes of northwestern Canada and Alaska*. Fisheries Research Board of Canada Bulletin 173: 381.

Moshenko, R. W. 1972. Ecology of the creek chub, *Semotilus atromaculatus atromaculatus* (Mitchill), in the Mink River, Manitoba. Unpublished M.Sc. Thesis, University of Manitoba, Department of Zoology: 63.

Moyle, P. B. 1976. *Inland fishes of California*. University of California Press, Berkeley: 405.

Moyle, P. B. 1969. Ecology of the fishes in a Minnesota lake, with special reference to the Cyprinidae. Ph.D. Thesis, University of Minnesota, Minneapolis: 169.

Narita, T. 1970. Physiological, ecological and morphological differences between two forms of the ninespine stickleback *Pungitius pungitius*, in North America. Unpublished Ph.D. Thesis, University of Manitoba, Department of Zoology: 90.

Nelson, J. S. 1994. *Fishes of the world, 3rd Edition*. John Wiley & Sons, Inc., Toronto, ON: 600.

Nelson, J.S., Crossman, E.J., Espinosa-Pérez, H., Findley, L.T., Gilbert, C.R., Lea, R.N., and Williams, J.D. 2004. *Common and Scientific names of fishes from the United States, Canada, and Mexico*. Fifth edition. American Fisheries Society, Special Publication 29, Bethesda, MD. In press.

Newsome, G. E. 1975. A study of prey preference and selection by creek chub, *Semotilus atromaculatus*, in the Mink River, Manitoba. Unpublished Ph.D. Thesis, University of Manitoba, Department of Zoology: 80.

Parker, B. 1987. Ecology of the quillback (*Carpiodes cyprinus*) of Dauphin Lake, Manitoba. Unpublished M.Sc. Thesis, University of Manitoba, Department of Zoology: 143.

Raney, E. C. 1940. Comparison of the breeding habits of two subspecies of the black-nosed dace, *Rhinichthys atratulus* (Hermann). *American Midland Naturalist* 23 (2): 399-403.

Ratynski, R. A. 1978. Growth, population structure and diet of the troutperch *Percopsis omiscomaycus* (Walbaum) in the Grand Rapids Area of Lake Winnipeg. Manitoba Department of Renewable Resources, Fisheries Research Section Manuscript Report 78-63: 20.

Reed, K. M., Dorscher, M. O., Todd, T. N., and Phillips, R. B. 1998. Sequence analysis of the mitochondrial DNA control region of Ciscoes (Genus *Coregonus*): Taxonomic implications for the Great Lakes species flock. *Molecular Ecology* 7 (1998): 1091-1096.

Reed, R. J. 1954. Hermaphroditism in the Rosyface Shiner. *Copeia* 4 (1954): 293-294.

Remnant, R. A., Graveline, R. B., and Bretecher, R. L. 1997. Range extension of rainbow smelt, *Osmerus mordax*, in Hudson Bay Drainage waters of Manitoba. *Canadian Field-Naturalist* 111 (4): 660-662.

Renard, P. A., Hanson, S. R., and Enblom, J. W. 1985. Biological survey of the Red River of the North. Special Publication # 142. Minnesota Department of Natural Resources, Division of Fish and Wildlife, Ecological Services Section, St. Paul: 82.

Renard, P. A., Hanson, S. R., and Enblom, J. W. 1983. Biological survey of the Red Lake River. Special Publication # 134. Minnesota Department of Natural Resources, Division of Fish and Wildlife, Ecological Services Section, St. Paul: 110.

Robert, L. 1992. Upper Red River channel catfish tagging report. Unpublished Manuscript Report, Eastern Region, Fisheries Branch, Manitoba Department of Natural Resources: 20.

Robert, L. 1989-1991. Field notes on file at Fisheries Branch, Manitoba Department of Water Stewardship, Lac du Bonnet Regional Office, Provincial Highway 502, Lac du Bonnet, Manitoba R0E 1A0.

Robbins, C. R., Bailey, R. M., Bond, C. E., Brooker, J. R., Lachner, E. A., Lea, R. N., and Scott, W. B. 1991. *Common and scientific names of fishes from the United States and Canada*. Fifth edition. American Fisheries Society Special Publications 20. Bethesda, MD: 183.

Rowes, K. D. 1994. Temporal and spatial distribution of pelagic larval fishes of Dauphin Lake, Manitoba. Unpublished M.Sc. Thesis, University of Manitoba, Department of Zoology: 104.

Salfert, I. G. 1984. Filial egg-cannibalism in the brook stickleback, *Culaea inconstans* (Kirtland): A test of the Rhower hypothesis. Unpublished M.Sc. Thesis, University of Manitoba, Department of Zoology: 99.

Schlick, R. O. 1966. Food competition between trout and dace in the North Pine River, Manitoba. Unpublished M.Sc. Thesis, University of Manitoba, Department of Zoology: 43.

Schweitzer, R. D. 1968. Evidence for two sympatric forms of ciscoes (subgenus *Leucichthys*) in Cedar Lake. Unpublished M.Sc. Thesis, University of Manitoba, Department of Zoology: 54.

REFERENCES

Scott, W. B. and Crossman, E. J. 1979. *Freshwater fishes of Canada*. Bulletin 184, Fisheries Research Board of Canada. Minister of Supply and Services Canada, Ottawa, Canada: 966.

Scott, W. B. and Scott, M. G. 1988. *Atlantic fishes of Canada*. Canadian Bulletin of Fisheries and Aquatic Sciences # 219: 730.

Smart, H. 1979. Coexistence and resource partitioning in two species of darters (Percidae), *Etheostoma nigrum* and *Percina maculata*. Unpublished M.Sc. Thesis, University of Manitoba, Department of Zoology: 43.

Smith, G. R. 1992. Phylogeny and biogeography of the Catostomidae, freshwater fishes of North America and Asia. In R. L. Mayden (Ed.), *Systematics, Historical Ecology & North American Freshwater Fishes*. Stanford University Press, Stanford, CA: 778-826.

Snyder, T. P., Larsen, R. R., and Bowen, S. H. 1992. Mitochondrial DNA diversity among Lake Superior and inland lake ciscoes (*Coregonus artedi* and *C. hoyi*). *Canadian Journal of Fisheries and Aquatic Science* 49: 1902-1907.

Sprules, W. M. 1952. The Arctic char of the west coast of Hudson Bay. *Journal of the Fisheries Research Board of Canada* 9 (1): 1-15.

Stasiak, R. H. 1972. The morphology and life history of the finescale dace, *Pfrille neogea*, in Lake Itasca State Park, Minnesota. Unpublished Ph.D. Thesis, University of Minnesota, Minneapolis: 165.

Stephanson, B. 1942a. Minnows liberated into Morden Lake. Internal Memorandum of Manitoba Department of Mines and Natural Resources, Game and Fisheries Branch, July 25, 1942.

Stephanson, B. 1942b. Distribution of 21 adult and approx. 200 fingerlings largemouth black bass to Minnewashta Lake at Morden. Internal Memorandum of Manitoba Department of Mines and Natural Resources, Game and Fisheries Branch, October 3, 1942.

Stewart, K. W. 1988. First collections of the weed shiner, *Notropis texanus*, in Canada. *Canadian Field-Naturalist* 102 (4): 657-660.

Stewart, K. W., Franzin, W. G., McCulloch, B. R., and Hanke, G. F. 2001. Selected case histories of fish species invasions into the Nelson River System in Canada. In J. A. Leitch and M. J. Tenamoc (Eds.), *Science and Policy: Interbasin Water Transfer of Aquatic Biota*. Institute for Regional Studies, North Dakota State University, Fargo, ND: 63-81.

Stewart, K.W. and Lindsey, C.C. 1983. Postglacial dispersal of lower vertebrates in the Glacial Lake Agassiz Region. In J. T. Teller and Lee Clayton (Eds.), *Glacial Lake Agassiz, Geological Association of Canada, Special Paper* 26: 391-419.

Stewart, K. W. and Lindsey, C. C. 1970. First specimens of the stonecat, *Noturus flavus*, from the Hudson Bay Drainage. *Journal of the Fisheries Research Board of Canada* 27 (1): 170-172.

Stewart, K. W., Suthers, I. M., and Leavesley, L. K. 1985. New fish distribution records in Manitoba and the role of a man-made interconnection between two drainages as an avenue of dispersal. *Canadian Field-Naturalist* 99 (3): 317-326.

Stewart-Hay, R. K. 1954. A killifish in Manitoba. *Canadian Field-Naturalist* 68 (2): 94.

Swee, U. T. and McCrimmon, H. R. 1966. Reproductive biology of the carp, *Cyprinus carpio* L., in Lake St. Lawrence, Ontario. *Transactions of the American Fisheries Society* 95 (4): 372-380.

Tallman, R. 1980. Environments occupied, indices of maturity, feeding ecology, shoaling behaviour, and interactions with other species by pearl dace, *Semotilus margarita* (Cope) in Manitoba. Unpublished M.Sc. Thesis, University of Manitoba, Department of Zoology: 74.

Todd, T. N. 1981. Allelic variability in species and stocks of Lake Superior ciscoes (Coregoninae). *Canadian Journal of Fisheries and Aquatic Science* 38: 1808-1813.

Todd, T. N. and Smith, G. R. 1992. A review of differentiation in Great Lakes Ciscoes. *Polskie Archiwum Hydrobiologii* 39 (3-4): 261-267.

Trautman, M. B. 1957. *The fishes of Ohio with illustrated keys*. Ohio State University Press, Columbus, OH: 683.

Turgeon, J. and Bernatchez, L. 2003. Reticulate evolution and phenotypic diversity in North American ciscoes, *Coregonus* ssp. (Teleostei: Salmonidae): Implications for conservation of an evolutionary legacy. *Conservation Genetics* 4 (1): 67-81.

Turgeon, J. and Bernatchez, L. 2001a. Mitochondrial DNA phylogeography of lake cisco (*Coregonus artedi*): Evidence supporting extensive contact between two glacial races. *Molecular Ecology* 10 (2001): 987-1001.

Turgeon, J. and Bernatchez, L. 2001b. Clinal variation at microsatellite loci reveals historical secondary intergradation between glacial races of *Coregonus artedi* (Teleostei: Coregoninae). *Evolution* 55 (11): 2274-2286.

Turgeon, J., Estoup, A., and Bernatchez, L. 1999. Species flock in the North American Great Lakes: Molecular ecology of Lake Nipigon ciscoes (Teleostei: Coregonidae: *Coregonus*). *Evolution* 53 (6): 1857-1861.

Tyson, J. D. 1996. The effect of thermal effluent on overwintering channel catfish (*Ictalurus punctatus*) in the lower Red River, Manitoba. Unpublished M.Sc. Thesis, University of Manitoba, Department of Zoology: 121.

Valiant, H. 1975. Species diversity and within-stream distribution of stream-dwelling fishes from Western Manitoba. Unpublished M.Sc. Thesis, University of Manitoba, Department of Zoology: 63.

Van Oosten, J. 1937. The age, growth and sex ratio of the Lake Superior longjaw, *Leucichthys zenithicus* (Jordan and Everman). *Papers of the Michigan Academy of Science, Arts and Letters* 22 (1936): 691-711.

Waddell, J. M. 1970. *Dominion City facts fiction and hyperbole*. Derksen Press, Steinbach, Manitoba. Reprinted for the Franklin Museum, June 1997: 132.

Winn, H. E. 1958. Comparative reproductive behavior and ecology of fourteen species of darters (Pisces-Percidae). *Ecological Monographs* 28 (2): 155-191.

Wood, R. M., Mayden, R. L., Matson, R. H., Kuhajda, B. R., and Layman, S. R. 2002. Systematics and biogeography of the *Notropis rubellus* species group (Teleostei: Cyprinidae). *Bulletin of the Alabama Museum of Natural History* 22: 37-80.

SOURCES OF PERSONAL COMMUNICATIONS

Beyette
D.J. Beyette, Fisheries Technician
Fisheries Branch
Manitoba Department of Water Stewardship
Provincial Highway 502
Lac du Bonnet, Manitoba, R0E 1A0

Bruch
Ronald M. Bruch
Wisconsin Department of Natural Resources
625 E. County Road Y, Suite 700
Oshkosh, WI, 54901, U.S.A.

Derkson
A.J. Derksen, Fish Habitat Biologist
Fisheries and Oceans Canada
Central and Arctic Region
Freshwater Institute
501 University Crescent
Winnipeg, Manitoba, R3T 2N6

Franzin
Dr. W.G. Franzin, Research Scientist
Fisheries and Oceans Canada
Central and Arctic Region
Freshwater Institute
501 University Crescent
Winnipeg, Manitoba, R3T 2N6

REFERENCES

Hanke	Dr. G.F. Hanke, Curator of Zoology Manitoba Museum 190 Rupert Avenue Winnipeg, Manitoba, R3B 0N2
Matkowski	S.M.D. Matkowski Fisheries Branch Manitoba Department of Water Stewardship 200 Saulteaux Crescent Winnipeg, Manitoba, R3J 3W3
Murray	L. Murray, Graduate Student Department of Zoology, University of Manitoba Fisheries and Oceans Canada Central and Arctic Region Freshwater Institute 501 University Crescent Winnipeg, Manitoba, R3T 2N6
Nelson	Dr. J. S. Nelson, Professor Emeritus University of Alberta Current Chair, American Fisheries Society Committee on Names of Fishes Department of Biological Sciences CW 405, Biological Sciences Centre Edmonton, Alberta, T6G 2E9
O'Connor	Dr. J.J. O'Connor, Director of Fisheries Fisheries Branch Manitoba Department of Water Stewardship 200 Saulteaux Crescent Winnipeg, Manitoba, R3J 3W3
Parker	B. Parker, Graduate Student Department of Biological Sciences University of Alberta 114 Street - 89 Avenue Edmonton, Alberta, T6G 2E1
Remnant	R.A. Remnant, Senior Fisheries Biologist/Principal North/South Consultants 83 Scurfield Boulevard Winnipeg, Manitoba, R3Y 1G4
Vanriel	P.J. Vanriel Canada North Environmental Services, Ltd. (CanNorth) #4-130 Robin Crescent Saskatoon, Saskatchewan, S7L 6M7
Wright	D.G. Wright, Coordinator, Environmental Affairs Fisheries and Oceans Canada Central and Arctic Region Freshwater Institute 501 University Crescent Winnipeg, Manitoba, R3T 2N6